Reflation and Austerity

In this volume, revised and brought up to date for this English language edition, the authors provide a well-documented analysis of the economic policy of the Mauroy and Fabius governments during the period 1981–6. From a Keynesian standpoint, they analyse French economic policy using quantitative data from their own econometric models as well as from other sources. They place their study firmly within the framework of the recessions brought on by the two oil crises of the 1970s, and of the constraints imposed by the international environment, particularly United States fiscal policy. They examine closely, in a comparative perspective, the three devaluations of the Mauroy government, and the way employment policies introduced before 1981 were continued and reinforced. The question of whether the austerity policy was necessary is squarely addressed. The success of the Left government in bringing down inflation and public spending is shown to have put the French economy back on course by 1986, but the authors argue strongly for a co-ordinated European re-expansion as the major prerequisite of lasting world economic recovery. This book is arguably the most detailed examination available of the reasons for, and the development and lasting legacy of, a key period in recent French political and economic history.

Pierre-Alain Muet, Professor at the Institut d'Etudes Politiques de Paris, Lecturer at the Ecole Polytechnique, and Head of the Department of Econometrics, Observatoire français des conjonctures economiques (OFCE), Paris

Alain Fonteneau, Lecturer at the Institut d'Etudes Politiques de Paris and formerly chief forecaster in the Department of Econometrics, Observatoire français des conjonctures economiques (OFCE), Paris

Reflation and Austerity
Economic Policy under Mitterrand

Pierre-Alain Muet
and
Alain Fonteneau

Translated by
Malcolm Slater

BERG
New York / Oxford / Munich
Distributed exclusively in the US and Canada by
St Martin's Press, New York

English edition
first published in 1990 by
Berg Publishers Limited
Editorial offices:
165 Taber Avenue, Providence, RI 02906, USA
150 Cowley Road, Oxford OX4 1JJ, UK
Westermühlstraße 26, 8000 München 5, FRG

English edition © Berg Publishers Ltd 1990

Originally published as *La gauche face à la crise*.
Translated from the French by permission of the publishers.
© Presses de la Fondation Nationale des Sciences Politiques, Paris.

All rights reserved.
No part of this publication may be reproduced
in any form or by any means without the written
permission of the publishers.

Library of Congress Cataloging-in-Publication Data
Fonteneau, Alain.
   [Gauche face à la crise. English]
   Reflation and austerity: economic policy under Mitterrand / Alain Fonteneau and Pierre-Alain Muet: translated by Malcolm Slater.
     p.   cm.
   Translation of: La gauche face à la crise.
   Includes bibliographical references.
   ISBN 0-85496-644-7
   1. France—Economic conditions—1945- 2. France—Economic policy—1945- 3. Socialism—France. 4. Mitterrand, François, 1916- I. Muet, Pierre-Alain. II. Title.
HC276.2.F6713 1990
338.944′009′048—dc20   89-28948
                                                                                    CIP

British Library Cataloguing in Publication Data
Muet, Pierre-Alain
Reflation and austerity: economic policy under Mitterrand.
1. France. Economic policies, history
I. Title   II. Fonteneau, Alain   III. Gauche face à la crise. *English*
330.944
ISBN 0-85496-644-7

Printed in Great Britain by Billing & Sons Ltd, Worcester

A national economy open to the laws of competition and engaging in trade is subject, for as long as it is a market and in need of outlets, to the equilibrium of the surroundings in which it is steeped – the world economy. It is subject to a common law and a common practice, and if it too rashly disregards this universal code, every breach leaves it open to harsh sanctions in the commercial and monetary fields, and as a consequence of this, in the political field.

To avoid this the nation which wants to do things differently either cuts off communication with the outside, puts an end to the normal interplay of competition and trade, and confines itself resolutely within a despotic autarchy – as Soviet Russia and Nazi Germany have done – or else it agrees to become part of a larger whole and to incorporate its own activities in activity of a universal character. France is reluctant to adopt the first solution; she must therefore apply all her will to making the second one prevail.

If one casts one's mind back several years, one realizes that the Popular Front Government, set up in France in the middle of 1936 under Socialist leadership, was faced with this alternative, even though its programme did not include very sweeping social changes.

Léon Blum, A l'échelle humaine, 1941

Contents

List of Tables — ix

List of Figures — xiii

List of Insets — xvi

Preface to the English Edition — xvii

Introduction — 1

1. **Understanding the Economic Crisis** — 7
   The Oil Shocks: Keynesian Depression and
      Stagflation 9
   The First Oil Shock 39
   The Second Oil Shock: Recession Worsened by
      Restrictive Policies 49
   *Appendix 1.1 Keynes and Classical Economics:
      A Traditional Model* 61
   *Appendix 1.2 Analysing the Effects of an Oil Price
      Rise Using a Keynesian Model of an Open
      Economy* 63

2. **Reflation Runs Into Difficulties** — 66
   The Economic Situation in France in Spring
      1981 67
   The Reflation of 1981–2 75
   A Comparative Analysis of the Reflation of
      1981–2 101
   *Appendix 2.1 The Budget, 'Economic Budgets' and
      the Plan* 117

3. **Unavoidable External Constraints** — 119
   Deterioration of External Balances 121

Contents

Analysis of the Parity Changes 132
Measures Complementing the Devaluations 154
Devaluations are no Substitute for Economic Austerity 162
Foreign Debt and Financing the External Deficit 178

4. The Fight Against Unemployment 189
Shorter Working Hours 190
The Creation of Public Sector Jobs and Direct Aid for Jobs 213
Labour Force Management Policy 222
The Development of Employment Policy and its Effect on Unemployment 236

5. The Fruits of Austerity 246
Disinflation and the Return of Profitability 248
The Reduction of Budget Deficits 263
Tax Reduction: Myths and Realities 277
Arguments for a Co-ordinated Reflation 290

Conclusion 302
The Failure of Ideologies 302
Creditable Achievements in a Europe Hit by Recession 304
Absence of Vision in the Medium Term 305
Two Conditions for Reducing Unemployment: Go for Growth and Redistribute Working Time 307
European Economic Expansion 308

Bibliography 310

List of Tables

1.1	Impact of the oil price rise on the real income of OECD countries as a whole	20
1.2	The saving–investment equilibrium at world level	21
1.3	Analysis of the rise in inflation after the first oil shock: imported inflation and domestic factors	42
1.4	Impact of the first oil shock and farm price rises on American growth, 1973–5	44
1.5	Breakdown of the balance of central and local government spending, 1973–6	45
1.6	Current account balances of the main groups of countries between 1973 and 1978	47
1.7	Change in trade balances between 1973 and 1976	48
1.8	Change in budget balances between 1979 and 1982	50
1.9	Effect of the second oil shock and economic policies on the slow-down in growth in the OECD, 1978–81	55
1.10	Comparison of the two oil shocks	57
1.11	Influence of the international situation on the French economy	58
2.1	Public sector borrowing requirement and surplus in the major countries	71
2.2	Change in the real value of wages and social welfare benefits to mid-1981	72
2.3	Forecasts for 1982 made in Autumn 1981	73
2.4	Macro-economic effect of rises in real value of minimum wage	77
2.5	Change in retirement benefit from 1980 to 1983	80
2.6	Macro-economic effect of the social policy measures	83
2.7	Direct help for job creation, 1981–3	84
2.8	Capital grants to nationalized undertakings	87
2.9	Financial aid given to major state undertakings, 1979–82	88
2.10	Assessment of the budgetary cost of tax allowances on investment	89
2.11	Macro-economic impact of measures to help job creation and investment, 1981–3	92
2.12	The new tax measures introduced in 1981 and 1982	93
2.13	Resources available to social security organizations	94

List of Tables

2.14	Macro-economic impact of new taxes, the November 1981 increase in employers' social security contributions, and the UNEDIC (unemployment benefit fund) loan	96
2.15	Total *ex ante* amount of the 1981–2 reflation	97
2.16	*Ex ante* transfers between economic agents	99
2.17	Impact of the Barre and Mauroy reflations on the growth of GDP	100
2.18	Macro-economic impact of the total package of reflationary measures introduced by the Left, including increases in taxation	101
2.19	Total *ex ante* amounts involved in the 1975–6 reflation	103
2.20	Macro-economic impact of the 1975 package of reflationary measures	106
2.21	Impact on GNP and current balance of payments of reflationary measures introduced by West Germany in 1978–9	111
2.22	Impact of the 1978–9 West German reflation on the French economy	112
2.23	Impact of the worsening international situation on the French economy in 1982	116
3.1	Part played by changes in volume and terms of trade in the deterioration of the balance of payments between 1978 and 1982	122
3.2	Contribution of different factors to the development of the volume of French exports to West Germany	129
3.3	Evolution of the trade balance from 1978 to 1980	130
3.4	Elasticities in the major French macro-economic models	136
3.5	Increase in the perverse effect due to the oil shocks: a numerical example	139
3.6	Macro-economic effects of a 10% devaluation of the franc in 1985: findings of the major French models	142
3.7	Change in central rate and actual rate of currencies against the franc for the three devaluations	146
3.8	Macro-economic effect of parity changes in the EMS, ignoring induced effects on non-EMS currencies	151
3.9	Overall effect of currency realignments on inflation and current balance	153
3.10	Impact of the March 1983 austerity plan	163
3.11	Comparison of the effect of the international situation and economic policy on changes in the trade balance in 1982 and 1983	164
3.12	Part played by the main factors in industrial trade volume changes between 1981 and 1983	166
3.13	Changes in trade balances by groups of countries	169
3.14	The recovery of external trade in 1959, 1970 and 1983	174

List of Tables

3.15	France's balance of payments, 1980–6	179
3.16	Differing assessments of foreign debt as at 31 December 1983	183
3.17	Medium- and long-term changes in the external debt	184
3.18	Debt charges	185
4.1	Manual workers and white-collar workers (excluding large state undertakings): breakdown of weekly hours in each category	196
4.2	Change in yearly hours worked from 1981 to 1982	197
4.3	Effects of shorter working hours on employment practices	199
4.4	Effect on jobs of shorter working hours, according to the forecasting section of the Ministry of Employment	201
4.5	Impact of schemes linking government help with shorter working hours	206
4.6	Part-time work as % of total number of employed in major countries	208
4.7	Total number employed by central government between 1975 and 1984, as at 31 December (in thousands)	214
4.8	Total net new jobs in the public sector during the Interim Economic Plan (1981–3)	215
4.9	Job creation in the large state undertakings	218
4.10	Effect on unemployment of financial aid to boost employment	222
4.11	Employees taking early retirement as at 31 December 1979–84	224
4.12	Schemes in 1982 and 1983 linking government help with early retirement	226
4.13	Unemployment and early retirement benefits	229
4.14	Overall effect of 'jobs pacts' and the 'plan for the future of youth'	231
4.15	Help for youth employment 1982–6	233
4.16	Youth unemployment between 1979 and 1985	236
4.17	Impact of employment policies (excluding general economic policy) on change in unemployment	238
4.18	Breakdown of the annual change in the resident labour force, derived from number of people in employment at 31 March 1954–85	240
4.19	Annual average total of people in work, in France and other countries, between 1980 and 1984	244
5.1	Consumer prices in the major OECD countries	249
5.2	Factors explaining changes in hourly wage rate	254
5.3	Comparison of two assessments of the slow-down in rise of hourly wage rates in 1983–4	255
5.4	Production prices and costs of non-financial enterprises	259
5.5	Changes in retail prices, 1981–4	259

List of Tables

5.6	Quantitative assessment of the freeze and the policy of disindexation, 1981–4	260
5.7	Main factors in changes in the profits–value added ration for firms	261
5.8	Net lending by general government (including Currency Stabilization Fund) as % of GDP	265
5.9	Level and structure of interest payments by central government, excluding nationalizations	266
5.10	Changes in government spending after 1981 (excluding interest payments) in constant francs	266
5.11	Factors in the growth in welfare benefits	270
5.12	Net performance of nationalized undertakings	276
5.13	Rate of taxes and contributions as % of GDP	280
5.14	Factors in the change in the US federal deficit as % of GDP between 1981 and 1985	283
5.15	Contributions to change in real GNP in the United States from 1981 to 1984	285
5.16	Tax cuts in the 1985 and 1986 budgets	287
5.17	Planned reductions in government spending in the budgets of 1985 and 1986	288
5.18	Impact on the budget of the new measures in 1985 and 1986	289
5.19	Macro-economic impact of the 1985–6 budgetary measures	290
5.20	Growth, investment and consumption: changes in volume of the balance on goods and services between 1979 and 1984	292
5.21	Multiplier effect of an increase in public spending equal to 1% of GDP	294
5.22	Effect on the current balance of a budgetary expansion equal to 1% of GDP	295
5.23	Effect on the budget deficit of an increase in public spending equal to 1% of GDP	297
5.24	Actual rate of unemployment and the NAIRU	300

List of Figures

1.1	Effect of an increase in savings with propensity to consume of 0.5, and exogenous investment	13
1.2	Effect of an increase in savings when propensity to consume is 0.5 and 'propensity to invest' is 0.3	14
1.3	The depressive effects of a rise in relative import prices on a country the size of France	18
1.4	Cumulative effect of a rise in oil prices	19
1.5	Inflation and unemployment in the seven main OECD countries	24
1.6	Determination of prices and wages in neo-Keynesian models	26
1.7	Non-Walrasian equilibrium in the employment market	30
1.8	Disequilibria according to levels of real wages and autonomous demand	31
1.9	Persistence of Keynesian inflation when prices are downwardly inflexible	32
1.10	Probabilities of the different regimes	33
1.11	Changes in the proportion of profits in the value added of companies	35
1.12	Breakdown of changes in the proportion of profits in the value added of companies	36
1.13	Profit constraint and demand constraint on investment	38
1.14	World prices of raw materials imported by France	39
1.15	Annual change in consumer prices in the OECD as a whole	40
1.16	Changes in industrial production between 1972 and 1978	43
1.17	Effect of budget expansion and automatic stabilizers on the US recovery of 1975–6	46
1.18	Short-term interest rates in the United States, 1955–85	53
1.19	Money, growth and inflation in the United States, 1979–84	53
1.20	Industrial production in major OECD countries between 1977 and 1984	56
1.21	The worsening of France's international environment after the second oil shock	60
2.1	Consumer prices in the major countries from 1974 to 1981	68

–xiii–

List of Figures

2.2	Cover rate of external trade, i.e. ratio of exports (fob) to imports (cif), according to customs figures	70
2.3	Forecasting error in the change in the dollar rate, 1978–84	74
2.4	Change in the real value of the minimum wage since 1979	76
2.5	Changes in level of investment by central government, local authorities and social security organizations since 1960	86
2.6	Change in average gross income of agricultural holdings	89
2.7	Change in GDP, consumption and investment in France from 1973 to 1984	91
2.8	World demand for and exports of French manufactured goods	105
2.9	Change in GDP, investment and consumption in West Germany from 1973 to 1984	110
2.10	Balance of trade between France and West Germany from 1972 to 1984	114
2.11	Change in GNP of France and its main trading partners from 1973 to 1984	114
3.1	Part played by changes in volume and terms of trade in the deterioration of the balance of payments between 1978 and 1982	122
3.2	Value of the Deutschmark and Franco-German competitivity	125
3.3	Factors in changes in French exports of manufactured goods to West Germany	125
3.4	Pressures on the franc: money market rate and Euro-franc rate	131
3.5	10% devaluation of the franc against all currencies; change in the total external balance and the energy and industrial balances	141
3.6	Direct and induced effects of devaluation	143
3.7	Effect of three kinds of depreciation of the franc on the current external balance	144
3.8	Realignments of central rates and exchange rate changes of EMS currencies	147
3.9	Difference between the franc and the green franc	150
3.10	Monthly change in consumer prices, 1978–84	159
3.11	Difference between inflation in France and in six main trading partners (consumer prices), 1978–84	159
3.12	Real exchange rate (franc), 1978–84	159
3.13	Cover rate and cyclical gap in relation to France's main trading partners, 1978–83	168
3.14	Balance on current account as % of GDP	171
3.15	Factors explaining changes in external trade from 1950 to 1979	173

List of Figures

3.16	Indicator of real exchange rate against the Deutschmark	176
3.17	Balance on current account as % of GDP (Sweden, Spain and France)	177
3.18	Industrial production (Sweden, Spain and France)	177
3.19	Quarterly balance of direct investment and portfolio investment	180
3.20	Financing the deficit from current transactions and 'spontaneous' movements of capital	181
3.21	Medium- and long-term changes in the external debt	188
4.1	Reduction in the working week since the 1890s	192
4.2	Changes in the length of the working week since 1950 in firms employing more than ten people	194
4.3	Actual annual working hours in France and other countries	210
4.4	Length of working week in the United States, in the non-agricultural private sector	212
4.5	Unfilled vacancies at end of month	227
4.6	Number of people in employment, 1980–7	241
4.7	Unemployment, 1980–8	242
4.8	Comparison of unemployment rates in France and certain OECD countries	243
5.1	Price–wage loop and the mechanics of disinflation	252
5.2	Prices and wages	255
5.3	Investment by firms and savings by companies	262
5.4	Public debt at year-end and as % of GDP	265
5.5	Social welfare benefits as % of GDP	271
5.6	Social welfare benefits by category as % of GDP	272
5.7	Resources for social welfare provision by category and % of GDP	273
5.8	Apparent welfare contribution rates	274
5.9	Rate of taxes and welfare contributions	281
5.10	US federal budget – structural and cyclical deficit per calendar year, 1972–85	283
5.11	Change in GNP, household consumption and investment in the United States from 1973 to 1984	284

List of Insets

2.1	Family welfare benefit measures introduced between July 1980 and January 1983	79
2.2	Experiences of reflation in West Germany between 1974 and 1981	107
3.1	Econometric estimate of an export function, France to West Germany	127
3.2	Policies complementing the three currency realignments	156
3.3	The austerity programme of March 1983	160
4.1	Shorter working hours and worktime patterns: employees' wishes	204
4.2	Schemes linking government help with early retirement	225
5.1	A core model to analyse disindexation	257
5.2	Conditions for stabilization of the public debt/GDP ratio	267
5.3	The cost of the nationalizations	278

Preface to the English Edition

The French edition of this book was written mainly during the period 1984–5, at a time when the move away from reflation to a policy of austerity was perceived by public opinion as the failure of socialism *à la française* and of Keynesianism. Increased unemployment seemed inevitable and the Left's adoption of economic liberalism, austerity and a stable exchange rate of the franc against the Deutschmark seemed so sudden that there appeared to be no possible alternative to the attractive West German model of slow, 'virtuous' growth.

In accepting the constraints of an open economy, conveniently forgotten in 1981, the Left in France gradually came round to supply-side economics, at the same time giving its own explanation of the failure of reflation: French industry, starved of investment over many years, had been unable to meet increased demand. Because of this, there was a need to develop the supply side, and to 'stimulate saving to boost investment'. Throughout Europe, the classical approach prevailed: whether in terms of 'wage gap', 'classical unemployment' or the non-accelerating inflation rate (NAIRU), unemployment was rising simply because too much value added went on wages, and economic ills could only be cured by the medicine of austerity. However, in contrast with mounting unemployment in Europe, the United States' economy, stimulated by one of the strongest surges in demand since 1945, took only a few short years to get back to full employment.

Since we supported the shift from reflation to austerity in France in 1982–3, our aim in analysing this crucial period was to show that the results of France's go-it-alone reflation were no more than could be expected, given the international context at the time, and, moreover, that although austerity was necessary to boost firms' profits, bring down inflation and restore external balances, it needed to be dispensed with as soon as these aims were achieved. However, a purely national solution was no longer possible, at least in a context where there was no possibility of a competitive devaluation (certainly risky and above all uncooperative). As we saw it, the problem

Preface to the English Edition

with continental Europe was not inadequate supply (which, with firms' profit margins restored, depends, through investment, on how demand is likely to move, especially in the medium term), but slow growth in demand because of a severe and prolonged period of austerity. And the reason why austerity lasted so long was that European countries did not co-ordinate their response to the second oil shock and to the interest rate and dollar rise. The danger was that austerity would continue if there was no concerted action to re-expand European economies.

Considerations of this nature dictated our approach in this book: we examined the two oil shocks, then analysed successively the 1981–2 reflation, external constraints and austerity policy, as well as the various employment policies applied during the period, and concluded by stressing the need for a concerted re-expansion in Europe to move away from the mass unemployment which was a characteristic at the time and which even today remains as the legacy of fifteen years of slow growth.

When we were asked by Berg Publishers in late 1986 to update the book for an English edition, France was in the middle of an unusual 'cohabitation' between a left-wing president and a right-wing government. Its short-lived nature was not apparent at the time, but our view was that the key period for an understanding of economic and political changes in 1980s France still remained the first half of the decade, which saw the switch from reflation to austerity and – more fundamentally – from French-style utopian socialism to European-style social democracy. Because of this, in updating the book, we did not extend the period of analysis or change its basic structure. From today's perspective, it is clear that this period was in fact crucial, in the political as well as in the economic field. It introduced into France the possibility of a smooth alternation of power between the moderate Left and the moderate Right, such as has long existed in the English-speaking world and in Northern Europe. Moreover, the realization of the constraints of an open economy led to greater emphasis on establishing a consensus in France about the need for closer co-operation in Europe.

Such a consensus is not totally unambiguous. Some people (ourselves included) see Europe as a means to break out of the position of non-co-operation in which EEC member-states have become locked, and, by finally applying expansionist policies, to move back to full employment. The prospect of an eventual monetary union has, however, also served as an excuse for a policy of austerity within a European Monetary System (EMS) dominated by

Preface to the English Edition

West Germany. It is true that the concerted re-expansion which we called for in 1985 has partly materialized, not through political will, but because fiscal policy reacted passively to an external shock – the beneficial oil shock of 1986. The transfer of revenue stimulated consumption and investment, and the extra tax revenue from this was spent gradually by governments, so that economic recovery was compounded by the relaxation of fiscal policy. This delay in the reaction time of fiscal policy and the (short-lived) relaxation of monetary policy following the Autumn 1987 stock-market crash were responsible for the gradual accelaration of growth in 1988–9. However, the return to restrictive monetary policy in European countries in 1989 showed how difficult it was for the countries of continental Europe to break free of a decade of austerity.

Apart from a short period of activism during 'cohabitation' (1986–8), which was more verbal than real, French macro-economic policy in the second half of the 1980s was in fact merely a passive reaction to an improvement coming from outside, and this was in strange contrast to the activism of the first years of the left-wing government. Gradually, French activism in this area carried over into Europe, as is shown by François Mitterrand's phrase: 'France is our country, but Europe is our future.' It was this development which, clearly, was one of the truly positive legacies of the period 1981–6.

Pierre-Alain Muet
Alain Fonteneau
January 1990

Introduction

Though the Mauroy government came to power in 1981 on a programme of economic expansion, less than two years afterwards, it had to align with the austerity policies practised by most Western countries. Was it a case of the failure of left-wing Keynesianism? Or of a socialist government which did not follow its chosen path to a logical conclusion? Or of a level of state control incompatible with the dynamics of present-day societies? Much of the writing on this theme has tried to show, often by making free with the facts, that the economic crisis could have been solved in some miraculous way.

As participants in the debates provoked by the arrival of the Left in power, the authors of this book sometimes assumed the role of Cassandra, and sometimes overestimated the freedom of manoeuvre which was available; in the five years after 1981 we observed, compared and quantified the succession of plans and measures. We thought it right, therefore, to add our contribution to the study of the longest experiment of left-wing government that France, up to that time, had undertaken.

This book has no simple miracle solution to offer, but it does aim to show that the analytical approach which has inspired contemporary economic theory, and its quantitative manifestation – macro-economic modelling – can be used to describe what happened and to set a framework for economic policy, even to suggest the conditions for the lasting recovery of economic growth in Europe. Furthermore, we hope that an assessment of the extent to which the world environment allows freedom of manoeuvre for economic policy, and a systematic use of quantitative and comparative analysis, will throw rather calmer, subtler and more useful light on this subject than the approach of those who have too readily forgotten the constraints of power, or else never accepted that they existed.

Any study of the five years of left-wing government in France must begin with an examination of the crisis affecting the world economy after the mid-1970s. By one of the greatest paradoxes of history, this crisis, which is a striking illustration of some of the basic principles of Keynesian theory, came at a time when this theory was being called into question. At a period when, because of the excess of savings at a world level brought on by the oil price rises, Western economies were sinking into the greatest Keynesian depression of the post-war era, the inability of national policies to right the imbalances caused by the oil shocks was interpreted as a defect of Keynesian analysis.

This led many observers to think that the simultaneous increase in inflation and unemployment, to which the name 'stagflation' was later given, clearly proved the need for a new theory. Their view was that previous macro-economics, amounting to a fine-tuning of the economy between inflation and unemployment, could not explain the phenomenon. However, nearly all the neo-Keynesian models of the 1960s and 1970s were capable of describing correctly the stagflationary consequences of the oil shocks, as well as the difficulties which can be caused by reflation in isolation.

An understanding of the economic crisis is therefore a prerequisite of the study of economic policies, and this is doubly important since the fact that reality appeared to lack any order led to a host of unrefined theories. The success of monetarist, neo-liberal and some Marxist theories is due to a large extent to the simplicity of their diagnosis and of the remedies they suggested. Whereas the practitioners of economic policy were making patient and cautious progress in understanding phenomena, ordinary discourse remained dominated by ideology. In parallel, economic theory was moving further and further away from reality; considerations of relevance were gradually being pushed out by the desire for originality and novelty.

The fact that a crisis caused partly by untrammelled economic liberalism, which presided over the internationalization of production and capital and brought to an end regulation by individual countries, led to the triumph of the liberal doctrine, is eloquent testimony of how far opinion was in disarray. Greater deregulation and flexibility can, of course, favour development, but they are not capable of righting the macro-economic imbalances which restrain world growth.

The dominant part played by liberalism in discourse is not matched when it comes to the real world. Regardless of their ideological inspiration, French governments in the forty years after the war constantly followed a policy of massive state intervention, not only by regulating demand, but also through industrial policy. In the early 1980s, the Reagan administration applied the first part of the classical liberal creed by a huge reduction in taxation; but it refrained from applying the second one – cuts in government spending. The result was that, in the guise of supply-side economics, the United States underwent the strongest Keynesian reflation of demand in the forty years since 1945.

Marxism followed roughly the same course; though the official doctrine of communist parties, and the implicit approach of a fraction of the socialist Left, it has never, in developed capitalist countries, gone beyond the status of ideology. As 'working-class parties' achieved power, as an exceptional event before the war, but on a regular basis since, Marxism ceased to inspire theory in those countries where the Left held power long and often enough for doctrine to merge into practice. It is true that Marxist economists thought that the difficulties in the decade after 1974 amounted to the crisis of capitalism which they had always predicted. Moreover, the drop in firms' profitability in some countries before the oil shock, and in all countries afterwards, gave new life to the 'law of the downward trend in profit rates', and meant that the Marxist analysis which attributed the economic crisis to a fall in profits came curiously close to the classical liberal diagnosis. However, as in the case of many other phenomena – for example, the rise in external and budget deficits, and in inflation – the fall in profits was both a consequence and a cause of the economic crisis. The truth is that because of the interdependence of economic phenomena, a couple of stylized facts can always be picked out to corroborate a simple thesis.

Lack of technological progress and the decline of European economies were other arguments put forward by some Marxist and classical liberal analysts. This happens frequently in times of economic recession. At the end of the 1930s, Keynes denounced those over-pessimistic people who attributed the economic crisis to the decline of the West. More recently, just before the first oil shock, economists were noting the sluggishness of US growth compared with Europe, and spoke of an 'American decline' which would last to the end of the 1970s. By the mid-1980s, the same people (now joined by others) were saying that European economic problems were caused by technological backwardness in the face of US dynamism.

Europe, however, was no more backward than the United States in the mid-1980s than it was in the early 1970s. Its problem is that it is divided into states which no longer have individual influence on a global economy dominated by *laissez-faire*. An individual European country cannot apply on its own a policy of economic expansion in the manner of the US economy, which is less open to foreign competition and which has the advantage of a world currency to finance its external deficit. Moreover, one has only to look at the wider context to see that policies based on competitive supply-side economics merely export problems to other countries.

If, as seems to be the fashion, we have to summarize our conclusions in a simple formula, we would say that the difficulties caused by the economic crisis showed how the market was unable satisfactorily to ensure full employment and the smooth functioning of the economy; and that this demonstrates the need for macroeconomic regulation of the economy. In the thirty years after 1945, the effect of economic regulation at the national level and the international monetary system was to preserve the stability of exchange rates and make sure that productive activity was not hampered by speculators and *rentiers*. However, the internationalization of production and capital led to the gradual break-up of the system, which put it at the mercy of the slightest jolt. Then the oil shocks occurred, to send the world economy into stagflation and recession.

The Keynesian approach, which was in part that of the Left in France, was one way out of the economic crisis, provided it was applied to the world economy as a whole or at least to Western Europe as a whole. What Léon Blum wrote in the dark hours of the occupation of France is still relevant today. It could easily apply to the difficulties faced by the Left forty years later.

The reader is therefore invited to accompany us in an analysis of the economic crisis and the economic policy of the Left in the years 1981–6. We have tried to write for the general reader, but macro-economics is complex, and we wanted to avoid any distortion through over-simplification. Several difficult detours are therefore necessary, though these can be omitted from a first reading.

The book is based on the numerous quantitative findings by our own econometric models, but we have tried to make the conclusions as firm as possible by calling on other tools of analysis, to indicate where there are differences or uncertainties. Where possible therefore, we have compared our findings with the assessments of government economic departments.

The first of the five chapters offers a theoretical analysis of the economic crisis, then a quantitative description of the way the world economy developed since the early 1970s. It shows in particular that the macro-economic imbalances caused by the oil shocks were not insignificant, as some superficial analyses led people to believe.

When the Left came to power, the French economy was already embarked on a recovery in domestic demand which had been

Introduction

underestimated for a long time, inflation was high, and the external deficit resulting from the second oil shock had not been cleared. In a situation of this nature, was it reasonable to go for reflation? The answer is less simple than is generally assumed. The world economy began to take off again in the first half of 1981, and all forecasters, in France and elsewhere, anticipated that growth would continue into 1982, and that the dollar would stabilize after the sharp rise since the middle of 1980. But instead of this recovery there was another recession, brought on by US restrictive monetary policy, and France's external deficit worsened because of a cyclical gap.

Chapter 2 examines the role played by the international environment and domestic policy in the events of 1981–2, then compares this with the Chirac reflation of 1975 and the various West German reflation policies between 1974 and 1979. Reflation came to grief through external constraints, not because of the competitivity losses which they caused, but because external trade was highly sensitive to changes in income. If price competitivity had played the part traditionally attributed to it, external constraints would have been easily countered by the government's devaluations. But the effect which parity changes had on the economy had been altered significantly by structural changes since the oil shocks and by the fact of floating exchange rates.

What was the effect of changes in the value of the franc within the EMS? Should the first devaluation have been earlier and bigger? Could economic austerity have been avoided? Is the level of debt a constraint for the future? These questions are examined in Chapter 3. The answers to them are primarily based on a quantitative analysis of the parity changes through devaluation, and of the factors leading to a worsening and then an improvement of the external balance; comparative reference is also made to previous devaluations in France (1958 and 1969) and abroad (Spain in December 1982 and Sweden in October 1982).

Bringing down unemployment by macro-economic mechanisms alone would have required a growth higher than 5% a year, which was out of the question given the world situation. Accordingly, it was necessary to continue, and develop further, specific employment policies applied during the 1970s, particularly in the fields of youth training and lowering of retirement age. At the same time, the Left tried to promote a new distribution of work, designed especially to increase the number of jobs, but also to achieve a better balance between work and leisure. Features of this policy were the reduction of the standard working week to thirty-nine hours, the introduction in 1982 of a general right to five weeks' paid holiday, and adjustments in working hours so that the way production was organized could be tied in with the shorter working week. Chapter 4 examines how effective these measures were, and looks at their effect on unemployment.

Paradoxically, the Left government succeeded where it was least expected – in bringing down inflation. The expectation of a continuing rise in the inflation rate was stopped by a particularly effective freeze on prices and incomes, followed by the policy of 'disindexation', and this led from 1983 to a significant fall in inflation and a recovery of firms' profits, which within a period of three years cancelled out the effects of two oil shocks. Bringing down the external deficits and the inflation rate was buttressed by the fall in domestic demand resulting from the new fiscal policy introduced in March 1983. The reduction in public and social spending was all the greater in that the government tried simultaneously to limit the public deficit to 3% of GDP, and to reduce taxes and social security contributions.

In its five years of power, the French Left succeeded, with fewer problems than elsewhere, in stabilizing the economy, which was one of the prerequisites for lasting recovery from the economic crisis. But this cannot be achieved by the market alone, and cannot rest on reflation by one country alone. Only a co-ordinated European reflation, based on overall medium-term programmes, can allow us to emerge finally from the economic crisis and ensure that the efforts to put the French economy back on course have not been in vain. These are the themes of the final chapter.

–1–

Understanding the Economic Crisis

The dubious assumption that understanding difficulties is the same thing as solving them has led many people to see the economic crisis as a clear indication of the inadequacies of contemporary economic theory. Perhaps there is an element of justice in the fact that economists, who have reaped unjustifiable benefits from this assumption during thirty years of growth, should now be experiencing the reverse side of the coin. Progress comes undoubtedly from questioning accepted ideas, but knowledge can be increased only if an effort is also made to see whether existing theories can account for observed phenomena. Those economists who had patiently forged the instruments needed for quantitative analysis of macroeconomic phenomena did of course make such an effort, but others took advantage of the apparent lack of order in reality to develop the most unlikely theories.

As happens often under such circumstances, the new ideas produced were little more than an updated version of the old ones. Thus all those keen to see an end to the Keynesian era[1] in terms of both economic thought and practice saw the economic crisis as an opportunity to question the wisdom of government intervention and to advocate a return to reliance on market forces alone. With market regulation in crisis, the call was for deregulation and less government intervention.

Others saw the economic crisis as reflecting the gradual collapse of the 'Fordist model' based on harmonious growth of productivity and real earnings. The recession of the 1930s had stemmed from the contradiction between greatly increased productivity and stagnant real earnings, thus leading to lack of demand and Keynesian depression. That of the 1970s, on the other hand, was due to lower productivity gains and a reduction in the return on capital. By this means, the traditional theory that there is a downward trend in profit levels, which is more or less implied in many Marxist analyses, came closer to the classical (in the Keynesian sense) theory of

1. The phrase was used by Jacques Rueff in *Le Monde*, February 1976.

unemployment whereby growth comes to a standstill when the level of real earnings is too high.

As is often pointed out in studies of the economic crisis, productivity gains in a number of countries began to slow as soon as post-war recovery[2] came to an end but, as with the consequent decline in profitability, this slackening off made itself felt only after the oil shocks, and as a result of them.[3]

The fact that many analysts of the economic crisis have been able to regard these effects as insignificant is a clear indication of the strong need for a quantitative analysis to show that the economic crisis is fundamentally macro-economic in nature, even though certain structural factors have played a part in its propagation.

In fact, the economic crisis which by 1985 had persisted for more than ten years can be seen to have two main causes:

1 The gradual disappearance of national and international macro-economic methods of market regulation (Bretton Woods system) as a result of the increasingly international nature of trade and capital.
2 The disequilibria produced by the two oil shocks: on the one hand, a sharp rise in prices accompanied by increased external deficits among importing countries and, on the other hand, the dampening effect of an increase in savings world-wide caused by the transfer of income from countries with a high propensity to spend to countries with a high propensity to save. This depression led to increased unemployment, greater public deficits and lower profits for firms. The weakness in demand and – to a lesser extent – in profitability led in turn to a weakness in investment and contributed to the lasting nature of the economic crisis. Inflation, external deficits and national income deficits militated against the separate adoption by the various governments of policies to stimulate demand. The situation was ripe for the industrialized economies and with them the rest of the world, including Eastern countries, to plunge into economic crisis. All these factors will be

2. These periods were much longer than the time needed to return to pre-war levels of production. The difference between the development capacity of economies in ruin and the actual production level lasted about fifteen years. On this point, see, for example, F. Janossy, *La fin des miracles économiques* (An end to economic miracles), Paris, Seuil, 1972.
3. Although economists have written extensively on the economic crisis, few in France have analysed correctly the effects of the oil shocks. One of the clearest analyses is by Raymond Barre in a chapter of his book *Une politique pour l'avenir* (A policy for the future), Paris, Plon, 1981, pp. 100–14 and in an interview published in *Le Quotidien de Paris*, 13–14 February 1982.

analysed firstly from a theoretical standpoint and secondly by examining the consequences of both oil shocks.

The first part of the chapter is essentially theoretical. Readers who are interested mainly in the crisis from a narrative viewpoint will miss nothing by reading the introduction to this first part and then going straight to the second section beginning on p. 39.

The Oil Shocks: Keynesian Depression and Stagflation

The most obvious consequence of an oil shock is its effect on inflation. In the case of the first oil shock, this aspect was generally anticipated without difficulty. But the most significant effect – the transfer of income from high-spending countries to high-saving countries, which brought about the ensuing economic crisis – tended to be missed at the time. The rise in oil-based product prices in 1974–5 and 1979–80 meant for OECD countries a loss of income of the order of 2% of GDP.

If the oil shocks had gone no further than transferring income in this way – in other words if the oil-exporting countries had immediately spent this extra money on goods and services – the loss of income would have been cancelled out by a corresponding increase[4] in real GDP in the oil-importing countries. But because of the low capacity of absorption of oil-exporting countries, particularly those of the Middle East, this transfer of income brought about a significant increase of world-wide saving, and the depressive consequences described in Keynesian theory. No economic crisis has had a more 'Keynesian' beginning than that which started in 1974. Of course, an analysis of its longer-term effects has to be more sophisticated than that offered by the basic Keynesian model, but before studying these effects we must first have a sound understanding of the mechanisms involved.

Classical economic theory, which is more or less implicit in many macro-economic analyses, suggests that excess savings always end up by being re-spent in some way, so that the downturn in demand caused by an increase in saving is only temporary. It is easy to see that hoarding leads to a downturn in demand, but it would seem logical that the recycling of petrodollars – monetary flows created by the savings of OPEC countries and invested in the financial

---

4. Assuming that the production capacities of the importing countries were able to adapt quickly to the demand.

markets of industrialized countries – ends up by stimulating investment because it leads to a drop in interest rates. Like the classical theory from which it is derived, this way of looking at things is based on the idea that saving determines investment. However, if investment is basically dependent on anticipated demands, which are particularly quiet when consumption dips, then the effect of increased saving is exactly the opposite. This is one of the basic lessons of Keynesian theory which will be evoked. It will then be shown that the usual extension of Keynesian theory to include an open economy is sufficient to explain both the qualitative and quantitative aspects of the dampening effects of oil shocks.[5]

Saving and Investment: A Return to Keynes and Classical Economics

Keynesian principles can be illustrated using the basic example of a closed economy consisting of three economic agents (firms, households and government) and two markets (the market in goods and services and the financial markets as a whole defined as the balance between saving and investment) – see Appendix 1.1.

The accounting process ensures that the *ex post* equilibrium of the market in goods and services:

Production = Consumption + Investment

matches that of saving and investment:

Total saving = Total investment

According to classical theory, this adjustment of saving and investment is brought about by interest rates. Production is therefore never held back by demand since, by balancing saving and investment, variations in interest rates automatically adjust demand to match supply of goods (law of markets, or Say's Law). Competition between manufacturers therefore leads to production at a level which provides maximum opportunity for profits to be made by firms and for the workforce to be fully employed, provided that prices and wages are sufficiently flexible.[6] Change in the consump-

---

5. The various points covered in this section are taken from P.-A. Muet, *Théories et modèles de la macro-économie* (Theories and models in macro-economics), Vol. 1, Paris, Economica, 1984.
6. Where there is not enough flexibility, there would be 'classical unemployment' with profitable production capacity limited by real wage levels which were too high.

Understanding the Economic Crisis

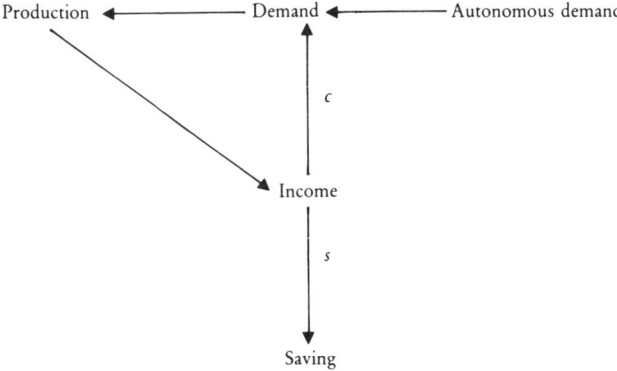

tion–saving share in favour of saving reduces consumption but also gives lower interest rates and increases investment without decreasing production.

Keynesian theory, on the other hand, describes a situation where production is limited by the level of demand and where there can be at the same time surplus usable capacity (firms could increase their profits by raising production if demand were greater) and surplus available labour (unemployment).

Such a situation may emerge because, contrary to classical theory, saving depends mainly on income, and investment is determined essentially by businesspeople's forecasts of future demand, which play a much greater role than interest rate changes.[7] If in the first instance exogenous investment is assumed, as in the basic form of Keynesian theory, then the level of production is determined by the level of autonomous demand (investment and public spending) through the multiplier, in accordance with the traditional circuit (as shown above).

Thus, unemployment is caused by insufficient autonomous demand and/or too low a propensity to consume. Without an increase in the propensity to consume or in autonomous demand, there is no reason for the economy to move towards full employment. If firms increased production without any other element changing, demand would rise by only a fraction (c) of the growth in production (the remainder $1 - c$ being saved) and, consequently, firms could not dispose of the additional output.

In other words, the equilibrium position of Keynesian underem-

---

7. These two hypotheses have been fully confirmed by econometric estimates.

ployment is stable and can be altered only by a policy of increased government spending or a change in business forecasts.

An ex ante rise in saving produces a reduction in income . . . According to classical theory, an increase in saving leads to a reduction in interest rates and therefore increases investment; in a situation of Keynesian underemployment, however, its only effect is to reduce consumption, income and production. Moreover, the new equilibrium does not affect the level of saving since, *ex post*, this is bound to be equal to the level of investment, which has not changed. As Keynes said, 'it is . . . impossible for the community as a whole to save *less* than the amount of current investment, since the attempt to do so will necessarily raise incomes to a level at which the sums that individuals choose to save add up to a figure exactly equal to the amount of investment'.[8]

This mechanism can be shown numerically by taking, as a simple example, a marginal propensity to consume of 0.5. If households shift from consumption to saving to the tune of 10 billion francs, production and income are reduced until a new equilibrium between supply and demand is reached, i.e. when production and income have gone down by 20 billion francs. This drop is equal to the *ex ante* reduction in demand (10 billion francs) together with the reduction caused by the halving of income – another 10 billion francs (see Figure 1.1).

The same result is obtained when *ex post* saving is taken to be the same as investment. Since investment is taken as unchanged, the secondary effect on saving of a drop in income (*s* times the drop in income) must be exactly equal to the original increase (10 billion). So the drop in income is equal to the product of the *ex ante* increase in saving by the multiplier (equal to the inverse of the rate of saving).

The initial rise in saving therefore leads *ex post*, that is after market adjustment, to a drop in supply and demand of 20 billion and a level of saving which is unchanged.

. . . which can bring about a fall in investment . . . Keynes however goes further in his analysis: 'The act of saving not only reduces present consumption, it can further weaken investment'.[9] If, in fact, forecasts about future demand are based largely on present demand,

---

8. J.M. Keynes, *The general theory of employment, interest and money* (The Collected Writings of J.M. Keynes, Vol. VII), London, Macmillan, 1973, p. 84.
9. Ibid., p. 212.

Understanding the Economic Crisis

Figure 1.1 Effect of an increase in savings with propensity to consume of 0.5, and exogenous investment

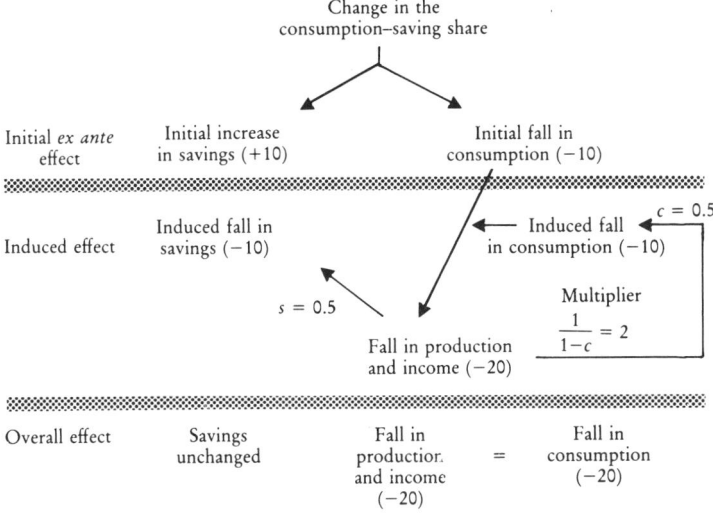

a rise in saving which reduces production will lead to a fall in investment. This is confirmed by econometric studies which show clearly the importance of the acceleration effect in explaining fluctuations in investment.

The relationship between increase in demand and increase in investment is complex. When demand rises, firms will invest if several conditions are present. Firstly, the increase in demand must be seen as likely to be permanent, in order to justify an increase in productive capacity. Secondly, there must not already be spare productive capacity in relation to demand. Finally, the increase in production must make marginal profit at least equal to the financial cost of the investment. Ordinary economic models generally take account of these different factors, so that the relationship between increase in demand and investment is far from being as automatic as is assumed in the following example.[10]

Let us assume that all the conditions mentioned are met and that demand increases by 1 billion francs. Since the relationship of capital to production (coefficient of capital) is on average 1.5 in the economy as a whole, investment ought to increase by 1.5 billion francs if capital is adjusted during the period. In fact, this effect is

10. See also p. 37.

Reflation and Austerity

Figure 1.2 Effect of an increase in savings when propensity to consume is 0.5 and 'propensity to invest' is 0.3

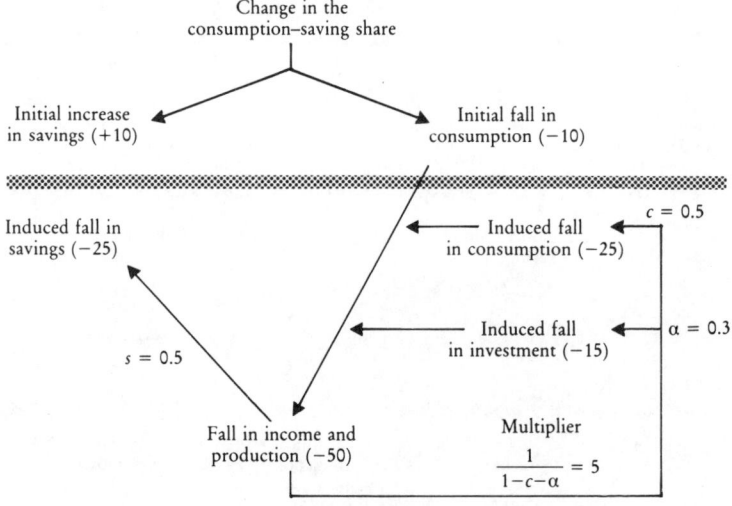

much less marked because of delays in capital adjustment and because forecasts are based on permanent variations of demand. On average, an increase in demand of 1 billion francs increases investment by only 0.3 billion to 0.5 billion in the short run, that is, over a year. This is shown in simulations by French models given in Appendix 1.2.

So let us take the figures in the last example and assume a marginal propensity to invest of 0.3. The *ex ante* increase in saving of 10 billion francs leads to a much bigger drop in income because the multiplier effect becomes 5 with the addition of the propensity to invest.[11] This reduction in income – of 50 billion francs – leads to a further drop in consumption of 25 billion francs ($c = 0.5$) and in investment of 15 billion ($\alpha = 0.3$), giving a total fall in demand of 50 billion (10 *ex ante* and 40 brought about by the fall in income).

... and an ex post *reduction in saving* The reduction in income of 50 billion brings about a reduction in saving of 25 billion ($s = 0.5$), so that the *ex ante* rise in saving becomes *ex post* a 15 billion drop in saving and investment (see Figure 1.2).

This example shows that *ex post* findings cannot be interpreted

11. It is clear that a multiplier effect of 5 is exaggerated in relation to a real economy. This is because we are ignoring stabilizers such as taxation and imports, which will be introduced in the next section.

without taking into account macro-economic interrelations. In a case where, in a given year, the only exogenous change over the previous year has been that certain households have saved 10 billion francs by reducing their consumption, the macro-economic effect will be a drop of 15 billion in saving and investment. But a superficial analysis of these results will lead to the conclusion that saving has fallen by 15 billion bringing about a reduction in investment of the same amount, whereas this drop was in fact caused by a 10 billion surplus of *ex ante* saving over investment and public spending.

This shows how important it is to use a theoretical framework which is consistent and quantified when analysing past developments. Many factors have an effect on the figures as they appear *ex post* and it is unusual for these factors, which have had a bearing on the results, to be identified by unrefined analysis of the figures.

The 10 billion *ex ante* discrepancy between supply and demand or between saving and investment could have been cleared, without any reduction in income, by a budget increase of 10 billion francs financed by loans or an increase in money supply – in other words, by a deficit of the same amount. This budget increase would have offset the drop in consumption by avoiding a fall in production and income. But the compensation would have been that excess saving would have been absorbed on the financial market by a public deficit in the form of a fall in government saving.

Having surveyed what Keynesian theory would be expected to show, it will now be applied to the analysis of an open economy and of the rise in oil prices.

Open Economy and Rise in Oil Prices: Lessons From a Keynesian Model

An oil price rise is equivalent to enforced saving In an economy open to international trade, the equilibrium between aggregate supply and demand is:

$$\text{Production} + \text{Imports} = \text{Consumption} + \text{Investment} + \text{Exports}$$

and the equilibrium between saving and investment brings in the current figure for balance of payments, appearing on the saving side if it is in deficit or on the investment side if it is in surplus:

$$\text{Domestic saving} + \text{Deficit in the current balance} = \text{Investment}$$

A rise in oil prices brings about a sharp deterioration in the terms of trade and in the deficit in the current balance of oil-importing countries. The effect of this, analysed as an increase in saving, is to accelerate inflation and depress domestic demand, and this will be examined by developing the Keynesian model outlined earlier. The figures under consideration (for income, saving, investment, etc.) are expressed in real terms, that is, adjusted for change in domestic demand prices. In fact, because of imported inflation, nominal figures rise in response to the shock whereas real ones fall. This reversal of the normal situation is characteristic of stagflation, and will be examined in more detail later.

The change in the terms of trade also causes a divergence between changes in real GDP and those in real national income, defined as nominal income adjusted by the index of domestic demand prices. The immediate effect of a worsening of the terms of trade is a fall in the purchasing power of national income. This brings about a contraction of demand and therefore a reduction in real GDP and investment. The total reduction in real income is therefore equal to the initial drop (external price rise) plus the fall in real GDP.

A simple model to analyse induced effects on the French economy   The previous model will be further refined by distinguishing between the effect of real income and of real GDP on the principal components of demand. The formal model and the value of the coefficients are shown in Appendix 1.2. National income is made up of firms' disposable income (net saving or self-financing), disposable income of households and government revenue in the form of taxation. On the assumption that a change of 1 billion francs in national income brings about a change in self-financing of a billion (taking a as 0.1) and in net transfer taxation of t billion ($t = 0.3$), then the change in disposable income of households will be $1 - a - t$, or 0.6 billion francs.

Taking, in relation to disposable income, a marginal propensity to consume (c) as 0.8 and to save (s) as 0.2, a change of 1 billion francs in real national income will bring about a change in consumption of:

$$c(1 - a - t) = 0.48 \text{ billion}$$

and in real saving of:

$$s(1 - a - t) = 0.12 \text{ billion}$$

As before, the assumption is that investment depends mainly on real

Understanding the Economic Crisis

GDP, and the marginal propensity to invest is taken as 0.5

Finally, the volume of imports is also a function of changes in the volume of production and domestic demand. Since a large proportion of imports is made up of intermediate goods and capital goods, it is more convenient to link the volume of imports with real GDP than with real income. Simulations by French models show that the net marginal propensity to import (m) is higher than the average propensity (i.e. the relationship of imports to GDP, about 30% in 1984) and represents between 40% and 50% of the increase in GDP. The figure for this marginal propensity is therefore put at 0.45.

At these values, the multiplier effect of an exogenous increase in a component element of demand is, in the simplified model (see Appendix 1.2):

$$\frac{1}{1 + m - c(1 - a - t) - \alpha} = 1.5$$

while each unit of reduction of real national income induces a fall in GDP of:

$$\frac{c(1 - a - t)}{1 + m - c(1 - a - t) - \alpha} = 0.7$$

These multiplier coefficients give an appropriate order of magnitude for knock-on effects in the short to medium term, that is, when these effects reach their culmination – about two years after the initial impact.

Dampening effect and restoration of equilibrium between saving and investment The externally induced price rise stemming from the rise in the terms of trade was on average, in the two oil shocks, of the order of 2% of GDP for the main oil-importing countries of the OECD. This price rise induces an initial fall in real income of 2%, which causes a drop in consumption and a decrease in real GDP and investment (see Figure 1.3). Since the impact coefficient of real income on real GDP is 0.7 in the case of our simplified model, GDP goes down by 1.4%, which causes a total drop in real national income of 3.4% – a 2% loss of purchasing power plus 1.4% loss from the fall in GDP. Since the values of the parameters have been previously introduced, it is easy to calculate the secondary effects expressed as percentage points of GDP, as Figure 1.3 shows.

Household consumption goes down 1.6 percentage points,

–17–

Figure 1.3 The depressive effects of a rise in relative import prices (in % of GDP) on a country the size of France

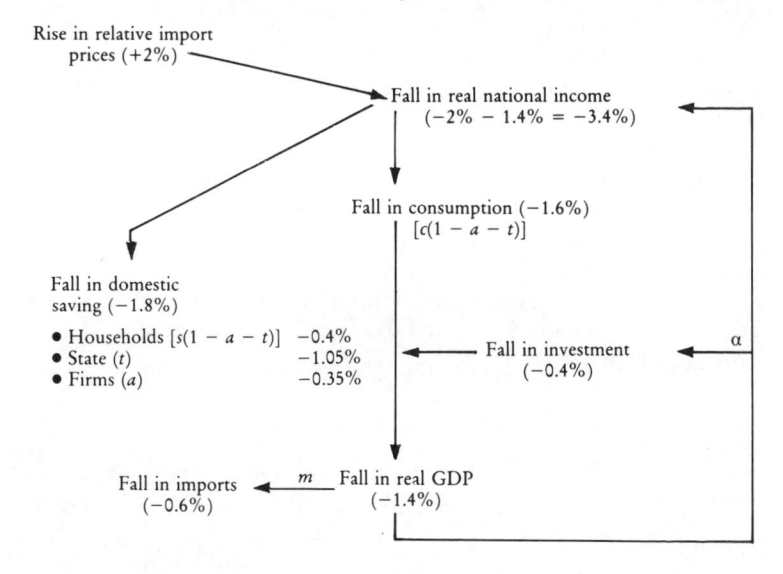

```
Rise in relative import
    prices (+2%) ─────────────► Fall in real national income ◄──────────┐
         │                         (−2% − 1.4% = −3.4%)                 │
         │                                │                             │
         │                                ▼                             │
         │                       Fall in consumption (−1.6%)            │
         │                            [c(1 − a − t)]                    │
         ▼                                                              │
    Fall in domestic                                                    │
    saving (−1.8%)                                                      │
    • Households [s(1 − a − t)]  −0.4%                                  │
    • State (t)                  −1.05%    Fall in investment          α│
    • Firms (a)                  −0.35%  ◄──── (−0.4%) ◄────────────────┤
                                │                                       │
                                ▼                                       │
         Fall in imports  ◄──m── Fall in real GDP                       │
            (−0.6%)               (−1.4%) ────────────────────────────┘
```

investment 0.4 points, giving a total reduction in demand of 2 points. Supply goes down by the same amount – 0.6 points in imports and 1.4 points in GDP.

The *ex ante* excess of external saving equivalent to 2% of GDP is wiped out partly by the drop in domestic saving of 1.8 points, which is made up of a reduction in household saving of 0.4 points, in firms' saving of 0.35 points and in government saving of 1.05 points, and partly by the drop in imports which reduces the *ex ante* deficit by 0.6 points. As in the previous example, the *ex ante* increase in external saving causes an *ex post* fall in total saving equal to the reduction in investment (0.4 points):

Ex post external deficit	1.4% of GDP
Reduction in real domestic saving	−1.8% of GDP
= Decrease in investment	−0.4% of GDP

Contraction of World Trade and Worsening of the Recession

In our calculation, which relates to the French economy, the initial balance of payments deficit of 2% of GDP was partly offset by the 0.6% drop in imports, due to the depressive effect. This in fact

Figure 1.4 Cumulative effect of a rise in oil prices

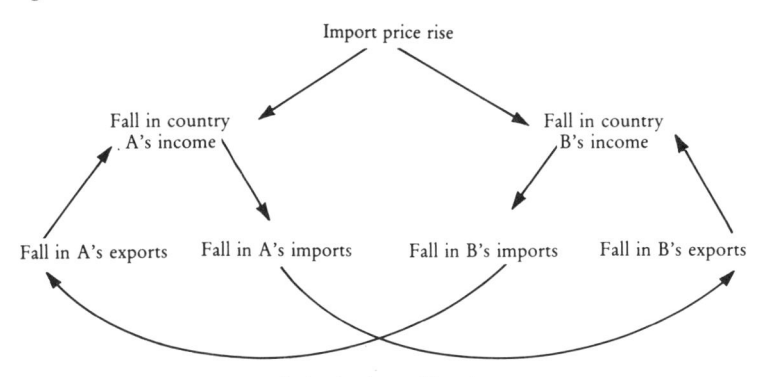

```
                        Import price rise
                       ↙              ↘
         Fall in country              Fall in country
          A's income                    B's income
        ↗            ↘                ↙            ↘
Fall in A's exports  Fall in A's imports  Fall in B's imports  Fall in B's exports
         ↖_____╳_____↗
                   Reduction in world trade
```

would have been the case if France's chief trading partners had not also been hit by the oil shock. However, the fact that they also suffered a drop in imports meant that this offset practically disappeared and at the same time the depressive effect was magnified because external markets declined, as Figure 1.4 shows.

A worsening world recession A rough idea of the total depressive effect of an oil shock can be gained by applying the previous model to oil-importing countries as a whole. If the coefficients previously determined for the French economy are used for the different countries of this group, it is easy to arrive at the model applicable to the whole group, by ignoring intra-group trade; the only change needed is in the propensity to import – this now relates only to oil imports, i.e. about 5% of GDP ($m = 0.05$).

The depressive effect of a unit reduction in national income is then 1.77 instead of 0.7, so that an oil price rise of 2% brings about, for oil-importing countries as a whole, a drop in GDP of 3.5% and in real income of 5.5%. Consumption and investment fall by 2.7% and 1% of GDP respectively. The reduction in the external deficit is no more than the reduction in oil imports caused by the economic crisis, amounting to only 0.18% of the group's GDP.

Confirmation of this brief outline comes from simulations carried out by the OECD using the INTERLINK multinational model (see Table 1.1). According to these, the drop in real income caused directly by the oil shock (revenue transfers and fall in GDP because of saving by OPEC) was 6% of GNP for the whole of the OECD in 1981, that is, the same order of magnitude as the results given by our theoretical model (5.5%).

Table 1.1 Impact of the oil price rise on the real income of OECD countries as a whole (in % of GDP)

	Theoretical model (m = 0.05)	OECD estimate 1980	OECD estimate 1981
Worsening of the terms of trade	2	1.75	1.75
GDP losses because of savings by OPEC	3.5	3	4.25
Overall effect on real income	5.5	4.75	6

Source: 'The cost of OPEC II', *OECD Observer*, 115, March 1982, p. 37.

Where did all the petrodollars go? The idea that saving by OPEC countries simply disappeared into thin air and had no equivalent in terms of investment goes so much against natural intuition that we must again refer to the *ex post* re-establishment of an equilibrium between saving and investment. The surplus of saving by OPEC countries over investment (capital expenditure within their own countries), equivalent to their financial surplus, was estimated at 2% of the GDP of importing countries. How was this surplus offset?

The coefficients used in our model allow us to calculate the secondary effect of a fall in world income and GDP on the saving and investment of oil-importing countries. Investment fell by 1% of GDP, and tax revenue and therefore public saving by 1.6% of GDP; the drop in firms' saving was 0.3% and saving by households fell by 0.7% of GDP (see Table 1.2). Excess saving by OPEC countries was slightly offset by a drop in oil imports amounting to 0.18% of the GDP of importing countries.

It is clear therefore that petrodollars looking for somewhere to be invested are not simply lost in the sand; through Swiss, US and UK banks, they were used to finance public and private deficits caused by oil price rises. From the financial point of view, they helped finance oil-importing economies; they did not however lead to a rise in world investment, which in fact fell because of the recession. All they did was to form a substitute for saving by oil-importing countries, which also fell because of the economic crisis.

This analysis needs to be refined by reference to the effects of nterest rate changes brought about by economic agents changing heir portfolios, though these effects were marginal until inconsistencies between budgetary deficits and tight money supply as the result of 'monetarist' policies brought a sharp rise in real interest rates.

Table 1.2 The saving–investment equilibrium at world level – theoretical model (changes as % of GDP of importing countries)

	Ex ante	Effects induced by the world recession[a]	Ex post
Surplus saving by OPEC	+2	−0.18	+1.82
Savings by oil-importing countries:			
Households $s\,(1-a-t) \times 5.5\%$		−0.66	−0.66 ⎫
States $t \times 5.5\%$		−1.65	−1.65 ⎬ −1.05
Firms $a \times 3.5\%$		−0.35	−0.35 ⎭
Investment by oil-importing countries: $\alpha \times 3.5\%$		−1.05	−1.05

[a] Fall in real income 5.5%, fall in GDP 3.5%.

Without the recycling of petrodollars, oil-importing countries would not have been able to finance their external deficit over several years, and would have been forced to reduce their income more than was the case, in order to wipe out more quickly the deficit caused by oil price rises. Conversely, whereas excess saving by OPEC was to a large extent recycled, it is not clear exactly how the implications of the behavioural relationships used in our simplified model gave rise to a fall in demand. What is implied is that, for an economic agent, a loan is not the same as income, because savings have to be constituted in order to repay it.[12] If we take all importing countries as a single agent, then the oil shock is equivalent to an extra tax of 2% on income plus a loan offer of the same amount if the petrodollars are immediately recycled. Why should this apparently neutral transfer bring about a reduction of demand on the part of the agent? Quite simply because, being conscious that the extra tax and the corresponding loan are permanent features, the agent has in the nature of things to generate saving to pay back the loan and the interest on it. In other words, the drop in income has a simultaneous effect on spending and saving; it is not limited to a reduction in saving. This is all the more true in that economic agents such as firms and households, who see their real income going down, are not the same as those such as banks who benefit from loans. This leads to a depressive multiplier effect since, in an

12. See *The Life Cycle Hypothesis*, (Modigliani Nobel lecture, 1985).

exchange economy, the reduction in spending of one agent leads inevitably to the reduction in income of another. The first mechanism shows at the macro-economic level in the rigid relationship between consumption and income (propensity to consume), and the second in the relationship between world income and world demand.

The Worsening of Deficits

The dampening effect of the second oil shock was aggravated by restrictive policies aimed at stemming both inflation and the rise in external and budget deficits. The inflationary impact will be dealt with in the next section, but the way in which deficits worsened because of the crisis can be illustrated by our simplified model.

With a marginal rate of tax of 0.3, the drop of 5.5% in real income led to a fall in tax revenue of 1.65% of GDP almost all of which, because of the inflexibility of spending, worked through to increase the budget deficit. The initial increase in the external deficit of importing countries as a whole was only marginally compensated by the recession and continued at 1.8% of GDP. This led inevitably in all countries to the introduction of restrictive fiscal, then monetary, policies. Fiscal policies will be looked at initially, since their effects are easily simulated.

The simultaneous application of restrictive policies cancelled out their beneficial effect on external deficits... If a restrictive policy is applied by only one country, it can certainly reduce budget and external deficits, as well as inflation, though at the price of a significant recession. But when all countries simultaneously adopt restrictive policies, beneficial effects on trade balances are cancelled out, and the ensuing recession is so serious that the resulting losses of tax revenue more or less cancel out the beneficial effects on the budget deficit. An analysis, using our theoretical model, of the effect of a reduction equal to 1% of GDP in government spending on goods and services shows that the multiplier effect of such a policy is to reduce GDP by 1.5% if France applies it alone and by 3.7% if it is applied by oil-importing countries as a whole. This multiplier is:

$$\frac{1}{1 + m - c(1 - a - t) - \alpha} = \begin{cases} 1.5 \text{ for } m = 0.45 \text{ (France)} \\ 3.7 \text{ for } m = 0.05 \text{ (importing countries as a whole)} \end{cases}$$

The effect of a restrictive policy on the external deficit is to reduce it by 0.7% (1.5 × 0.45) when it is applied by one country and by only 0.2% (3.7 × 0.05) when it is applied by importing countries as a whole. Trying to reduce the external deficit stemming from the oil shock by the use of restrictive policies is absurd. Why should the GDP of importing countries be reduced by 400% in order to eliminate the 2% of external deficit caused by the rise in oil prices? It is obviously more efficient to keep on trying for energy saving and replace fossil fuels by more modern sources, which was fortunately one aspect of the policies which were tried.

... and on budget deficits When restrictive policies are applied by all countries, they have little effect on reducing budget deficits. Where the depressive multiplier effect on national income *is higher than the marginal rate of tax, a cut in spending makes the deficit bigger rather than smaller.* This is precisely the result given by our simplified model (see above) for a situation where restrictive policies are adopted by all countries – a drop in income of 3.7% leads to a fall in tax revenue higher than the cut in spending (1.1%), making the deficit bigger, the marginal rate of tax (t) being 0.3.

	Ex ante reduction (in %)	Loss of tax revenue caused by fall in income (in %)	Ex post increase or decrease (in %)
Policy applied by one country	−1	1.5 × 0.3 = 0.4	−0.6
Policy applied by all countries	−1	3.7 × 0.3 = 1.1	+0.1

Simulations by OECD's INTERLINK model confirm these figures. A reduction in public spending of 1% of GDP by a single country brings down the budgetary deficit after three years, in the case of the United States by 0.3%, of West Germany by 0.6% and of France by 0.7%; the reduction in tax revenue is greater in the United States because the multiplier is higher. When the same measures are taken simultaneously by OECD countries as a whole, the deficit is not reduced but increased in the three countries.[13] The simultaneous nature of these policies as well as the rise in interest charges explain why significant budget deficits as a result of the oil

13. OECD, 'Simulations of fiscal policy using the OECD model of international links', *OECD Economic Outlook, Special Studies*, July 1980.

Figure 1.5 Inflation and unemployment in the seven main OECD countries

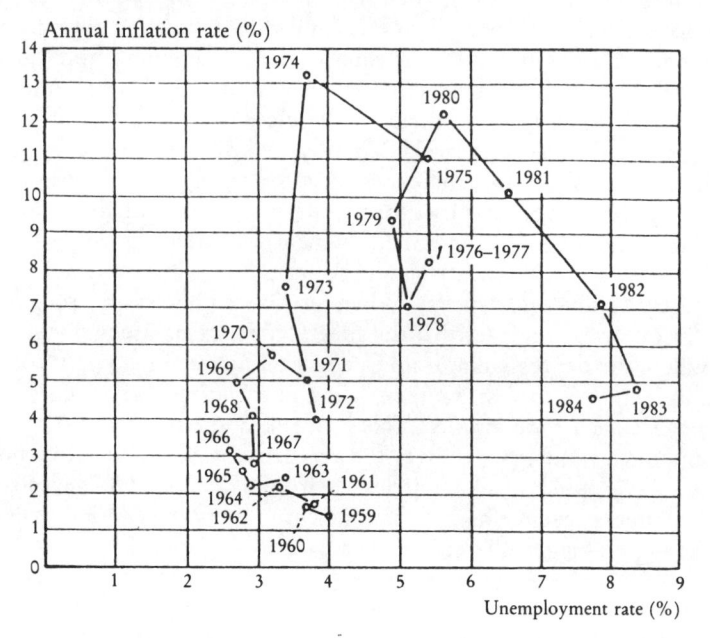

shocks were so persistent. The only notable success of simultaneous restrictive policies was in slowing down inflation – policies applied after the second oil shock in fact meant that the inflation brought about by the two shocks was stemmed, though at the price of a serious recession.

Inflation and Unemployment: The 'Paradox' of Stagflation

Many observers regarded the phenomenon of stagflation, involving the simultaneous worsening of inflation and unemployment, as proof of the inadequacy of traditional macro-economic theory. This theory had developed in the 1960s on the basis of the Keynesian model by the addition of a mechanism for determining prices and wages in a way which took account of disequilibria between supply and demand in the goods market and labour market. It was clear that the ordinary macro-economic models using the traditional Phillips curve – that is, a decreasing relationship between wage rates and unemployment rates – could easily be used to describe the opposite correlation observed during the 1960s between inflation and unemployment (see Figure 1.5). But without complete revision, the model seemed unable to describe the simultaneous rise in inflation and unemployment which occured in the 1970s.

This view was still very widespread in the 1980s: François Simon, writing in *Le Monde* in 1984 said that a decreasing relationship had been evident since 1980 and that 'Phillips might be right once again'. But such a view fails to take account of the mechanisms involved in a full macro-economic model, where the apparent relationship between inflation and unemployment goes beyond the Phillips curve and takes in the totality of macro-economic interactions. Thus an unchanged model with unchanged coefficients can, depending on exogenous shocks, give a decreasing relationship between inflation and unemployment, or an increasing one. This was shown by Laurence Klein using simulations carried out with the Wharton model, but his work can be subsumed within the neo-Keynesian approach, which is the common framework of most econometric models.[14]

Figure 1.6 shows the classic structure of the main macro-economic models. It can be divided into four blocks: a 'real block' which determines production according to the exogenous components of demand and the multiplier; two 'tension blocks' which describe the disequilibria existing in the markets for goods and labour – capacity utilization rate and unemployment; and a last block describing how prices and wages are determined (the price–wage loop).[15]

The general price level depends on capacity utilization rate (demand inflation) and costs – wage costs and, possibly, the price of imported raw materials, though the effect of this is small because it involves value added and not production. Wage rates are a function of consumer prices and the rate of unemployment. The conclusion is that the main cause of imported inflation is that the rise in import prices works through and has an effect on consumer prices and, as a consequence, on wage and GDP price levels. This effect is very marked when the indexation of wages on prices and prices on wages is high; if it is a total indexation, the whole of a rise of 1% in import prices is carried through to the general price level, wage rates and consumer prices.

In the 1960s, economic fluctuations were mainly caused by fluctuations in demand. When demand increased during periods of boom, unemployment fell, and production and employment rose,

---

14. Cf. his article 'Longévité de la théorie économique' (The longevity of economic theory), *Cahiers du séminaire d'économétrie*, 20, 1979.
15. Cf. P.-A. Muet, 'La modélisation macro-économique' (Macro-economic modelling), *Statistiques et études financières*, Special Number, 1979.

Figure 1.6 Determination of prices and wages in neo-Keynesian models

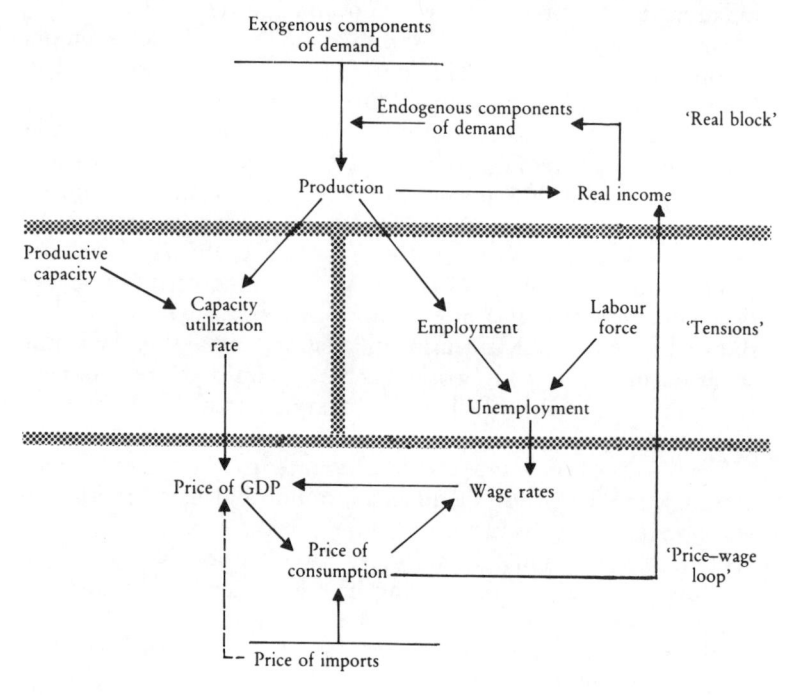

but so did inflation, through demand inflation (tension in the market for goods) and increases in costs (wages increased because unemployment decreased). Conversely, a slackening of demand caused inflation to fall and unemployment to rise. There was indeed a negative correlation between inflation and unemployment, but this correlation could occur even when there was no Phillips curve, simply through demand inflation.

In the 1970s, economic fluctuations were mainly the result of sharp rises in the price of energy and imported raw materials. This led to a rise in consumer prices, a fall in real incomes and a slowing down of production and employment, causing a simultaneous rise in inflation and unemployment. Figure 1.5 shows that, taking into account the need for adjustment of demand to income and of employment to production, the effect on inflation always showed itself before unemployment rose, which is why the 'curve' of the two oil shocks is where it is – moved upwards and to the right.

Between 1981 and 1983 the increased use of restrictive policies led to the reappearance of the negative correlation characteristic of deflation – drop in demand, increase in unemployment and slackening of inflation. This point will be raised again when disinflation is examined.

Figure 1.5 shows however that since the 1960s the increase in inflation was already accompanied by a rise in unemployment. This was the result of a lack of structural adjustment between the supply of and the demand for labour which did not have an inevitable effect on wages. Moreover, tensions over income distribution which appeared at the end of the 1960s had a greater effect on the rise of inflation, in that exchange rate fluctuations and then the end of fixed parities from 1971 made it easier for inflationary trends to work through by partly removing the constraint which foreign competition provided.

The Nature of Unemployment Since 1974

We have been examining in detail the depressive effect of the oil shocks on demand in importing countries. But supply also decreased as firms' profitability fell and as capital accumulation slowed down precisely because of a drop in profitability and demand. Accordingly, though unemployment undoubtedly rose because of a slackening of economic growth – though some economists deny that unemployment was enforced and refer to a change in attitudes to work to explain the millions of unemployed in OECD countries – its nature is nevertheless more problematical, whether looked at from the Keynesian perspective of insufficient world demand, or from the classical one of insufficient supply.

Traditional macro-economic models, the structure of which has been briefly outlined, bring both supply and demand to bear in examining macro-economic processes, so that the situation they describe falls between classical unemployment and Keynesian unemployment. The distinction between these, however, is basic to the theory of 'fixed price equilibria' or 'non-Walrasian equilibria' developed for the most part in France from about the mid-1970s.[16] This theory has done a great deal to show clearly the links between the situation of under-employment described in Keynesian theory and the Walrasian general equilibrium of traditional micro-economic theory. It retains the hypotheses of micro-economic theory about behaviour (maximization of firms' profits and consumer utility). By

16. See, for example, Edmond Malinvaud's book *Unemployment Theory reconsidered*, Blackwell, 1983, and the article by J.-P. Benassy, 'Théorie du déséquilibre et fondements micro-économiques de la macro-économie' (The theory of disequilibrium and the micro-economic basis of macro-economics), *Revue économique*, 27 (5), 1976, pp. 756–804.

rejecting, however, the hypothesis that markets immediately adjust to price variations, it gives us a description of various configurations of the economy in which for example, as in Keynesian theory, unemployment (excess supply in the labour market) can exist alongside excess productive capacity (excess supply in the market for goods). In a more general sense, the combination of disequilibria in the market for goods and the market for labour gives rise, apart from the Walrasian equilibrium situation, to four 'disequilibrium' configurations:[17]

1 The Keynesian unemployment situation, in which there is excess supply of both goods and labour markets.
2 The classical unemployment situation, in which supply of labour and demand for goods are in surplus.
3 The repressed inflation situation, in which demand is in surplus in both markets.
4 The under-consumption situation, in which demand for labour and supply of goods is in surplus.

In the Keynesian unemployment situation, firms' production is limited because demand is inadequate. There is an excess of supply in the market for goods: the level of production which would maximize firms' profits, taking into account available capital and the value of real wages (profitable productive capacity), is higher than demand. Firms could therefore increase production, employment and their own profit if demand was higher. Similarly, there is excess supply in the labour market – the number of people seeking work at this wage-level is higher than the number of workers needed for the relevant level of production (involuntary unemployment). This Keynesian unemployment situation or generalized excess supply is inefficient, compared with the Walrasian equilibrium which is an optimum in the Pareto sense, that is, the situation of one economic agent cannot be improved without worsening that of another. Because demand is inadequate, firms are rationed in their supply of goods, which leads them to limit their demand for labour and to ration households in the labour market. This rationing of households leads in turn to inadequate consumer demand and consequently contributes to the rationing of firms in the market for goods. The existence of multiplier effects is a consequence of this

---

17. The term 'disequilibrium' refers to potential supply and demand. Actual supply and demand are obviously the same, this equilibrium being established by rationing.

double rationing: by increasing spending, the government can free firms from constraints in the market for goods, and they can in turn increase the level of production and the number of jobs, thereby freeing households from constraints in the labour markets, increasing consumption, and further freeing firms. . . . This is clearly a case of the demand multiplier which characterizes a Keynesian unemployment situation.

The mirror image of a Keynesian unemployment situation, *repressed* inflation, or generalized excess demand, is also inefficient. There is excess demand in the labour market, and firms are limited to the supply of labour by households (full employment). Because of this constraint, firms' production levels are lower than investment demand and consumption demand (there is excess demand in the market for goods), which leads to household consumption being rationed. In other words, the rationing of firms in the labour market leads to the rationing of households in the market for goods. Wage earners, unable to satisfy their potential consumption, tend to scale down their activity, which reinforces the rationing of firms in the labour market. Such a situation of generalized excess demand is not found very often in market economies, because the surplus is taken up by inflation, as indicated in the next section. On the other hand, it is common in planned economies where the phenomena of enforced saving and absenteeism, the consequence of rationing consumers, are often quite marked. As before, the possibility of multiplier effects exists. An increase in the supply of labour by households would free firms from constraints in the labour market and the corresponding increase in production would free households from constraints, leading them to increase their supply of labour, and so on. The supply multiplier in a situation of generalized excess demand takes the place of the demand multiplier in a situation of generalized excess supply.

In the classical unemployment situation, production and employment depend on the profitability of productive capacity, that is, on whether wages are too high and/or there is insufficient capital, giving excess supply in the labour market (unemployment), but excess demand in the market for goods. Increased government spending has therefore no effect on the level of production and employment. A policy of wage restraint, on the other hand, improves the profitability of firms; because of this, production can be increased and unemployment reduced.

The final possible configuration, that of under-consumption, is inherently a temporary one, since it assumes that firms are constrained in the labour market and the market for goods at the same

Reflation and Austerity

Figure 1.7 Non-Walrasian equilibrium in the employment market

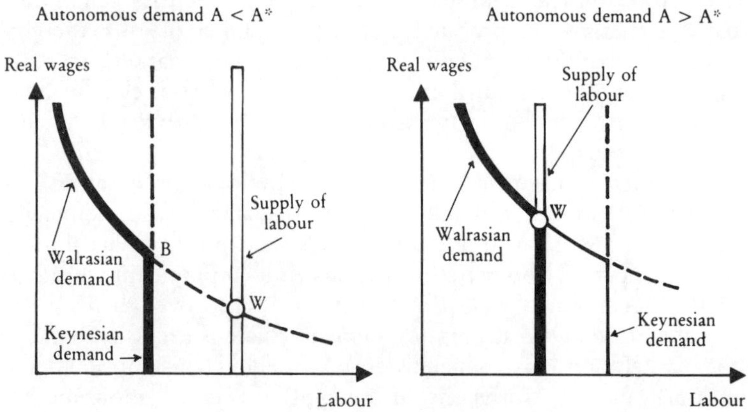

Autonomous demand A < A* *Autonomous demand A > A**

[Two diagrams with axes Real wages (vertical) and Labour (horizontal). Left: Walrasian demand curve, Keynesian demand, Supply of labour, points B and W. Right: Walrasian demand, Keynesian demand, Supply of labour, point W.]

time. If there are no inventories and if labour can adjust readily to production, this situation appears only in exceptional circumstances. In fact only one of the constraints in this configuration applies, because the firm can always adjust the level of production to constraints in the labour market or the level of employment to constraints in the market for goods. It is easy to imagine this being brought about if a sudden and temporary drop in demand happens when all the working population is in employment – the excess supply of goods would be stocked and firms would not reduce their employment levels; that is, there would be no Keynesian unemployment situation. Clearly, such a situation is temporary, and arises either because adjustment is not immediate or because the drop in demand is itself regarded by firms as temporary.

The situation in which the economy finds itself at any one time depends on the level of autonomous demand and on price and wage levels. A simplified example would be where there is an immediate adjustment of employment to production and of production to demand (which rules out an under-consumption situation) and where the supply of labour by wage earners is independent of real wages. With the axes representing real wages and labour, as in Figure 1.7, the supply of labour is a vertical straight line, but there are two possible outcomes of the demand for labour depending on the situation in which firms find themselves. If there are no constraints on their markets, the demand for labour which maximizes their profits is a declining function of real wages. If on the other hand there are constraints on the market for goods, the demand for labour is a function of autonomous demand, and possibly of the

–30–

Figure 1.8 Disequilibria according to levels of real wages and autonomous demand

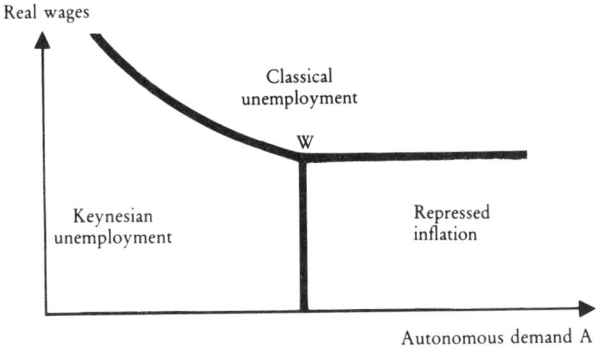

```
Real wages
    │
    │╲          Classical
    │ ╲        unemployment
    │  ╲
    │   ╲_____W_____
    │                │
    │  Keynesian     │   Repressed
    │ unemployment   │   inflation
    │                │
    └────────────────────────────→
                          Autonomous demand A
```

level of prices if demand depends on this, so is also represented by a vertical straight line in this diagram (Keynesian demand). For a given general level of prices, the economic situation depends on only two variables – the level of autonomous demand and real wages. When autonomous demand is lower than the level which would give full employment (the left-hand diagram in Figure 1.7), there is unemployment. This unemployment is Keynesian if real wages are lower than the marginal productivity of labour – corresponding to point B where Keynesian demand and Walrasian demand meet – because in this case employment is limited by autonomous demand; but it is classical unemployment when wages are higher than this point, and employment is determined by Walrasian demand. When autonomous demand is higher than the level which would give full employment (the right-hand diagram in Figure 1.7), two outcomes are also possible depending on the level of real wages. If this is lower than the level where Walrasian supply and demand for labour are equal (point W), the economy is in a situation of repressed inflation (full employment). But if real wages are above this point, this gives a situation of classical unemployment.

The argument just outlined can be summarized in a graph where the axes are 'autonomous demand' and 'real wages' (see Figure 1.8). Keynesian unemployment occurs when both autonomous demand and real wages are low, classical unemployment when real wages are high, and repressed inflation when autonomous demand is high and real wages lower than the Walrasian equilibrium level. A situation of under-consumption occurs only on the line between repressed inflation and Keynesian unemployment.

Reflation and Austerity

Figure 1.9 Persistence of Keynesian depression when prices are downwardly inflexible

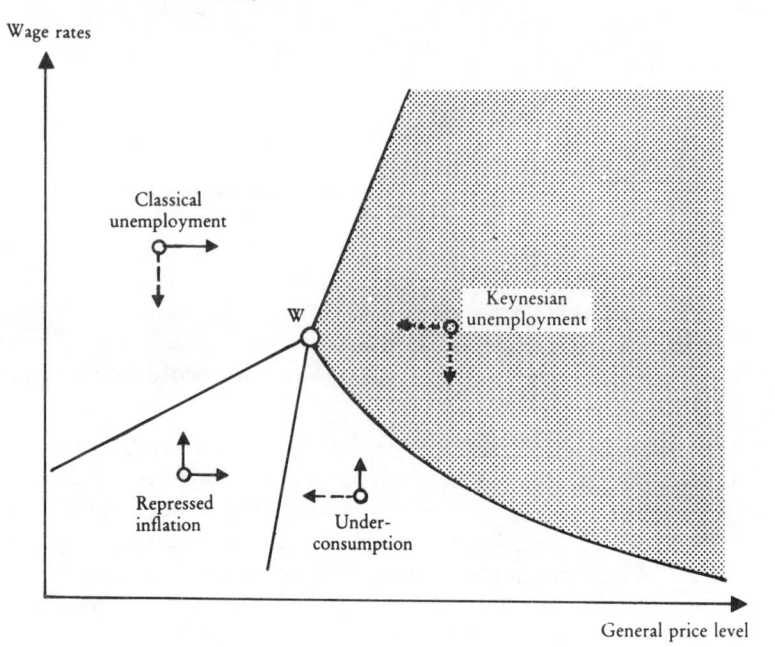

Note: The arrows show the upward or downward trend of prices and wages, and consequently the development of the overall situation. When prices are downwardly inflexible, the shifts shown by dotted lines are impossible.

In a similar way, various economic situations can be shown using the levels of wages and prices, with autonomous demand taken as fixed (see Figure 1.9). Bearing in mind that the general level of prices and autonomous demand have opposite effects on overall demand, this graph is based on the previous one, but the areas of Keynesian unemployment and repressed inflation are changed round. In the real world, prices are not rigid, but adjust slowly to disequilibria, rising when there is excess demand, falling when there is excess supply. The arrows in Figure 1.9 show the directions in which prices and wages tend to move in each situation – a general fall in the case of Keynesian unemployment, a general rise in an inflation situation.

If prices are able to move upwards as well as downwards, the economy will tend to move to the Walrasian equilibrium in all situations. If however prices are able to rise but not fall, as is partly

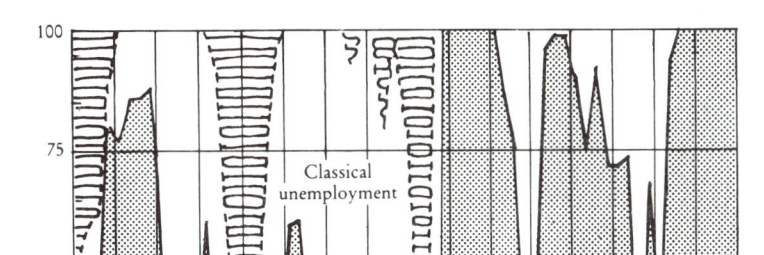

Figure 1.10 Probabilities of the different regimes

[Figure: Graph showing probabilities of Classical unemployment and Keynesian unemployment regimes in France from 1966 to 1981, with y-axis from 0 to 100.]

the case in the real world, Figure 1.9 shows that every situation will tend to disappear except that of Keynesian unemployment *which thereby becomes a permanent phenomenon.*

The development of the econometrics of rationing models has gradually made it possible to estimate the probability of each of the situations.[18] Figure 1.10 gives the results for France for the period 1966–81 obtained by P. Artus and S. Avouyi-Dovi. It is clear that Keynesian unemployment has been the dominant phenomenon in the economic crisis, except for brief periods when growth in production and employment was also held back by lack of productive capacity. In this way, there was classical unemployment briefly during 1976 when economic recovery both nationally and worldwide loosened constraints on demand (compare the analysis of the 1975 recovery in Chapter 2), and at the end of 1979 and the beginning of 1980 when the second oil shock occurred. The West

---

18. In France, M. Vilares is responsible for the first empirical applications; see his 'Un modèle macro-économique pour l'étude des changements structurels: théorie et application à l'économie française' (A macro-economic model for the analysis of structural change: theory and application to the French economy), in J.-P. Fitoussi and P.-A. Muet (eds), *Macrodynamique et déséquilibre*, Paris, Economica, 1985; see also P. Artus, G. Laroque and G. Michel, 'Estimation of a quarterly macro-economic model with quantitative rationing', *Econometrica*, 52 (6), November 1984, pp. 1387–414.

German reflation of 1979 (see Chapter 2) meant that the depressive effect on demand in France was less strong, so that at the beginning of the second oil shock the impact which wage rises (pushed up by consumer price rises) had on the supply of goods was initially more important than the drop in demand.

Fall in Profits and Accumulation of Capital*

The first oil shock led, in most industrialized countries, to a significant deterioration in the profitability of firms. Since then, it has become common to say that it was firms which paid the increased oil bill. It has often been thought that this low level of profitability was the main obstacle to world economic recovery and a lasting recovery of investment. However there is no automatic connection between investment and profits despite Chancellor Schmidt's well-known formula: 'Today's profits create investment tomorrow and jobs the day after tomorrow.' In a period when the growth of demand is slowing down, market prospects can dampen down investment at least as much as an inadequate level of profitability. This point will be examined by using recent studies of constraints on investment, after looking at factors which have led to a decrease in the proportion of value added represented by profit.

Decrease in firms' profits Figure 1.11 shows three indicators of the proportion of value added of companies which is made up of profits. The broadest approach includes all non-wage income (value added less total wage bill, including social welfare contributions). A more restricted approach excludes taxes net of subsidies, and the narrowest one goes no further than self-financing.

The way these three indicators developed is roughly the same – a steep drop from 1973 to 1976, slight recovery until the second oil shock, another fall in 1979–80, then recovery starting in 1982.

The fall was due to a combination of three factors. Firstly, the slowing down of growth had an impact on the productivity of labour and on real wages. Productivity of labour is reduced when growth stops or slows down, because firms adjust staff levels only slowly. Conversely, the fact that wages are determined by institutional factors means that the rise in real wage levels slows down only as the employment situation worsens. Secondly, the deteriora-

---

* This section is based on the article by P.-A. Muet and H. Sterdyniak, 'Rétablissement des profits et stagnation de l'investissement: un paradoxe?' (Recovery of profits and stagnation of investment: a paradox?), *Lettre de l'OFCE*, 25, 28 May 1985.

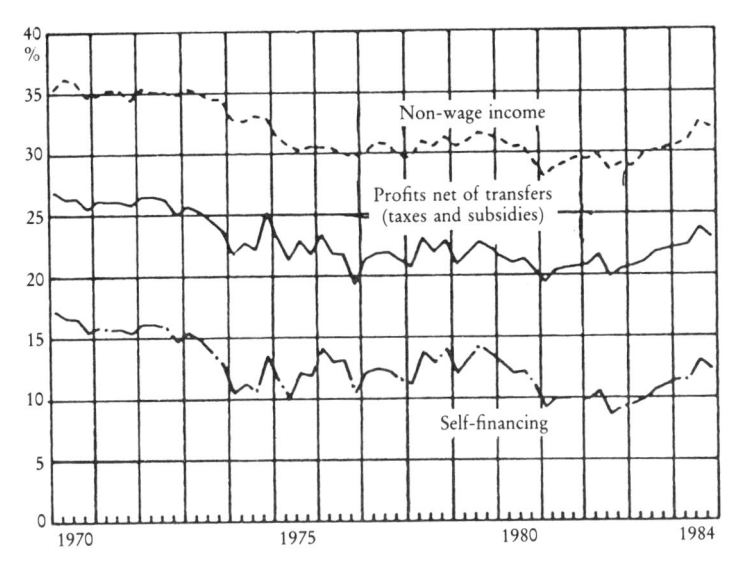

Figure 1.11 Changes in the proportion of profits in the value added of companies

tion in the terms of trade led to a rise in consumer prices (on which wages are indexed) which was more rapid than that of value added (which determines how much value added there is to share out between wages and profits). Finally, a rise in the rate of social welfare contributions paid by employers meant a further reduction of profits. In fact, this rise in employers' contributions partly offset the increase in social welfare spending as a proportion of GDP brought on by the slowing down of growth.

Figure 1.12 shows the part played by each of these factors in the development of the proportion of non-wage income since the beginning of the 1970s. Before the first oil shock, growth in labour productivity and in real wages was roughly at the same rate; slight changes in the terms of trade tended to be favourable and compensated for slight increases in social security contributions, so that the share of profits, in the broadest sense, remained the same. After the first oil shock, however, the share of profits in GDP fell by more than five percentage points (curve 4). More than two-thirds of this fall was accounted for by the difference between the growth rate of labour productivity and real wages (curve 1). But the adverse effect in 1974 of worsening terms of trade caused by the oil shock was in fact offset during the years after 1974 by domestic inflation so that, at least until the second oil shock, relative prices between

Figure 1.12 Breakdown of changes in the proportion of profits in the value added of companies

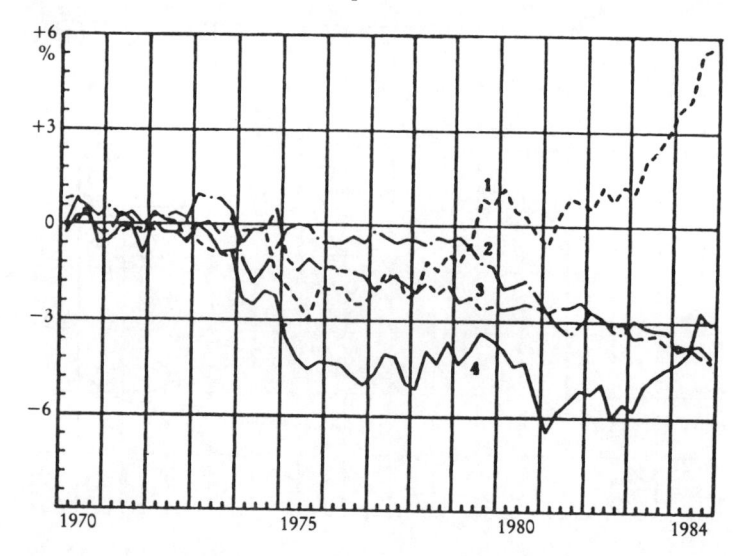

Note: Changes in the proportion of non-wage income in the value added of companies (4) are broken down into:
(1) growth curve of productivity of labour and real wages;
(2) relative price of value added and consumption;
(3) rate of employers' social security contributions.

Source: P.-A. Muet and H. Sterdyniak, 'Rétablissement des profits et stagnation de l'investissement: un paradoxe?' (Recovery of profits and stagnation of investment: a paradox?), *Observations et diagnostics économiques, Lettre de l'OFCE*, 25, 28 May 1985.

consumption and value added (curve 2) had no effect one way or the other on the wage–profit distribution.

From 1977, however, the rise in real wages was always lower than the rise in labour productivity, apart from a brief period of recession caused by the 1980 oil price rises. Figure 1.12 shows that if the rise in labour productivity in relation to the rise in real wages had been the only factor in the way the wage–profit distribution developed, then the proportion of value added going to profits would have reached pre-first oil shock levels by 1979 and would have been nearly six percentage points higher than these levels by the end of 1984. However, this recovery was hindered by the constant rise in employers' contributions throughout the whole of this period (curve 3) and, from 1979 onwards, by the worsening of the terms of trade due to the oil shock and the rise in value of the dollar (curve 2). It was only in 1983 that the recovery got under way, when labour productivity began to increase at a time when real wage levels were stable (see Chapter 5).

Market prospects as the main constraint on investment The decision to invest is a complex process which assumes that several conditions are met:

1 The firm must be in a position to sell anything extra produced by the investment, and so an increase in its markets must be observed or anticipated.
2 The marginal profit brought about by the investment must be at least equal to the return on financial assets.
3 There should be finance available for the investment, without increasing borrowing in a way which would jeopardize future profitability. This consideration usually leads firms to pay for the investment from their own financial resources, by ploughing back profits.

Traditional econometric models generally take these conditions into account by bringing into play three things at the same time – changes in demand (acceleration effect), labour and capital costs, and finally actual profits made. Numerous econometric studies undertaken in the 1980s show that anticipation of demand (the acceleration effect) is very important, that cost factors play a relatively minor role – the rise in real interest rates in particular seems to have had no significant effect on productive investment – and finally that the influence of actual profit levels is more temporary.[19] However, with this kind of approach, combining different variables with fixed coefficients, it is not possible, in any satisfactory way, to take account of how predictions about growth or inadequate profit levels can have a dampening effect on investment. In fact, a low level of self-financing can have the effect of not dampening investment if growth in demand is itself very low and does not lead to favourable market forecasts.

Recent developments in econometric methods can estimate these models by identifying the constraint which is holding down investment in each period – in the present case, anticipated demand and actual profit levels.

---

19. See especially P. Artus and P.-A. Muet, 'Un panorama des développements récents de l'économétrie de l'investissement' (A survey of recent developments in the econometrics of investment), *Revue économique*, 35 (5), September 1984; and by the same authors, *Investment and Factor Demand*, North-Holland, 1990.

Reflation and Austerity

Figure 1.13 Profit constraint and demand constraint on investment

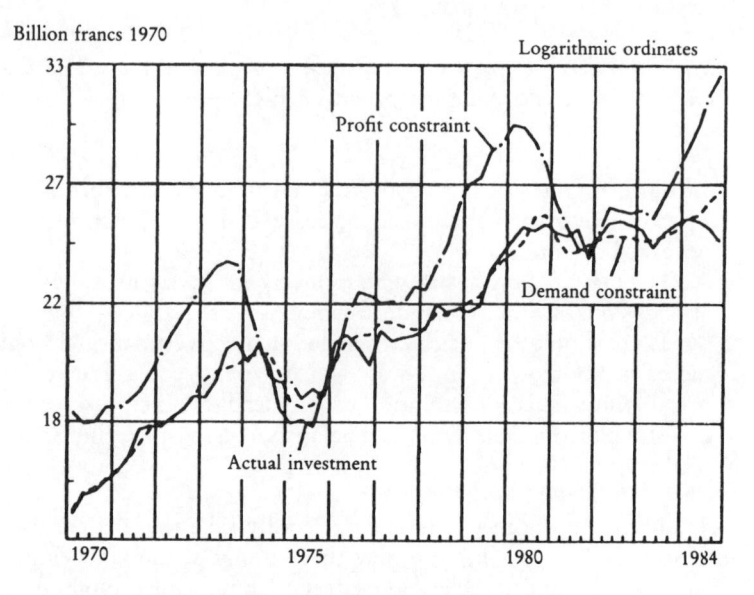

Note: The model is in the form of $I = \text{Min}(D, P)$ where D is investment determined by demand and P is investment determined by profit. The minimum for the two functions is estimated using the method called 'CES approximation'.
Source: Muet and Sterdyniak, 28 May 1985.

Figure 1.13 shows actual investment and the two constraints. Profit levels held back investment only during the recession after the first oil shock, and then again in 1981 and the beginning of 1982. During 1982 and up to the beginning of 1983, it was anticipated demand which held back investment, though the constraint of profit levels came a close second and a more marked growth in demand would inevitably have come up against the problem of inadequate level of profits. Finally, after the middle of 1983, when profits again reached their previous levels, it was principally anticipated growth which held back investment.

In this way, Keynesian theory and its modern developments make it possible to analyse the economic crisis brought about by the oil shocks, the simultaneous rise in unemployment and inflation (stagflation), the way in which investment stagnated and profits fell, and the difficulties national policies had in coping with the economic crisis. The foregoing analysis leads us to a quantitative description of the consequences of the first oil shock.

Understanding the Economic Crisis

Figure 1.14 World prices of raw materials imported by France

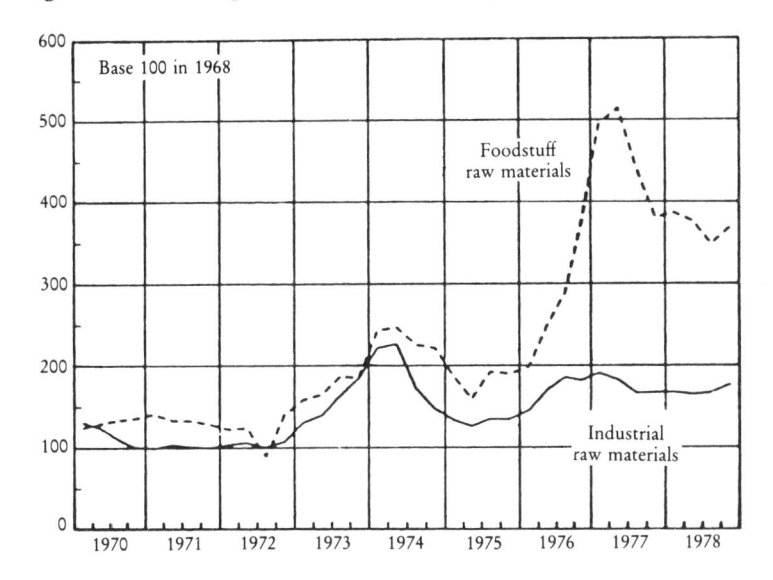

[Graph: Base 100 in 1968, years 1970–1978, showing Foodstuff raw materials and Industrial raw materials]

The First Oil Shock

Immediately prior to the oil shock, the world economy had entered a phase of rapid growth which came about because the economic cycles of the main OECD countries were in step. The recovery which followed the recession of 1970–1 had culminated in considerable expansion during 1973, when speculation on the commodity and exchange markets played a role unprecedented since the Korean War.

Inflation, which had been gathering pace since the end of the 1960s and had scarcely been checked by the 1970–1 recession, was already high even before the oil crisis broke. A particular cause of the rise in inflation had been the gradual disappearance of exchange rate stability following the collapse of the Bretton Woods system at the beginning of the 1970s. At the same time, internationalization of production and trade had been accompanied by the unprecedented development of international financial markets (Euro-dollars, in particular). This had the effect of encouraging speculative moves on the money, gold and commodity markets which led to a tremendous explosion of certain world prices (see Figure 1.14) when, for example, the cost to France of imported raw materials went up by 80%.

Figure 1.15 Annual change in consumer prices in the OECD as a whole

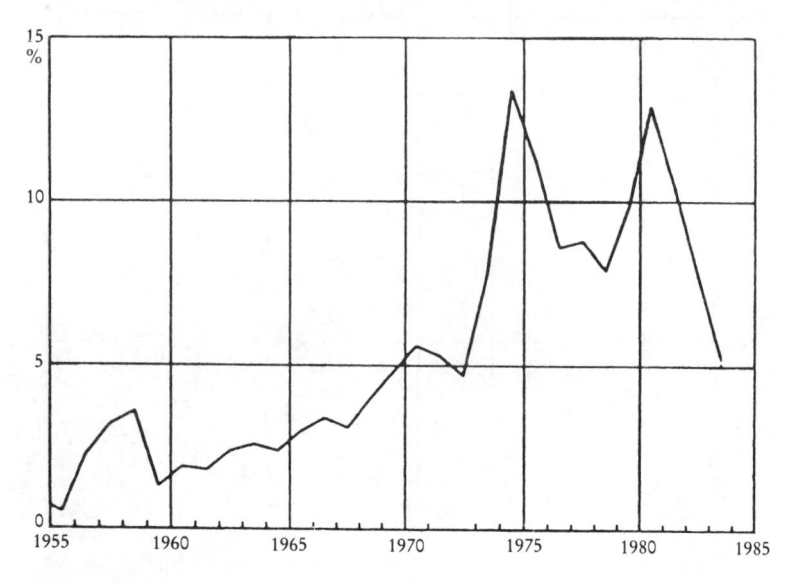

Source: OECD.

According to a study carried out by the OECD, the jump in inflation in member countries from 4.8% in 1972 to 7% in 1973 seemed to be wholly accounted for by rises in the price of raw materials (see Figure 1.15).[20] It was in this very troubled atmosphere that the oil crisis broke in Autumn 1973 and led in two stages to a four-fold increase in the price of crude oil.

Contrasting Effects on Inflation

The rise in inflation caused by the oil shock can be seen clearly from Figure 1.15. In 1974 the increase in consumer prices was 14% in the major OECD countries and it was only in the mid-1980s that it returned to below 7% or 8%.[21]

This overall trend applied differently in individual countries. Inflation in West Germany peaked at 6.5% in 1974 before falling to a level below that of the late 1960s from 1977 onwards, while in Japan it rose very sharply in 1974 (a 25% increase on the previous

20. *OECD Economic Outlook*, 14, December 1973.
21. See Figure 2.1 in Chapter 2.

year) and then in 1977 dropped back to levels lower than the 1970–2 period. In France the rate of inflation reached 14% in 1974 before slowing to around 10%.

For a more detailed analysis, reference needs to be made to simulations by econometric models. A comparative study of the five major OECD countries was carried out by Patrick Artus using the usual formulas for the determination of wages and prices outlined at the end of the previous section. These simulations isolate two groups of factors – firstly, the rise in import costs and internal factors as a whole and, secondly, capacity utilization rates, unemployment rates and productivity growth. A reduction in the rate of productivity growth increases the wage bill per unit produced and fuels inflation, but this effect is partially offset, particularly in West Germany and the United Kingdom, by the sensitivity of wage rates to productivity gains.

The impact of these two groups of factors on the development of consumer prices is shown in Table 1.3. It has been calculated by taking as the base the average trend for the period immediately prior to the first oil shock, i.e. 1970–2.

Imported inflation (due to the oil shock and exchange rate fluctuations) was high in Japan, the United Kingdom and France, accounting for about 9 to 10 points of the percentage increase in inflation experienced by these countries in 1974. It was less marked in the United States (5.6% in 1974) despite devaluations of the dollar, because imports played a smaller role in domestic demand. In West Germany, a rising Deutschmark curbed the increase in import costs (30% increase between the beginning of 1973 and the end of 1974 compared with 60% to 80% in the other countries) and this meant that the increase due to imported inflation did not exceed 2.6% following the oil shock.

The curb on growth had the effect in all the countries of producing higher unemployment, an easing of demand on production capacity and a drop in productivity gains. The first two factors acted as a brake on inflation while the third encouraged it so that the combined effect of the three was very different.

For example, in the United States, the rise in wage costs resulting from a slowing of the rise in the productivity of labour was greater than the curb on wage rises brought about by rising unemployment, so that the resulting internal changes helped to fuel inflation at a time when the impact of imported inflation was waning. Thus the delayed effects of imported inflation and the fall in productivity gains played an equal part in keeping inflation high in 1977 and 1978.

Table 1.3 Analysis of the rise in inflation after the first oil shock: imported inflation and domestic factors

	Base 1970–1972	\multicolumn{6}{c}{Change in consumer prices on previous year (in %)}
	Base 1970–1972	1973	1974	1975	1976	1977	1978
United States							
Inflation	4.8	7.3	11.0	6.1	4.9	5.9	7.8
Imported inflation	0.0	+2.4	+5.6	+3.3	+2.7	+3.1	+2.6
Domestic factors	0.0	+0.3	+2.1	+2.8	+2.1	+2.1	+2.3
West Germany							
Inflation	4.7	7.2	6.5	5.6	4.0	3.5	2.4
Imported inflation	0.0	+0.6	+2.6	+1.9	+1.9	+1.5	+0.5
Domestic factors	0.0	−0.3	−1.3	−2.5	−3.0	−3.0	−3.2
France							
Inflation	5.6	7.9	14.0	10.0	10.1	8.4	9.4
Imported inflation	0.0	−0.1	+8.5	+8.9	+7.6	+7.2	+5.2
Domestic factors	0.0	−0.1	−0.9	−2.7	−2.4	−3.0	−3.6
United Kingdom							
Inflation	7.6	10.3	18.3	25.3	15.0	13.0	8.1
Imported inflation	0.0	+4.9	+9.0	+8.7	+6.6	+3.6	+1.5
Domestic factors	0.0	+0.1	+1.4	+2.3	+2.3	+2.0	+1.2
Japan							
Inflation	6.1	16.5	24.6	8.5	9.4	6.0	3.4
Imported inflation	0.0	+3.0	+10.1	+4.7	+4.6	+3.1	+1.4
Domestic factors	0.0	+3.9	+1.8	−3.1	−6.0	−9.0	−11.2

Source: P. Artus, 'Formation conjointe des prix et des salaires dans cinq grands pays de l'OCDE' (Joint determination of prices and wages in five OECD countries), *Annales de l'INSEE*, 49, January–March 1983, p. 41. The effect of imported inflation and domestic factors is estimated in relation to a base position established by the average change in these factors during 1970–2. The figures on the second line in each case show, for example, that the rise in import prices in 1973 compared with the trend in 1970–2 increased US inflation by 2.4% in 1973, 5.6% in 1974, etc.

The situation in the United Kingdom was similar. Imported inflation did not last as long as in the United States but the fact that the influence of unemployment on wage levels was not strong and the abolition in 1974 of wage controls meant that domestic developments helped to maintain high inflation following the oil shock.

Understanding the Economic Crisis

Figure 1.16 Changes in industrial production between 1972 and 1978

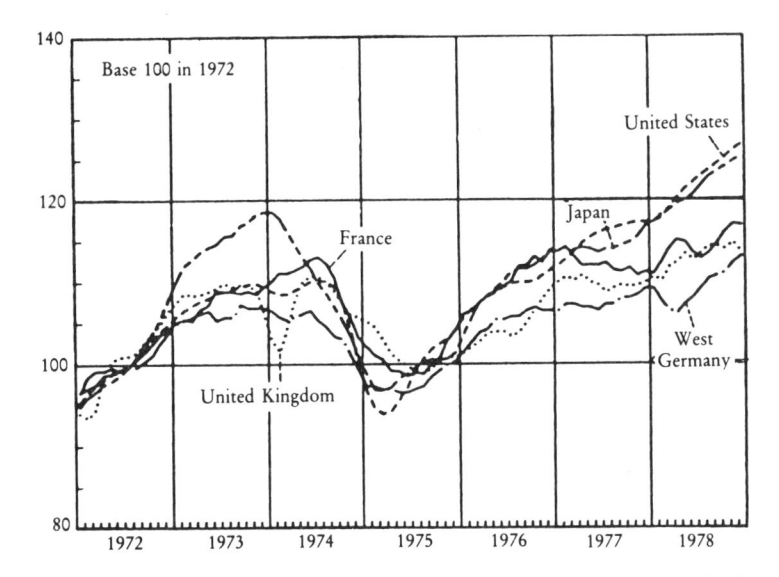

In West Germany, France and Japan, rising unemployment had a greater effect than falling productivity and helped to curb inflation. This disinflation produced by slower growth was not enough in France, however, to offset the effect of imported inflation. Inflation in France remained high because wages were closely tied to prices and the franc was falling, which meant that imported inflation stayed high. In West Germany and Japan, on the other hand, the disinflation factors produced by the recession led, surprisingly, to a lower rate of inflation three years after the oil shock than in the period immediately preceding it. Thus, while the direct effects of the oil shock were highly inflationary, its induced effects on real variables generally tended to reduce the initial impact in the years immediately afterwards, though with widely differing results from one country to the next.

The Recession Aggravated by Parallel Economic Cycles and Rising Farm Prices

The recession which followed the first oil shock was severe but short-lived: industrial production fell in all countries between the second half of 1974 and the first quarter of 1975 (see Figure 1.16) but recovery was rapid due to the expansionary budget policies applied in most countries. The extent of the 1974–5 recession was

–43–

Table 1.4 Impact of the first oil shock and farm price rises on American growth (in %), 1973–5

	1973	1974	1975
Actual growth of GNP	5.5	−0.6	−0.7
Effect of farm price rises	+0.9	−1.9	+0.8
Effect of the oil crisis	+0.3	−2.9	−2.4
Total of the two effects	+1.2	−4.8	−1.6

Source: *Growth in GNP*, OECD. Simulation: O. Eckstein, *The great recession*, North-Holland, 1979, p. 67 and p. 119. Since actual growth in 1974 and 1975 has been drastically revised since the publication of this book, we have taken the estimated impact as a 'variation' and not as a 'level'.

not due to the oil shock alone but to the fact that it coincided with the synchronization of the economic cycles of the major economies.

The recovery which followed the 1970–1 recession culminated in very marked growth in 1972 and 1973. Excess demand led to increased inflation in all countries and a steep rise in the cost of raw materials. An additional factor, following poor harvests in Asia and the Soviet Union, was the imbalance between supply and demand in world agricultural markets which led to a very sharp increase in farm prices.

The 1974–5 recession in the United States is covered in depth by O. Eckstein in his book *The Great Recession*. According to his assessments, based on DRI model simulations, the oil shock accounted in 1974 for almost 3% of the reduction in the US GNP and the rise in farm prices for about 2% (see Table 1.4).

Both factors led to speculative stockpiling in 1973 followed by a drop in demand, the impact of which was heightened by an off-loading of stocks in 1974. The two shocks thus added to growth by 1 point in 1973 and curbed it by almost 5 points in 1974, which more or less tallies with the slow-down observed. The recession was therefore worsened by fiscal policy and, above all, monetary policy when this took a restrictive turn in 1974.[22] But from 1975 onwards the United States, in common with most of the major OECD countries, adopted a policy of budgetary expansion which allowed economic activity to recover during the summer of 1975.

---

22. The author's estimates of the impact of monetary policy seem exaggerated in view of actual events and also in comparison with the findings of other US models.

Table 1.5 Breakdown of the balance of central and local government spending (as % of GDP), 1973-6

	1973	1974	1975	1976
Seven major OECD countries:				
actual balance	0.0	−0.8	−4.3	−2.9
Economic cycle component	+0.6	−0.6	−2.3	−1.6
Structural component	−0.6	−0.2	−2.0	−1.3
OECD countries as a whole: actual				
balance	0.1	−0.6	−3.9	−2.7
Economic cycle component	+0.5	−0.5	−2.2	−1.5
Structural component	−0.4	−0.1	−1.7	−1.2

Source: Article by R.W.R. Price and P. Muller, 'Structural budget indicators and the interpretation of fiscal policy stance in OECD economies', *OECD Economic Review*, 3, Autumn 1984, p. 27. The seven major OECD countries are the United States, Canada, Japan, West Germany, France, the United Kingdom and Italy.

Economic Recovery and Increase in Budget Deficits

The recessionary spiral was halted by economic policy. West Germany, which had followed a restrictive policy in 1973 in response to the boom, adopted a more expansionist policy in 1974. French economic policy was more uneven: a restrictive policy until mid-1974 (a plan to combat inflation in December 1973, then a plan to reduce the external deficit in June 1974), followed by a highly expansionist policy in 1975. The United States, Japan, Italy and Canada also followed an expansionist policy in 1975. Budgetary expansion in this year was equivalent, according to OECD estimates, to a 'deliberate' budget deficit of 2% of GNP for the whole of the seven major OECD countries. The policy adopted by smaller OECD members, however, was much less expansionary, so that the 'deliberate' public spending deficit for the whole of the OECD did not increase by as much − 1.7% of GDP in 1975.

Tax revenue and spending associated with unemployment vary with economic activity, so that the budget deficit gets worse during a recession and improves in periods of expansion (automatic stabilizer). The effect of variations in economic activity in relation to a growth potential, estimated by the OECD at just over 4% a year is provided for by the cyclical element of the budget balance. The remaining structural element mainly reflects deliberate measures of fiscal policy aimed at supporting economic activity. Table 1.5 shows that half of the increase in budget deficit, which in 1975 had reached 4.3% of GDP in the seven major OECD countries, was due to the

Reflation and Austerity

Figure 1.17 Effect of budget expansion and automatic stabilizers on the US recovery of 1975-6

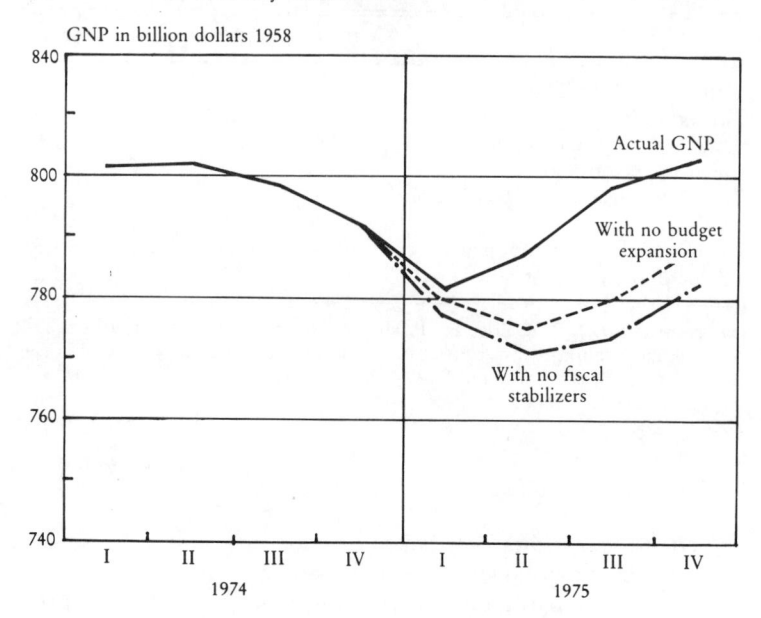

Source: O. Eckstein, 1979.

slow-down in economic activity, and half to the recovery measures implemented after the first oil shock.

These recovery measures proved effective. They accounted for between 2 and 3 percentage points of the recovery which began in mid-1975. The automatic stabilizer factor and budgetary expansion played a decisive part in limiting the recession, as is clear from the simulations on the United States economy produced by O. Eckstein. American recovery measures took the form of tax reductions on an unprecedented scale (the Taxes Reduction Act of May 1975) combined with the creation of 320,000 jobs in the public sector. Budgetary and fiscal incentives amounted to 23 billion dollars, that is, 1.6% of GNP. Automatic stabilizers represented an injection of 5 billion dollars in 1974 and 17 billion dollars in 1975. Without incentives and automatic stabilizers, the fall in GNP would still have been halted in the second half of 1975 but the recovery would have been more uncertain, as can be seen from Figure 1.17.

During the period 1975-8, however, economic growth was never sufficient to bring about a significant reduction in unemployment. Among OECD countries as a whole, unemployment rose from 3%

Table 1.6 Current account balances of the main groups of countries between 1973 and 1978

	1973	1974	1975	1976	1977	1978
OECD	10	−28	3	−17	−25	9
OPEC	5	66	32	37	28	1
Developing countries	−6	−22	−31	−18	−13	−23
Eastern bloc countries	−3	−7	−14	−10	−7	−13
Others	0	−3	−4	−2	−1	0
Adjustment	−6	−6	+14	+10	+18	+26

Source: OECD.

to 5% between 1973 and 1978. And there were soon wide differences between the current balance deficits of oil-importing countries, mainly because of the differing economic policies followed from 1976.

The Gradual Reduction of External Deficits

The increase in oil prices produced a transfer of annual income of about 150 billion dollars to OPEC. This transfer which, because of the low propensity to spend of OPEC countries, lies at the root of the contraction in world demand, led to OPEC having a current account surplus. This was gradually cancelled out as a result of increased imports of goods and services by the OPEC countries and a reduction in the volume of oil imports. The adjustment process lasted some four years, as is shown in Table 1.6. But the imbalances were very unevenly distributed between groups of countries. The deficit of OECD countries disappeared in 1975 because of the major recession, but this was only a short-term improvement, since the imbalance reappeared in 1976 with the economic recovery. Moreover, recovery in the current balance of the OECD countries was partly at the expense of those developing countries which were not oil producers and of countries in Eastern Europe; the 1975 deficits were, respectively, 31 billion and 14 billion dollars.

Just before the second oil shock, the balance of payments between OPEC and the OECD countries had got back into equilibrium, but the developing countries' deficit, and to a lesser degree that of the countries of Eastern Europe, was still running at a high level, at least if no account is taken of the statistical gap (adjustment) which became significant at that time.

Within the OECD itself, there was wide variation in the level of deficit, mainly due to differing trends in domestic demand and in

Table 1.7 Change in trade balances between 1973 and 1976 (in billion dollar)

	Change in trade balance	Breakdown of the change 1973–76 Volume effect	Terms of trade effect
Japan	+6	+20	−14
United States	−10	+4	−14
Italy	0	+7	−7
France	−5.5	−3	−2.5
West Germany	1	−1	+2.0
Seven major OECD countries	−10	+25	−35
Total for small OECD countries (except Norway)	−14	+1	−15
Total for OECD	−26	+26	−53

Source: OECD Economic Outlook, 21, p. 99.

the organization of external trade. As stated in an OECD study, it seems that exchange rate movements or changes in competitivity did not have a major influence on external balances following the oil shock.[23] This observation is in keeping with conclusions in Chapter 3 on the effect of devaluations of the franc.

A breakdown of the variations in trade balances from 1973 to 1976, distinguishing between those caused by changes in volume of trade and those arising from changes in the terms of trade, shows up a wide variety of situations within the OECD (see Table 1.7). Whereas for the whole of the OECD, a 26 billion dollar improvement in the volume of trade offset half of the 53 billion dollar deterioration in the terms of trade between 1973 and 1976, the volume effect for the small OECD countries was insignificant and differed in the larger ones.

The main beneficiary of recovery in volume of trade was Japan, where a 14 billion dollar worsening of the terms of trade was more than offset by a considerable improvement (20 billion dollars) in the volume balance. The recovery was also significant in Italy, though it

23. *OECD Economic Outlook*, 21, July 1977, p. 95ff.

was much more modest in the United States. In France, because there was a growth in domestic demand which was more marked than in the case of its trading partners, a worsening balance in the volume of trade compounded the unfavourable effect arising from the terms of trade.

The biggest paradox is in the case of West Germany, where favourable shifts in the terms of trade resulted in an improvement in trading surplus. The worsening in the terms of trade caused by the oil shocks and a slight deterioration due to changes in volume were offset by a rise in value of the Deutschmark and economic specialization, which was particularly favourable.

The Second Oil Shock: Recession Worsened by Restrictive Policies

The second oil shock which, like the first one, caused a 2% fall in the real income of OECD countries, occurred at a time when imbalances brought about by the first shock had not yet been corrected. Inflation took off once more, reaching 13% on average in the OECD in 1980. Current balance and public spending deficits worsened, and unemployment continued to rise. The reaction as far as economic policies were concerned was very different from what happened in the first shock. The desire to combat inflation, to reverse the sharp fall in firms' profitability, and to reduce external and public deficits, led most countries to revise their fiscal policy, and then (under US influence) their monetary policy, in extremely restrictive directions.

Fiscal policy: Tight Control in Europe, A Looser Approach in the United States

Table 1.8 analyses the way in which changes in budget balances were influenced by changes in economic activity, increases in interest charges and deliberate structural changes. It indicates that all the major OECD countries, with the exception of the United States and France in 1981–2, followed restrictive budgetary policies. Indeed, in the United Kingdom budget cuts amounted to the unprecedented figure of over 6% of GNP between 1979 and 1982 although this did not lead to a comparable reduction in the actual deficit, which fell by only 1.1% of GNP.

Efforts to reduce public deficits were, in fact, hindered by the fact that restrictive policies were being followed generally, and by the

Table 1.8 Change in budget balances between 1979 and 1982 (in % of GNP, a minus sign indicates a worsening)

	1979 balance (a)	1982 balance (b)	Actual change (c)=(b)−(a)	Effect of economic activity (d)	Effect of rise in interest charges (e)	Structural or deliberate change (f)
United Kingdom	−3.2	−2.1	+1.1	−5.4	−0.2	+6.7
Japan	−4.8	−3.4	+1.4	−0.1	−0.7	+2.2
Canada	−1.8	−5.3	−3.5	−4.9	−0.9	+1.3
West Germany	−2.7	−3.5	−0.8	−2.2	−0.6	+2.0
France	−0.7	−2.6	−1.9	−2.1	−0.3	+0.5
Italy	−9.5	−12.5	−3.2	−0.9	−2.3	0.0
United States	+0.6	−3.8	−4.4	−3.5	−0.7	−0.2
Average for seven major OECD countries	−1.7	−4.0	−2.3	−2.7	−0.7	+1.1

Source: The breakdown shown in this table uses estimates appearing in the article by Price and Muller (*OECD Economic Review*, 3, Autumn 1984).

(c) = (d) + (e) + (f).

rise in interest charges. As has been shown, policies aimed at reducing deficits can succeed when they are followed in isolation but are ineffective when applied simultaneously, as was the case after the second oil shock. Because of the effect of automatic stabilizers, the reduction in economic activity resulting from the oil shock and from budgetary restrictions actually led to a worsening of the deficit which was greater than the planned reduction.

The second factor hindering the recovery of public finances was the increase in interest charges resulting from higher rates and increased debt. This had less impact, however, than the reduction in economic activity. In the case of the seven major OECD countries, reduced economic activity accounted on average for almost 3% of GNP in the worsening of public deficits while higher interest charges accounted for only 0.8%. Both these factors were only slightly offset by budgetary restrictions (1.5% of GNP), which meant that the public finance deficit rose from 1.7% of GNP in 1979 to 4% in 1982.

Monetary policies, which had been expansionist in the 1970s to accompany the budgetary expansion which followed the first oil shock, gradually became restrictive under US and UK influence.

The Contradictions of US Monetarism and the Rise in Interest Rates

In October 1979 the US monetary authorities decided to abandon interest rate controls and to concentrate instead on quantitative goals. More fundamentally, this change marked the transition from a policy based on interest rates which was not strict to one based on money supply which was restrictive. This signalled the discreet entry of monetarism on to the US scene before it came out into the open combined with the supply-side economics of the Reagan policy package. This policy led to numerous deregulation measures concerning raw material prices and the banking system. But the most important measures from the point of view of their macroeconomic consequences were tax reductions aimed at 'boosting investment and private saving', not because they had an effect on these two variables, but because the contradiction between an expansionary fiscal policy and a restrictive monetary policy brought about, quite in keeping with the lessons of post-Keynesian macroeconomic theory,[24] a rise in interest rates which was without

---

24. The IS-LM model and its extension to an open economy, which appears in all the textbooks.

precedent in the post-war period. As a result, the dollar went up in value, and the extension – more forced than deliberate – of restrictive monetary policies in industrialized countries led to a return of very high real interest rates in those countries and to considerable financial difficulties in the developing countries, which were already heavily in debt.

The way the US economy has developed in recent times is easily understood using the normal neo-Keynesian models, without having to resort to monetarist arguments or the incantatory formulas of supply-side economists.[25]

Until Summer 1982, when some flexibility was introduced to avoid the financial breakdown threatened by bank failures and a default on loan payments by Mexico, all that the tough policy on money supply growth did was to make interest rates rise when demand was rising and fall when it was slackening. The rise in nominal interest rates and then in real rates when inflation eased (see Figure 1.18) had a significant dampening effect at first, to add to the recession brought on by the oil shock. The US GDP fell by 2% in 1982, whereas the Reagan administration was expecting a rise of 4%.

The recession led to a very sharp rise in unemployment, reaching a US total of 12 million by December 1982. The coincidence of the longest recession which the United States had experienced since the Second World War, of a wages policy restricting nominal rises, and of an unprecedented rise in the dollar, brought about a very rapid disinflation which was not really connected, as Figure 1.19 shows, with the growth in money supply. Monetary policy certainly played a part in this disinflation – not through monetarist short-cuts, that is, where money supply is supposed mainly to affect prices rather than quantities (Figure 1.19 would lead to the opposite conclusion if one failed to remember that demand for money depends on the level of economic activity and that supply is difficult to control even when Paul Volcker is in charge), but through the recession which monetary policy brought about and perhaps also through the effect it had on expectations. This latter of course is not verifiable, but due acknowledgement must be given to the rational anticipation school of thought.

---

25. See especially H. Lenormand and D. Vallet, 'Les responsabilités de la politique monétaire américaine dans les difficultés économiques mondiales' (The responsibilities of US monetary policy in time of world recession), *Economie prospective internationale* (Journal of the CEPII), 18, 2nd quarter 1984, pp. 49–50; and D. Miqueu, 'La politique économique des Etats-Unis' (US economic policy), *Les Cahiers Français*, 218, October–December 1984, p. 8ff.

Understanding the Economic Crisis

Figure 1.18 Short-term interest rates in the United States, 1955–85

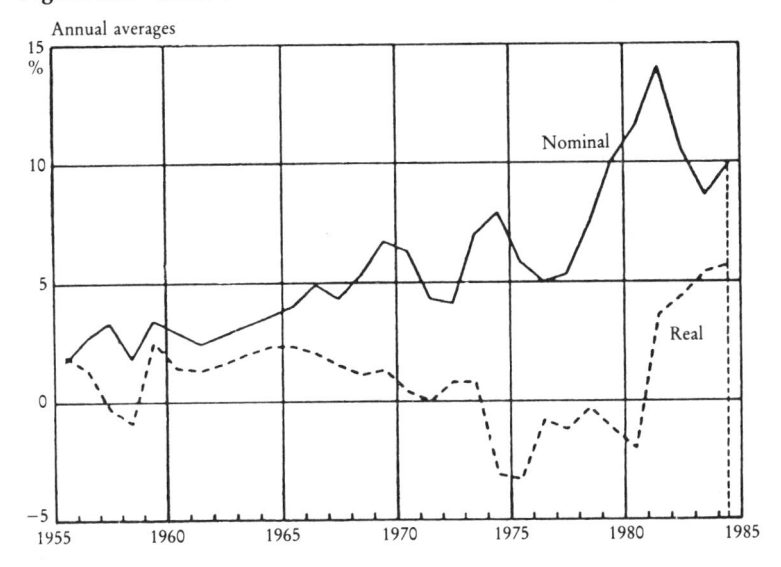

Source: Federal Reserve System.

Figure 1.19 Money, growth and inflation in the United States, 1979–84

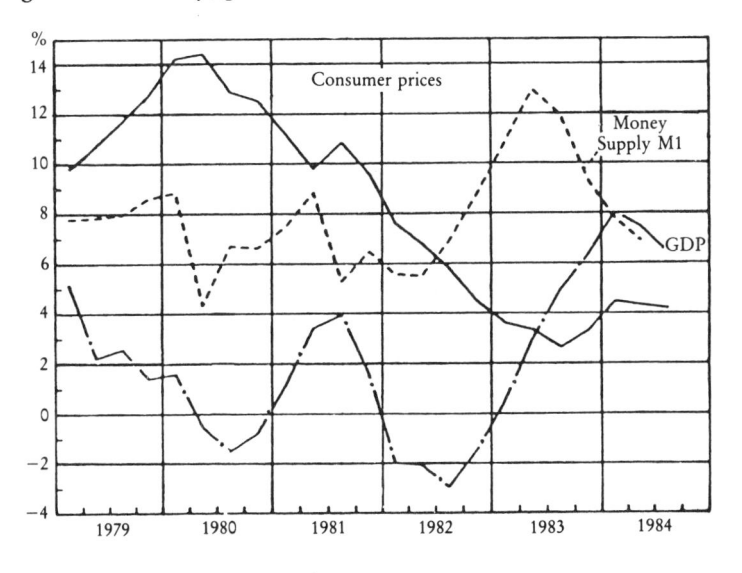

Shifts in exchange rates also played an important part in disinflation in the United States (and conversely in keeping inflation higher in Europe). Studies by CEPII – Centre d'Etudes Prospectives et d'Informations Internationales (Centre for forecasting studies and international data) – based on the normal formulae for determining prices and wages, show that exchange rate shifts between 1979 and 1983 accounted annually for 2.5% of US disinflation in 1981–3, whereas in France and West Germany they contributed 1.4% a year to the *prevention* of disinflation.[26]

The US recovery of 1983–4 had no more to do with supply-side economics than disinflation had with monetarist arguments. Tax reductions and disinflation brought a rise in the income of households which led to a sharp rise in consumption and an exceptional upswing in house buying.[27] Recovery in demand, and the fact that firms' profit levels improved as wage rises slowed, led in the classic manner to an increase in productive investment.

The Recession of 1979–82 in Quantitative Terms

The first oil shock coincided with the appearance of the first retrospective quantitative studies of economic activity using macro-economic models. Eckstein's work on the US economy marked the beginning of 'cliometry', that is using models for retrospective analysis rather than for forecasting. At the time, however, comparable multinational studies were not available. The development of multinational modelling after the mid-1970s and the increasing use of these tools by international organizations, particularly OECD and the EEC, allowed a much more satisfactory analysis of the second oil shock. From two recent studies based on simulations of multinational models, it is possible to evaluate the role of the second oil shock and of economic policy in the recession which followed.

Using its INTERLINK model, the OECD has been able to quantify the effect of the main factors which affected growth in the OECD in 1979–81 (see Table 1.9)

The dampening effect of the rise in oil prices reached a peak in

---

26. See CEPII, *Economie mondiale 1980–1990: la fracture?* (The world economy in the 1980s: the final breakdown?), Paris, Economica, 1984.
27. This recovery was largely the result of the fall in nominal rates. It did happen, despite the rise in real rates, which shows the importance of nominal rates in the investment decisions of households. The burden of annual repayments is largely appreciated by banks and households, and the yearly repayments are tied to the nominal income in the same period, ignoring corrections for anticipated inflation which a rational economic calculation would suggest.

Table 1.9 Effect of the second oil shock and economic policies on the slow-down in growth in the OECD, 1978–81

	1978	1979	1980	1981
Actual change in GNP	4.0	3.1	1.2	2.0
Oil crisis	0.0	− 0.5	− 2.3	− 0.5
Budgetary policies	+ 0.5	− 0.5	− 0.5	− 1.5
Monetary policies	0.0	− 0.5	0.0	− 0.7
Overall effect	+ 0.5	− 1.5	− 2.8	− 2.7

Source: INTERLINK and OECD simulations published in J. Llewellyn, 'Resource prices and macro-economic policies: lessons from the two oil shocks, *OECD Economic Review*, 1, p. 229. For actual changes: OECD, *OECD Economic Prospects*, July 1984, statistical appendices.

1980, adding more than 2% to the slow-down in growth, and then slackened from 1981, mainly because of the sharp rise in the volume of imports by OPEC members, and a more favourable shift in the terms of trade. But fiscal and monetary policies from 1981 onwards took over from the oil shock as the factor which kept growth down.

By removing the effect of the oil shock and economic policies from the picture as it developed, figures are obtained giving the annual growth which OECD countries would have had without the shock and the policies. Over the period 1979–81, this would have been on average 4.3% instead of 2%, that is, of the same order of magnitude as that of the previous period (1976–8), when it was 4.2%.

The recession which followed the second oil shock was characterized by two distinct phases: first, a recession in 1980–1 caused by the oil shock, but made worse by restrictive policies, and followed by a short recovery in mid-1981 which was more evident in the United States than in Europe, being fuelled in particular by the optimistic outlook of the new Reagan administration; second, another recession in 1982 for which US monetary policy was essentially responsible (see Figure 1.20). This second recession brought about a stagnation in economic growth throughout the three years following the second oil shock; from 1979 to 1982 the average annual growth in GDP was only 0.2% in the United States and 0.4% in the EEC, compared with 1.2% and 1.8% respectively in the three years after the first oil shock.

H. Lenormand has done a detailed quantitative comparison of the economic policies in operation during the two periods, using the European Communities' COMET multinational model. His study

Figure 1.20 Industrial production in major OECD countries between 1977 and 1984

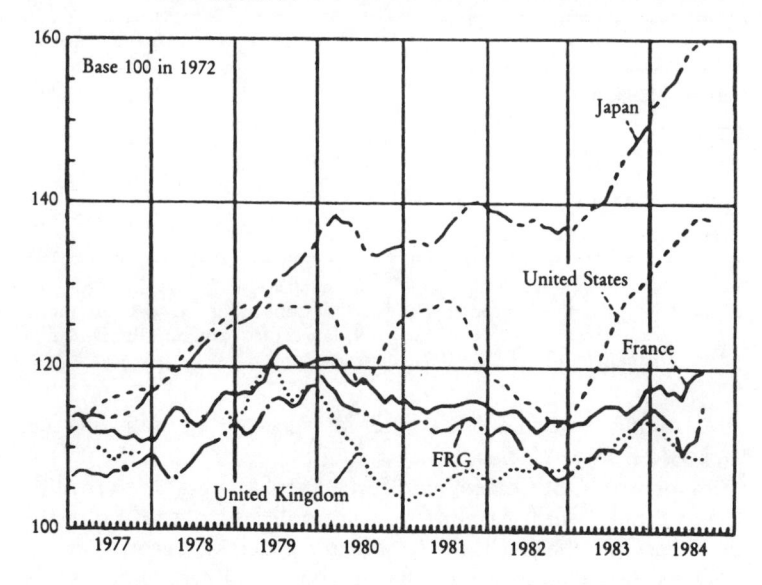

differentiates between the effect of fiscal policies (slightly expansionist in the United States, restrictive in Europe), the effect of monetary policies made necessary by restrictive policy in the United States, and the impact of the slowing down of wage rises. The most important results are shown in Table 1.10. The extent to which economic policies were restrictive is measured by comparing them with what they had been during the first oil shock. A negative influence indicates a policy which was more restrictive than for the first shock.

US monetary policy affected the world economy because it passed on the effect of its interest rate rises and a stronger dollar. The former was a greater factor for the United States (−1.1% of growth) than for Europe (−0.5%). As for the stronger dollar, it has already been mentioned that this was disinflationary for the United States and inflationary for Europe. The loss of competitivity which it brought about reduced US growth by 0.6% per year during this period. For European countries, there were two contrasting effects – competitive advantages created expansion, but import price rises had the effect of an oil shock in causing considerable stagflation. Lenormand's simulation shows that the overall effect was virtually nil for European growth. A more indirect consequence for Europe of US monetary policy was the reduction of imports by developing

Table 1.10 Comparison of the two oil shocks

	United States	EEC
Average annual growth between 1973 and 1976	+1.2	+1.8
Average annual growth between 1979 and 1982	+0.2	+0.4
Difference (at annual average rate)	−1.0	−1.4
Effect of economic policies on 1979–82 growth (compared with 1973–6)		
Monetary policies		
Interest rate rise	−1.1	−0.5
Dollar rise	−0.6	+0.1
Third World debt	−0.1	−0.2
Fiscal policies	+0.5	−1.0
Slow-down in wages	−	−0.3
Overall effect of economic policies	−1.3	−1.9

Source: Actual growth – OECD and EEC; effect of economic policies – H. Lenormand, 'Une analyse des causes de la stagnation économique mondiale' (An analysis of the causes of world economic stagnation), paper given to the conference on multinational modelling, Brussels, 8–9 December 1983. The simulations used the COMET model.

countries due to an increased need to service debts. Between 1978 and 1982, the total interest paid by developing countries practically trebled not only because the total debt rose but also because the average interest rate on this debt almost doubled. The rise in interest charges brought about by the increased rate accounted for an average fall of 3% per year in the volume of imports by developing countries and a loss of growth of 0.2% per year for EEC countries.

Monetary policy was responsible for about a third of the economic downturn, the other two-thirds being accounted for by fiscal policy and a slow-down in wage rises. In the United States, monetary policy had a dampening effect through the operation of all three factors, though about a quarter of this was offset by budgetary expansion.

The reason therefore that the recession after the second oil shock was so long and extensive was that there were changes in economic policy, as is shown by comparing the difference in growth in the period 1974–9 (−1.0% in the United States, −1.4% in Europe) with the overall impact of post-1979 economic policy (−1.3% in the United States, −1.9% in Europe).

Table 1.11 Influence of the international situation on the French economy

	1979	1980	1981	1982
Actual annual growth of GDP (%)	3.4	1.2	0.5	1.8
Effect of:				
Change in oil and raw materials prices	−0.2	−1.1	−1.8	−0.9
Change in dollar against the ECU	+0.1	+0.2	+0.2	−0.1
Fall in world demand	−	−0.3	−1.6	−2.8
Rise in foreign interest rates	−	−0.2	−0.3	+0.1
Actual annual inflation rate (price of GDP in %)	10.4	12.0	12.0	12.5
Effect of:				
Change in oil and raw materials prices	+1.3	+3.5	+3.0	+1.0
Change in dollar against the ECU	−0.8	−1.3	+0.1	+1.4
Fall in world demand	−	0	−0.2	−1.0
Rise in foreign interest rates	−	+0.7	+0.6	−0.1
Actual trade balance (goods and services in billion francs)	−3	−56	−55	−100
Effect of:				
Change in oil and raw materials prices	−19	−60	−34	−25
Change in dollar against the ECU	+12	+10	−19	−20
Fall in world demand	−	−3	−16	−30
Rise in foreign interest rates	−	+3	+10	+5

Source: A. Fonteneau and P.-A. Muet, 'Let poids de la contrainte extérieure sur la France' (The impact of international constraints on France), *Lettre de l'OFCE*, 3, 23 March 1983. The simulations were made using the OFCE-annual model. The figures have been adjusted since March 1983.

The Effect on France of External Constraint: From Stagflation to Deflation

The quantitative analysis of the impact of the international environment on the development of the French economy leads to similar conclusions. Table 1.11 outlines the effects on growth, inflation and external balance of the four main ways in which the world recession affected the French economy:

1 Increase in the price of oil and raw materials.
2 Changes in the dollar value of the ECU.
3 Fall in world demand.
4 Rise in foreign interest rates.

Understanding the Economic Crisis

World inflation has not been shown as an independent factor, but has been taken into account when looking at the effects of the oil shock and the effects of the fall in world demand.

The base point for examining the impact of each of these four factors is the average situation for each, in the period between the two oil shocks. More specifically, in the case of rise in world demand, the average rise between 1974 and 1980 has been taken as the base. For the rise in oil prices the base of an assumed annual rise since 1978 is obtained from the rate of world inflation – 7.5% per year. For foreign nominal interest rates, it is the average rate for 1979, that is, 10%. And finally, to measure the influence of dollar rates on the French economy between 1979 and 1983 independently of the devaluation of the franc against other European currencies, the value of the dollar is expressed in ECUs, the base value being the average value between 1979 and 1982. The difference in this base is because the dollar was relatively undervalued in 1979–80 and overvalued in 1981 and 1982. These base values, and the way the various factors evolved, are shown in Figure 1.21.

The effect of the external environment on the annual increase in GDP, the annual rate of inflation and the balance in value of trade in goods and services are shown in Table 1.11. The figures show that the oil shock, with its inflationary effect on the world economy, accounted for around 3% of inflation in France from 1980 onwards, the highest point being in 1981. The impact was not immediate because effects on incomes and prices in France and abroad took time to filter through. The slow-down in the growth of GDP caused by oil price rises was around 1% per year, with once again a peak in 1980–1. The consequent balance of payments deficit reached 60 billion francs in 1980 but then came down because imports fell with the dampening effect of the oil shock and also because raw material prices fell.

The rise in the value of the dollar in 1981 and 1982 had the same stagflation effect as the oil shock. The fall in value in 1979 and 1980 had partly offset inflation caused by oil price rises, whereas its rise fuelled inflation in 1982. The influence of the value of the dollar on the external deficit was weaker than that of oil prices, both because the rise in the dollar was itself smaller, and because it brought about increased competitivity which partly offset the unfavourable effect. In all, however, the consequences of the dollar rise were unfavourable for both growth and external deficit.

The slow-down in French growth and the balance of payments deficit were mainly a direct result of the oil shock of 1980 and 1981. In 1982 however these unfortunate phenomena were helped along

Figure 1.21 The worsening of France's international environment after the second oil shock

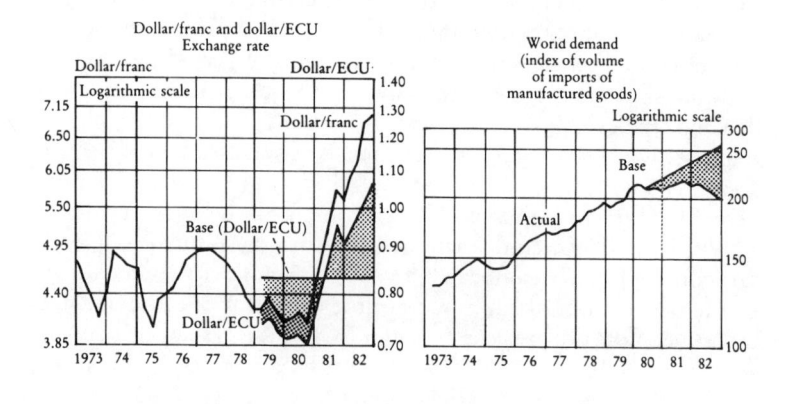

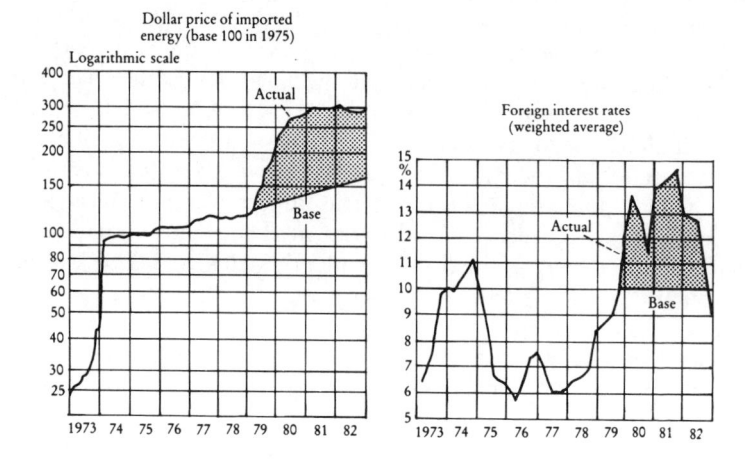

by a fall in world demand, which, since it slowed inflation at the same time, brought the international environment from stagflationary to deflationary.

The influence of the rise in foreign interest rates was not as great. It affected rates on French money and bond markets, which reduced investment, increased firms' costs and raised general price levels. However, it improved the balance of trade, since the effects of a slow-down in demand offset the worsening of competitivity caused by price rises. An attempt to assess the impact of interest rates not on the current balance but on currency movements would involve

	1979	1980	1981	1982
Growth (%)	+3.5	2.6	4.0	5.5
Inflation (%)	9.9	9.1	8.5	10.2
External deficit (in billion francs)	+4.0	−6.0	+4.0	−30.0

also looking at how French rates and foreign rates affected capital flows.

The importance of external constraint for the French economy can be understood by calculating what the levels of growth, inflation and external deficit would have been if the international environment had been the same as in 1975–9. By removing from the actual picture the effect of the factors given in Table 1.11, the above figures are obtained.

Even though this is only a rough calculation, it shows that if the international environment had not been unfavourable, the economy would have developed in keeping with what could have been expected from successive economic policies – restrictive in 1980, expansionist in 1981–2. This will be examined in detail in the next chapter.

APPENDIX 1.1

Keynes and Classical Economics: a Traditional Model

Assume that there is a closed economy and, to simplify the analysis, that saving by firms is nil and that only firms invest. Since prices and wages are constant, levels are expressed indifferently in either value or volume. Since the economy is closed, the price of production is the same as that of demand. The current social account gives the variables of the model as: Q = production, I = investment by firms, C = consumption by households, G = government spending, Y = national income, T = taxes net of government transfers, S_m = saving by households, S_g = government saving (deficit if negative).

Uses			Operations	Resources		
Firms	Households	Government		Firms	Households	Government
I	C	G	Goods and services	Q		
Y			Incomes		Y − T	T
	S_m	S_g	Saving/investment	I		

Reflation and Austerity

The budget balance for each economic agent is:

Firms: $Y = Q$ (1.1)

(saving by firms is taken as nil, so that production all goes to households and the government).

Households: $C + S_m = Y - T$ (1.2)

Government: $G + S_g = T$ (1.3)

These three equations ensure that there is equivalence between the equilibrium in the market for goods (1.4) and the equilibrium of saving and investment (1.4a):

$$\text{(1.1) to (1.3)} \quad Q = C + I + G \Leftrightarrow S_m + S_g = I \quad (1.4, 1.4a)$$

In classical theory, saving adjusts to investment through changes in the interest rate r. Equilibrium in the goods market is then ensured at any level of production (Say's Law):

$$S_m(r) + S_g = I(r) \Leftrightarrow \forall Q, Q \equiv C + I + G$$

Demand never constrains production which is determined by full employment. For Keynes, on the other hand, investment is exogenous ($\bar{I}$) and consumption depends on income (c = propensity to consume, C_0 = exogenous consumption in the short run, s = propensity to save):

$$C = c(Q - T) + C_0 \Leftrightarrow S_m = s(Q - T) - C_0 \quad (1.5, 1.5a)$$

The equilibrium in the goods market (or between saving and investment) then determines production through the multiplier:

$$\left. \begin{array}{l} \text{(1.1) to (1.3), (1.4) and (1.5)} \\ \quad \text{or} \\ \text{(1.1) to (1.3), (1.4a) and (1.5a)} \end{array} \right\} \Leftrightarrow Q = \frac{\bar{I} + \bar{G} - cT + C_0}{1 - c}$$

An *ex ante* increase in saving ($\Delta C_0 < 0$) therefore leads to a fall in production and consumption, without altering investment $\bar{I}$:

$$\Delta Q = \Delta C = \frac{\Delta C_0}{1 - c} < 0$$

When investment is dependent on anticipated growth and anticipation

−62−

Understanding the Economic Crisis

based on actual demand (flexible accelerator):

$$I = \sum_{i=0}^{n} \alpha_i (Q_i - [1 - \delta] Q_{i-1}) = \alpha \cdot Q + I_0 \tag{1.6}$$

The multiplier becomes:

$$\text{Equations (1.1) to (1.6)} \Leftrightarrow Q = \frac{I_0 + G - cT + C_0}{1 - c - \alpha}$$

An *ex ante* increase in saving leads to a fall in production and an *ex post* reduction in saving and investment:

$$\Delta Q = \frac{\Delta C_0}{1 - c - \alpha} < 0 \qquad \Delta S = \Delta I = \frac{\alpha}{1 - c - \alpha} \Delta C_0 < 0$$

APPENDIX 1.2

Analysing the Effects of an Oil Price Rise Using a Keynesian Model of an Open Economy

The same notation is used as in Appendix 1.1, but this time the presence of external trade means that a distinction must be made between the price of production and that of domestic demand. Let X and M be the volume of exports and imports, and p_x and p_m the corresponding prices; p_c is the price of domestic demand (it is taken to be identical for the three components of domestic demand) and p is the price of production.

The volume equilibrium of goods and services is:

$$I + C + G + X = Q + M \tag{1.7}$$

As for the value equilibrium, this serves to determine the price of domestic demand on the basis of the prices of production and external trade:

$$p_c (I + C + G) + p_x X = p Q + p_m M \tag{1.8}$$

The magnitudes in value which appear in the current social account are all expressed in real terms, that is to say, deflated by the price of domestic demand p_c. For example, in the current social account, there are:

– real income $Y = \dfrac{p}{p_c} \cdot Q$

– the external deficit in real terms $D = \dfrac{p_m M - p_x X}{p_c}$

Uses				Operations	Resources			
Firms	House-holds	Govern-ment	External		Firms	House-holds	Govern-ment	External
I	C	G		Goods and services	Y			D
Y – A				Incomes		Y–A–T	T	
A	S_m	S_g	D	Saving/Investment	I			

Volumes are expressed in prices of the period before the oil shock, so that all initial price indexes are unit. Let D_v be the external deficit in volume ($D_v = M - X$). The volume of production equals the volume of domestic demand less the volume of the external deficit:

$$Q = C + I + G - D_v \qquad (1.9)$$

Real income is equal to the difference between the volume of demand and the external deficit expressed in real terms:

$$Y = C + I + G - D \qquad (1.10)$$

In order to simplify the presentation of the model, it will be shown as changes (or more accurately in a differentiated form). Change in the real external deficit is broken down into volume change of the deficit and change due to the terms of trade ($d\, D_p$):

$$d\,D = d\,D_v + d\,D_p \qquad (1.11)$$

From this is deduced the relationship between the change in real income and that of the volume of GDP:

$$d\,Y = d\,Q - d\,D_p \qquad (1.10a)$$

The other equations of the model are:

Real self-financing	$dA = a \cdot dY$	(1.12)
Taxes net of subsidies	$dT = t \cdot dY$	(1.13)
Government account	$dS_g = dT - dG$	(1.14)
Households' account	$dS_m + dC = (1 - a - t)\,dY$	(1.15)
Consumption by households	$dC = c\,(1 - a - t)\,dY$	(1.16)
Investment by firms	$dI = \alpha \cdot dQ$	(1.17)
External deficit in volume	$dD_v = m \cdot dQ$	(1.18)

The model has ten equations and twelve variables (the nine variables of the current social account plus the volume of GNP [Q], and the volume-price breakdown of the external deficit [D_v and D_p]). The two exogenous variables are public spending ($\bar{G}$) and the terms of trade ($\bar{D}_p$). This gives the normal multiplier:

$$dQ = \frac{\overline{dG} - c(1 - a - t)\,\overline{dD}_p}{1 + m - c(1 - a - t) - \alpha}$$

In this way, we get the reflation effect of an increase in public spending ($dG \geqslant 0$) and the depressive effect of a worsening of the terms of trade ($dD_p > 0$). The numerical values used come from the apparent propensities of the principal French models summarized in the following table. The propensities indicated correspond to the impact in the short run (one year) and in the medium run (five years). The date in brackets is the year when public spending was increased. The multiplier effect has in fact been weaker in recent years because of the increasing openness of the French economy. The apparent marginal propensity to consume is stronger in the medium run than in the short run because of delays in the adjustment of consumption to income. The marginal propensity in the external deficit is, on the other hand, stronger in the short run than in the medium run, where it tends towards the average propensity. Finally, the apparent propensity to invest also goes down in the medium run because of the accelerator effect. The values used are mid-way between the short and the medium run.

Apparent propensities and multiplier in the main French models

	Value used	\multicolumn{4}{c}{Value after one year}	\multicolumn{2}{c}{Value after five years}
		DMS 1 (1965)	METRIC 1 (1969)	OFCE-annual (1981)	OFCE-quarterly (1984)	DMS 1 (1965)	OFCE-annual (1977)
Multiplier	1.50	1.10	1.38	1.07	0.94	1.60	1.30
Apparent propensities:							
– external deficit (m)	0.45	0.50	0.43	0.46	0.59	0.30	0.30
– investment (α)	0.30	0.32	0.48	0.28	0.32	0.10	0.20
– consumption $c(1-a-t)$	0.48	0.28	0.22	0.24	0.21	0.60	0.30

Source: For DMS and METRIC, we have used the breakdown of multipliers given in the article by P. Artus and P.-A. Muet 'Une étude comparative des propriétés dynamiques de dix modèles américains et cinq modèles français' (A comparative study of the dynamic properties of ten American and five French models), *Revue économique*, 31 (1), January 1980.

–2–

Reflation Runs Into Difficulties

> A strong growth and a different kind of growth is necessary to achieve these objectives ... We want growth which is egalitarian, autonomous and creative.
> *Projet socialiste* (Socialist Party policy statement), 1980

Most of the economic measures proposed by François Mitterrand in 1981 had been included in the manifesto of the left-wing parties since the joint programme for government was signed in 1972.[1] At that time, growth was strong (between 5% and 6% a year), public finances were in balance, profits high and external debt virtually nil; in these circumstances, it was not too hard to find the money for welfare provisions and a rise in real wages.

However, the first oil shock in 1973 halved growth to 3%, and it was again halved by the second shock,[2] casting doubt on the credibility of the measures proposed by the Left, which were posited on strong growth. Michel Rocard showed that he was well aware of this when in 1978 he suggested that policies should be adapted to new global economic conditions. A change of this kind however involved political risks which François Mitterrand and the French Socialist Party were unwilling to take.

Their reaction to the slow-down in growth was to say that 'the Plan will establish a high growth rate'.[3] But macro-economic theory shows that there is always a risk that a strong dose of reflation will founder on external constraints and budget deficits. Mitterrand's economic advisers argued that this was not true because the theory would be overtaken by the structural changes which the Left would

---

1. See, for example, Chapter 1 of the book by Michel Beaud, *Le mirage de la croissance* (The mirage of growth), Paris, Syros, 1983
2. Cf. Chapter 1.
3. Parti Socialiste, *Propositions pour l'actualisation du programme commun de gouvernement de la gauche* (Proposals for updating the joint programme for government), Paris, Flammarion, 1978, p. 63.

bring about.[4] Most of the Left refused to countenance the obvious fact that economic behaviour and the way the economy works cannot be changed in a short space of time, if at all. They thought, or gave the impression of thinking, that all that was needed to reduce, for example, the share of imports in the GNP, was political will.[5]

Nevertheless, some degree of reflation was necessary in June 1981. For political reasons, the Left could not be seen to take power merely to outdo the Right in economic austerity. Moreover, unemployment had been growing significantly since Summer 1980 and, except in 1975, the budget had not been used to support growth, whereas the West German government had boosted the economy four times between 1974 and 1981.[6] It is true that the trade balance was still largely in deficit in Spring 1981, but external debt was relatively low and, most significant of all, international organizations were forecasting an upsurge in the world economy with a probable sustained growth in exports to offset increased imports due to economic recovery.

The economic situation at the time and the structural parameters of the French economy, however, called for extreme care with regard to policy choices and the extent of reflation. But whereas policy options had unfortunately been determined for some time, the extent of the reflation, as we shall see, was relatively modest. This will be seen by a detailed examination of the measures taken and of their macro-economic effects, and by a comparison of these with what happened in other examples of reflation and with the worsening international environment.

The Economic Situation in France in Spring 1981

The situation in France in May 1981 was examined by the Commission du Bilan (Commission on the state of the nation),[7] so only a brief reminder is necessary of the position regarding the main

---

4. In general, politicians and certain economists of the Left found the models too 'conservative'. Experience showed that economic and social inflexibility was greater than they thought or hoped in 1981.
5. Point 20 of Mitterrand's 1981 presidential election manifesto stipulated that 'by 1990, the proportion of foreign trade in GDP will be brought down to below 20%'. In 1984, imports represented 28% of GDP as against 23% in 1980 – an increase of 5 percentage points in five years.
6. See below.
7. Commission du Bilan, *La France en mai 1981* (France in May 1981), Paris, La Documentation Française, 1981.

Reflation and Austerity

Figure 2.1 Consumer prices in the major countries from 1974 to 1981

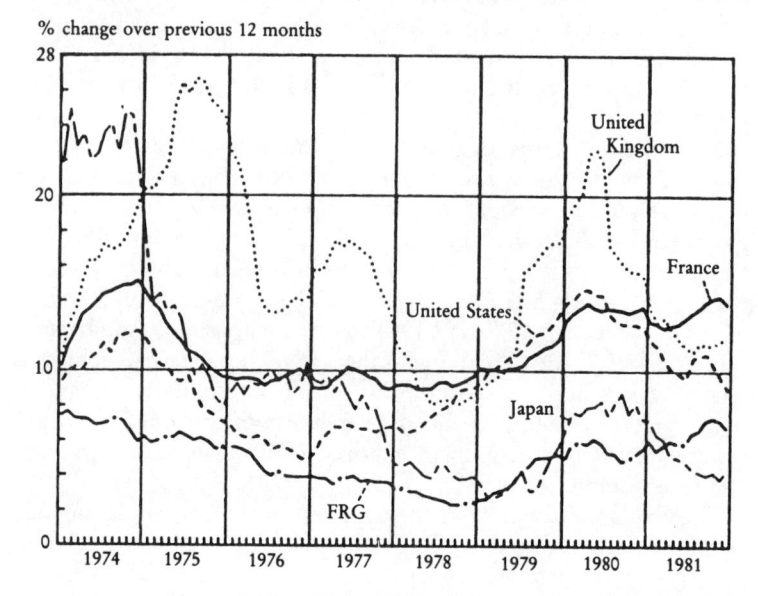

macro-economic variables. This will be followed by reference to the Barre government's pre-electoral reflation, which went largely unnoticed, and by an examination of the forecasts about the world economy made at the beginning of Summer 1981.

The Main Equilibria

What was the situation with regard to the main economic variables – prices, level of unemployment, foreign trade and public finances – in Spring 1981? How did they compare with those in the other major industrial countries?

Price rises were greater in France than in other countries Consumer prices had risen considerably in all Western countries in 1979 following the second oil shock (see Figure 2.1). But, from mid-1980 onwards, restrictive policies applied by most of these countries had brought about a gradual reduction in inflation.[8] Disinflation had been compounded in the United States, in the United Kingdom and in Japan by appreciation of the currency, but in France and West Germany it had been held in check.

8. See Chapter 5.

Reflation Runs Into Difficulties

The figure of 2 million unemployed was fast approaching Between November 1980 and June 1981, the number of registered unemployed was increasing on average by 37,000 a month. By July 1981 there were 1.8 million as against 1.43 million a year previously; if that rate continued, the figure of 2 million would be reached by the end of the Autumn. The rise in unemployment is explained by an increase in the number of people available for work, a reduction in the number of jobs available beginning in the second quarter of 1980, and a far from energetic employment policy at the time (see Chapter 4). Nevertheless the French unemployment rate was about average for the EEC countries as a whole; Belgium (10%) and the United Kingdom (11%) were much higher and West Germany (around 4%) much lower. The United States rate remained steady between mid-1980 and mid-1981, but this level was nevertheless high (7.5% of the labour force).

The trade deficit brought about by the second oil shock had not been overcome Although there had been a severe recession since mid-1980, the deficit in foreign trade was still in evidence in Spring 1981. It is true that the export/import ratio had risen to about 85%, as against 82% in the second and third quarters of 1980 (see Figure 2.2). This improvement had been brought about by a reduction of the deficit with non-EEC OECD countries, with OPEC countries and with the developing countries. On the other hand the export/import cover rate with EEC countries was significantly lower than in 1979 (90% as against 96%).

This situation was in the main due to the appreciation of the franc in real terms against the Deutschmark. The differential rate of inflation in France and West Germany had not been corrected by a devaluation of the franc since the setting up of the EMS in 1979. The resulting loss of competitivity had grievous implications for French exports until the second devaluation of the franc in mid-1982.[9]

Public finances were in balance but... Between 1973 and 1980, OECD countries had reacted in different ways to the negative effect which the slow-down in growth had on public finances. After the first oil shock, all had experienced an increase, which was more or less automatic or deliberate, in general government net lending (see Table 2.1). Certain countries, and France was one of them, had deliberately kept their deficit in check by means of an increase in taxes. Others, such as Italy, Japan, West Germany and the United

---

9. See Chapter 3.

Reflation and Austerity

Figure 2.2 Cover rate of external trade, i.e. ratio of exports (fob) to imports (cif), according to customs figures (the balance of trade is in equilibrium when the cover rate of exports to imports is 95.5%)

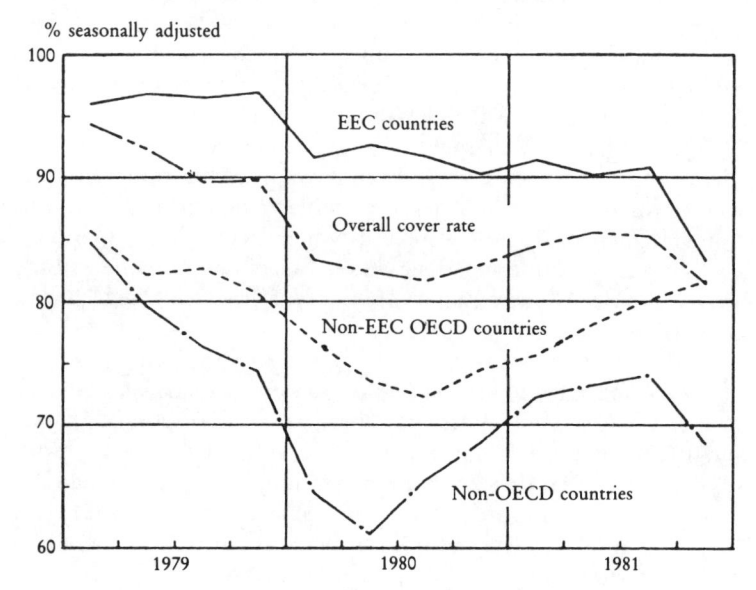

Source: *Comptes de la Nation 1981* (National accounts 1981), Vol. II.

Kingdom had tolerated significant deficits in an attempt to stem the rise in unemployment and alleviate the effect of taxation on economic activity.

By 1980, there was again a financial surplus in France for government spending (0.3% of GDP), but this situation was a precarious one since it was the result of rather short-term economic factors. The fact that national income accounting showed a low government borrowing requirement (10.7 billion) was due to a large extent to accounting procedures;[10] in terms of what was needed to implement the budget, disregarding the IMF and the Currency Stabilization Fund, the deficit was 30 billion francs as against 38 billion in 1979. The improvement shown in 1980 was therefore small and was due especially to the significant increase in tax receipts brought about by growth during 1979.[11] The third reason that the government had

10. It was due mainly to the demonetization of the 50 franc piece and to profits made by the Currency Stabilization Fund.
11. The West German reflation of 1978–9 was favourable to French growth in 1979 and 1980 (see below).

Reflation Runs Into Difficulties

Table 2.1 Public sector borrowing requirement (−) and surplus (+) in the major countries (as % of GDP)

	1973	1974	1975	1976	1977	1978	1979	1980	1981
France	1.2	0.6	−2.2	−0.7	−0.8	−1.7	−0.7	0.3	−1.8
West Germany	1.2	−1.3	−5.7	−3.4	−2.4	−2.5	−2.7	−3.1	−4.0
United Kingdom	−3.5	−3.8	−4.9	−5.0	−3.4	−4.3	−3.2	−3.2	−2.1
Italy	−7.0	−7.0	−11.7	−9.0	−8.0	−9.7	−9.4	−8.3	−11.9
United States	1.0	0.5	−3.5	−1.5	−0.3	0.0	0.6	−1.3	−1.0
Japan	0.7	0.4	−2.8	−2.9	−3.8	−5.5	−4.8	−4.2	−3.9

Source: *Comptes de la Nation 1982* (National accounts 1982), Vol. 1, p. 128.

more money at its disposal was that the social security fund surplus increased from 18.1 billion in 1979 to 26.7 billion in 1980. This increase is almost exactly the sum raised by an emergency increase in contributions introduced in August 1979.

... this achievement was not very solid The fragility of the achievements of 1980 became glaringly apparent during the first half of 1981. When the Left came to power, the supplementary budget had to increase the 30 billion originally envisaged as a deficit to 52 billion – the extra 22 billion was to 'sort out what we inherited'. As we shall see, the reflation policy applied by the Barre government just before the election had led to an increase in the level of general government spending and a drop in revenue of a parafiscal nature.

Before May 1981: The Reflation which Tends to be Forgotten

In Spring 1981 the French economy was, contrary to widespread belief, already in a situation where domestic demand was being stimulated; the importance of this was for a long time underestimated by the new socialist government. Barre's austerity policy had been considerably softened in the run-up to the elections by a series of measures taken during the Winter of 1980/1. The two most important ones were, first, the abolition in February 1981 of the employees' sickness insurance surcharge introduced on 1 August 1979, and second, the hand-out to farmers of 4.1 billion francs in the supplementary budget of December 1980, to maintain their 1980 income levels. In January and February 1981, there was a significant increase in the retirement pension and certain other payments to handicapped people and old age pensioners. Furthermore, the budget for 1981 had further increased tax advantages on investment by firms, first introduced in 1979. Up to 1 October 1980, the

Table 2.2 Change in the real value of wages and social welfare benefits to mid-1981 (% rate of change per quarter)

	1980(1)	1980(2)	1980(3)	1980(4)	1981(1)	1981(2)
Gross wages	−0.1	0.6	0.1	0.2	0.6	−0.1
Wages net of employees' social contributions	−0.4	0.5	0.1	0.2	1.4	0.3
Welfare benefits	0.2	−0.5	1.6	0.9	1.6	1.8
Households' disposable income	−1.0	0.2	0.6	0.3	1.8	1.1

Source: *Comptes de la Nation 1981* (National accounts 1981), Vol. I.

advantage was in respect only of the *increase* in investment over the previous year, but after that date, it was the *level* of capital investment between 1 October 1980 and 31 December 1985 which counted. At the same time, car tax and the tax on oil-derived products were not increased in the budget for 1981, whereas they had been increased in line with inflation in previous years.

The final point is that during the first few months of 1981, the government did not immediately pass on to the consumer in public utility charges all of the increased cost of imported energy, as had been its practice in the two previous years. Consumer energy prices had to be raised sharply in July and August 1981 by the incoming socialist government. The boost given to the economy by the Barre government is clearly apparent in the way wages and welfare benefits fared in each quarter between the beginning of 1980 and the middle of 1981 (see Table 2.2). Employees' real incomes net of social security contributions went up by 1.7% in the first half of 1981 as against 0.1% in the first half of 1980; for welfare benefits the equivalent figures were a rise of 3.4% compared with a drop of 0.3% in 1980.

The cost to public finances of the 'Barre reflation' was approximately 20 billion francs, of which 10 billion went on social security. These measures stimulated growth by about 0.4 percentage points in 1981 and worsened the trade balance by 8 billion francs.

The International Situation in Summer 1981 and the Forecast for 1982

At the beginning of Summer 1981, international forecasting bodies expected world economic recovery, which had begun during the first half of the year, to continue and grow in 1982. In June, the OECD was forecasting for 1982 a growth of 2% in real GNP and a

Table 2.3 Forecasts for 1982 made in Autumn 1981

	Budget for 1982[a]	Average of unofficial forecasts in Autumn 1981[b]	Actual outcome[c]
International environment			
Real GNP of OECD countries	1.8	2.0[d]	−0.5
World demand for French manufactured goods	4.8	6.25[d]	0.4
Dollar/franc exchange rate	n.a.	5.5	6.58
France			
Annual average growth rate			
GDP	3.3	2.75	2.0
Imports	5.1	5.7	2.9
Household consumption	2.5	2.8	3.0
Investment by firms	3.0	−0.6	−1.2
Exports	4.9	4.5	−2.5
Inflation rate (household consumer price deflator)	12.9	13.5	11.7
Balance of trade (goods and services in million francs)	−61.0	−66.0	−100.5

(a) Budget for 1982, *Annexe au rapport économique et financier* (Appendix to the economic and financial report), September 1981.
(b) These are forecasts by the OECD and the EEC as well as by the following French institutes or publications: BIPE (Bureau d'Information et de Prévision Economique); Centre d'Observation Economique de la Chambre de Commerce de Paris; Crédit Lyonnais; GAMA (Groupe d'Analyse Macro-économique Appliquée); REXECO (Recherches pour l'Expansion de l'Economie); *Expansion; Nouvel Economiste; Vie Française*.
Source: A. Fonteneau 'Les erreurs de prévisions économiques pour 1982' (Errors in economic forecasting for 1982), *Observations et diagnostics économiques*, 4, June 1983.
(c) Provisional national accounting statistics for 1982, published in the report on the accounts for 1984. Volume is calculated at the prices of the preceding year (1981).
(d) Forecast by the OECD only, see *OECD Economic Outlook*, 29 July 1981.

6% increase in imports for OECD countries as a whole. Forecasts prepared for the 1982 budget (the bill passed in Autumn 1981) as well as those by almost all French forecasting organizations came up with more or less the same figures (see Table 2.3).[12] Moreover, the

12. See A. Fonteneau, 'Les erreurs de prévisions économiques pour 1982' (Errors in economic forecasting for 1982), *Observations et diagnostics économiques*, 4, June 1983.

Figure 2.3 Forecasting error in the change in the dollar rate, 1978–84

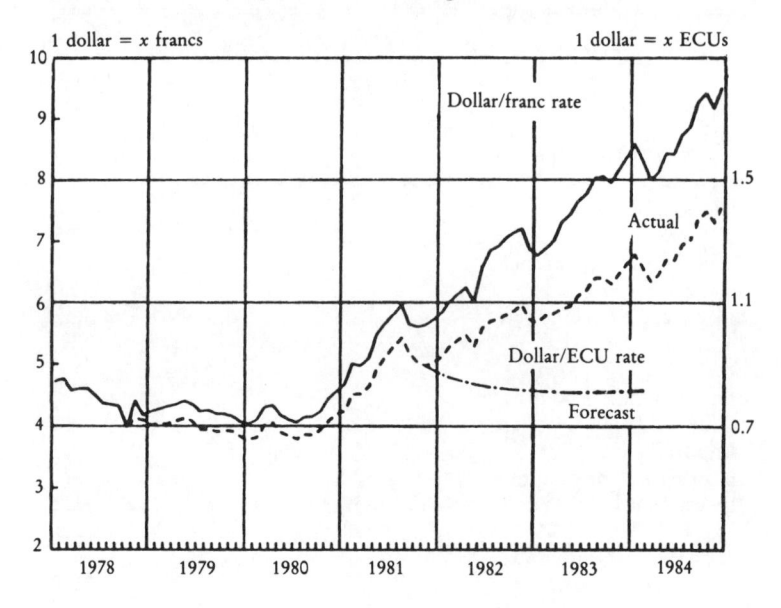

forecasts were for a stable dollar, even a slight fall, after the sharp rises in the first nine months of 1981.

In this context, according to official forecasts and most unofficial ones, the reflation of the French economy would bring about a growth in the economy greater than that of its main trading partners, and create as a consequence a relatively large trade deficit (between 60 billion and 70 billion francs). This, however, appeared to be acceptable in the short term because of the expected recovery in the world economy and the fairly low level of France's external debt. But the way the world economy in fact developed did not bear out the forecasts made during the summer of 1981. The GNP of OECD countries as a whole dropped by 0.5% in 1982 whereas a rise of 2% had been forecast. The volume of world trade remained the same when forecasts reckoned on a growth of between 4% and 6%. Furthermore, the contradiction between US monetary policy and its fiscal policy led to a continuous rise in the dollar. It was worth 7 francs at the end of 1982 whereas a rate of about 5.5 had been forecast (see Figure 2.3).

Reflation Runs Into Difficulties

The Reflation of 1981-2

The reflation of 1981-2 was based mainly on increases in the minimum wage, a rise in welfare benefit payments and the boost given to the economy through fiscal policy. At the same time, new taxes on wealth and top incomes were introduced and a new plan for the social security fund was implemented.

A Higher Guaranteed Minimum Wage

In keeping with its promises the socialist government, as soon as it took office, applied its policy of increasing low pay. The Council of Ministers meeting on 3 June 1981 agreed on a 10% rise in the minimum wage;[13] further, less spectacular rises were introduced subsequently, so that the minimum wage rose 38% in money terms between 1 June 1981 and March 1983. Whereas the minimum wage had risen in real terms by only 1.5% in 1979 and 1.8% in 1980, it rose 5.8% in 1981 and 4.2% in 1982. At the same time, the government reduced some employers' social security contributions to offset about half of the extra costs (wages and contributions) arising from the 10% increase in minimum wage. This compensation consisted of an across-the-board reduction of 6.5 percentage points in contribution rates for incomes up to 1.2 times the minimum wage; it ceased to apply when the minimum wage reached a figure 20% higher than its 31 May 1981 level. The net loss in social security contributions, amounting to the difference between the revenue shortfall because of the concession and the increase in revenue from the significant rise in the minimum wage, was met by the State. To cover this, the sum of 2.6 billion francs was included in the supplementary budget of August 1981 and a further 2 billion in the budget prepared for 1982. However, the real cost to the budget of this particular measure turned out to be less than expected – 3.5 billion over the two years 1981-2.[14]

The effects of increases in the minimum wage were modest In order to measure the effects of increases in the minimum wage, we

---

13. 3.5% is due to the rise in prices and 6.5% to increase in purchasing power.
14. According to the 'final settlement laws' confirming the implementation of the budget, the cost to the budget of these exemptions was 2.53 billion francs in 1981 and 1 billion in 1982. Taking into consideration accounting delays and advances to social security funds made by the government, allowances actually given to firms are estimated at 1.5 billion in 1981 and 2.1 billion in 1982 by the joint employers' association/government report on firms' social security contributions.

Figure 2.4 Change in the real value of the minimum wage since 1979

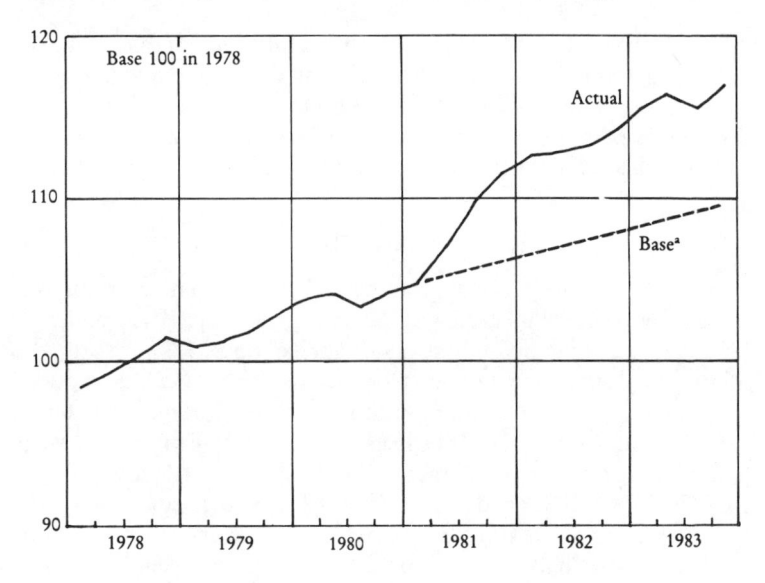

[a] The base is the average rise in 1979–80 of 0.4% per quarter.
Source: INSEE, *Comptes Trimestriels* (Quarterly accounts).

must take a base situation, calculate the number of wage-earners involved and work out the effects on incomes as a whole.

To establish the base, we have assumed that if there had not been a deliberate policy to increase low pay, the rise in real terms in the minimum wage would have been what it was during 1979–80, i.e. slightly more than 0.4% per quarter (see Figure 2.4).

The study carried out by the Ministry of Employment in July 1981 shows that 8% of the employees of firms employing ten or more people *directly benefited* from the June 1981 rise, as against only 3.7% from that in July 1980. If firms employing fewer than ten people are included, INSEE (the national statistical office) put the total number of employees paid at roughly the minimum wage in trade, industry and services at 1.5 million in July 1981 – that is, about double the number estimated for July 1980.[15]

The overall results of the Ministry of Employment's quarterly studies, taken for each job category and for each industry, suggest that the *induced effect* on higher incomes of rises in the minimum

---

15. Cf. F. Bourit, P. Hernu, M. Perrot, 'Les salaires en 1981' (Wages in 1981), *Economie et statistique*, 141, February 1982.

Table 2.4 Macro-economic effect of rises in real value of minimum wage

	1981	1982	1983
Impact on annual growth rate (%)			
Real GDP	+0.1	+0.05	−0.1
Household consumption (volume)	+0.2	+0.1	0.0
Total investment (volume)	−0.2	+0.1	−0.1
Consumer prices	0.1	+0.2	+0.3
Real disposable income	+0.3	0.0	−0.05
Impact on level (annual average)			
Employment (thousands)	+4.0	+6.0	0.0
Unemployment (thousands)	−2.0	−3.5	+2.0
Balance of trade (billion francs)	−1.0	−1.5	−1.5
Public borrowing requirement or surplus (billion francs)			
ex ante	−2.55	−1.0	−0.0
ex post	−1.9	+0.2	+0.8

Source: Simulations by the OFCE-annual model.

wage in 1981 was in the end very small. The effect of the June 1981 rise went no further than unskilled workers (according to an 'income structure' study, the average wage of an unskilled worker was 1.3 times the minimum wage in 1978). During the third and fourth quarters of 1981, the induced effects were similarly very modest. The rise in firms' costs brought about by this exceptional rise in the minimum wage was calculated at 550 million in 1981 and 2.9 billion in 1982 by the joint employers' association/government report on firms' costs.

The increase in wages gave only a temporary boost to the economy Table 2.4 shows the macro-economic impact of the rise in the minimum wage during 1981–3, taking into account the temporary reduction in employers' social security contributions.[16] The rise in the minimum wage led to an increase in wage earnings in 1981–2, which itself brought about a more sustained growth in household consumption (0.2% in 1981 and 0.1% in 1982), and in the level of economic activity. However, according to econometric simulations

16. The real value of the remuneration of government employees and of welfare benefits for unemployed and retired people is taken as unchanged in the simulation whereas in general it automatically follows a rise in incomes. Rises in social welfare benefits are analysed later.

by the OFCE-annual model (and others), the rise in production described a bell-shaped curve: as the rise in the minimum wage worked its way through and as soon as the compensation for half the increased costs came to an end, price rises speeded up, which put a brake on exports and increased imports; the result was that at the end of the two years during which wages gained ground, production was again down.

Investment by firms was stimulated by the upsurge in the demand for consumer goods, and by the increased cost of labour (capital was substituted for labour in the medium term), but the shrinkage of profits was the deciding factor, and firms' gross fixed investment became permanently lower than its base level. The end result was that any economic recovery effect of rises in the minimum wage was particularly short-lived, especially for industry, which suffered the direct consequences of a fall in competitivity and investment. The employment situation improved only very slightly (5,500 more jobs) and for a short time only. From 1982 the fall in industrial production and capital–labour substitution led to a decrease in industrial jobs.

Nevertheless, the *ex post* cost to the budget was significantly lower than the direct cost of compensating half of firms' extra outlay: the reason for this was, first, that because consumption rose more rapidly there was a rise in VAT receipts and, second, that social security contributions went up with wages. Table 2.4 shows that the net cost to the budget of this policy measure was, *ex post*, practically nil. If the policy of compensating firms had gone on for longer or if it had been, say, 75% or 100%, then firms' profits would not have been affected, investment by firms would have been higher and the effect on inflation would have been negligible.

The conclusion is that although rises in the minimum wage in 1981–2 had only a slight reflationary impact in the short term, and a negative effect in the medium term,[17] they nevertheless made it possible to reduce salary differentials to a small extent.

Social Policy Measures

Nearly all the social policies in the Left's manifesto were put into

---

17. For wage rises to have a lasting reflationary effect on the economy, the structural parameters of the economy would have to be such that foreign trade is not very sensitive to competitivity, that households' propensity to consume is very much higher than firms' propensity to spend profits, and that prices adjust slowly to unit costs of production. These conditions were not satisfied (or only partially satisfied) in 1981.

> **Inset 2.1**
>
> *Family welfare benefit measures introduced between July 1980 and January 1983*
>
> 1 July 1980: 5,000 franc rise in maternity allowance for third child
> 1 January 1981: introduction of minimum family income level
> 1 July 1981: 25% increase in child benefit and housing benefit; 20% increase in allowance for handicapped adults
> 1 December 1981: 25% increase in housing benefit
> 1 February 1982: 25% increase in child benefit for two-child families
> 1 July 1982: 14% rise in tax allowance for families

effect during the first year of Mitterrand's presidency. They were mainly directed towards families and retired people. There were also other less far-reaching measures to help low-income farmers, people in rented accommodation and workers on short time. The money for these measures came from the central government's budget and from the various social security funds.

Family welfare benefits were increased substantially and permanently In order to halt the drop in the birth rate, the Barre government had introduced a 'third child' policy in 1980, consisting of an increase in child benefit, higher tax allowances for dependants, and an increase of 5,000 francs in maternity benefits (see Inset 2.1).

When the Left took office, they wanted to base the family benefits system on 'rights for children'. 'A child is a creditor, is owed a debt by society, simply by being a child. All children have this right, whatever their position in the family, whatever the income or matrimonial status of their parents.'[18] The new government therefore proposed in 1981 a gradual and complete overhaul of family policy.[19] To halt the decline of family benefits as a proportion of the welfare budget, immediate and substantial rises were introduced. Child benefit rates were increased by 25% in July 1981 and by a further 25% in February 1982 for families with more than one child.

18. See *Le Plan intérimaire: stratégie pour deux ans (1982–83)* (The provisional Plan: strategy for the next two years), Paris, La Documentation Française, 1981.
19. In fact, it was not until November 1984 that a comprehensive reform of family welfare benefits began to be applied. It was characterized by two important innovations – a young children's allowance and an allowance towards the costs of education (see *Lettre de Matignon*, 128, 19 November 1984).

Table 2.5 Change in retirement benefit from 1980 to 1983[a]

	Annual increase (in %)				Monthly amount in francs in July 1983
	1980	1981	1982	1983	
Non-contributory benefit (AVTS)	13.6	17.0	17.3	9.8	980
Extra payment (FNS)	11.5	30.9	46.2	8.8	1,318
Guaranteed minimum level	12.6	23.8	32.4	9.2	2,298

[a] The guaranteed minimum level of the various retirement and invalidity benefits is made up of two distinct elements. A non-contributory benefit is paid to people whose contributions record does not entitle them to a retirement pension; for employed persons, this would be the AVTS (*allocation aux vieux travailleurs salariés*), which in 1980 was paid to 4.35 million people. The second element is the extra allowance paid from the FNS (*fonds national de solidarité*) which brings the total of all other allowances up to the level fixed as the guaranteed minimum. It is financed by the government and in 1980 was paid to 1.76 million people.
Source: *Comptes de la Nation 1983* (National accounts 1983), Vol. 2.

Taken in conjunction with rises for inflation, these rises represented a benefits increase of 43% in real terms between 1981 and 1983, for a family with two children and 14% for a family with three children. At the same time, housing benefit was raised by 25% in July 1981 and 20% in December 1981.

The overall estimate is that these policies led to an increase in welfare payments to families of around 3 billion francs in 1981 and 10 billion in 1982, over and above the rises which would have happened if previous legislation had remained in force. The impact of these 1981–2 measures was somewhat reduced when in 1983 the method of calculating the date of entitlement to family welfare benefits was changed and the extra payment for a third child was halved. Nevertheless, the real value of family benefits continued to rise – by 1.8% for families with two or three children. The conclusion is that the policies introduced by the Left when it took office improved the lot of families, particularly families with two children, substantially and on a long-term basis. After the 1983–4 standstill further measures introduced in November 1984 to help large families and families with young children increased the standard of living for families from 1985.

The retirement pension went up by 62% in two years There had been a considerable effort during President Giscard's term of office to help the most impoverished old age pensioners; on 1 January

1974 the annual retirement pension was equal to 46% of the minimum wage, but by 1 January 1980, this figure had reached 57.6%. The Left gave added impetus to this trend – between May 1981 and July 1983 the monthly individual rate of retirement pension went up from 1,416 to 2,300 francs, a rise of 62% in two years (Table 2.5).

The extra spending needed for rises in retirement pension can be estimated at 1.5 billion in 1981 (the July 1981 supplementary budget put the cost for 1981 at 1.44 billion) and around 5 billion in 1982. During 1981–3, policies specifically aimed at retired people were introduced, the most important being, in April 1983, the lowering of the age of full entitlement to retirement pension to 60, a measure costing 1.3 billion francs in 1983 and 5.4 billion in 1984.[20] Moreover, the faster rise in incomes in 1981 due to the increase in the minimum wage led to a rise in the real value of retirement pensions paid by the social security system of 2.2% in 1982, as against a fall in 1979–80 and no change in 1981.[21]

Overall, the extra benefits due on the one hand to more favourable legislation, and on the other hand to rises paid by the State (August 1981) and by the social security system (in 1982) which increased the real value of retirement pensions, can be put at 2.3 billion in 1981 and 9 billion to 10 billion in 1982–3. On the basis of the previous legislation, the total paid out by the retirement insurance fund would have increased by about 2% a year in real terms, because of changing population structure, greater life expectancy and the fact that the system of retirement benefits had reached maturity. As a result of the new measures, the increase was in fact 2.8% in 1981, 6.8% in 1982 and 5.1% in 1983.

Social policy in other areas There were many other policy decisions in the social field during 1981–2, but mention will be made only of the three most important from the cost point of view. The first was housing benefits for rented accommodation: the sum

---

20. Cf. Chapter 4.
21. The decree of 29 December 1982 (*Journal officiel*, 30 December) changed the rules on raising the basic retirement pension, but kept the principle that changes in retirement pensions follow wages. Until 1982, indexation took place on 1 January and 1 July each year on the basis of the change *in the previous year's average wage*. The decree provided that the January and July increases were to be a function of the rise, *as envisaged in the draft budget*, in the average annual gross wage per employed person paid by non-financial, non-agricultural firms. Any adjustment on the basis of the *actual* rise is applied retrospectively at the end of the year. This change explains why there was a fall in the basic retirement provision in 1983.

allocated in the budget to the national housing aid fund and also individual housing aid were increased by 355 million francs in the August 1981 supplementary budget and by 2.2 billion in constant francs in 1982. The second concerned farmers in the lowest income bracket, who received 440 million in 1981 through social policy measures. The third was the improvement in benefit for workers on short time. From 1 August 1981, the number of hours per year for which this was payable went up from 400 to 600, and it was extended to cover 70% of gross hourly remuneration instead of the previous 50%; a further rise was introduced on 1 November. The approximate cost of these measures can be put at 200 million francs in 1981 and 800 million in 1982.

Macro-economic effects of the social policy measures The *ex ante* cost to the government of all the social policy measures so far considered was around 6.3 billion francs for the second half of 1981 and 24 billion in 1982 and 1983 (see Table 2.6). For households, these figures represent 0.3 percentage points of the increase in real disposable income in 1981 and 0.8 points in 1982.[22]

The GDP multiplier associated with this kind of stimulation of demand is relatively small in the short term, because of the time taken for consumption to adjust to income (consumer habits) and for employment to adjust to production (productivity cycle). For every 10,000 jobs created or saved with this kind of policy measure, about 4.3 billion a year on average has to be spent, and an extra annual external deficit of 2.2 billion has to reckoned with.[23] Nevertheless, the increase in social welfare benefits was substantially more effective as far as employment was concerned than the rises in the minimum wage, since it meant that, in all, 60,000 jobs were created or saved (Table 2.6).

New Policies to Create Jobs and Stimulate Investment

The rises in the minimum wage and the social policy measures just outlined were inspired by a desire for social justice and for a

22. Households' disposable income increased, at face value, by 2.9% in 1981 and 2.7% in 1982.
23. These figures are obtained from Table 2.9 by dividing the annual average cost (15.4 billion domestic deficit and 7.8% billion external deficit) by the average number of jobs created over the three years (35,000). This annual cost is lowest in the third year, when the multiplier effect achieves its biggest impact on employment (60,000 jobs) and when tax revenues reduce the domestic deficit (18 billion). Thus, for every 10,000 jobs created, a domestic deficit of 2 billion and an external deficit of 3 billion are needed.

Table 2.6 Macro-economic effect of the social policy measures (difference in relation to projected change)

	1981	1982	1983
Impact on annual growth rate (%)			
Real GDP	0.1	0.4	0.15
Household consumption (volume)	0.2	0.7	0.2
Total investment (volume)	0.1	0.3	0.4
Consumer prices	−0.1	−0.1	−
Real disposable income	0.3	0.8	−
Impact on level (annual average)			
Employment (thousands)	+7.0	+40.0	+60.0
Unemployment (thousands)	−4.0	−22.0	−32.0
Balance of trade (billion francs)	−2.1	−8.9	−12.3
Public borrowing requirement or surplus (billion francs)			
ex ante	−6.3	−24.0	−24.0
ex post	−6.3	−22.0	−18.0

Source: Simulations by the OFCE-annual model.

reduction of income inequalities. To combat unemployment, the Mauroy government established three priorities for government spending in the period 1981–3:

1 To create public sector jobs and give direct encouragement to employment and training.
2 To provide more public amenities and subsidized housing.
3 To increase production capacities by a massive research effort and a dynamic industrial policy.

Apart from these, certain measures to help farmers were brought in, aimed at maintaining the level of their income and encouraging them to invest.

The creation of public sector jobs and new measures to help employment The employment policy followed after 1981 and its effect on unemployment will be analysed in detail in Chapter 4. For now, we will simply look at the stimulus effect of extra public spending on new measures to help employment, of which there were two kinds – the creation of public sector jobs and direct government aid to create jobs.

Between July 1981 and December 1983, around 110,000 new jobs

Table 2.7 Direct help for job creation, 1981–3

	Budget for 1981	Supplementary budget 1981	Budget for 1982	Draft budget 1983	% change 1981–3
Youth training programmes	3.9	–	4.8	5.7	46.2%
Established measures for job creation and training	8.9	–	11.9	13.1	47.2%
Funds earmarked for new job creation measures	–	2.0	2.0	5.9	–
Total	12.8	2.0	18.8	24.7	93.0%

In billion francs

were created by budgetary and non-budgetary means, to which must be added state funding for certain bodies, leading to the creation of 20,000 jobs through local action and 8,700 in the social and cultural fields.[24] The cost of these initiatives to the general budget has been put at 800 million francs in 1981 and 7.1 billion in 1982.[25] Our own calculations put the figure at 10 billion for 1983. At the same time, money from social security and social welfare authorities led to the creation of 35,000 new jobs in hospitals, and health care and welfare establishments. Taking into account the induced effect, the total gross income accruing to households from all new public sector jobs examined here (i.e. ignoring new jobs in large state undertakings and local authorities) was 1.1 billion francs in the second half of 1981, 12.5 billion in 1982 and 20 billion in 1983.

The total sum allocated in the budget for direct help towards job creation was 24.7 billion in 1983 compared with 12.8 billion in the first draft of the budget for 1981 – an increase of 93% in nominal terms and 57% in real terms. The new measures implemented by the Mauroy government in September 1981 and also during 1982–3 represented an aggregate cost to the government of 10 billion francs (see line 3 of Table 2.7) of which 3 billion went on special aid projects and 1.9 billion when the government agreed to pay part of employers' social security contributions in the textile and clothing industry.

Public sector job creation came in for much criticism. However, of all the measures for economic recovery which we have looked at, it was by far the most effective in terms of the number of jobs

24. Cf. Chapter 4.
25. Source: supplementary budget of August 1981 and budget for 1982.

created per unit cost to the budget. The extra contributions made and the extra tax revenue meant that the actual cost to the government departments involved was about half. The simulations presented in Table 2.11 show that for 10,000 public sector jobs created on average between 1981 and 1983, the *ex post* annual cost to central funds was 0.5 billion francs. For each job, this cost is four times lower than that of job creation (in the private sector) by budgetary expansion (spending by government departments and local authorities) and nearly ten times lower than job creation through the social policy measures just analysed.

Investment by central and local government Government capital expenditure in the civil and military fields did not increase in 1981. The allocations in the budget for 1982 were significantly higher (27% and 17% respectively); however, ministerial decrees during 1982 cancelling various programmes (22 February, 16 July, 18 October) meant that the rise in government capital investment for that year was in the end very small. On the other hand, investment by local authorities – which makes up 80% of the total investment by the administration – gave a significant boost to economic activity in 1981–2 (see Figure 2.5). This increase can be explained by three factors more or less directly attributable to budgetary expansion: the sharp rise in transfers from the government to local authorities – 16% in 1981 and 21% in 1982; increase in borrowing (by 25% in 1982); and the local council elections. Statistics since the beginning of the 1960s show that local authorities invest much more in the three-monthly periods before local elections (1965, 1971, 1977, 1983, 1989). It is likely that local councils were prompted to give a boost to economic activity by the arrival of the Left in power at a time when these councils had many socialist and communist members.

Spending on housing Since the steep rise in real and nominal interest rates in 1980 had brought about a significant drop in investment in family housing, efforts were made as part of the reflation policy to end the slump in the construction industry. These were directed towards improving the existing stock of publicly owned housing (142,000 units were refurbished in 1982 as against 102,000 in 1981); increasing the number of subsidized housing loans (75,000 were made in 1982); and means-tested loans for home buying (170,000). The extra costs involved in this new spending on 'bricks and mortar' was 250 million francs in 1981 and 3.1 billion in 1982. As a proportion of budget allocation for housing

Figure 2.5 Changes in level of investment by central government, local authorities and social security organizations since 1960 (in constant francs)

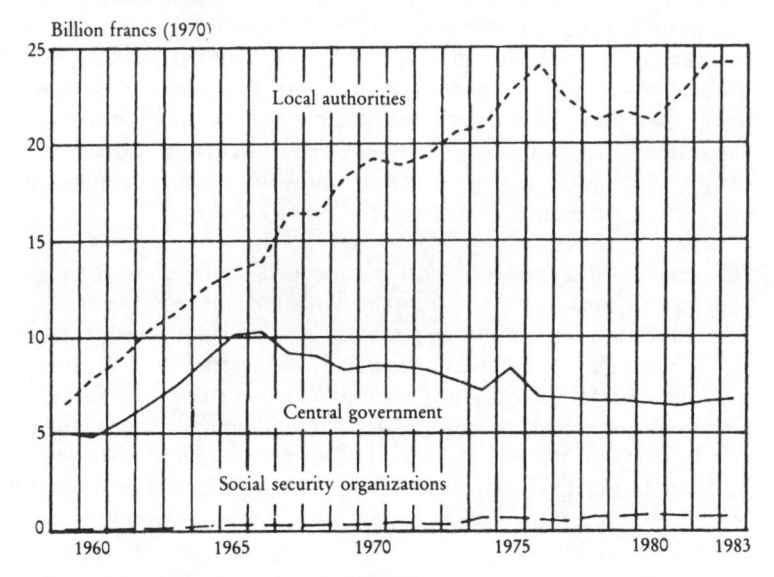

Source: INSEE, *Comptes de la Nation* (National accounts).

subsidies (11.3 billion in 1983), these sums are large, though they are not large in relation to other reflationary measures. It would have been better to spend much more on housing, particularly in the field of energy saving measures, since any expansion in house-building has an insignificant effect on imports.

Industrial policy and financial aid to nationalized industries May 1981 saw the replacement of a niche strategy (*politique de créneaux*) – seeking international niches in specialized areas of nuclear power, aeronautics, telecommunications, military hardware – by one of vertical integration (*politique de filières*) based on the idea that there were no industries in inexorable decline, merely that some technologies were out of date. This led to emphasis being put on general financial aid to industry rather than help for specific industries or for exports. There was a large increase in the budget allocation for non-military research into technological programmes. Funds for ANVAR (Agence Nationale de la Valorisation de la Recherche – national agency for the development of research) rose by 76% in 1982; spending on the electronics and computer industries increased

Table 2.8 Capital grants to nationalized undertakings[a] (in million francs)

	1980	1981	1982	1983	1984
(1) *Total grants* from:	2,460	4,825	14,083	13,342	19,181
budget	1,650	720	2,500	11,150	14,150
supplementary budget	265	3,797	9,317	2,124	1,116
previous year	545	308	2,266	68	3,915
(2) *Grants actually made*		2,152[b]	2,559[c]	14,015	9,457	16,300
(3) *Carried over to following year,* i.e. (1) − (2)	308	2,266	68	3,915	2,881

[a] Grants actually received by firms vary from those appearing in the budget because of accounting delays.
[b] Not including 12.358 billion francs in loans from the FDES (Fonds de Developpement Economique et Social) to the EDF (Electricité de France)
[c] Not including 13.804 billion francs in loans from the FDES to USINOR-SACILOR.
Source: Budget legislation.

five-fold between 1981 (350 million) and 1983 (1.85 billion); on aeronautics from 1.3 billion to 2.8 billion, a rise of 115%; and on the space programme, involving Ariane and the placing of satellites in orbit, by 60%, 2.26 billion being authorized in 1983. There was also a significant increase in funds for the development of solar energy, but a small drop in spending on the electro-nuclear programme.

A further point is that nationalized firms received very large capital grants – 26 billion francs in the period 1981–3 (see Table 2.8), which was more than for the whole of the Giscard presidency. About two-thirds of these grants went to industrial firms in areas of strong competition. Moreover, the big state undertakings, particularly Charbonnages de France[26] (the national coal undertaking) (see Table 2.9), received increased subsidies for running costs, whereas there had been no rise in 1979–80.

There was a significant extension of new loans to industry at favourable rates of interest, from organizations such as the Fonds Industriel de Modernisation (industrial modernization fund) and the Fonds de Développement Economique et Social (economic and social development fund). Discounting agriculture, these stood at 17

26. The unrealistic aims of the 'coal plan' were abandoned in 1983.

Table 2.9 Financial aid given to major state undertakings[a] 1979–82

Undertakings	1979	1980	1981	1982
Electricité et Gaz de France	2,178	1,957[b]	678	1,554
Charbonnages de France	4,072	4,052	4,330	6,184
SNCF and RATP	13,278	14,109	17,444	18,934
Air France and Air Inter	598	501	456	881
PTT	92	151	169	63
Total	20,218	20,770	23,077	27,616
(including capital grants)	(1,000)	(1,000)	(1,529)	(2,180)

[a] Financial help is made up principally of subsidies on operating costs.
[b] Not including 12.358 million francs of loans from the FDES (Fonds de Developpement Economique et Social) to the EDF (Electricité de France).
Source: J.-C. Dutailly, 'Aides aux entreprises: 134 milliards en 1982' (Government help for business: 134 billion in 1982), *Economie et statistique*, 169, September 1984.

billion in 1980, but had risen to 51 billion by 1983. Favourable interest rate schemes accounted for a third of investment credit outstanding in 1983; the cost to the State of this interest rate relief rose from 1.4 billion in 1980 to 3.6 billion in 1983.

The tax allowance on investment spending introduced by the Barre government in October 1980 was raised from 10% to 15% in 1982 as a special measure, though this applied only to firms which had not reduced the total number of their employees. This restriction was not of great significance however, since tax returns show that the allowances gave firms 5.6 billion francs in 1981, 10.3 billion in 1982 and 6.9 billion in 1983 (see Table 2.10). Because many firms were running at a loss, the cost to the government was fairly small – 1.3 billion in 1981, 2.6 billion in 1982 and 1.8 billion in 1983, amounting to about 25% of the allowance, whereas in theory it could have reached 50% since the allowance reduced the proportion of profits subject to tax at 50%.

Financial aid to agriculture Faced with a continual drop in farmers' incomes from 1974 (see Figure 2.6), the Barre government finally took action in December 1980 (see the section on 'the reflation which tends to be forgotten', pp. 71–2). The Mauroy government gave them another 5.5 billion in December 1981, half being paid for by the Caisse Nationale du Crédit Agricole (national bank for agricultural loans) from surpluses it had accumulated when it was exempt from company tax, and the other half being met by the government. Because agricultural production and farmers' in-

Table 2.10 Assessment of the budgetary cost of tax allowances on investment

Year	1979	1980	1981	1982	1983	1984
Allowances declared (million francs)	1,975	4,029	5,565	10,300	6,872	653
Budgetary cost (million francs)			976	1,352	2,575	1,810

Source: P.A. Muet and S. Avouyi-Dovi, 'L'effet des incitations fiscales sur l'investissement' (The effect of tax incentives on investment), *Observations et diagnostics économiques*, 18, January 1987.

Figure 2.6 Change in average gross income of agricultural holdings (in constant francs)

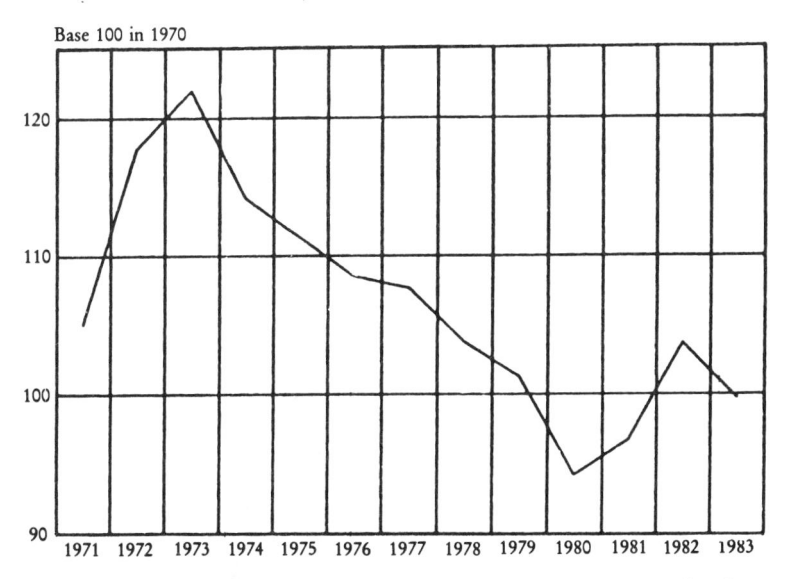

Source: *Les Comptes de l'Agriculture Française en 1983* (French Agricultural accounts for 1983), *Collections de l'INSEE*, series C, 121.

comes improved more than expected, the sums which were in fact paid out were smaller (1.7 billion francs by the government and 1.4 billion by the agricultural loans bank). About one-third of this money was invested in agricultural equipment, and the rest went to paying off loans taken out by young farmers who had got into debt, to improving mountain areas and to improving trading practices where exports were concerned.

Macro-economic effects To help us analyse their macro-economic implications, the budgetary expansion measures to create jobs and encourage investment can be grouped under three headings. The first are those which had a direct effect on the *labour market* (more jobs in the public sector and direct financial aid for job creation). The second involves those measures which mainly helped to sustain demand for construction and public works programmes (gross fixed capital investment by government departments and local authorities, and money for investment in housing). The third heading subsumes all the financial aid which was given to public and private companies (capital grants, grants for research and innovation, industrial policy, low interest loans), or which propped up the income level of individuals (help for farmers).

Table 2.11 shows that, according to simulations by the OFCE-annual model, measures to promote job creation and investment helped the growth of GDP by 0.6 percentage points in 1982 and 0.5 points in 1983, in other words about a third of the increase in 1982 and a half of that in 1983. Compared with the increases in minimum wage and the social welfare measures, budgetary reflation proved to be much more effective in terms of job creation. The number of jobs created or preserved – in relation to the base position – was nearly 200,000 in 1982 and 300,000 in 1983 as against 40,000 and 60,000 respectively in the case of increases in social welfare benefits.

New Fiscal and Parafiscal Measures

To stop the budget deficit getting out of hand, the Mauroy government introduced certain new taxes from July 1981 onwards. Furthermore, a new plan for financing social security had to be introduced in November 1981.

New taxes on the wealthy In accordance with socialist principles, the new taxes introduced by the Left were conceived in a spirit of national solidarity. In the supplementary budget of August 1981 two kinds of tax revenue were brought in:

1 Measures affecting the wealthiest sections of the population (special rate of tax on higher incomes, and an increase in tax on certain luxury items).
2 Measures affecting companies (tax on certain general expenses) and the windfall profits of banks and credit institutions (because of the rise in interest rates) and of oil companies (because of the rise in oil prices).

Reflation Runs Into Difficulties

Figure 2.7 Change in GDP, consumption and investment in France from 1973 to 1984 (at constant prices)

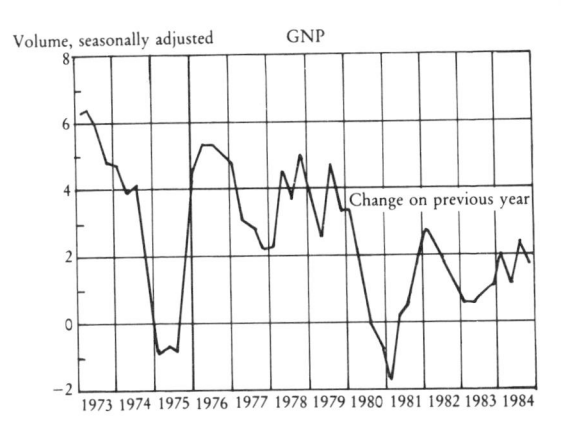

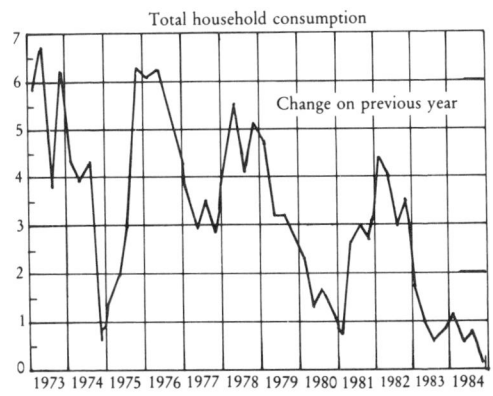

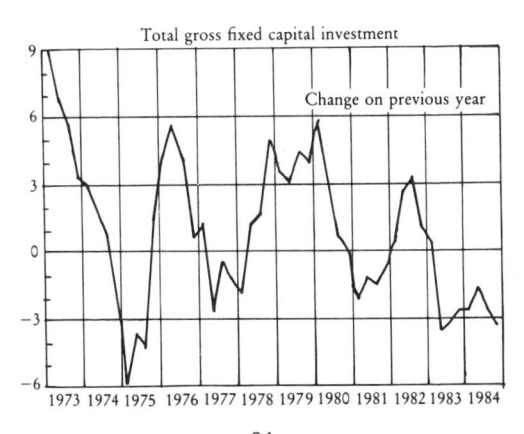

Table 2.11 Macro-economic impact of measures to help job creation and investment, 1981–3

Measures	Job creation in the public sector and direct help for employment 1981	1982	1983	Investment by government departments and help for public housing 1981	1982	1983	Help for firms in the public and private sectors and measures to help agriculture[a] 1981	1982	1983
Impact on annual growth rate (%)									
Real GDP	0.05	0.15	0.15	0.1	0.2	—	—	0.2	0.3
Household consumption (volume)	0.1	0.3	0.3	0.05	0.1	0.05	—	0.2	0.1
Total investment (volume)	—	0.1	0.2	0.6	1.3	0.1	0.2	1.0	1.4
Consumer prices	—	0.05	0.1	—	−0.1	0.1	—	−0.2	−0.3
Real disposable income	0.1	0.5	0.2	0.1	0.1	—	—	0.3	—
Impact on level (annual average)									
Employment (thousands)	16	140	200	10	36	49	2	20	50
Unemployment (thousands)	−8[b]	−75[b]	−110[b]	−5	−16	−23	−1	−10	−28
Balance of trade (billion francs)	−0.8	−4.7	−8.7	−1.6	−5.5	−6.2	−0.8	−6.7	−13
Public borrowing requirement or surplus (billion francs)									
ex ante	−2.4	−13.0	−19.0	−4.1	−13.0	−14.3	−3.2	−23.0	−18.0
ex post	−2.1	−7.6	−8.8	−2.9	−8.7	−7.9	−3.0	−21.0	−13.0

[a] It is extremely difficult to quantify the effect of this set of measures. The figures given here should be taken as very approximate.
[b] The impact on unemployment includes the total effect (direct and indirect) of the creation of jobs in the public sector as well as the knock-on effect of public spending brought about by direct help to stimulate employment. The individual impact on unemployment of policy measures on training, early retirement, retirement at 60 and reduction of the working week will be analysed in detail in Chapter 4.
Source: Simulations by the 'OFCE-annual' model.

Table 2.12 The new tax measures introduced in 1981 and 1982 (in billion francs)

	1981 Estimate	1981 Actual revenue	1982 Estimate	1982 Actual revenue
Emergency tax increase on top incomes	3.4	3.7[a]	5.7[b]	5.3[c]
Introduction of wealth tax	–	–	4.5	3.8
Taxation of windfall profits				
– One-off levy on banks and credit institutions	1.0	0.9	1.5	1.9
– One-off payment by petroleum product manufacturers	1.0	0.9	0.75	0.75
Taxation of certain business expenses	1.2	0.6	4.5	1.6
General	0.2	0.2	2.1	1.3
Total	6.8	6.3	19.1	14.7

[a] 3.3 billion was paid by households in 1981 and 0.4 billion in 1982.
[b] 'Solidarity' tax to pay for half of the UNEDIC (unemployment benefit fund) deficit in 1982.
[c] 4.9 billion was paid in 1982 and 0.4 billion in 1983.

The revenue expected from these new taxes (see Table 2.12) had been fixed at a level which would cover the cost of the new policies for job creation and investment introduced in the second half of 1981.

The budget for 1982 retained, and indeed increased, the 'special taxes' applied in 1981. Furthermore, a wealth tax was introduced. It was expected that the amount of extra tax revenue would be 19.1 billion francs, of which 6 billion (from the increased tax on higher incomes) would pay for a special government subsidy to UNEDIC (unemployment benefit fund).[27] In fact these 'treasures yet to be tapped' proved to be smaller than expected – the wealth tax brought in 3.8 billion instead of the 4.5 envisaged and the taxing of firms' general expenses (presents, travel, entertainment, etc.) 1.6 billion

27. To cope with its deficit, UNEDIC also raised a loan of 6 billion francs, guaranteed by the government.

Table 2.13 Resources available to social security organizations

	1971–4	1974–80	\multicolumn{2}{c}{Amount and percentage in 1982}	
	Average annual growth rate (by volume)	Average annual growth rate (by volume)	Billion francs (current)	%
Total resources of social security departments	6.9	7.7	793	100.0
Employers' actual social security contributions	6.7	6.1	445	56.2
Employees' social security contributions	10.2	11.4	165	20.8
Self-employed social security contributions	1.5	8.1	47	5.9
Transfers between government departments	3.2	10.4	111	14.0
Various	–	–	25	3.1

Source: *Comptes de la Nation* (National accounts).

instead of 4.5 billion. The overall contribution of the new taxes to keeping down the budget deficit is put at 8.7 billion, not counting the 6 billion which the government made over to UNEDIC.

The implications of these new taxes for consumption were not very great in that it is reasonable to assume that higher income earners mainly drew on savings to meet their higher tax bills for 1981 and 1982.

The Autumn 1981 plan for financing social security As mentioned earlier, in the discussion of 'the reflation which tends to be forgotten', the Barre government abolished in February 1981 the sickness insurance surcharge introduced in August 1979. However, the winter of 1980/1 saw spending on health care beginning to rise again after a levelling out during 1980. As a result, a funding deficit was expected by the end of 1981. The government therefore came up with a new plan in November 1981 designed to put straight the 1981 situation as well as to equalize revenue and expenditure for 1982 (see Table 2.13). The plan put into operation on 10 November 1981 involved an increase in contributions for wage earners, the self-employed and employers, which brought in 1.5 billion in 1981 – 0.9 billion from wage earners and 0.6 from employers. In a full year, it was expected to raise 10.6 billion from wage earners and 6.6 billion from employers.[28]

The new government's economic policy was not responsible for all of these measures. Despite having a surplus in 1980, a 5.3% fall in the real value of contributions after the abolition of the surcharge meant that the Caisse Nationale d'Assurance Maladie (national sickness insurance fund) could have balanced its books in 1981 only by limiting any increase in health spending to 2.5% in constant francs. In fact, the actual rise in spending on health care was 4.3%. It follows that a new book-balancing exercise would have been necessary in any case at the end of 1981.

From the macro-economic point of view, these measures have to be weighed against the reduction of 1 February and the rise in health care benefits paid to households,[29] since these have not been included in the survey of reflationary social welfare measures. Accordingly, in trying to quantify the macro-economic effects of the new social security plan, only the increase in employers' contributions has been taken into account (0.6 billion in 1981 and 6.6. billion in 1982).

Macro-economic effects The effects of the new taxes introduced in 1981–2 and of the November 1981 plan for financing social security are summarized in Table 2.14. Bearing in mind the working hypotheses mentioned earlier, fiscal and parafiscal increases slowed growth in GDP by only 0.15 percentage points in 1982, contributed to the rise in inflation by 0.4 points and increased unemployment by 17,000. In return, the *ex post* deficit of government departments was reduced by 6.4 billion in 1981 and by 16 billion in 1982 (excluding the UNEDIC loan and increases in employees' social security contributions).

The Macro-Economic Balance Sheet of Reflation

After a detailed look at the reflationary measures taken by the Left and the new taxes which were introduced, it is now possible to make a final analysis of the *ex ante* cost of reflation, of the kind of transfers between economic agents which it brought about, and of its overall macro-economic effects.

The total ex ante cost of the measures was slightly less than 2% of

28. Cf. *Comptes de la Nation* (National accounts), 1983, Vol. I, p. 35.
29. Spending on health increased by 5.2% in real terms in 1982, as against 2.9% in 1981 and 0.8% in 1980.

Table 2.14 Macro-economic impact of new taxes, the November 1981 increase in employers' social security contributions, and the UNEDIC (unemployment benefit fund) loan (difference in relation to base situation)

	1981	1982	1983
Impact on annual growth rate (%)			
Real GDP	−0.05	−0.15	−0.10
Household consumption (volume)	−0.05	−0.2	−0.1
Total investment (volume)	−0.1	−0.25	−0.3
Consumer prices	0.05	0.4	0.2
Real disposable income	−0.2	−0.3	−0.05
Impact on level (annual average)			
Employment (thousands)	−3.0	−17.0	−36.0
Unemployment (thousands)	1.5	10.0	20.0
Balance of trade (billion francs)	0.9	4.7	6.3
Public borrowing requirement or surplus (billion francs)			
ex ante	6.9	21.3	22.0
ex post	6.4	16.0	12.0

[a] The unemployment benefit fund loan of 6 billion does not alter the government's revenue and expenditure position in the national income accounting sense, since it is a financial operation.
Source: Simulations by the OFCE-annual model.

GDP   We estimate that the net effect of new spending and taxation was 0.25% of GDP in 1981, and 1.45% in 1982 because of additional measures and because it was the first full year for decisions taken in the second half of 1981 (see Table 2.15). The government, through the budget, met around 70% of the cost in 1981 and 80% in 1982, the rest being met by social security organizations and firms (rise in minimum wage).

Significant redistributive effects   Two kinds of redistributive effects were set in train by reflation – on the one hand between households, firms, the State, the social security organizations and the local authorities; and on the other hand between the top end and the bottom end of the income scale, and between public undertakings and private firms. Table 2.16 shows the *ex ante* transfers between economic agents for 1982.

– The lowest-income households received 30 billion francs (increases in minimum wage and social welfare benefits), and new

Table 2.15 Total *ex ante* amount of the 1981–2 reflation[a]

Measures	1981 Total amount	1981 including ex ante budgetary cost	1982 Total amount[b]	1982 including ex ante budgetary cost	Total 1981–2 Total amount[b]	Total 1981–2 including ex ante budgetary cost
1. Increase in expenditure						
(a) Increase in real value of minimum wage	2.5[b]	2.5	6.0[b]	1.0	8.5[b]	3.5
(b) Social policy measures						
– benefits paid to families	3.0	0.3	10.0	1.5	13.0	1.8
– benefits paid to retired people	2.3	2.3	10.5	7.0	12.8	9.3
– other benefits (agriculture, etc.)	1.0	1.0	3.5	3.5	4.5	4.5
(c) Measures to promote job creation and investment						
– creation of jobs in the public sector	1.0	0.8	9.5	7.1	10.5	7.8
– direct help to employment	1.4	1.4	3.5	3.5	4.9	4.9
– investment by government departments	1.0	1.0	3.0	3.0	4.0	4.0
– housing subsidies	0.2	0.2	3.1	3.1	3.3	3.3
– help for industry (including favourable rates of interest)	0.4	0.4	2.1	2.1	2.5	2.5
– capital grants to nationalized firms	1.8	1.8	12.0	12.0	13.8	13.8
(d) Measures in December 1981 to help farmers	–	–	3.1	1.7	3.1	1.7
Total expenditure: (a) + (b) + (c) + (d)	14.6	11.7	66.3	45.5	80.9	57.2

continued on p. 98

Table 2.15 continued

Measures	1981 Total amount	1981 including ex ante budgetary cost	1982 Total amount[b]	1982 including ex ante budgetary cost	Total 1981–2 Total amount[b]	Total 1981–2 including ex ante budgetary cost
2. Increase in taxation and social welfare contributions (November 1981)						
– taxes paid by households	3.7	3.7	9.1	3.1	12.8	6.8
– taxes paid by firms	2.6	2.6	5.6	5.6	8.2	8.2
– employers' social welfare contributions	0.6	–	6.6	–	7.2	–
Total revenue	6.9	6.3	21.3	8.7	28.2	15.0
3. Difference between expenditure and revenue (1 − 2)						
– in billion francs	7.7	5.4	45.0	36.8	52.7	42.2
– as % of 1981 GDP	0.25	0.17	1.45	1.18	1.70	1.35

[a] Based on actual outcome. The quantification of certain measures should be regarded as approximate, given the methodological difficulties involved e.g. minimum wage, and money to help industry or stimulate job creation.
[b] Extra gross income of employed persons.
Source: Assessments based on budget final settlement legislation.

Table 2.16 *Ex ante* transfers between economic agents (in billion francs)

	Households	Firms	Government	Social security and unemployment fund
(1) Transfers received[a]	41.1	27.6	8.7	12.6
(2) Transfers disbursed[a]	9.1	18.2	48.3	14.4
(3) Net position (1 − 2)	+32.0	+9.4	−39.6	−1.8

[a] Including the effect of the minimum wage.
Source: Based on the assessments in Table 2.15.

public sector employees, trainees, and people taking early retirement received 11.1 billion (9.5bn + 1.6bn). In return, better-off individuals paid out 9.1 billion in increased taxation. The net figure for all households is therefore 32 billion francs.

– Nationalized undertakings received 12 billion, public housing authorities 3.1 billion, farmers 3.1 billion and private firms 9.4 billion, of which 1.9 billion went to the textile and clothing industry and 1 billion to offset the cost of rises in the minimum wage; but these groups paid 5.6 billion in extra taxation (of which 1.9 billion was paid by banks and credit institutions), 6.6 billion extra social welfare contributions and 6 billion in wages because of the rises in the minimum wage. Overall, therefore, they received more (29 billion) than they had to pay out (18.2 billion). It is true however that private firms lost out, though far from the famous '100 billion' claimed by Yvon Gattaz, President of the Confédération Nationale du Patronat Français (national employers' confederation) from 1981 to 1986.[30] Moreover, *ex post*, by improving firms' profits, budgetary expansion partly offset the initial costs it incurred.

– Spending by government departments was divided as follows: the net figure for government spending was 39.6 billion francs, and social security organizations paid out 14.4 billion and received 12.6 billion in contributions (including 6 billion for UNEDIC). To these transfers should be added 3 billion of central government spending on capital equipment and 7 billion by local authorities.

Reflation by the Barre and Mauroy governments stopped the French

---

30. It will be seen in Chapter 4 that the shorter working week was not very expensive for firms, given the prevailing emphasis on productivity.

Table 2.17 Impact of the Barre and Mauroy reflations on the growth of GDP

	1981	1982	1983
Actual growth (annual % rate)	+0.5	+1.8	+0.7
Impact of the reflations:			
– Barre	+0.4	+0.2	0.0
– Mauroy	+0.3	+0.9	+0.5
Contribution of some factors to the growth of GDP:			
– External trade	+0.8	−2.0	+1.1
– Variations in stocks	−1.8	+1.4	+0.8

economy going into recession in 1981–2 Reflation by the Left following policy measures by the Barre government undoubtedly stabilized the general economic situation in 1981–2. Without measures to support the economy, there would have been virtually nil growth in France over the two years 1981–2. However, the 2% growth seen in 1982 is not attributable exclusively to reflation by the two governments. The exceptional volume of agricultural production, and restocking by firms (see Table 2.17) played a part in it as well.[31]

In fact, it seems that not only forecasters but also firms overestimated foreign demand. This difference between expected and actual demand shows up in the movement of stocks which explains 1.4% of the increase in GDP. Because of the irreversible nature of several of the measures, and the time taken to adjust to them, reflation also helped growth in 1983 by 0.5 of a percentage point. In all, over the three years 1981–3, the Mauroy reflation contributed 1.7 percentage points to GDP, 2.3 points to consumption, 4.8 points to investment and created 320,000 jobs (see Table 2.18). In other words, without the expansionary policies, aggregate growth in the three years 1981–3 would have been about half as strong (1.3 points as against 3 points), investment would have fallen by 9.5 points instead of 4.7 points and the French economy would have lost 320,000 more jobs. The overall achievement in terms of stimulating growth and job creation is therefore far from negligible.

The other side of the picture is that the total volume of imports rose and their rate of penetration in relation to production in-

---

31. Without agriculture, growth would have been only 1.3%.

Table 2.18 Macro-economic impact of the total package of reflationary measures introduced by the Left, including increases in taxation

	1981	1982	1983	Total impact[a] 1981–3
Impact on annual growth rate (%)				
Real GDP	0.3	0.9	0.5	1.7
Household consumption (volume)	0.5	1.2	0.6	2.3
Total investment (volume)	0.6	2.5	1.7	4.8
Consumer prices	0.1	0.6[b]	0.4	1.1
Real disposable income	0.6	1.5	0.2	2.3
Impact on level (annual average)				
Employment (thousands)	36	225	323	323
Unemployment (thousands)	−19	−117	−171	−171
Balance of trade (billion francs)	−4.5	−23	−36	−36
Public borrowing requirement or surplus (billion francs)				
ex ante	−11.6	−53	−54	−54
ex post	−9.8	−43	−35	−35

[a] The total impact is obtained by aggregating the effect on annual growth rates.
[b] Including the inflationary effect of the reduction in the working week (+0.3 percentage points).
Source: Simulations by the OFCE-annual model.

creased; and exports fell because there was less incentive to export when the domestic market expanded and competitivity worsened – the reflation added 0.6 of a percentage point to price rises in 1982. Overall, without the 'corrective' measures taken from June 1982 onwards, *reflationary policies would have worsened the trade balance by 23 billion in 1982 and 36 billion in 1983.* As will be shown, the rise in the dollar and the fall in world trade made the situation worse in 1982.

A Comparative Analysis of the Reflation of 1981–2

Was the reflation of 1981–2 different from or comparable with other experiences of reflation? How far was it reflation and how far was it the international situation which was responsible for the way the

Reflation and Austerity

French economy developed in 1981–2? An answer to these two questions will be preceded by an analysis of two other experiences of reflation – the Chirac reflation of 1975–6 and those applied by the West German Social Democrats between 1974 and 1981.

The Reflation of 1975–6*

To get rid of the balance of payments deficit and combat price rises brought about by the first oil shock, the French government had introduced during 1974 a plan to cool down the economy (short-term revenue measures, emergency tax increases, slowing down of the rate at which public spending was brought on stream, etc.). By the end of 1974, the balance of payments deficit had virtually disappeared, but production was falling fast and unemployment rocketing. To correct its aim, and after several piecemeal measures (early introduction of some benefit increases, early repayment of the surcharge on income tax imposed in 1974) and help for specific sectors (housing aid, help for farmers), Chirac's government introduced two plans to boost the economy, the first in April 1975 and the second in September 1975.

Significant but short-term measures The 15.7 billion plan in April to boost productive investment involved a programme of capital equipment in the telephone service of 4.2 billion over two years, a 5 billion loan on preferential terms (interest rate of 8.5%, repayment postponed for five years) to boost investment and employment, an increase of 1.25 billion in grants made by the Fonds de Développement Economique et Social (social and economic development fund) to state undertakings, and temporary 10% subsidies for items of capital equipment, provided they were ordered before 31 December 1975.

The 30.5 billion plan for 'development of the French economy' adopted in the supplementary budget of 15 September 1975 involved measures to give an urgent boost to consumption, a programme of public works and industrial infrastructure, an increase in tax benefits for productive investment (on orders placed before 7 January 1976) and a six-month postponement of direct taxes paid by firms.

Table 2.19 summarizes the expected and actual figures from the

---

* For a more detailed analysis, see A. Fonteneau and A. Gubian, 'Comparaison des relances françaises de 1975 et 1981–82' (Comparison of the French reflation of 1975 with that of 1981–2), *Observations et diagnostics économiques*, 12, July 1985.

Reflation Runs Into Difficulties

Table 2.19 Total *ex ante* amounts involved in the 1975–6 reflation (in billion francs)

	Expected total amount	Actual amount		Total actual amount
	1975–6	1975	1976	1975–6
(1) Stimulation of consumption	10.0	9.3	0.2	9.5
(2) Public authority housing	1.35	0.8	0.55	1.35
(3) Investment by government and local authorities	9.6	4.6	4.0	8.6
(4) Telephone service investment programme and major industrial projects	5.3	2.5	2.4	4.9
(5) Tax incentives to productive investment	5.8	1.3	8.2	9.5
Total of (1) to (5)				
– in billion francs	32.05	18.5	15.35	33.85
– in % of 1975 GDP	2.2%	1.3%	1.0%	2.3%
(6) Loans at favourable rates by:	12.25	6.7	2.6	9.3
– FDES	(4.25)	(0)	(1.3)	(1.3)
– Linked loan for investment and employment	(5.0)	(3.8)	(1.2)	(5.0)
– Preferential finance for firms' export efforts	(3.0)	(2.9)	(0.1)	(3.0)
(7) Postponement of payment of direct taxes by firms from 15 September 75 to 15 April 76	(9.6)	7.4	−7.4	(7.4)
Total of (1) to (7)	53.9	–	–	50.55

Source: A. Fonteneau and A. Gubian, July 1985.

whole of this reflationary policy. Measures to stimulate consumption cost 9.5 billion (line 1 of Table 2.19), investments 14.85 billion (lines 2 to 4), tax benefits for investment 9.5 billion (line 5) and loans at favourable rates 9.3 billion (line 7). Ignoring loans and delays for taxes to work through, the measures implemented to stimulate the economy represented 1.3% of the GDP in 1975 and 1.0% in 1976, a total of 2.3% for the two years.

There were four central features in the reflation policy of 1975–6:

1 The main effort was towards *investment*. More than four-fifths of the extra money went on public investment (government and local authority spending, the telephone service, the big state undertakings) and on private investment (tax benefits, postponement of tax payments, low-interest loans).
2 The measures were concentrated in a short space of time, being either very specific (emergency increases in benefit payments) or temporary (tax benefits, tax postponements).
3 Virtually the whole cost was met by the government through the budget.
4 Direct stimulus through the budget was complemented by *monetary and financial policy*. The percentage of deposits on call required to be backed by reserves fell from 17% in January to 2% in September 1975, the base lending rate from 13% to 8%, the maximum term for borrowing was extended, the proportion to be found by the borrower reduced, the amount outstanding on personal loans by banks raised, and loans to local authorities increased.

The 1975 reflation went with *the economic cycle* The idea of the 1981 reflation was to anticipate the world economic recovery expected in 1982 by most international forecasting organizations. Since this recovery did not happen in 1982 but in 1983–4, the recovery of the French economy in fact went against the economic cycle. The economic policy measures taken in 1974 and 1975, on the other hand, had gone *with* the economic cycle. The plan to take the heat out of the economy adopted in June 1974 dampened down economic activity until the end of the first half of 1975, during the time when the world economy was in recession. Similarly, the reflationary measures taken during 1975 stimulated production from Summer 1975 at a time when the world economy was coming out of recession and world demand was taking off again (see Figure 2.8). Economic policy in France therefore accentuated the world economic cycle.

Reflationary measures involving government spending and household consumption had a speedy effect on economic activity, but it was only during the course of 1976 that tax benefits for investment bore fruit, because of the time taken by the investments to work through the economy.[32] Overall, in relation to the base position, the

---

32. The extent of the aid given meant that investment was strongly stimulated. However, the extra investment produced by fiscal stimulation measures in 1975 did not cover its budgetary cost, whereas investment brought about by all such

Figure 2.8 World demand for and exports of French manufactured goods

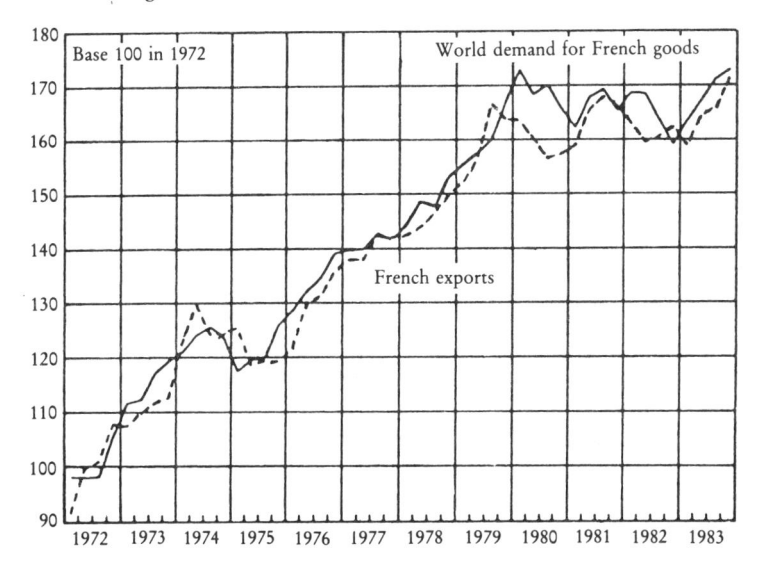

[Chart: Base 100 in 1972; World demand for French goods; French exports; years 1972–1983; y-axis 90 to 180]

Source: Customs statistics (for exports); OFCE (for world demand).

level of GDP was increased by 1.2 percentage points in 1975 and 1976 (see Table 2.20).

This extra growth meant that 160,000 jobs were created or preserved during the two-year period 1975–6. However, all other things being equal, the balance of payments worsened by 11 billion francs at current prices, or 0.75% of GDP. The drought of Summer 1976 added to the deficit.

Reflation in West Germany between 1974 and 1980

During the period 1974–80 there were four occasions when West German economic policy had recourse to budgetary tools to stimulate growth and employment[33] – in 1974–5, 1977, 1978–9 and 1980–1 (see Inset 2.2).

---

measures over the twenty years up to 1985 was on average 1.8 times the cost to the budget. See P.A. Muet and S. Avouyi-Dovi, January 1987.
33. At the same time, monetary policy, for which the Bundesbank is responsible, was used principally for exchange rate management. Cf. P.-A. Baudet, 'Dix ans de politique économique en RFA' (Ten years of economic policy in FRG), *Les Cahiers Français*, 218, October–December 1984.

Table 2.20 Macro-economic impact of the 1975 package of reflationary measures

	1975	1976
Impact on annual growth rate (%)		
Real GDP	1.2	0.0
Household consumption (volume)	1.3	−0.4
Total investment (volume)	4.0	1.7
– public	8.1	3.2
– private	5.2	1.5
Impact on level (annual average)		
Employment (thousands)	117	162
Balance of trade (billion francs)	−10.7	−11.2
Ex post public borrowing requirement (billion francs)	−21.6	−0.2

Source: A. Fonteneau and A. Gubian, July 1985.

A gradually increasing emphasis on tax cuts Measures introduced in 1974 and 1975 to try to bring the economy out of the recession caused by the first oil shock were directed towards boosting consumption (by tax cuts of 4 billion Deutschmarks and increased transfers to households of 10 billion Deutschmarks), public spending (an increase of 2.6 billion) and private investment (temporary 7.5% subsidies for capital equipment, and a programme to boost construction).

Stimulative measures introduced during 1977 were less extensive and were designed to compensate for the decline in economic activity in Spring 1977 after the strong recovery during 1976.

The circumstances of the November 1978 measures, part of the 'concerted action programme', were different because they were the result of pressure by West Germany's partners at the Bonn summit in July.[34] The total amount of this reflation was 15.75 billion Deutschmarks, or 1.25% of GNP for 1978. The main thrust of these measures was towards a cut in taxes on households (11 billion) and on firms (4.75 billion). In return, VAT rates were raised on 1 July 1979.

In July 1980, a new round of tax cuts amounting to 16.4 billion

34. In June 1978, ministers meeting in the Council of the OECD had agreed on an international 'concerted action programme' to 'bring about faster economic growth, greater price stability, improvement in the balance of payments and more vigorous energy policies'. At the Bonn summit in July, the big seven industrialized countries approved this programme, and West Germany agreed to play the role of 'locomotive'.

Inset 2.2

Experiences of reflation in West Germany between 1974 and 1981[a]

Measures	Amount in billion Deutschmarks[b]
1. *The reflation of 1974–5*	
Measures passed at the end of 1974:	
– reduction of direct taxes on households	4.0
– increase in transfers to households	10.0
– extra public spending, federal and local	2.6
– 7.5% subsidy on orders for capital equipment placed between December 1974 and mid-1975	n.a.
Measure passed in August 1975:	
– programme of aid to the construction industry	5.75
2. *The reflation of 1977*	
Measures passed in March and June:	
– postponement of attempts at medium-term budgetary retrenchment	n.a.
– rise of 1 point, not 2, in the VAT rate increase due on 1 January 1978	n.a.
– reduction in direct taxes	1.0
Measures passed in September:	
– reduction in direct taxes on households	8.0
– 10.1% rise in federal government spending in 1978, instead of expected 7.5%	n.a.
– relaxation of the system of gradually reducing repayments	1.5
3. *The reflation of 1978–9*[c]	
Measures introduced on 1 January 1979:	
– reduction of direct taxes on households	11.0
– extra federal government spending	2.75
– increase in tax allowances for dependent children	1.75
Measures introduced on 1 July 1979:	
– greater entitlement to early retirement	1.0
– increase in maternity allowances	0.75
– increase in VAT rate	−6.5

continued on p. 108

Inset 2.2 *continued*	
Experiences of reflation in West Germany between 1974 and 1981[a]	
Measures	Amount in billion Deutschmarks[b]
Measures introduced on 1 January 1980: – increase in personal tax allowances and tax allowance for education expenses – net reduction of company taxation, apart from profits tax	2.25 2.75[d]
Total cost of the measures	15.75
4. *The tax reduction programme of July 1980*[e] – increase in tax allowance on end-of-year bonuses – raising of the federal scale applicable to expenses for child-minding – change in income tax bands – increase in allowance for housing costs – increase in allowance for dependants – increase in exemptions for single parents – extension of special allowances – other measures	 1.4 2.1 6.1 0.6 2.0 0.3 3.6 0.3
Total cost to the budget	16.4

Notes:
[a] Source: *OECD Economic Outlook*, July 1975, December 1975, December 1977, July 1979 and December 1980.
[b] A minus sign indicates a contraction effect.
[c] Annual amount.
[d] The gross amount of this reduction is 4.75 billion.
[e] Cost to the budget in the first full year.

Deutschmarks was introduced in order to offset the slow-down in economic activity resulting from the second oil shock.

There were three main features of reflationary policies in West Germany during 1974–80:

1 There was a gradually increasing emphasis on alleviating the

tax burden, either by reducing direct taxes for all households or by increasing tax allowances to which families were entitled. At the same time, there was a gradual switch from a policy of increasing transfers to households to one of raising indirect taxation (VAT).

2 The increase in government spending went on capital investment rather than on more jobs in the public sector or on paying government employees more.

3 Financial help to firms for investment purposes had to be used primarily for reducing capital costs. The main element in the regulation of labour costs was a wages policy agreed on by both sides of industry.

Reflation stimulated domestic growth... Figure 2.9 shows that the budgetary expansion measures in fact stimulated demand and production, though this took one or two three-monthly periods to work through.

The OECD secretariat ran its INTERLINK model of international linkages to simulate the effects on production and on the external balance of the reflationary package of 1978–9.[35] This exercise showed that the measures introduced by West Germany increased the *level* of GNP by around 0.8% in 1979 and 1.4% in 1980 (see Table 2.21). On the other hand, the balance of payments worsened by 4.35 billion Deutschmarks in 1979 and by 7.55 billion in 1980 – the equivalent of 17 billion francs at the average 1978 exchange rate. The second oil shock, by increasing the cost of energy imports, compounded the worsening of the external situation caused by reflation: the surplus on the balance of trade fell from 25 billion dollars in 1978 to 17 billion in 1979 and 10 billion in 1980; moreover, there was a heavy deficit (17 billion dollars) on the current transactions balance in 1980, as against a surplus of 9 billion in 1978.

... and had a beneficial effect on the French economy The INTERLINK multipliers allow us to calculate the effects of the West German budgetary expansion on other countries of the OECD, and particularly on the French economy (see Table 2.22). Measures taken as part of the 'concerted action programme' led to a 0.1% increase in the *level of GDP* in France in 1979 and 0.3% in 1980 while at the same time improving the net balance on current

---

35. See OECD, 'Simulations of fiscal policy using the OECD model of international links', *OECD Economic Outlook, Special Studies*, July 1980.

Reflation and Austerity

Figure 2.9 Change in GNP, investment and consumption in West Germany from 1973 to 1984 (at constant prices)

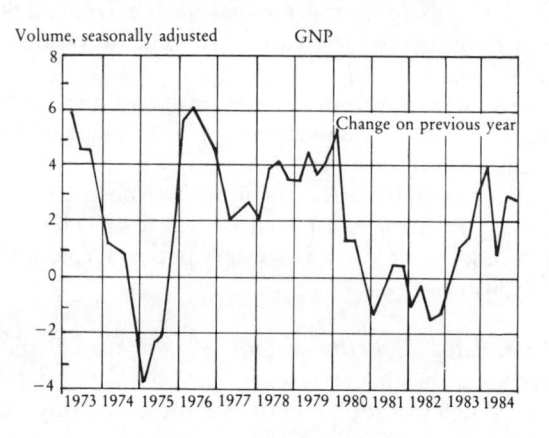

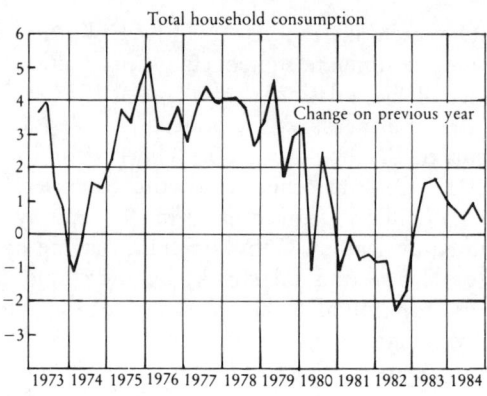

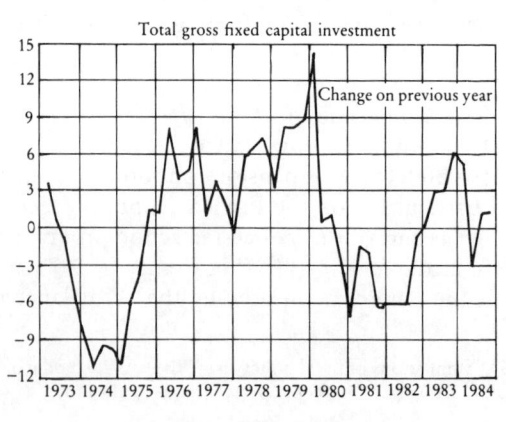

Table 2.21 Impact on GNP and current balance of payments of reflationary measures introduced by West Germany in 1978–9

	Federal government spending	Taxes on households	Taxes on firms	Indirect taxes (VAT)[a]	Total
1. Aggregate multipliers on GDP:					
First year	1.35	−0.57	−0.27	−0.58	—
Second year	1.96	−1.15	−0.67	−1.20	—
2. Average annual amount of the measures, in % of GNP:					
1979	0.22	−1.07	0.00	0.25	1.04
1980	0.22	−1.31	−0.22	0.51	1.24
3. Impact on GNP (% increase on 1978 level)[b]					
1979	0.30	0.61	0.00	−0.14	0.77
1980	0.43	1.37	0.06	−0.46	1.40
4. Net effect on current balance of payments (in billion Deutschmarks, at 1978 prices):					
1979	−1.70	−3.47	0.00	0.82	−4.35
1980	−2.25	−7.44	−0.34	2.48	−7.55

[a] The effect of a rise in the VAT rate is calculated by assuming that all of it is carried through to market prices. If this does not happen, the figure should be divided by two.
[b] The impact on GNP is obtained from the value of the multiplier (section 1) and the cost of the measure expressed as a percentage of GNP (section 2).

Source: Simulations by the fiscal INTERLINK model, *OECD Economic Outlook, Special Studies*, July 1980.

Table 2.22 Impact of the 1978–9 West German reflation on the French economy

Measures	% increase in French GDP 1979	% increase in French GDP 1980	Net effect* on the French current balance of payments 1979	Net effect* on the French current balance of payments 1980
Federal government spending	0.04	0.09	0.70	0.75
Taxes on households	0.09	0.24	1.40	2.65
Taxes on firms	–	0.01	–	0.15
Indirect taxes (VAT)	−0.01	−0.04	−0.15	−0.45
Total	0.11	0.30	+1.95	+3.10

* Effects are measured in billion francs and are calculated on average prices and exchange rate in 1978 (1 Deutschmark = 2.24 francs).
Source: Authors' calculations from multipliers of the fiscal INTERLINK model, see OECD, *Special Studies*, July 1980.

payments by 2 billion and 3 billion francs in those years.[36] These figures may seem rather low, but their importance is apparent when the effects of all four West German reflations are aggregated. Without them, economic growth in France between 1975 and 1980 would have been appreciably lower and the external deficit higher. The Barre government had, to a certain extent, to thank Chancellors Brandt and Schmidt, just as Chancellor Kohl had to thank President Mitterrand.

The Particular Features of the 1981–2 Reflation Compared with the Other Cases

Analysis of the French reflation of 1975 and the West German experiences allows us to highlight the particular features of the Left's reflation of 1981–2. There are, we would argue, three specific elements – the first concerns the means used, the second is in its 'structural' nature and the third is that it happened in international isolation.

There was emphasis on higher spending In reflating immediately after the first oil shock, governments used a combination of in-

36. These figures must be taken as very approximate, given the extent of aggregation in the method used and the fact that the assumptions tended towards simplification.

creased spending and tax cuts to boost the economy. Gradually, however, it was the second approach which was used overwhelmingly or indeed exclusively, as in the West German reflation of 1980.

Compared with this development, the French reflation of 1981–2 seems particularly untypical since government revenue (taxes and social security contributions) went up at the same time as spending was significantly increased. This feature of the 1981–2 reflation is partly explained by its distributive aspects and by the low level of direct taxation in France. But it also anticipates to a certain extent the opposite approach tried in 1984–5 – the reduction of direct taxes and contributions, dealt with in Chapter 5.

Most of the measures were of a structural nature The second particular feature involves the 'structural' nature of the measures introduced, on the one hand because they tried to reduce income differentials and on the other hand because they could not easily be reversed once they had taken effect. This irreversible character is apparent when they are compared with Chirac's reflationary measures of 1975–6. Most of these were either piecemeal or temporary, and when they had ceased to be applicable, the situation reverted to normal. This was the case with social welfare benefits (a one-off extra payment), reduced tax rates and postponement of tax payments. The situation was quite different in the case of the 1981–2 measures, which involved a permanent increase in the sums transferred – social welfare benefits, creation of jobs in the public sector, the early retirement scheme and to a certain extent industrial policy (capital grants to nationalized undertakings). On the other hand, new taxes imposed to pay for certain expenditure were all of a temporary nature.

France was the only country to reflate In 1975–6, most of the big Western countries had introduced expansionary budgetary and monetary policies in order to cope with the economic crisis. The 'concerted action programme' of the OECD countries adopted at the Bonn summit in 1978 envisaged co-ordinated economic recovery in the various countries, but gave West Germany the role of locomotive. In keeping with its commitments, West Germany introduced a budgetary reflation policy which stimulated growth. But, whereas the reflation experience of 1974–5 had not posed the problem of foreign trade, the second oil shock coupled with the strong reflation of 1979–80 reduced the trading surplus (see Figure 2.10) and caused a significant deficit in the West German current

Reflation and Austerity

Figure 2.10 Balance of trade between France and West Germany from 1972 to 1984

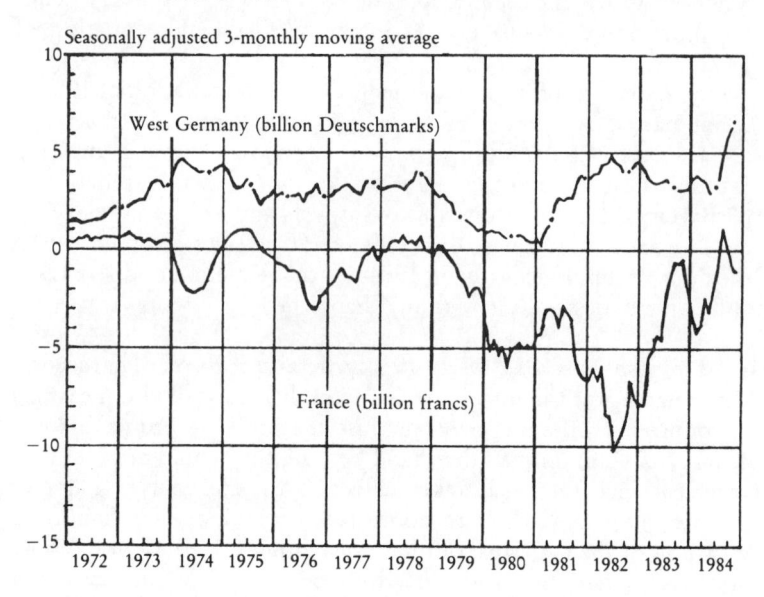

Figure 2.11 Change in GNP of France and its main trading partners* from 1973 to 1984 (change over previous twelve months)

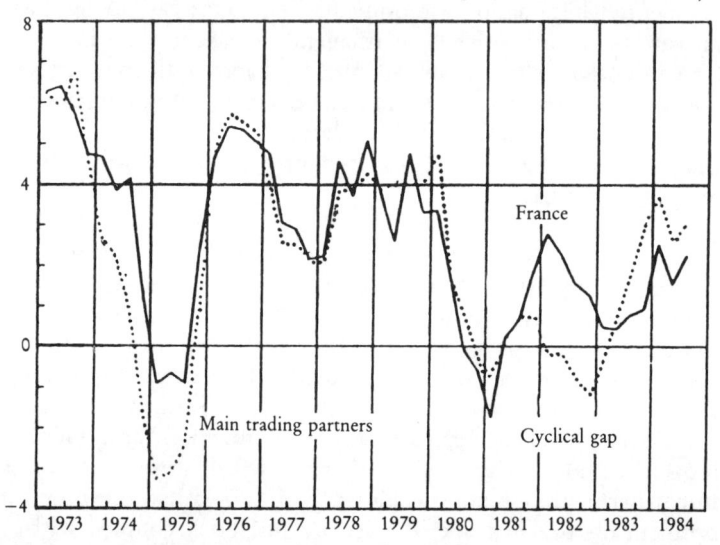

* GNP of France's main trading partners weighted by structure of French exports in 1979.

balance. More or less the same misfortune happened to the Left in 1981–2. Already handicapped by a 1980 foreign trade deficit of 60 billion, French economic recovery remained completely isolated, leading to a cyclical gap which had dire consequences for the balance of trade (see Figure 2.11 and Chapter 3).

Reflation Ran Into Difficulties Because of Restrictive Policies in Other Countries

It has been shown that the Left's reflation was comparable in extent with the Chirac reflation of 1975 and the West German reflation of 1978–9. It can also be examined in the context of the international environment, particularly during 1982.

The downturn in the world economy in 1982 increased the external deficit by 44 billion To assess the impact of the international environment in 1982, the forecasts made by the OECD in July 1981 have been taken as the base. The gap between what was forecast and what actually happened was about six points in the case of foreign demand for French manufactured goods and two and a half points in the case of the GDP of France's chief trading partners.

On inflation, the forecasters anticipated a moderate slow-down when the fall in energy prices and the effect of the restrictive policies were taken into account. But the fall in inflation in 1982 was greater than expected because of the severity of the economic crisis. As for the price of international trade, which directly affects French competitiveness, actual movement was one point lower than forecast.

To assess the impact of the rise in the dollar independently of the devaluations of the franc within the European Monetary System which can be attributed to economic policy (see Chapter 3), the value of the dollar in ECUs has been taken, using as a base its average value during the first nine months of 1981. This more or less corresponded to forecasts made at the time for 1982.

The drop in demand and the fall in world inflation put a strong brake on French growth and at the same time increased the deficit in foreign trade and public finances (see column 2 of Table 2.23). The rise in the dollar had more modest negative effects on growth and employment, though its effects on the external deficit and inflation were significant (column 3 of Table 2.23).

Overall, the worsening international situation, compared with the forecasts of Summer 1981, brought a 2% slow-down in French growth in 1982, a much worse government financial situation (since revenue depends on economic growth) and above all a greater

Table 2.23 Impact of the worsening international situation on the French economy in 1982

	Actual change* (1)	Impact: Drop in demand and fall in world inflation (2)	Impact: Rise in dollar against ECU (3)	Change if situation had been as forecast for 1982 (4) = (1)−(2)−(3)
% change over 1981				
Real GDP	1.8	−1.7	−0.3	3.8
Consumption by households (volume)	3.4	−0.3	−0.5	4.2
Total investment (volume)	0.7	−1.9	−0.9	3.5
Exports (volume)	−2.6	−7.0	+0.3	4.1
Imports (volume)	6.8	−4.5	−0.8	12.1
Consumer prices	11.2	−0.1	+2.0	9.3
Level				
Unemployment (thousands)	1,870	+90	+10	1,770
Balance on goods and services (billion francs)	−100	−20	−24	−56

*Volume is measured in 1970 prices. Actual changes in 1982 for investment, imports, and to a lesser extent consumption by households, differ from those measured by the previous year's prices. These variations stem from differences in weighting in the two methods of calculation.

external deficit of around 44 billion francs, or about twice as much as the deficit attributable to reflation.

What might have happened in 1982 if... An idea can be gained of what would have happened to the French economy if the international environment had turned out as forecast in Autumn 1981, by ignoring the effects of world deflation (column 2 of Table 2.23) and the rise in the dollar (column 3) when looking at what actually happened (column 1). Such an exercise shows that economic growth would have been slightly greater than forecast (4% as against 3.3%), partly because of unusually high agricultural production but also because of strong growth in household consumption which, even with an unfavourable environment, was already higher than forecast. The drop in investment and the deterioration of the trade balance are easily explained by the world situation.

If the forecasts about the international environment had been borne out, the increase in investment would have been 2.2%, and the rise in exports 4.5% and in imports more than 9%. This is indeed the situation which could have been expected from reflation. Moreover econometric analysis of each area shows that the traditional equations do in fact account for what happened in the period 1981–2. The fall in exports and the growth of imports are explained by the combination of strong domestic demand and depressed world demand. As for investment by firms, this was permanently higher than indicated by changes in demand and profitability of firms.[37] If investment did not reflect the upturn in consumption, as some people have claimed, this can be attributed to factors in the international environment.

APPENDIX 2.1

The Budget, 'Economic Budgets' and the Plan

The *Budget de l'Etat* is the description, in accounting terms, of future state revenue and expenditure, and is outlined in the *loi de finances* (finance law), which is presented to Parliament in draft form in the October before the year in question. The *loi de finances* is normally approved in December, for the following calendar year. Sometimes during the course of the year, one – or more – *loi de finances rectificative* (supplementary finance law) is approved, either when there is a change of government, or when the economy needs to be reflated or is overheating. Three years after a budget, confirmation of its implementation is published in a *loi de règlement* (final settlement law).

The *Budgets économiques* are macro-economic forecasts included in the *loi de finances*. They are made by the Government Accounting Department (inflow–outflow table, overall economic table, flow of funds account), and mean that a detailed quantified analysis can be made of future developments in balance of payments, public finances, incomes, monetary supply, etc. They are drawn up three times a year (in spring, summer and winter) by the forecasting section of the Ministry of Economy and Finance. Those drawn up during the course of the summer are published as an appendix to the *projet de loi de finances* (draft budget), under the title 'Economic and financial report for the year . . .'.

37. A. Bucher and H. Sterdyniak, 'Un investissement relativement soutenu' (An investment which was relatively sustained), *Observations et diagnostics économiques*, 5 October 1983.

The *Plan* is drawn up by the Commissariat Général du Plan. Its aim is to outline future scenarios and define medium-term (five-year) strategies. Its essential purpose is to study structural changes in the economy – modifications of the mechanisms of production (relative importance of the different sectors, relative prices, etc.), changes in the factors of production (capital stocks, employment, length of working week), France's place in the international division of labour (competitivity, foreign markets), changes in the importance of the public sector, etc. The principal formal instrument used in the preparation of the *Plan* is the DMS model of INSEE (government statistical service). In fact nowadays the *Plan* is essentially something which promotes analysis and concerted action.

–3–

Unavoidable External Constraints

The Left government's reflation came to grief because of external constraints; the reason was not, however, as is often said and thought, the loss of competitivity caused by reflation, but the high degree of sensitivity of foreign trade to changes in income. If the effect of price competitivity had been as great as analysts normally assume, external constraints would have been easily removed by the devaluations which were applied. However, whereas the normal mechanism had always managed to offset deficits caused by France expanding faster than her trading partners, it could not easily do this after the oil shocks and floating exchange rates had altered the structure of her foreign trade.

Any analysis of the external constraints must therefore be based above all on an understanding of the way in which the impact of devaluation had changed. A century of Franco-German rivalry and several centuries of keeping gold coins under the mattress have led to absurd connotations of the word 'devaluation' in France. Whereas the dollar responded to international speculation by more than doubling in value in only a few years, and this aroused no more attention than the weather forecast, the most minor adjustment of Franco-German parity was seen as a national calamity. For public opinion a strong franc means a strong French economy, and a stable currency means that economic policy is working, even if it leads to millions being unemployed.

Even worse is when certain French economists seem to think that the strength of the dollar, by weakening the Deutschmark and avoiding a 'devaluation' of the franc, in some way helps French disinflation. It is absurd to use the word 'devaluation' only for parity changes within the European Monetary System, and then to be happy with a rise in the dollar (and therefore a devaluation in relation to it) leading to a sharp increase in inflation and a fall in domestic demand, if this avoids devaluation against the Deutschmark, which is good for growth and the balance of payments and has only moderate inflationary impact.[1]

This in fact is one area where econometric studies can throw some light on present problems. Of course, even though the effects of currency changes on national economies are well understood, the same cannot be said of the way in which exchange rates are determined in a climate which is highly speculative; this is shown by a succession of forecasting errors over the dollar rate in recent times. This point however is not our concern here, and our main intention is to examine the consequences for France of exchange rate fluctuations imposed on her (a rise in the dollar against all other currencies), or which she partly decided, at least as far as the time scale was concerned (parity changes within the EMS).

The importance of this matter and the controversy which it aroused even inside the government warrants a brief examination of the consequences of parity changes before the three devaluations of the franc are analysed. This is necessary in order to understand what was new in these devaluations and the constraints put on socialist economic policy by the costly appreciation of the franc against the Deutschmark as a result of the 'strong franc' policy of 1979–80, and by the steady rise of the dollar. The exchange rate situation favourable to France's foreign trade (a weak dollar and a strong Deutschmark) was precisely the opposite of what the socialist government faced at the beginning of François Mitterrand's presidency. As for the new aspect of devaluation, this lay in the inability of parity changes to rectify the deficit caused by the coincidence of the 1982 cyclical gap and the rise in value of the dollar. The recognition of these constraints led inevitably to a situation where France had to fall in line with the austerity policy of others. This change-round happened in two stages: in June 1982, when devaluation was accompanied by a plan to fight inflation, and in March 1983, when an austerity policy was introduced which bore fruit, sometimes bitter fruit, in 1984 and 1985.

Should devaluation have been earlier and bigger? The question is important in that the French experiment served as an example for socialist governments which came to power afterwards and immediately introduced a competitive devaluation: Sweden in October 1982, Spain in December 1982 and Greece in January 1983. What happened in Sweden is a good illustration of the conditions necessary for success and of the difficulties which would have been encountered, both because of the short-term economic situation and for structural reasons, if the same thing had been done in France.

---

1. Especially if it was the result of a fall in the dollar.

Unavoidable External Constraints

Deterioration of External Balances

On the eve of the second oil shock, the deficit of OECD countries had been more or less wiped out. In 1978 France even had a 14 billion franc surplus on goods and services. After 1978 and until the record deficit in 1982, the net balance worsened because of two factors: the oil shock, followed by the dollar's rise from 1980; and a drop in the volume of trade in industrial goods caused by loss of competitivity between 1979 and 1981 in relation to France's main partners in the EMS, and by the short-term lack of adjustment in 1982.

The inheritance from the previous government included a poisoned chalice: a franc which had appreciated in real terms by more than 10% in relation to the Deutschmark since the setting up of the EMS, and which was to place over economic policy the sword of Damocles of the defence of the franc, even before the new government had taken power. The inheritance also included a nuclear energy programme which some elements on the Left had opposed vigorously, but which they were very glad to have when the external deficit appeared.

A Worsening Balance of Trade

The balance of trade can deteriorate either because of changes in volume (for example when the volume of imports increases faster than the volume of exports), or because the terms of trade worsen, as when import prices rise more quickly than export prices. The breakdown of changes in the balance of trade between those due to volume and those due to price gives a clear indication of the respective importance of the factors leading to a larger deficit (See Table 3.1 and Figure 3.1).

Two main factors are apparent: the worsening of the terms of trade for energy and the fall in trade in industrial goods.

To price rises for imported energy . . . The energy deficit increased from 63 billion francs in 1978 to 180 billion in 1982. This change was caused principally, in 1979 and 1980, by a rise in the dollar price of crude oil which was only slightly offset by a fall in the dollar against the franc. During these two years, the rise in energy prices accounted for 75 billion francs of the increased deficit, and the rise in volume imported added another 5 billion to this.

The oil shock was followed in 1980 by a steady rise in the dollar with the result that despite the levelling out and then the fall in the

Reflation and Austerity

Table 3.1 Part played by changes in volume and terms of trade in the deterioration of the balance of payments between 1978 and 1982 (in billion francs)

	Balance of payments		Breakdown of changes in the balance				
	1978	1982	1978–80		1980–1		1981–2
			volume	prices	volume	prices	volume prices
Agri-food	−2	+14	+10	+3	+6	+3	−7 +1
Energy	−63	−180	−5	−75	+18	−47	+9 −26
Industrial goods	+49	+28	−33	+18	+12	+8	−45 +20
Services	+30	+42	−3	+6	+5	−4	+5 +2
Total	+14	−96	−31	−48	+41	−40	−38 −3

Source: This breakdown, like that given in Figure 3.1, has been derived from series of quarterly national income accounts by applying the following formula to the annual averages from four consecutive quarters:
$$\Delta S = p_x \Delta X - p_m \Delta M + X_{-1} \Delta p_x - M_{-1} \Delta p_m$$
X, M, volume of exports and imports (annual average in 1970 francs)
p_x, p_m, price of exports and imports (annual average)
Since the results have been rounded to the nearest billion, the algebraic total of volume and price effects may differ slightly from the change in value from 1978 to 1982.

Figure 3.1 Part played by changes in volume and terms of trade in the deterioration of the balance of payments between 1978 and 1982

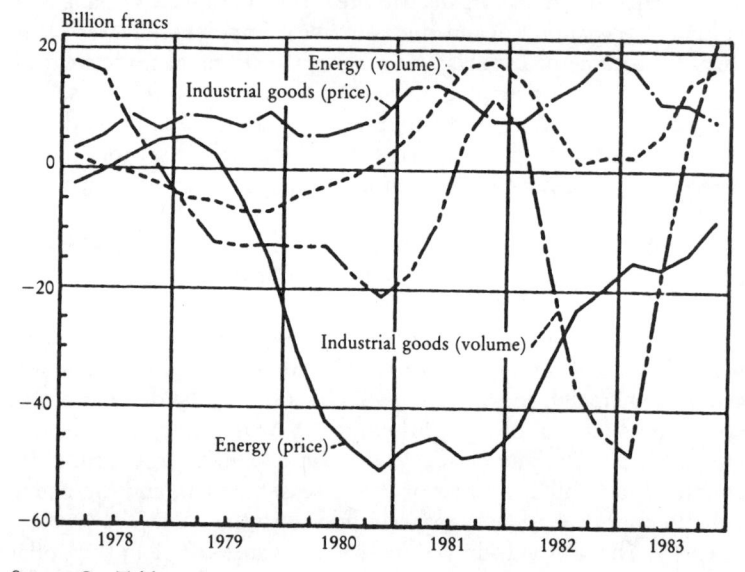

Source: See Table 3.1.

dollar price of oil from 1981, there was still a worsening of the net balance because of the terms of trade (47 billion from 1980 to 1981, 26 billion in 1982). The position would have been worse if it had not been for economies in imported energy made possible when the nuclear power programme begun during Giscard's presidency came on stream. The savings in energy costs from reduced imports amounted to 18 billion in 1981 and 9 billion in 1982.

... must be added the drop in trade in industrial goods The rise in energy prices was not the only factor in the worsening of the balance of trade. From 1978 to 1980, the overall worsening of the terms of trade accounted for 48 billion francs of the total deficit, whereas the worsening of the volume contributed 31 billion francs. In 1981, the two factors had equal weight; in 1982 only the volume factor played a part in the decline, since the worsening of the terms of trade for energy was offset by an improvement in the terms of trade for industrial goods.

The decline in volume of trade was particularly marked in the industrial sector: 33 billion francs from 1978 to 1980, then 45 billion during 1982. The cause of this between 1978 and 1981 was loss of competitivity brought about by the Barre government's exchange rate policy. This loss was offset in 1981 by the rise in exports to oil-producing countries and the developing countries (large capital equipment projects) and by the economic upturn which was starting to show at the beginning of 1981. In 1982 the worsening of the balance of trade was mainly caused by the cyclical gap, at a time when competitivity had been re-established by the devaluations of the franc and the appreciation of the dollar.

The Cost of the 'Strong Franc'

When France joined the EMS, this marked the end of a long tradition of competitive devaluations which brought real gains for French industry, and the beginning of a period when the franc appreciated in real terms (1979–81), with sometimes catastrophic consequences for sectors such as the automobile industry which were wide open to international competition.

The 'virtuous circle' did not happen The principle behind the 'strong franc' policy was simple; it also coincided with the view which regrettably tended to turn things on their head by thinking that a strong currency meant a strong economy. It concluded that since a depreciation of the franc meant imported inflation and further steady depreciation, all that was needed was to hitch the franc to the strong currencies of northern Europe to turn the vicious circle into a virtuous one of 'appreciation – disinflation' which had given West Germany such an advantage at the time of the first oil shock (see Chapter 1); the inevitable slow-down in growth of industrial production and national income would be offset by the appreciation of the franc.[2]

Several conditions must be met however before such a virtuous circle starts operating. Firstly there must be a pattern of exports which is not over-sensitive to price competition. Whereas this applies to West Germany where the main export is capital goods, it is not the case with France. The second condition is to be able to reduce domestic inflation quickly by taking advantage of 'imported disinflation'. Figure 3.2 shows that the virtuous circle did not happen: inflation in France continued to be higher than in West Germany (the difference was 4.6% per year in terms of industrial prices) and since the difference was not reduced by a depreciation of the franc, competitivity worsened by more than 10% until the first devaluation on 6 October 1981.

A quantitative analysis of the various parity changes shows up the illusory nature of this policy. Compared with the oil crisis and changes in the value of the dollar, the contribution of an overvalued franc to the limitation of imported inflation was a mere drop in the ocean. The direct disinflationary effect of a rise in the value of the franc in relation to the Deutschmark was negligible, as will be shown in the second section of this chapter. What of its indirect effect, through the way it affected the dollar?

Taking the most unfavourable hypothesis, where the devaluation of the franc against the Deutschmark affects the dollar/franc parity by the same amount (which is not always the case – see p. 146), the extra inflation would have been less than one percentage point per year. This hypothetical saving on inflation, however, was very expensive for French importers.

The fall in exports to West Germany It is nothing new for French firms to lose a share of the German market. Since the first oil crisis, France's share of German imports fell by 38% (Figure 3.3a). This deterioration over a long period cannot be attributed to currency changes since throughout the period the relationship between

---

2. This was precisely the West German position in the 1970s – lower growth than that of its main trading partners (including France), but increased value of currency reserves through a rising Deutschmark.

Figure 3.2 Value of the Deutschmark and Franco-German competitivity

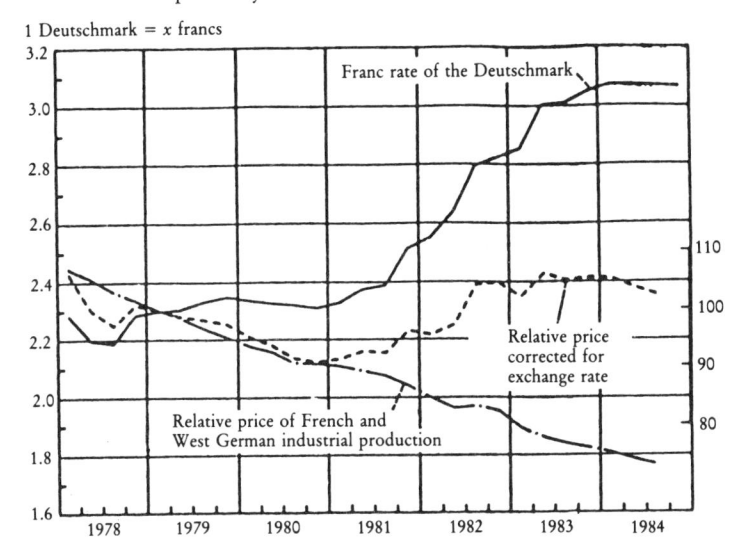

1 Deutschmark = x francs

Note: An increase indicates an improvement in French competitivity.

Figure 3.3 Factors in changes in French exports of manufactured goods to West Germany

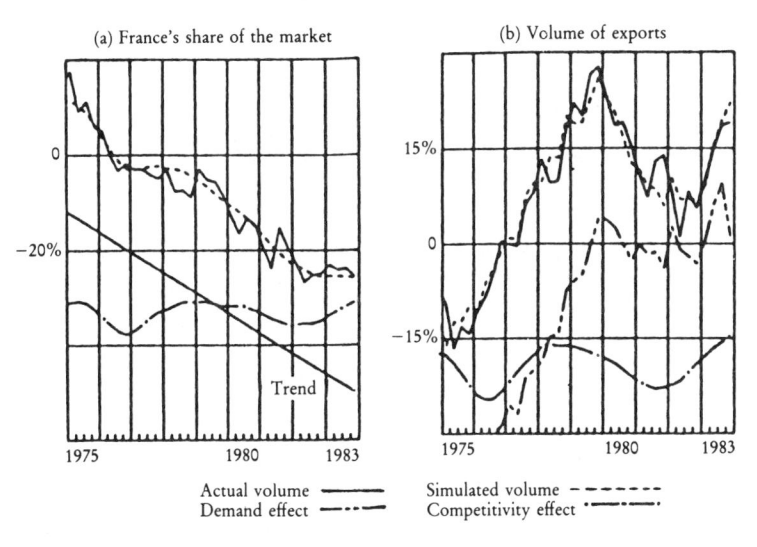

(a) France's share of the market
(b) Volume of exports

Actual volume ———
Demand effect —··—
Simulated volume − − − − − −
Competitivity effect ·—··—·

Sources: See Inset 3.1.

French industrial prices and West German industrial prices adjusted to take account of the exchange rate never significantly altered. However econometric analysis shows that the times when France's share of the market sank rapidly (from the first oil shock to the second half of 1976, and from the beginning of 1979 to the second half of 1982) coincided with a worsening of French competitivity, whereas there was little change in market share when an improvement in competitivity occurred (1977–8 and after the devaluation of 1982). Econometric analysis (see Inset 3.1) is able to indicate the respective effect of competitivity, market growth and structural factors on the volume of French exports of manufactured goods to West Germany. Market growth is shown by the volume of West German imports of manufactured goods. The index of competitivity used is that of a comparison of industrial prices adjusted to take account of the exchange rate. So what is measured is both the 'competitivity' effect and the 'export margin' effect: when French industrial prices expressed in Deutschmarks increase less rapidly than West German prices, the result is either that competitivity improves, if exporters use this advantage to lower their prices on the West German market, or an increase in export profits if they charge the same as their West German competitors. In either event, exports are boosted. The narrowing of France's share of the market is shown by a trend over time, and was quite significant: 3.6% per year throughout the period 1974–83. One notable cause was the arrival of new competitors in the West German market such as Japan and South-East Asia.

Figure 3.3b shows the development of exports of French manufactures to West Germany, as well as the respective influence of West German demand for imports and of price competitivity on this development. All econometric studies of foreign trade show the same result – that income effects are much more important than competitivity effects. Exports to West Germany rose sharply between 1975 and 1979, then fell sharply until 1982, and then rose again in 1983. Whereas the main reason for the 1975–9 rise was a bigger total market, quite a large part of the post-1979 fall was attributable to an overvalued franc and the resulting loss of competitivity. Table 3.2 gives the detailed breakdown of the development over this period as shown in Figure 3.3b.

During 1979, the growth in the volume of West German imports brought about by increased domestic demand (see Chapter 2) was in the region of 10%. The volume of French exports to West Germany however increased by only 5.7%. The simulation of the trading relationship for the same period gives the same result – an increase

Unavoidable External Constraints

Inset 3.1

Econometric estimate of an export function, France to West Germany

Statistics used

The value of exports is determined by customs statistics. The volume has been calculated by using as the price index a weighting of the price of West German imports and of the price in Deutschmarks of French exports to the EEC. There was a check to make sure the findings were not significantly modified when the weightings were changed. The statistical series were seasonally adjusted.

Econometric estimate

The model covered the period between the last quarter of 1974 and the last quarter of 1983, giving the following formula (the 'Student' Ts of the coefficients are shown in brackets):

$$\text{Log Ex} = \underset{(13.0)}{1.05 \text{ Log } Ia} + \underset{(5.0)}{0.80} \sum_{i=0}^{6} \alpha_i \text{ Log}\left(\frac{ep_e}{p}\right)_{-i} \underset{(6.8)}{-0.0036\, t} + \underset{(4.1)}{1.89}$$

$R^2 = 0.93$ Standard error = 3%   DW = 1.7

The quarterly series used are respectively:

- Ex : volume of French exports to West Germany
- Ia : volume of West German imports
- p_e : price of West German industrial goods
- e : rate of exchange (1 Deutschmark = e francs)
- p : price of French industrial goods
- t : time
- α_i : distributed lags in competitivity effect estimated by Almon's method (14%, 17%, 18%, 17%, 15%, 12%, 7%)

Figure 3.3b shows that over the whole period the effect of changes in competitivity is much weaker than that of the total volume of West German imports. Moreover the negative trend term shows a structural reduction in France's share of the West German market which is independent of price competitivity.

Estimate by market share

This econometric estimate shows that there is almost unit elasticity

continued on p. 128

> **Inset 3.1** *continued*
>
> *Econometric estimate of an export function, France to West Germany*
>
> of French exports to West German imports. The model can be looked at again from the viewpoint of 'market share' (France's share of West German imports). A final point is that to avoid an arbitrary volume–price split, market shares have been calculated by value (relationship of exports to West Germany expressed in Deutschmarks to West German imports in Deutschmarks). The estimated model is:
>
> $$\text{Log } P_m = -\underset{(22.2)}{0.0043}\, t + \underset{(3.5)}{0.46} \sum_{i=0}^{6} \alpha_i \text{ Log}\left(\frac{ep_e}{p}\right)_{-i} + \underset{(14.0)}{2.7}$$
>
> $R^2 = 0.94$ DW = 1.7   Standard error = 3%
>
> α_i in % (–18, 2, 18, 26, 30, 26, 16)
>
> The distributed lags of the competitivity effect (α_i) show up in this case as the traditional J-curve since the market share P_m is expressed as a value. The coefficient of the first quarter is negative because a fall in the franc bringing about a fall in the price in Deutschmarks provokes initially a drop in France's market share. Then, when competitivity gains show, the rise in the volume of exports increases the market share.

of 5.7%, consisting of the favourable effect of the growth of West German imports (since there was practically unit import elasticity, this effect is also around 10%) offset partly by loss of competitivity (1.4%) and the deteriorating trend (2.7%). From the last quarter of 1979 to the second quarter of 1981, exports to West Germany fell by 20%. The model is able to account for only 16%, made up of fall in demand (5.7%), loss of competitivity (4.9%) and the downwards trend (5.4%). Thus, for this period, half of the short-term drop in French exports to West Germany was due to the fall in demand and half due to loss of competitivity from an overvalued franc. The three parity adjustments within the EMS, by offsetting almost entirely the downwards trend, meant that from the second quarter of 1983, competitivity was re-established and the French share of the West German market was kept up (column 3 of Table 3.2).

Analyses of specific sectors confirm the problems arising from the strong franc policy. In those areas facing keen competition such

Table 3.2 Contribution of different factors to the development of the volume of French exports to West Germany (in %)

	From 1st quarter 1979 to 4th quarter 1979	From 4th quarter 1979 to 2nd quarter 1981	From 2nd quarter 1981 to 4th quarter 1983
Actual change	+5.7	−20.5	+11.8
Simulated change	+5.7	−16.0	+12.2
'Demand' effect	+9.8	−5.7	+13.5
'Competitivity-price' effect	−1.4	−4.9	+7.8
'Trend' effect	−2.7	−5.4	−9.1

as the car industry, export margins were compressed both by the rise in domestic prices and costs, and by the fact that prices in the West German market remained steady.

Compression of export margins: the example of the car industry This is a sector where there is a vast difference between the large European countries where domestic manufacturers play a central role in determining prices, and small countries where European manufacturers face Japanese competitors selling at much lower prices. In Italy, West Germany, France and the United Kingdom, domestic manufacturers dominate the market and Japanese competition is contained by limits of various kinds. European importers adjust their prices to those of domestic manufacturers and, apart from the United Kingdom, market conditions are similar. In 1982 the pre-tax selling price of French cars was more or less the same in France, Italy and West Germany, whereas it was on average more than 20% higher in the United Kingdom. On the other hand, in smaller EEC countries with strong Japanese penetration, French cars sold at prices 20–30% less, at existing exchange rates, than those in France. In these countries, European manufacturers had to adjust to Japanese competition or risk being forced out of the market.

Since prices of exported cars had to match those of competitors in foreign markets, a faster rise in domestic prices not offset by a devaluation of the franc led inevitably to a reduction in export margins. An analysis of a sample of seven mass production car models showed that the factory gate price in francs of cars exported to West Germany, which in October 1979 was already 1% higher than the price of cars sold in France, had by October 1980 become 12% lower. Despite the currency adjustment of October 1981, the gap was still 13% just before the June 1982 adjustment. By this date

Table 3.3 Evolution of the trade balance from 1978 to 1980

	Balances (billion francs)			Change 1978–80 (billion francs)
	1978	1979	1980	
Balance of goods and services[a]	+14	−3	−55	−69
Customs balance cif–fob, excluding military equipment[a]	−24	−42	−101	−77
– all EEC	−8	−8	−22	−14
– all four countries (FRG, Netherlands, US, Japan)	−26	−35	−56	−30
– oil-producing countries	−23	−39	−64	−41

[a] The balance of trade in goods and services in the national accounts measures imports and exports in a symmetrical way and therefore gives an indication of the surplus (if it is positive) or the actual deficit (if it is negative). The customs balance cif–fob, excluding military equipment, is the only one which gives a breakdown by country, but it exaggerates the actual deficit since there is a different accounting system for imports and exports, and military equipment is not included.

the only French car exports which were showing a profit were those to the United Kingdom. In all other European markets, profit on exports was lower than that on domestic sales, the difference being as high as 30% in the case of Belgium.

Deterioration in trade with industrialized countries The poor competitive showing of French goods was the main reason for the worsening of French trade with developed countries. As previously emphasized, the oil shock was not the only factor in the deterioration of the net trade balance in the period 1978–80. Trade in industrial goods with EEC and OECD countries also fell into sharp deficit. The trade deficit with the EEC as a whole rose from 8 billion in 1979 to 22 billion in 1980; the worst deficits were with West Germany, the Netherlands, the United States and Japan. In the period 1978–80, the French deficit with these four countries alone was almost as great as that in trade with the oil-producing countries (see Table 3.3).

Speculation against the Franc

The problem of the devaluation of the franc had already arisen before the Left government came to power, since the franc, overvalued against the Deutschmark, was being carried along by the

Unavoidable External Constraints

Figure 3.4 Pressures on the franc: money market rate and Euro-franc rate

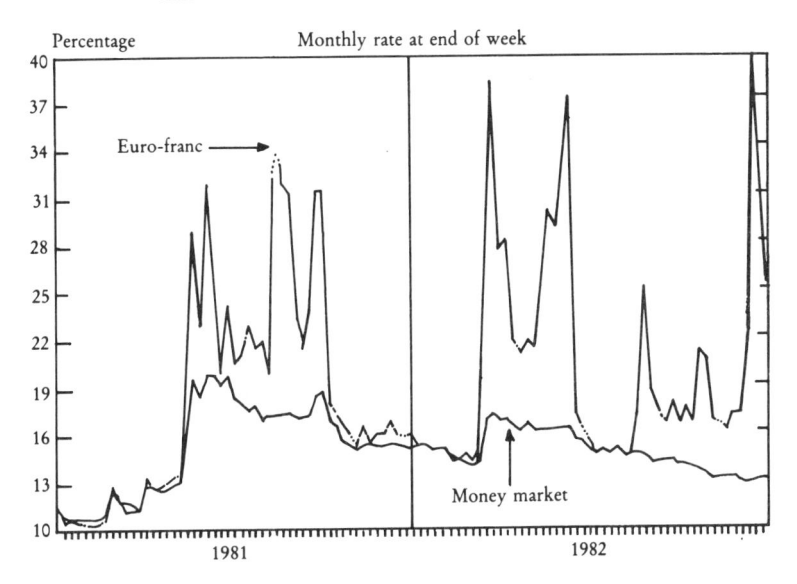

Source: Report by the Conseil National du Crédit.

'confidence' which international financial circles had in the Barre government's resistance to devaluation. However, this position became more difficult from March 1981 because of the impending election and after this date the franc was always at the lowest point of its permitted margin of fluctuation against the Deutschmark. Pressures on the franc increased with the probability of a Left victory, and just after Mitterrand won the presidential election, the Barre government raised the base rate which went from 13% to 19% in one week. An idea of the pressures on the franc is gained from a comparison between the money market rate and the Euro-franc rate (see Figure 3.4). The Euro-franc market is in fact a very narrow one which is subject to wide changes in rates. When there is lack of confidence in the franc, foreign dealers operating into francs increase their forward cover. Because they cannot borrow from French banks, which are not allowed to lend to non-residents, they borrow on the Euro-franc market, which affects the rates. The difference between the Euro-franc rate and the base rate is therefore indicative of the pressures on the franc during this period.

The drop in currency reserves which had started in a minor way in February rapidly gained momentum and reached one billion

Reflation and Austerity

dollars a day in the week of 18 to 22 May *before* the Mauroy government was installed. In a book covering the events of his first year of office,[3] Mauroy described the rapid succession of events affecting the franc which coincided with the victory ceremony at the Pantheon in Paris, and the decision which he took, against the advice of certain people including Michel Rocard, to defend the franc. His view was that 'the victory of the Left should not be celebrated by a devaluation'; there was no doubt that the existence of currency speculation offered the rare opportunity for a devaluation to restore competitivity very rapidly, though this would have been risky, and despite what certain economists still believe would not have solved all problems. As it happened, devaluation was merely delayed by introducing traditional exchange control measures. The drain on reserves, which had reached 43 billion between the end of February and the end of May 1981, was temporarily halted and a slight recovery of 4.3 billion was registered in June and July. However, there was renewed speculation just before 15 August and in September when, despite the rise in the base rate, measures to support the franc caused a further loss of 18 billion. The flight of capital did not really stop until the adjustment on 5 October 1981, and in the last quarter of that year reserves rose by 18 billion.

The flight of capital has always had a significant impact on public opinion. But purely speculative capital movements, though dramatic, have little long-term effect on foreign debt or gold and currency holdings because the effect is reversed when the aim (devaluation) has been achieved. On the other hand a persistent deficit in the balance of current transactions is much more serious because, unless it is offset by a permanent influx of capital as in the United States, it inevitably leads to a drop in reserves and/or an increase in external debt. This problem will be looked at again at the end of the chapter; the analysis of external constraints now continues with a comparison of the macro-economic effects of the three parity adjustments.

Analysis of the Parity Changes

Economists have long been aware that devaluations do not necessarily bring the trade balance back into equilibrium. Normally, a devaluation is supposed to rectify the net balance of trade because competitivity improves in domestic and foreign markets. However,

---

3. *C'est ici le chemin*, Paris, Flammarion, 1982.

the initial effect of a devaluation is to make imports (as expressed in the home currency) dearer, and therefore to increase the external deficit – the 'perverse' effect of devaluation. This perverse effect has to be offset by gains in competitivity if there is to be an improvement in the trade balance. This area was first analysed in the 1930s when economists came up with a simple condition for the price elasticities of foreign trade known as the 'Marshall–Lerner condition' which is still the basis of any quantitative study of a specific devaluation.

But the macro-economic impact of a change in parity is not just a matter of the direct effects of currency values on the trade balance. A better competitive position stimulates production and employment, whereas externally induced price rises brought about by the worsening of the terms of trade has a dampening effect. Imported inflation eventually cancels out increased competitivity, so that the overall effect on the trade balance should be looked at as a function of macro-economic interactions as a whole. A final point is that in a situation where the exchange rate is fixed within the EMS but floats against other currencies, the concept of devaluation is less important than when all rates are fixed. Moreover, because of the structure of French trade with other countries, a fall in the value of the franc against the Deutschmark has fundamentally different effects from a fall against the dollar.

These points will be looked at in the light of the findings of the main French macro-economic models, and then the three parity adjustments will be analysed.

Analysis of Devaluation

We will begin by examining the direct effects of a devaluation on the trade balance, ignoring the way it affects inflation and boosts economic activity. How far devaluation increases competitivity and how far it worsens the terms of trade (perverse effects) is obviously highly dependent on the movement of export prices.

The Marshall–Lerner condition The traditional version of this has been to assume that when parities are adjusted export prices expressed in the currency of the exporting country remained unchanged. Improved competitivity in domestic markets depend on the price elasticity of demand for imports (ε) and exports (ε'). These elasticities indicate how far the volume of trade is sensitive to variations in the relative prices of external trade. A 1% devaluation of the franc has the following effects:

1 A 1% rise in the franc value of imports.
2 No change in the price of exports in francs, but a 1% fall in the price of exports in foreign currency.
3 An ε% fall in the volume of imports as a result of a 1% loss of competitivity by importers in the French market.
4 An ε'% increase in the volume of exports as a result of a 1% gain in competitivity in foreign markets.

The first effect (dearer imports) worsens the trade balance expressed in francs, whereas the last two improve it. For the devaluation to succeed, the favourable effects from increased competitivity must be greater than the perverse effects from dearer imports. The breakdown of the *change in the balance of trade*, expressed in francs, is as follows:

Favourable effect	Totals involved in a 1% devaluation
Increase in the volume of exports	Initial value of the exports $\times \varepsilon'$%
Fall in the volume of imports	Initial value of the imports $\times \varepsilon$%
Offset by perverse effect	
Increase in the price of imports	Initial value of the imports $\times 1$%

If the initial deficit is not too high the total exports can be assimilated to the total imports and the change in the trade balance can be calculated:

$$\frac{\text{Change in the}}{\text{trade balance}} = \frac{\text{Initial amount}}{\text{of exports}} \times (\varepsilon' + \varepsilon - 1)$$

The devaluation therefore improves the trade balance if the sum of the price elasticities of foreign trade is higher than 1. This is the Marshall–Lerner condition.

However, if the initial deficit is not insignificant in relation to the level of external trade, the condition for re-establishing equilibrium by devaluation is narrower: this is because one of the components of the favourable effect – the rise in exports – is applied to a total (exports) which is lower than that involved in the perverse effect (imports). Where Θ is the rate at which imports are covered by exports, the change in the trade balance becomes:

$$\frac{\text{Change in the}}{\text{trade balance}} = \frac{\text{Initial amount}}{\text{of exports}} \times (\Theta.\varepsilon' + \varepsilon - 1)$$

Choice between improving margins and improving competitivity
Analysis of the way foreign trade prices react to exchange rate shifts shows that the usual hypothesis that export prices in the home currency remain the same does not correspond to what happens in reality. In fact when demand-price elasticity is low, it is better for firms to fall in with prices abroad by improving their export margins. Any loss of competitivity is more than offset by domestic price rises expressed in home currency. This price adjustment reduces gains in competitivity but also means that the perverse effect is reduced. In a case where export prices are totally in line with prices abroad, the gains in competitivity would disappear completely and the perverse effect of the rise in import prices would be replaced by the favourable effect of the rise in export prices.

The real situation is between the two: in econometric models, foreign trade prices are the geometric averages of domestic and foreign prices. Where a' and a are the respective elasticities of prices of exports and imports to foreign prices expressed in francs, a devaluation of the franc by 1% has the following consequences:

1 A rise of a% in the price of imports in francs (a is about 0.7 for industry as a whole – see Table 3.4).
2 A rise of a'% in the price of exports in francs and a fall of $(1 - a')$% in the price in foreign currency (a' is about 0.3 for industry as a whole).
3 A rise of $(1 - a') \cdot \varepsilon'$% in the volume of exports, because of a fall of $(1 - a')$ % in the price of French exports in foreign markets.
4 A fall of $a \cdot \varepsilon$% in the volume of imports because of a price rise of a% in imports in francs.

Maintaining the previous assumption that the initial deficit is not very large, the change in the balance of trade brought about by the devaluation will be:

Change in the trade balance	=	Initial amount of imports	×	$[(1 - a') \varepsilon' + a \varepsilon$	$- (a - a')]$
				Competitivity gains	Change in the terms of trade

The formula in square brackets represents the elasticity of the cover rate of imports and exports to a variation in the exchange rate. It quantifies the effect of a devaluation and thus the amount necessary to offset a trade deficit, disregarding course-induced effects.

Table 3.4 Elasticities in the major French macro-economic models (long-term elasticities)

	DMS base 1971				Trade in industrial goods			All goods and services FMV 1951–79
	Intermediate goods	Capital goods	Consumer goods	METRIC	OFCE-annual	OFCE-quarterly		
Price elasticity of volume of trade								
Exports (ε')	2.5	0.4	1.3	1.6	1.8	1.3		1.4
Imports (ε)	0.0	0.0	0.8	0.7	0.7	0.9		0.5
Foreign price and exchange rate elasticity of external trade prices								
Exports (a')	0.4	0.0	0.2	0.5	0.3	0.25		0.5
Imports (a)	0.8	0.3	0.7	1.0	0.7	0.7		0.75
Exchange rate elasticity of export/import cover rate, divided between:								
Competivity gains $[\varepsilon(1 - a') + \varepsilon a]$	1.1	0.1	1.1	1.0	1.35	1.15		0.8
	1.5	0.4	1.6	1.5	1.75	1.6		1.07
Terms of trade effect ($a' - a$)	−0.4	−0.3	−0.5	−0.5	−0.4	−0.45		−0.25

Source: For DMS – *Revue économique*, September 1980, pp. 930–80; for METRIC – INSEE volume 1981, p. 132; for OFCE-quarterly – R. Topol and M.-A. Boudier, 'Les mauvais résultats du commerce extérieur industriel pèsent sur la croissance' ('Poor external trade figures stifle growth'), *Observations et diagnostics économiques*, 5, October 1983; for FMV 1951–79 – F. Fournelle, P.-A. Muet and P. Villa, 'Le commerce extérieur en France depuis 1950' (External trade in France since 1950) *Annales de l'INSEE*, 49, January–March 1983.

Unavoidable External Constraints

The relative uniformity of the relations determining volumes and prices of foreign trade in the French models means that the different elasticities can be calculated. The estimated values for these elasticities in four of the main French econometric models are shown in Table 3.4. They take into consideration all trade in industrial goods (METRIC, OFCE-annual, OFCE-quarterly), each of the three big industrial sectors (DMS model), and the whole of trade in goods and services (the FMV model by F. Fournelle, P.-A. Muet and P. Villa of estimated foreign trade for the period 1951–79).

The first observation is that price competitivity figures rather prominently for consumer goods and intermediate goods but has only a very small role in the capital goods sector. Rather than price, international competition in this sector is more and more through the extension of the range of products and their adaptation for specific needs. A further observation is that there is a big difference between the price elasticity of imports (about 0.7 on average throughout industry) and that for exports (around 1.6), but this is normal for an economy as a whole since imports consist for the most part of goods not produced by the importing country. The competition therefore between domestic production and imported goods is always relatively weak. On the other hand, competitivity on price plays a much larger role for exports since in foreign markets French exporters are competing not only with the producers of the countries to which they are selling but also with all other exporters.

The obvious conclusion is that competitivity gains from devaluation will show more in foreign markets and only slightly in domestic markets. In other words, devaluations are not the way to win back domestic markets.

On the basis of the values of the elasticities involved, it is easy to calculate the direct effect of a devaluation on the net balance of trade in industrial goods. Table 3.4 gives values which vary little between the different models. On average, a devaluation of the franc, disregarding knock-on effects, brings about an improvement in the cover rate of industrial goods which is slightly higher than the percentage devaluation: this coefficient is 1.35 in the OFCE-annual model, 1.15 in the OFCE-quarterly model, 1 in METRIC and less than 1 in the DMS model. For all external trade the estimated average elasticity over the period 1951–79 is 0.8, though it has fallen considerably since the oil shocks.

Perverse effect compounded by the oil shocks   Although the direct effect of a devaluation of the franc is favourable to the balance of trade in industrial goods, its impact on the overall trade balance is much weaker because of the added importance of the energy factor in the balance of trade since the oil shocks. This increase in the perverse effect can be highlighted by assuming what is implicit in the models taken together – that elasticities in the industrial sector have not changed during the period of the oil shocks. To simplify the calculations, a distinction is made between trade in industrial goods, energy imports and the balance on other goods and services; in the case of the latter, the assumption is made that the competitivity effects and the terms of trade effects cancel each other out, and that the value of this balance does not alter with a change in parity. For energy imports, substitution effects are ignored since they appear only in the long run, and the assumption is made that the rise in the price of the imported energy is the same as the amount of the devaluation and that there is no fall in the volume of imports.[4]

The first two columns of Table 3.5 show the structure of France's external trade as a percentage of total imports. Energy imports accounted for 11% of total imports in 1970 and 25% in 1981. The reverse trend is shown by exports of industrial goods which accounted for 68% of total French imports in 1970 but only 59.6% in 1981.

This structural change had important consequences for external constraints, as is evident by comparing the effect of a 10% devaluation of the franc on the 1970 structure with that on the 1979 structure. The elasticities previously discussed make it possible to calculate the change, expressed as a percentage of total imports, of each of the elements, and by adding them algebraically, the effect on the overall balance (again expressed as a percentage of total imports). The calculation was made using the elasticities of the OFCE-quarterly model which fall between those of the OFCE-annual model and those of the METRIC model. The values of these elasticities are quoted in column 3 of Table 3.5 and the change in each element brought about by devaluation is shown in the last two columns.

Since the assumption is that changes in other balances can be ignored, devaluation has only three effects – a favourable effect on industrial exports, a practically nil effect on industrial imports and an extremely unfavourable effect on imports of energy. The increase in the value of industrial exports is the result both of the rise in the price of exports expressed in francs and the increase in volume because of increased competitivity (the split between these depends on marginal behaviour shown by the coefficient a'). The elasticity of

---

4. Induced effects are analysed in the next section.

Table 3.5 Increase in the perverse effect due to the oil shocks: a numerical example

	Structure of foreign trade (as % of total imports)		Exchange rate variation elasticities*					Effect of a 10% devaluation on the external balance (as % of total imports)**	
	1970	1981	Price effect	+	Volume effect	=	Overall effect	Structure 1970	Structure 1981
Industrial exports	68.0	59.6	a'	+	$\varepsilon'(1-a')$	=	+1.2	+8.2	+7.1
Less									
Industrial imports	−62.6	−52.4	a	−	εa	=	+0.1	−0.6	−0.5
Energy imports	−11.3	−25.6	+1	−	0	=	+1.0	−1.1	−2.6
Plus									
Other balances	+7.6	+11.2	0 by definition					0.0	0.0
Trade balance	+1.7	−7.2						+6.5	+4.0

* The values of the elasticities a', a, ε, ε', are taken from the OFCE-quarterly model.
** The effect of each entry expressed as a % of imports is derived from the following formula: Impact in % = proportion of total imports × elasticity × rate devaluation.
For example, the effect on the external balance of the change in the value of industrial exports equals:
0.68 × 1.2 × 10 = +8.2% in 1970
0.59 × 1.2 × 10 = +7.1% in 1981

the value of exports to changes in the exchange rate is 1.2, but because of a lower cover rate of industrial goods (due to the oil shocks), the part played by industrial exports in rectifying the overall trade balance dropped from 8.1% in 1970 to 7.1% in 1981.

The effect of the devaluation on the value of industrial imports is virtually nil: the rise in the franc price of imports ($a = 0.7$) is more or less offset by increased competitivity ($\varepsilon \cdot a = 0.6$) so that the impact on the trade balance is only -0.6% in 1970 and -0.5% in 1981. As for the 10% rise in imported energy prices as a result of the devaluation, this worsens the balance by 1.1% of total imports in 1970 and 2.6% in 1981. Overall, the improvement in the external balance from the direct effect of variations in the exchange rate, which in 1970 would have been 6.5% of imports for a devaluation of 10%, would have been only 4% in 1981. The difference of 2.5% represents 19 billion francs in 1981.

Moreover, when the slowness of competitivity gains and induced effects on inflation and growth are taken into account, the improvement in the external balance brought about by devaluation is seen to be much smaller. Estimates made during the setting up of the main econometric models show that increased competitivity takes a long time to work through, and that the first consequence of devaluation is the perverse effect from the worsening of the terms of trade. The way the external balance develops is the traditional 'J-curve' – deterioration during the first year, and improvement after that.

Figure 3.5 shows how the external balance would evolve with a 10% devaluation against all currencies (on 1 January 1985), as simulated by the OFCE-quarterly model. The initial deficit would worsen by 7 billion francs in the first quarter, but then would be wiped out to give a surplus after a year. The energy sector deficit would keep on increasing by 4 billion to 6 billion francs a quarter whereas the industrial balance would improve after the second quarter. But this improvement would not offset the worsening energy deficit until fully two years after the devaluation. The length of this J-curve, characteristic of the French situation after the oil shocks, goes a long way to explain the difficulties there are in trying to rectify rapidly the external balance by devaluation (an identical curve is found in Figure 3.7 which shows the simulation done with the METRIC model).

Table 3.6 which summarizes how the main French models have simulated the macro-economic effects of a hypothetical 10% devaluation on 1 January 1985, shows that there is a 20 billion franc worsening of the external deficit in the first year. This gives way to an improvement of 6 billion in the second year and 15 billion in the

Figure 3.5 10% devaluation of the franc against all currencies; change in the total external balance and the energy and industrial balances

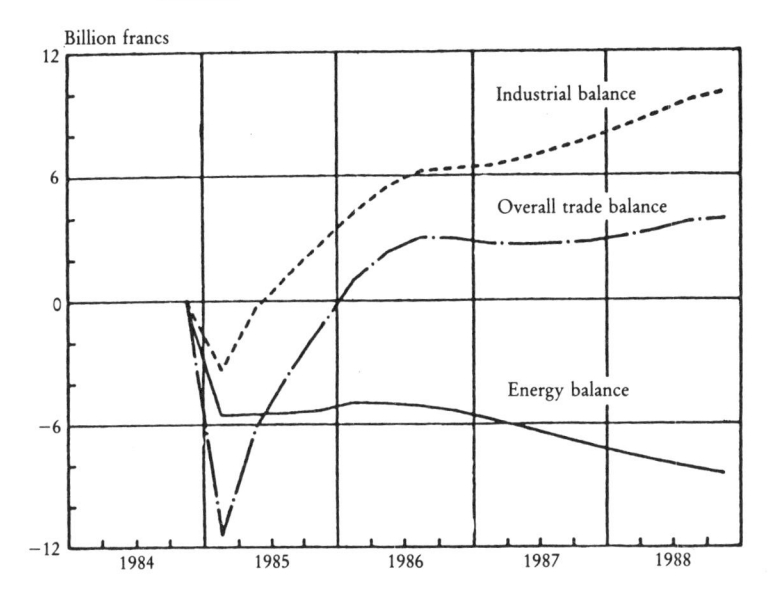

Source: Simulation by OFCE-quarterly model.

third year. The original deficit is wiped out therefore only after three years.

Induced effects: inflation and reflation ... A 10% devaluation brings an immediate rise in import prices of between 6% and 8%, depending on the model used, which is passed on to prices for intermediate and finished consumer goods. Wage indexation and the fact that rises in costs such as wages and intermediate consumer goods are passed on to prices means that there is an inflationary spiral which can, when wages are fully indexed, in the long run cancel out the improved competitive position arising from the devaluation. This is roughly the long-term situation described by the main French models.

In the short term, over one year, the rise in consumer prices is between 1% and 2% depending on the model. In the third year, consumer prices are on average 4% to 5% higher and, after five to six years, if prices and wages are not subject to control after the devaluation, imported inflation almost totally cancels out competitivity gains.

Table 3.6 Macro-economic effects of a 10% devaluation of the franc in 1985: findings of the major French models (differences of level in relation to base)

	METRIC-DP	COPAIN	DMS	ICARE	OFCE-annual	OFCE-quarterly
Import prices (%)						
1st year	8.0	5.7	7.1	7.2	8.0	7.7
3rd year	8.7	5.9	9.0	9.0	8.3	8.2
Consumer prices (%)						
1st year	1.8	0.2	2.5	1.2	2.5	0.9
3rd year	4.0	2.3	5.6	4.5	4.8	3.9
Volume of GDP (%)						
1st year	0.3	0.6	0.8	0.5	0.6	0.8
3rd year	0.9	0.25	0.5	1.3	1.3	2.3
Trade balance (billion francs)						
1st year	−18	−17	−26	−25	−24	−22
2nd year	+6	+2	−7	+6	+7	+9
3rd year	+16	+13	+10	+13	+20	+11

Sources: Simulations presented to the Commissariat Général du Plan technical group on 'the medium-term macro-economic outlook'.

In the medium term, competitivity gains cause an increase in exports and a fall in imports, and therefore through the normal Keynesian multiplier a rise in production and in incomes. As in the case of an oil shock, dearer imports reduce the real value of household incomes and firms' financial margins; there is a depressive effect on consumption and, because profits fall, on investment. What happens to incomes and production depends on the respective importance of these two effects which both compound the direct effects of the devaluation (see Figure 3.6).

Stagflation (caused by imported inflation and the depressive impact of externally induced price rises) is the result of the perverse effect of the devaluation, whereas an increase in economic activity, like an improved trade balance, is the result of the favourable effect.

In the case of a devaluation of the franc against all currencies, the stimulus effect is greater than the stagflation effect of externally induced price rises. The GDP rises by 0.6% in the first year and by

Figure 3.6 Direct and induced effects of devaluation

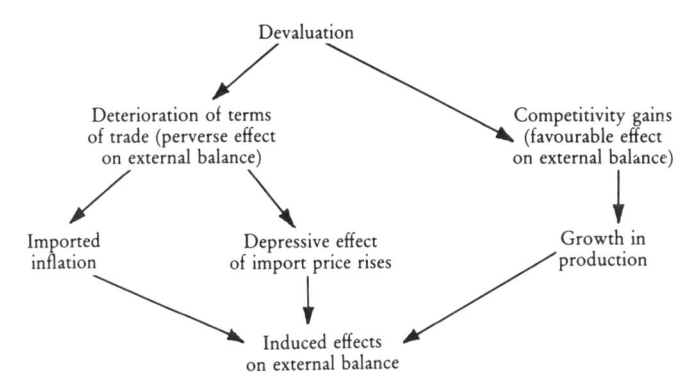

```
                         Devaluation
                        ╱          ╲
    Deterioration of terms         Competitivity gains
    of trade (perverse effect      (favourable effect
    on external balance)           on external balance)
       ╱         ╲                        ↓
   Imported   Depressive effect       Growth in
   inflation  of import price rises   production
         ╲         ↓         ╱
          Induced effects
          on external balance
```

1%, taking the average of the models, after three years. The knock-on effects are more varied when the parity change involves only the Deutschmark or the dollar.

... differ, according to whether the depreciation is against the Deutschmark or the dollar The macro-economic effects of a devaluation of the franc have been analysed in detail by M. Debonneuil and H. Sterdyniak using the METRIC model of INSEE (the French national statistical office).[5] One of their important findings was that, regarding inflation, the effect of an exchange rate move on economic activity and the external balance is significantly different depending on whether the franc has depreciated against the dollar or against the Deutschmark.

All imported energy and two-thirds of industrial raw materials are in fact quoted in dollars. For agricultural imports, 65% is quoted in dollars, the rest being in ECUs, the European currency of which the Deutschmark and the guilder constitute about half the value. If a parity change does not affect the price of raw materials in their quoted currency, a 10% appreciation of the dollar causes a 10% rise in the price of imported energy and about a 6.5% rise in the price of industrial and agricultural raw materials. On the other hand, a 10% rise in the Deutschmark does not change the franc price of imported energy and raw materials and increases the price of agricultural imports by only 1.5%, assuming 'green' parity follows real parity. The overall cost of energy and raw material imports would have risen, in 1981, by 27 billion francs in the first

---

5. M. Debonneuil and H. Sterdyniak, 'Apprécier une dévaluation' (Assessment of a devaluation), *Economie et statistique*, 142, March 1982.

Reflation and Austerity

Figure 3.7 Effect of three kinds of depreciation of the franc on the current external balance

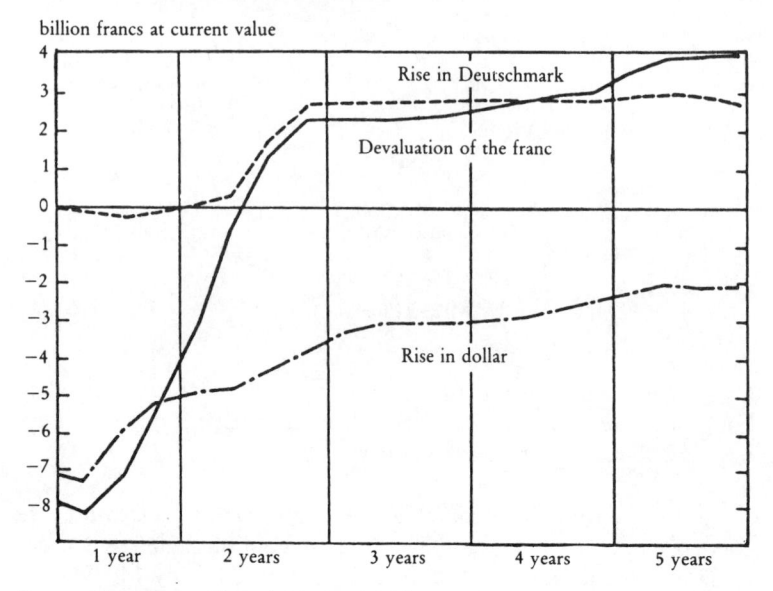

Source: M. Debonneuil and H. Sterdyniak, March 1982. Simulations using the METRIC model.

hypothesis and by less than 1 billion in the second. This basic difference is the reason that the two parity changes have totally different macro-economic effects.

A rise in the dollar has a stagflationary impact comparable to that of an oil shock, as simulations in Chapter 1 and 2 have shown: the external deficit grows, inflation gains momentum, and the real incomes of domestic economic agents fall. A rise in the value of the Deutschmark on the other hand has virtually no inflationary effect. The perverse effect and therefore the externally induced rise in prices is very weak and the depressive impact is largely offset by the economic stimulus effect of gains in competitivity, so that the real incomes of domestic economic agents rise, boosting production and investment. The perverse effect is quickly cancelled out by gains in competitivity and the trade balance shows a surplus during the second year following the parity change.

Figure 3.7 shows that in the case of a devaluation of the franc against all currencies, the J-curve initially follows the dollar curve (perverse effect) then coincides with the one showing the appreciation of the Deutschmark and the guilder (favourable effect).

Unavoidable External Constraints

A devaluation of the franc against all currencies was the actual situation in the 1950s and 1960s, but since the end of fixed exchange rates and the setting up of zones such as the European Monetary System (EMS) where rates are fixed but adjustable, the concept of devaluation has not had the same meaning or the same impact.

Parity Realignments Within the EMS

The European Monetary System which started operating on 13 March 1979 consists of an exchange rate mechanism (ERM), with parities which are fixed but adjustable, linking the currencies of the European Community with the exception of those of the United Kingdom, Greece, Spain and Portugal. Currencies in the EMS have a central rate in European currency (ECU) which determines bilateral central rates around which member states must keep their actual rates, with a margin of fluctuation of ± 2.25% (± 6% for the Italian lira). Central banks are therefore obliged to intervene when a bilateral rate reaches the edge of its margin of fluctuation; the currencies are then said to be divergent and the intervention is in the divergent currencies.[6]

Realignments are triggered by a slide in exchange rates Between March 1979 and Autumn 1985, eight exchange rate realignments were introduced. Five of them concerned only a limited number of currencies, whereas those in October 1981, June 1982 and especially March 1983 involved almost all currencies. Table 3.7 shows the percentage variation in the central rates against the ECU which each of these realignments introduced. The fact that there are rather large margins of fluctuation means that currency readjustment no longer has the stark character which devaluations used to have, since the gradual movement of currencies within the fluctuation margins usually brings a change in the central rate.

The currency realignment of 4 October 1981 revalued the mark by 5.5% and devalued the franc by 3% as against their previous ECU values, giving an overall 8.5% devaluation of the central rate of the franc as against the Deutschmark. However, as Table 3.7 shows, the actual devaluation of the franc as against the Deutschmark between 2 October and 5 October was only 4.4%. The 8.5% devaluation of the franc against the Deutschmark had in fact been happening gradually from the uncoupling of March 1981 up to that

---

6. This intervention system existed in the snake, and was added to by various provisions which are detailed in *Economie européenne*, 12, July 1982.

Reflation and Austerity

Table 3.7 Change in central rate and actual rate of currencies against the franc for the three devaluations (in %)

	From 2 to 5 October 1981 Central rate	From 2 to 5 October 1981 Actual rate	From 11 to 14 June 1982 Central rate	From 11 to 14 June 1982 Actual rate	From 18 to 22 March 1983 Central rate	From 18 to 22 March 1983 Actual rate
Dutch guilder	+8.5	+5.0	+10.0	+6.2	+6.0	+2.3
Belgian franc	+3.0	+2.6	+5.75	+4.9	+4.0	+3.3
Deutschmark	+8.5	+4.4	+10.0	+6.0	+8.0	+3.4
Lira	0.0	+1.3	+3.0	+4.4	0.0	+3.9
Danish kroner	+3.0	+2.5	+5.75	+4.6	+5.0	+5.0
Irish pound	+3.0	+2.0	+5.75	+4.7	−1.0	−1.0
Dollar/franc	−	+2.1	−	+7.0	−	+3.9
Dollar/Deutschmark	−	−2.3	−	+1.0	−	+0.5
Dollar/ECU	−	+0.6	−	+2.1	−	+1.1

of April 1982 (see Figure 3.8).

On 12 June 1982 also, the franc was devalued by 5.75% and the Deutschmark revalued by 4.25%, giving a 10% revaluation of the central rate of the Deutschmark against that of the franc. The actual revaluation of the Deutschmark between the last day on which the money markets were open before the realignment (11 June) and the reopening of the markets on 14 June was only 6%.

If the notion of a large dramatic devaluation is not strong in the EMS context, it is logically much more so where currencies outside the EMS are concerned. The October 1981 realignment was set off by speculation involving the Deutschmark and the Swiss franc but temporarily ignoring the dollar, which fell against all European currencies during September. The consequence of this realignment was that the dollar rose 2% against the franc and fell 2.3% against the Deutschmark, while its rate in ECUs was virtually unchanged. With the 12 June 1982 adjustment, the dollar rose 7% against the franc and 1% against the Deutschmark. There was a similar effect with the 21 March 1983 realignment, which led to an 8% revaluation of the central rate of the Deutschmark against the franc. Between 18 March and 22 March, the Deutschmark rose by 3.4% and the dollar by 3.9% against the franc.

It is therefore clear that the three parity adjustments did not happen when the dollar was moving in the same direction; it fell against the Deutschmark with the first realignment, and rose slightly with the second and third, reflecting longer-term trends (a continuous rise in the dollar against European currencies, inter-

Unavoidable External Constraints

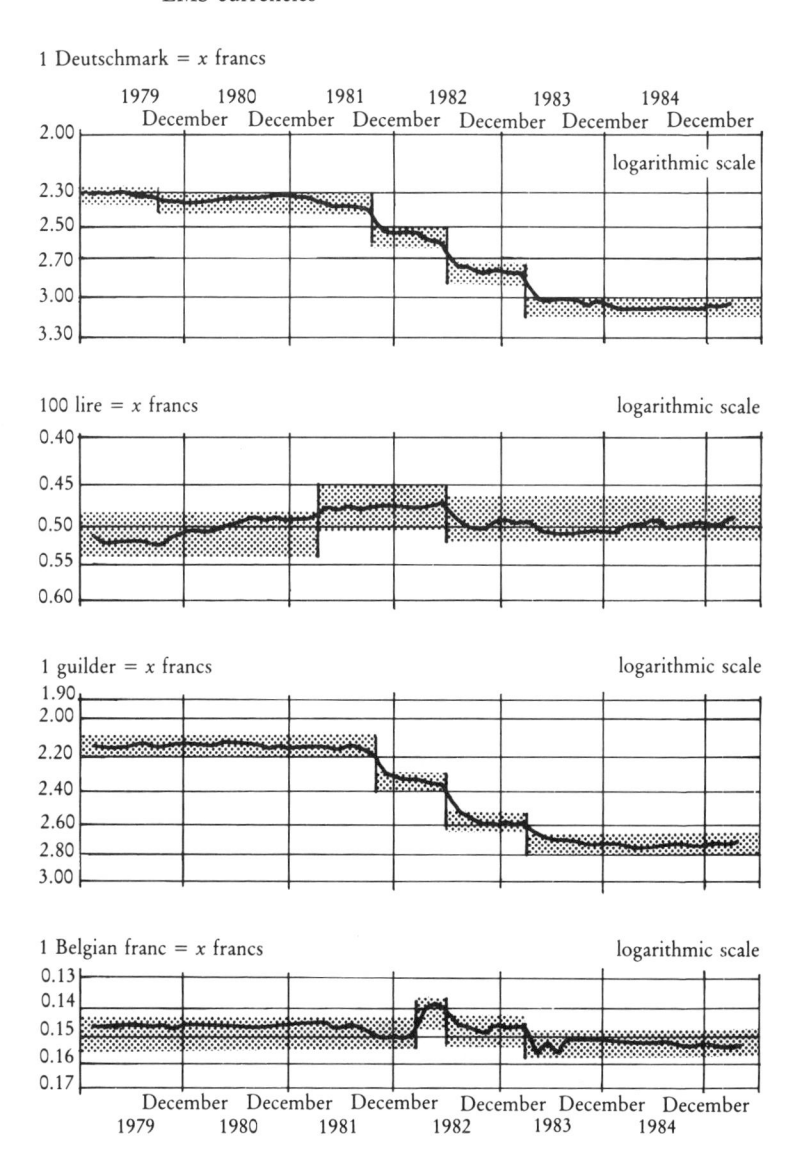

Figure 3.8 Realignments of central rates and exchange rate changes of EMS currencies

rupted by brief periods when it fell). Although it is relatively easy to analyse actual shifts in exchange rates, it is much more difficult to isolate the overall effect of adjustments within the EMS. As far as EMS currencies are concerned, Figure 3.8 shows that over a fairly long period, changes are roughly similar to those of the central rates and that adjustment is a continuous process.

In order to maintain consistency in analysing the impact of 'devaluations' of the franc within the EMS, it will be assumed that the ECU values of these currencies represent their 'true evolution'. In this way, account will be taken, in looking at parity changes, of the effect of the devaluations of the franc as against the ECU on the values of non-EMS currencies.

Parity adjustment and farm prices: compensatory amounts A further point is that the effect of devaluations is totally skewed in the case of agriculture because of the system of monetary compensatory amounts introduced when the franc was devalued in 1969. To prevent a rise in inflation, the French government of the time was reluctant to increase farm prices on the domestic market, even though this would have been the normal effect of a 10% depreciation of the franc as against the European unit of account used to determine common prices. In order to maintain the principle of undifferentiated prices and to stop French products transferring their price advantage to foreign markets, a tax (or negative compensation amount) was put on French exports, equal to the difference between the Community price and the French price, expressed in ECUs. Subsequently, whenever the Deutschmark was revalued, West German farm prices were not lowered by a similar proportion in order to protect farmers' incomes; West German exports to the rest of the Community attracted a positive compensatory amount from the EEC. Compensation payments were a system of subsidizing exports to support domestic prices in countries which revalued (positive MCAs) and of taxing exports to offset the gain in competitivity when domestic prices in countries which devalued dropped below Community prices (negative MCAs); but they completely distorted competition to the advantage of countries with a strong currency. Here, artificially high farm prices became a strong incentive to raise output and produce surpluses. On the other hand, in a country which devalued, the imposition of negative compensatory amounts whereby farm prices did not feel the benefit of devaluation (in other words, the 'green' franc was not devalued) means that domestic producers lose out since their prices in national currency do not rise, whereas they are paying more for imported intermediate goods. The end result is that not only do devaluations not have a competitivity effect, because there are single Community prices, but also, when there is no subsequent devaluation of the 'green' franc, any potential improvement of farmers' profits in domestic currency in fact accrues to the Community and to those countries attracting positive compensatory amounts.

Although they were conceived as a temporary measure to stagger the effect of parity changes on a rise or fall in domestic farm prices, compensatory amounts became, especially during the period of floating exchange rates in the 1970s, a permanent feature sometimes reaching very high levels. In the period after 1971, West Germany had positive compensatory amounts of 5–10%, and France and Italy applied negative compensatory amounts sometimes exceeding 20% (Italy from 1976 to 1979, France in 1977 and 1978). An example would be the intervention price for butter and powdered milk, which at the end of 1983 was 11.8% higher in West Germany and 5% lower in France than what it should have been if the Community price had applied. The gap was made up by a subsidy paid to West German exporters and a tax imposed on French exporters equal to these percentages, after allowing for exemptions.

Compensatory amounts in France were gradually abolished by the Barre government between 1978 and 1981, as one of the advantages of the 'strong franc', but they were later reintroduced because of the three parity adjustments (Figure 3.9). In March 1984, when France occupied the EEC presidency, it was decided to abolish compensatory amounts in three stages. The French figure stood at 10.8% and reductions were envisaged of 3 percentage points from 1 April 1984, 5 points from 1 January 1985 and the remainder (2.8 points) by 1 April 1987 at the latest. The agreement precluded new positive compensatory amounts in the event of currency realignments. Such a reduction in positive compensatory amounts is more difficult in that it involves a reduction of farmers' incomes in the countries concerned. Figure 3.9 shows that the gap between the actual franc/ECU exchange rate and the 'green' exchange rate which had opened up when the franc was devalued within the EMS, disappeared during the course of 1984.

The Macro-economic Impact of the Three Currency Adjustments

In line with the previous approach, a distinction will be made between the impact of parity changes within the EMS and the effect of the depreciation of the franc in relation to the ECU on currencies outside the EMS.

Reflation and Austerity

Figure 3.9 Difference between the franc and the green franc (franc value of the ECU)

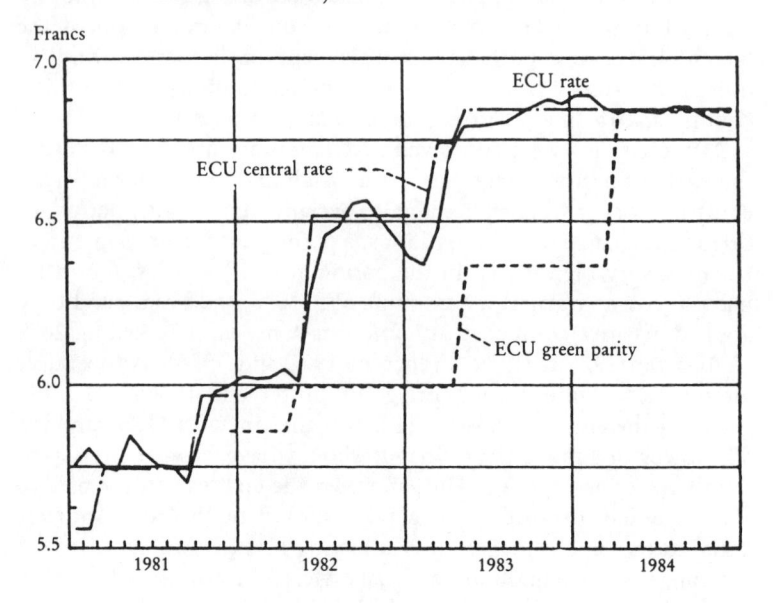

The beneficial effect of the fall in the franc against EMS currencies... Table 3.8 summarizes the effects of parity changes within the EMS. The values given are the percentage differences from a base point which is the situation if parities had remained unaltered since the first quarter of 1981.

The first line of Table 3.8 gives the effective exchange rate of the franc against a basket of the currencies of France's main trading partners. There has been a gradual depreciation of the franc, though three more pronounced breaks correspond to the devaluations – the quarters concerned are shown by an asterisk. Following the three parity adjustments, the effective exchange rate of the franc fell by 8.7%, a depreciation which by the end of 1984 raised import prices by 7% and export prices by 3%. The increase in consumer prices by the end of 1984 was a modest 1.3%, as a result of additions to the annual inflation rate of 0.3% in 1982 and 0.5% in 1983 and 1984.[7]

The way in which indicators developed is a reflection of the importance of competitivity gains from adjustments within the

---

7. The OFCE-quarterly model used in these simulations describes a fairly slow process of imported inflation, in contrast to the OFCE-annual model which gives in the short term an inflation rate twice as high. In the longer term however the two sets of findings are close, as we have seen.

Table 3.8 Macro-economic effect of parity changes in the EMS, ignoring induced effects on non-EMS currencies (% difference in relation to base level)

	1981				1982				1983				1984			
	1	2	3	4*	1	2	3*	4	1	2*	3	4	1	2	3	4
Effective exchange rate	0	−0.5	−0.6	−2.5	−2.7	−3.2	−6.5	−6.4	−6.3	−8.3	−8.2	−8.5	−8.7	−8.7	−8.7	−8.7
Effect on volumes																
GDP	—	—	+0.1	+0.2	+0.3	+0.4	+0.7	+0.9	+1.2	+1.5	+1.8	+2.1	+2.3	+2.6	+2.9	+3.3
Imports	—	—	−0.1	−0.3	−0.4	−0.5	−0.8	−1.1	−1.1	−1.2	−1.3	−1.2	−1.1	−1.0	−0.7	−0.2
Household consumption	—	—	—	—	—	−0.1	−0.1	−0.1	0.0	0.0	0.0	−0.1	−0.1	0.0	+0.1	+0.4
Investment by firms	—	—	—	+0.1	+0.2	+0.4	+0.8	+1.1	+1.5	+2.1	+2.7	+3.2	+4.0	+4.9	+6.0	+7.1
Exports	—	—	+0.1	+0.4	+0.7	+0.9	+1.7	+2.0	+2.5	+3.1	+3.7	+4.1	+4.8	+5.5	+5.8	+6.4
Effect on prices																
Import prices	—	—	+0.4	+1.6	+1.9	+2.3	+4.6	+4.8	+4.9	+6.4	+6.6	+6.9	+6.8	+7.0	+7.1	+7.1
Consumer prices	—	—	—	—	+0.1	+0.1	+0.2	+0.3	+0.4	+0.5	+0.7	+0.8	+1.0	+1.1	+1.2	+1.3
Export prices	—	—	+0.2	+0.5	+0.7	+0.9	+1.6	+1.9	+2.1	+2.5	+2.8	+2.9	+3.0	+3.0	+2.9	+2.9
External balance (billion francs)	—	−0.3	−0.2	−1.1	−0.5	−0.6	−2.4	−0.6	+0.2	−0.2	−2.0	+2.7	+3.9	+5.0	+5.0	+6.0

Source: Simulations by the OFCE quarterly model. The base solution is of parities remaining unchanged since the first quarter of 1981. The differences are given in % in relation to the base, except for the external balance which is in billion francs.

EMS: there was a strong boost to exports; export sales and increases in firms' profits boosted investment; and the resulting growth offset, from 1984, the depressive effect on household consumption of a rise in import prices. The three devaluations arguably therefore increased GDP by 3.3% by the end of 1984, equivalent on average to an extra 1% growth per year since 1982.

The external balance describes a J-curve which is a combination of the curves stemming from the three devaluations. The worsening of the balance had reached one billion francs by the last quarter of 1981, with a recovery until the June 1982 devaluation which caused a new loss of 2.4 billion in the third quarter. This deficit was wiped out and a slight surplus was registered in the first quarter of 1983; a new deficit appeared after the March 1983 devaluation. However, from the following quarter, gains in competitivity from previous devaluations were stronger than the perverse effect of the last devaluation and the surplus grew in the second quarter and throughout 1984 (see Table 3.9).

... was partly offset by its effect on the dollar This recovery was much slower if the impact of devaluations of the franc on non-EMS currencies is also taken into account. Volume of trade was only slightly affected because the depressive effect of devaluations against the dollar is more or less offset by the beneficial effect of devaluations against the pound and the yen. However the increase in inflation and the perverse effect was quite large. The rise in inflation of 0.3% per year was in fact 1% if account is taken of the effect on other currencies. Moreover the external deficit rose significantly during 1982 and 1983. The overall worsening of the balance for goods and services was 6.7 billion francs in the third quarter of 1982 and almost 15 billion for the whole of 1982. It was still 3.5 billion in the second quarter of 1983 as a result of the effects of devaluation on non-EMS currencies. Taking 1983 as a whole, there was a 5 billion improvement in the balance from readjustments within the EMS, but overall the balance was negative because of an 8 billion deficit from effects on non-EMS currencies. The impact was even more unfavourable on the current balance because of the rise in interest rates brought about by the increased cost of entries expressed in foreign currencies and by extra debts incurred as a result of the perverse effect. The net increase in interest charges arising from the devaluations was 5 billion francs in 1983 and 6 billion in 1984. This increase was partly offset by receipts from tourism so that the difference between the balance on goods and services and the current balance is only 2 billion francs in 1982 and 3 billion in 1983.

Table 3.9 Overall effect of currency realignments on inflation and current balance

	1981		1982				1983				1984			
	3	4	1	2	3	4	1	2	3	4	1	2	3	4
Effect on consumer prices (% differences from base)														
– within EMS	–	–	+0.1	+0.1	+0.2	+0.3	+0.4	+0.5	+0.7	+0.8	+1.0	+1.1	+1.2	+1.3
– outside EMS (inc. pound)	–	+0.1	+0.2	+0.2	+0.5	+0.6	+0.6	+0.8	+0.9	+1.0	+1.4	+1.5	+1.6	+1.7
Total:	–	+0.1	+0.3	+0.3	+0.7	+0.9	+1.0	+1.3	+1.6	+1.8	+2.4	+2.6	+2.8	+3.0
Effect on external balance (in billion francs)														
Balance of goods and services	−0.2	−2.6	−2.1	−2.8	−6.7	−3.9	−1.6	−3.5	+0.3	+1.5	+1.5	+5.3	+6.2	+9.0
– within EMS	−0.2	−1.1	−0.5	−0.6	−2.4	−0.6	+0.2	−0.2	+2.0	+2.7	+3.9	+5.0	+5.0	+6.0
– outside EMS (inc. pound)	–	−1.5	−1.6	−2.2	−4.3	−3.3	−1.8	−3.3	−1.7	−1.2	−1.4	+0.3	+1.2	+3.0
Current balance inc. net interest to foreign countries	−0.2	−2.6	−2.3	−3.1	−7.1	−4.8	−2.5	−4.2	−0.7	+0.6	+1.8	+4.8	+6.0	+8.5
	–	–	−0.2	−0.4	−0.5	−1.0	−1.2	−1.2	−1.5	−1.6	−1.6	−1.5	−1.4	−1.3

Source: Simulations by OFCE-quarterly model.

Reflation and Austerity

These simulations are a good illustration of how an external deficit of the size of the one in 1982 cannot be wiped out by exchange rate changes. In fact it was not until the end of 1983 that the balance of trade saw an improvement.

This slowness in the J-curve is partly due to the fact that the three devaluations were so close, which tended to delay the appearance of their beneficial effects. Moreover the devaluations gave quite a strong boost to inflation because raw materials were more expensive and increased competitivity led to increased economic activity. Because price rises tend in the long term to cancel out gains in competitivity, it is vital to combat them by a policy of accommodating measures.

Measures Complementing the Devaluations

The three devaluations were stages in the rethinking of economic policy, leading in less than two years from reflation to austerity. The first occurred when there had been several speculative surges and came shortly after the Autumn 1981 budget confirmed the policy of reflation. The accommodating measures went no further than the partial freezing of certain prices and the suspension of 15 billion francs of government spending. This was a modest adjustment to the original budget and in fact the 15 billion was cancelled to keep the budget within its original limits. In November 1981 the Questiaux plan for financing the social welfare funds was another slight modification of the expansionist policy. In all, changes were very small in view of the difference which became apparent throughout 1982 between reflation in France and austerity elsewhere in Europe.

The second devaluation was the first real step towards a more deflationary policy. The policy measures complementing the devaluation of June 1982 put the fight against inflation as the first priority by introducing a prices and wages freeze which turned out to be very effective. The real turning point however was the March 1983 austerity plan which followed the third devaluation (see Inset 3.2).

June 1982: An Effective Prices and Incomes Freeze

The measures complementing the June 1982 devaluation contained three packages: a prices and incomes freeze, adjustment to VAT rates and the postponement of increases in certain welfare payments.

The prices and incomes freeze All prices and margins at all stages of production and distribution, with the exception of certain agricultural and oil-derived products, were frozen from 11 June to 31 October 1982. The freeze also affected public and private services and margins on imports, and applied to prices net of all taxes except for foodstuffs carrying the reduced rate of VAT.

The remuneration of all employees in the public and private sectors was frozen from 1 June to 31 October 1982, except for increases in the minimum wage,[8] normal promotions within career structures and increases agreed before 11 June. The freeze applied to fees and company dividends paid during 1982 and 1983 were subject to a ceiling.

Changes in VAT rates The standard rate of VAT was raised by 1 percentage point from July 1982 (17.6% to 18.6%) while the reduced rate on foodstuffs was lowered from 7% to 5.5%. This rise in VAT rate could not be passed on during the price freeze; it cost firms about 5 billion francs during 1982, but against this has to be set the reduction in corporation tax introduced in April 1982 which helped firms' overheads to the tune of about 11 billion francs in the following two years. The overall effect on firms' costs of these two measures was nil in 1982 and beneficial in 1983 since VAT rises were passed on to the consumer after the price freeze.

Economy measures in the field of social security The economy measures of 10 billion francs (2 billion of which came from the freezing of pharmaceutical prices and doctors' fees) were intended to limit the deficit arising from the growth in healthcare spending and from the expected fall in contributions (estimated at 4.5 billion francs) as a result of the prices and incomes freeze. The measures involved a postponement of certain benefit increases previously announced and savings in health care spending (hospitalization, drugs, etc.). Insofar as existing plans have been assessed on the basis of their effective implementation and not on spending levels announced *ex ante*, the new measures will be analysed separately from the prices and income freeze.

The impact of the freeze The freeze led to a significant slow-down in the growth of prices (see Figure 3.10) and wages. The price of manufactured goods, which had been rising 1% a month during the

---

8. The increases were partly offset by a 2.2 percentage point reduction in employers' social security contributions.

Inset 3.2

Policies complementing the three currency realignments

	October 1981	June 1982	March 1983
Currency realignments	Deutschmark and guilder revalued by 5.5%, franc and lira devalued by 3%.	Deutschmark and guilder revalued by 4.25%. Lira devalued by 2.75% and franc by 5.75%. In February 1982, Belgian franc had been devalued by 8.5% and Danish kroner by 3%.	Deutschmark revalued by 5.55%, guilder by 3.5%, Danish kroner by 2.5%, Belgian franc by 1.5%. Lira and French franc devalued by 2.5%, Irish pound by 3.5%.
Action on prices	Inflation target: 10% in 1982. Freeze on certain prices of 6 months for services, 3 months for basic foodstuffs. Post-freeze situation to be regulated by agreements. Average increase in public utility prices to be between 8% and 10%. Recommended 8% rise in industrial prices for 1982.	Inflation target: 8% in 1983. General price freeze from 10 June to 30 October, except energy and food. Post-freeze situation to be regulated by government in services and trade, by agreements in industry (commitment to keep rises down).	No change in general thrust of policy applied in second half of 1982. After Summer 1983, announcement of aim of 5% price rise for 1983. Timetable for public utility price rises changed (all concentrated into April 1983). Taxes on energy increased.
Action on incomes	Three recommendations: purchasing power to be maintained overall; reduction of inequalities; more work-sharing. New rules for setting wages tried in the public sector.	Purchasing power to be maintained overall for 1982–3; drive on incomes – rises to be planned on basis of 8% for 1983; recommendations generally accepted in negotiations during wage freeze (July–October 1982).	No change in incomes policy.

Fiscal policy: action on demand	Reserve of 15 billion francs set up in budget for 1982. The Questiaux Plan of 4 November looks for 21 billion savings or new revenue in field of social security.	Twenty billion reserve set up on government spending in 1982; budget deficit fixed at 3% of GDP for 1982 and 1983; 20 billion of extra revenue and spending cuts for social security, a quarter of which is accounted for by disindexation.	Public sector borrowing requirement reduced *ex ante* by 37 billion – 24 billion through cuts and 13 billion through revenue increases, mainly from households. People paying more than 5,000F in tax in 1982 obliged to lend to government 10% of 1982 tax, repayable in 1986 (14 billion); ceiling on 'A' and 'Blue' accounts in government savings bank increased; doubling of amounts able to be deposited in and lent by house purchase savings schemes (5 billion).
Monetary policy	Money supply growth norm (revised upwards in 1981 from 10% to 12%) fixed at 12.5% for 1982.	Money supply growth fixed at 10% for 1983.	Target for money supply increase lowered from 10% to 9%, and tightening of credit.
	Less pressure on the franc means base rate cut from September average of 17.7% to November and December average of 15.5%.	Base rate, raised in March to defend the franc, gradually brought down in second half of 1982 (16% average in June to 13% in December).	Little change in base rate after 1983 devaluation – average of 12.5%. Exchange control tightened.
	Low-interest loans to businesses increased from 17 billion to 22 billion for 1981. 50% increase in research grants by ANVAR.	Low-interest loans raised to 30 billion for 1982.	Low-interest loans raised to 40 billion for 1983.

Source: Jerome Vignon (*Cahiers francais*, October–December 1984, p. 65) and the chronologies of the *Rapports du Conseil National du Credit*.

first half of 1982, increased by only 0.5% to 0.6% a month during the freeze, giving a 2% reduction for the whole year. For services, the rise was only 0.2% a month during the freeze compared with 1% during the first half of the year, but it increased significantly after the freeze.

It is more difficult to assess the effect of the freeze on wages because the significant slow-down in the increase in hourly wage rates in the second half of the year was due partly to the freeze and partly to the end of the system whereby wages remained the same despite a reduction in the working week (it was this which had caused the steep rise in hourly wage rates for the first half of the year). A more detailed examination of the effects of the freeze on disinflation is undertaken in Chapter 5.

The prices freeze put an end to the situation where French inflation was, by the second quarter of 1982, 6% higher than the rate in other countries (see Figure 3.11), and allowed France to keep the gains in competitivity brought about by devaluation (see Figure 3.12).

The Austerity Programme of March 1983

The aim of the March 1983 austerity plan was to reduce overall demand and re-establish equilibrium in the balance of payments within two years. It had three main thrusts: an increase in taxes and other obligatory payments mostly affecting households, a reduction in government spending and various procedures to boost savings and limit the need to buy foreign currency. The principal measures are summarized in Inset 3.3.

New taxes and contributions The two most important measures were the enforced loan of 10% of income or wealth tax for households paying more than 5,000 francs a month in tax, and the 1% surcharge on taxable income, which went to the social security fund.

The enforced loan represented an extra payment of 14 billion francs, equal to 0.5% of the taxable income of households. Its macro-economic effect is difficult to assess because it depends on the way households reacted to it. Though it paid less than investments of the same kind it can nevertheless be classed as saving; as such it could have been merely one among several investment outlets, with no effect on consumption. However, because it was obligatory and because it coincided in June 1983 with the payment of a 1% tax surcharge, it is likely to have been thought of as a 'tax',

Unavoidable External Constraints

Figure 3.10 Monthly change in consumer prices, 1978–84

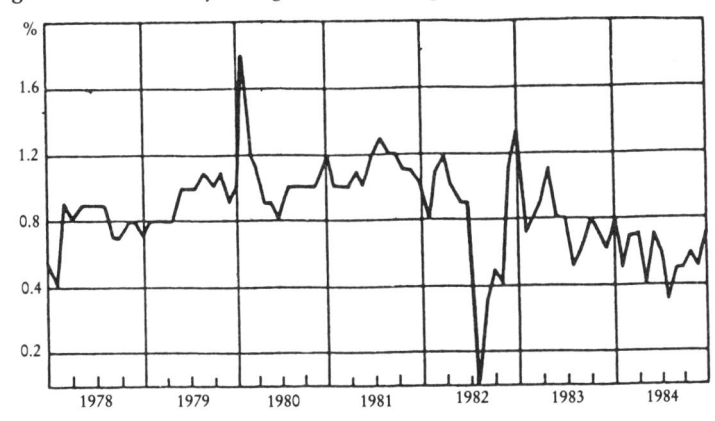

Source: INSEE.

Figure 3.11 Difference between inflation in France and in six main trading partners (consumer prices), 1978–84

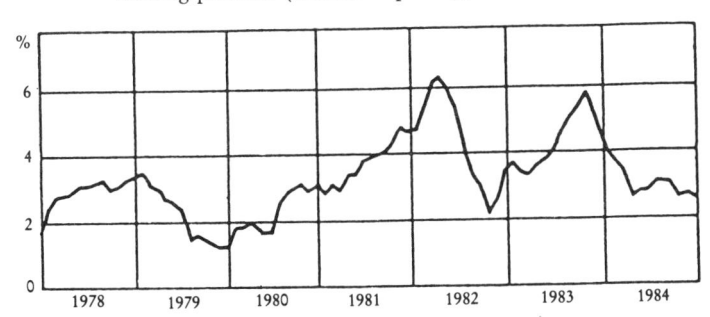

Source: INSEE.

Figure 3.12 Real exchange rate (franc), 1978–84

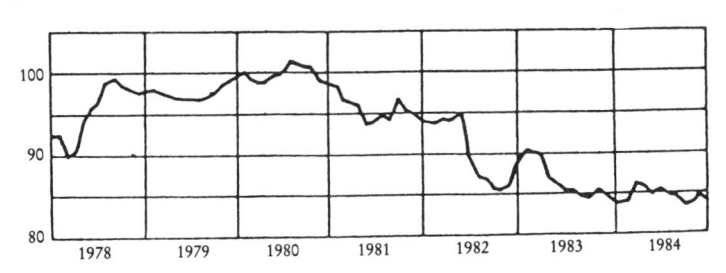

Source: INSEE.
Note (all figures): An increase indicates an improvement in competitivity.

Inset 3.3

The austerity programme of March 1983

	Estimated amount involved in 1983 (billion francs)
New taxes and obligatory payments	
Obligatory loan of 10% of income or wealth tax	14
1% surcharge on taxable income	8
Other measures to correct social security financing	2
Special tax on petroleum products	0.5
Earlier introduction of public utility price rises	2.5
Total:	27
Government and public sector spending cuts	
Cancellation of expenditure reserves	7
Deferment of government spending until 1984	3
Extra cuts in expenditure	5
Reduction in loans to local authorities	2
Savings by large state undertakings	7
Total:	24

Incentives for saving
Increased return on savings for house purchase (9% to 10%)
Doubling of deposits in and loans by savings schemes for house purchase
Increased ceiling for deposits in 'A' and 'Blue' accounts
Setting up of wage-contributory funds for industrial development

Tightening of exchange controls
2,000F per adult per year limit on currency transactions for tourism; use of credit cards abroad limited to business trips
Increase from 10 million to 50 million in authorization ceiling for borrowing from abroad

Source: Appendices to 38th *Rapport du Conseil National du Crédit*, p. 41 and *Chronique de conjoncture de l'INSEE*, February 1984, p. 18.

and to have had an effect on consumption.[9] In our simulation, it was assumed that one-third of the loan was a substitute for other forms of savings and two-thirds had, as far as the split between consumption and savings was concerned, the same effect as an extra tax.

The 1% surcharge on taxable income, which was renewable, was intended to finance on a permanent basis an equalization fund for the social security schemes; it was deducted at source in proportion to each income bracket. Though it was kept for 1984, in 1985 it was abolished as part of the policy of tax reductions (see Chapter 5). The total amount of 11 billion francs originally expected for 1983 turned out to be only 8 billion because of various exemptions.

The tax on spirits came into effect on 1 April and the 25% tax on tobacco on 1 July.[10] These measures, intended to fund social security, were complemented by a hospital charge of twenty francs per day introduced by the Bérégovoy Plan of November 1982. The total extra revenue was supposed to be 2 billion francs. The yield from the special tax on oil-derived products was significantly reduced by the rise in the dollar. It was introduced to prevent the oil price fall working through into the French market, but according to INSEE estimates it yielded only 0.6 billion francs instead of the 3 billion expected.

Bringing forward the introduction of price rises in public services and utilities – electricity and gas prices, railway fares and telephone charges went up by 8% on 1 April – brought in 2.5 billion francs extra revenue.

Spending cuts Reductions were effected in the spending of the big state concerns (7 billion francs) and in government spending where a cut of 15 billion in the budget deficit was obtained by cancelling 7 billion of the 20 billion put into the budget regulation fund set up in February 1983, by postponing spending plans involving 3 billion and by other budget savings amounting to 5 billion francs.

The quantification of the macro-economic impact of the austerity plan takes account only of reductions which can be pinpointed sufficiently to form part of the simulation, i.e. cuts of about 18 billion francs.

The other provisions of the package of accommodating measures These were principally concerned with boosting savings. Interest on

---

9. *Chronique de conjoncture de l'INSEE*, February 1984.
10. This was later abolished when the EEC Commission declared it in breach of Community regulations.

savings schemes for housing loans went up from 9% to 10%, and there was a doubling of the investment and loan limits associated with such schemes. Upper limits on investment in 'A' and 'Blue' savings accounts were raised and schemes for investing part of income in industrial development were introduced. Further provisions were that the money supply growth norm went down from 10% to 9%, exchange controls were strengthened by a foreign spending limit for French tourists of 2,000 francs per adult per year (plus 1,000 francs per trip), and the time during which foreign currency could be bought for a future international trade deal was reduced from three months to one week. At the same time, in an effort to help exporting firms and the balance of payments, the threshold for authorization of foreign loans was raised from 10 billion to 50 billion francs. Except for the interest rate increase on savings schemes for housing loans, the measures just mentioned have not been included in the simulation, and therefore there is a slight underestimate of the overall effect of the austerity plan.

The impact of the austerity programme This is summarized in Table 3.10. Apart from the enforced loan and the postponement of budget spending, all the measures were kept in the simulation for 1984 and subsequent measures were ignored, in order to gauge the impact of the plan not only on the year in question but also on the period afterwards. Fiscal policy for 1984 and 1985 is analysed in greater detail in Chapter 5.

The increase in taxes and other obligatory payments mainly affects household consumption and indirectly, through the reduction in market outlets, investment by firms. The increase in obligatory payments and the reduction in spending had more or less the same impact on economic growth, giving a combined reduction of 0.6% in 1983 and 0.4% in 1984. The fall in the external deficit brought about by the March 1983 budgetary measures was 12 billion francs in 1983 and 22 billion in 1984. A final point is that the slightly inflationary impact of the rise in public utility prices was very broadly offset by the policy of keeping down wage rises, which is not included in this simulation (see Chapter 5).

Devaluations are no Substitute for Economic Austerity

Among left-wing economists there has always been an underlying debate about how far one can break free of external economic constraints by a bolder exchange rate policy (some urge floating

Table 3.10 Impact of the March 1983 austerity plan

Impact on:	Increase in taxes and obligatory payments 1983	1984	Expenditure cuts 1983	1984	Total 1983	1984
Annual growth rate (%)						
Real GDP	−0.3	−0.2	−0.3	−0.2	−0.6	−0.4
Household consumption (volume)	−0.4	−0.3	−0.1	−0.1	−0.5	−0.4
Total investment (volume)	−0.3	−0.4	−1.5	−0.3	−1.8	−0.7
Consumer prices	0.2	0.1	0	0.1	0.2	0.2
Levels						
Employment (thousands)	−16	−34	−27	−46	−43	−80
Unemployment (thousands)	8	19	13	21	21	40
General government net lending (billion francs)	15*	13	12	17	27	30
Trade balance (billion francs)	4	10	8	12	12	22

*The enforced loan makes no difference to the surpluses of government departments in terms of national income accounting because it is a financial operation.

rates, others a competitive devaluation after leaving the EMS), and even by a policy of economic self-sufficiency. The irony is that this debate came to the surface in government circles at the very time that the government's freedom of action was most restricted, that is, just before the third devaluation. To have left the EMS and devalued competitively in May 1981 would certainly have entailed risks but would have had some advantages and would have been facilitated by the reserves then available. Such a policy however was much riskier at the beginning of 1983, given accumulated debt and a weaker currency reserve position. The fundamental point stemming from all these analyses is that economic austerity was inevitable in the international context which the Mauroy government had to face.

The trade deficit worsened by 40 billion francs in 1982 and improved by 50 billion in 1983. What part did the various factors play in these developments? The freedom of action available within economic policy can be illustrated by reference to two complementary analyses. The first uses the findings of a total model to focus on the impact of economic policy in isolation from that of the international environment; the second concentrates exclusively on external

Table 3.11 Comparison of the effect of the international situation and economic policy on changes in the trade balance in 1982 and 1983 (in billion francs)

	From 1981 to 1982	From 1982 to 1983
Previous year's balance	−54	−100
Impact as compared with previous year:		
– of the international situation (dollar, raw materials, world demand)	−23	+15
– of domestic policy, respectively:	−16	+8
1981–82 reflation	(−18)	(−13)
restrictive policies of June and November 1982, March 1983	(+2)	(+21)
– of the devaluations	−12	+11
– other factors	+5	+18
Following year's balance	−100	−48

trade relations to highlight the respective effect of competitivity and cyclical gap.

From the 46 Billion Franc Deterioration in 1982 to the 52 Billion Improvement in 1983

By using the same simulations as before, we can begin to explain the worsening of the external balance in 1982 and the recovery in 1983 (see Table 3.11). The deterioration in 1982 was 46 billion francs (a 54-billion deficit in 1981 increased to 100 billion in 1982), to which the international environment contributed 23 billion (the rise in the dollar and the drop in world demand were partly offset by cheaper oil and raw materials), domestic policy contributed 16 billion, and the devaluations 12 billion. Factors not taken into account, particularly the saving of energy, accounted for an improvement of 5 billion. The worsening of the deficit in 1982 therefore was caused half by the international situation and half by domestic reflation. The same division of responsibility can be seen for 1983, but of course with the opposite effect, since the deficit improved by 52 billion over 1982. The international environment contributed 15 billion (the effect of the recovery was stronger than that of the rise in the dollar), domestic policy contributed 8 billion (the retrenchment policies of June 1982, November 1982 and March 1983 cancelled out any remaining adverse effect of the reflation measures), and the devaluations contributed 11 billion – the impact of the devaluations on the external balance in 1983 was a negative one (minus 3 billion francs), but it had been minus 14 billion in 1982, so the improvement over the previous year was 11 billion. Cyclical factors helped to improve the 1983 trade balance, in particular a very favourable balance of agro-food produce and a considerable reduction in stocks of oil-derived products – which is why the figures in Table 3.11 under 'other factors' are so significant.

The inability of parity changes to cancel out deficits of the size of the one in recent years is basically caused by the fact that the volume of foreign trade is much more sensitive to income and demand changes than it is to price changes. Even in the industrial sector where price competition is traditionally strong, changes in competitivity have not been enough to offset the effect of cyclical gap.

Competitivity Effects Not Enough to Offset Cyclical Gap

We saw at the beginning of this chapter that the worsening of the 1982 deficit was brought about partly by the rise in the dollar but even more by the significant deterioration of trade in industrial goods. The relationships used in the OFCE-quarterly model to determine the volume of foreign trade will allow an analysis at a sub-annual level of the part played in this deterioration respectively by the ways in which foreign and domestic demand, tensions on capacity and competitivity developed.

Modelling these relationships is a way of assessing the effect of competitivity and cyclical gap on the development of industrial trade in 1981 and 1982. The cyclical gap is apparent in the reversal of the 'demand' effects and the stresses of mid-1981 to Autumn 1982 (see Table 3.12).

During the first half of 1981, the start of world economic recovery and the effects of the restrictive policy applied in 1980 (the Barre reflation came too late to have a significant influence on the overall economic situation in the first half of 1981) brought about a steep rise in exports and a fall in the volume of imports. The rise in exports was the result of a favourable trend in the three factors previously looked at: world recovery contributed 2.7%; the contraction of the domestic market in relation to capacities of production and the pressure of foreign demand contributed 1.7%;[11] and the improvement in France's competitivity compared with the

---

11. Capacity utilization rates abroad are included in the formula for determining exports.

Table 3.12 Part played by the main factors in industrial trade volume changes between 1981 and 1983

	% change over the period, on previous period		
	1st half of 1981 (2 quarters)	2nd quarter of 1981 to 3rd quarter of 1982 (5 quarters)	3rd quarter of 1982 to 4th quarter of 1983 (5 quarters)
Volume of exports (actual)	+5.5	−3.6	+8.3
(simulated)	+5.3	−4.8	+11.8
broken down into:			
– world demand	+2.7	−4.2	+7.9
– tensions	+1.7	−3.2	+1.9
– competitivity	+0.9	+2.6	+2.0
Volume of imports (actual)	−2.0	+12.4	−0.7
(simulated)	−2.6	+12.6	−0.6
of which:			
– domestic demand	−3.6	+6.5	−0.7
– tensions	−1.2	+2.0	−1.1
– competitivity	+0.4	−0.3	−2.8
– trend	+1.8	+4.4	+4.0

Note: Because of the interpenetration of economies, the growth of imports outstrips, over a long period of time, that of domestic demand. This gradual opening of frontiers is represented by a trend which appears only in the case of imports. For exports, the opening of frontiers is already taken into account in the demand indicator, which is a weighting of the imports of France's trading partners.

Sources: For data – INSEE quarterly accounts; and simulations of external trade formulae by OFCE-quarterly model. The equations are given in the article by R. Topol and M.-A. Boudier in *Observations et diagnostics économiques*, 5, October 1983.

average of her trading partners contributed 0.9%. This improvement was the result of the steep rise in the dollar, the pound and the yen since the middle of 1980 (delays in reacting are relatively long) which had a greater effect than losses of competitivity in relation to France's EMS partners.

The fall in imports, which at 2% was not very great, was caused essentially by the fall in domestic demand and the increase in surplus productive capacities, at a time when competitivity remained unchanged.

During the second half of 1981, the world economy sank into the 'monetarist' recession, whereas French reflation stimulated domestic demand. Imports went down by 3.6%, and the effect of the drop in world demand and the pressure of domestic demand was by and large greater than increased competitivity from a continuing rise in the dollar and the first two devaluations. Imports increased in volume by more than 12% under the influence of an increase in domestic demand (6.5%), stresses on capacity (2%), and the increasing interpenetration of economies (4.4%). Increases in competitivity were however, once again, not big enough to offset volume effects, and counted for minus 0.3%.

The respective influence of the cyclical disparity and increased competitivity can easily be summarized: from the second quarter of 1981 to the third quarter of 1982, the drop in exports and the rise in imports represented for the industrial sector a deterioration of the situation (in the sense of extra to the development due to the interpenetration of economies) of about 48 billion francs. The cyclical gap represented by differential developments in foreign and domestic demand and utilization rates caused a deficit of 60 billion francs, while increased competitivity from the two devaluations of October 1981 and June 1982 and the rise in the dollar was limited to 12 billion francs over this period. These two figures are a good illustration of the inability of parity changes to ensure, over a period of time, higher growth than France's partners.

The improvement in foreign trade which began in the third quarter of 1982 and continued right through 1983 and 1984 came from favourable trends in all the factors: recovery abroad, stabilization of domestic demand and increased competitivity. The growth of exports was nevertheless rather smaller than should have been the case when all factors were taken together.

External balances were highly sensitive to changes in domestic and foreign demand and this can be illustrated by putting on the same graph the import/export cover rate in France and her main trading partners (the solid line in Figure 3.13) and the comparison of domestic demand in France and her trading partners (the dotted line). The deterioration in 1982 and then the recovery in 1983 are clearly apparent. The way each element of the external balance developed is summarized in Table 3.13 and shows that the worsening of the deficit in 1982 was particularly significant in the case of industrialized countries – the deficit with EEC countries went up by 33 billion francs and with the rest of OECD countries by 15 billion. Even though subsequently the position improved in the case of OECD countries and particularly with the United States because of the US economic recovery and increased competitivity from the rise in the dollar, the deficit with France's EEC partners remained

Reflation and Austerity

Figure 3.13 Cover rate and cyclical gap in relation to France's main trading partners, 1978–83

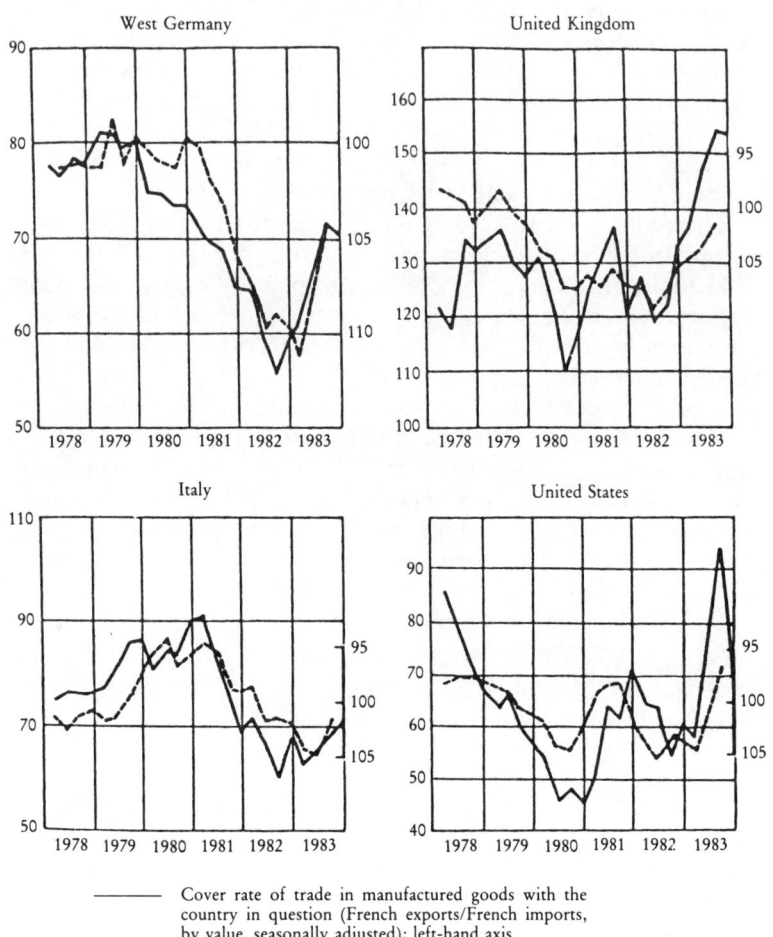

——— Cover rate of trade in manufactured goods with the country in question (French exports/French imports, by value, seasonally adjusted); left-hand axis

--------- Difference in demand (French domestic demand/foreign demand, by volume, seasonally adjusted); right-hand axis

Note: The axis of the difference in demand for goods and services is doubled to take account of the industrial trade volume elasticity, which is about 2. Moreover, both axes cover different numerical ranges depending on the country because of structural differences from the cover rate. The analysis is limited to major countries with quarterly national income accounts.
Source: *Rapport sur les Comptes de la Nation de l'année 1983*, p. 109.

Table 3.13 Changes in trade balances by groups of countries

	1981	1982	1983	1984	Changes 1981–2	1982–3	1983–4
Balance of goods and services (national income accounting)	−54	−100	−48	−16	−46	+52	+32
Customs balance (cif–fob), excluding military equipment	−105	−151	−105	−90	−46	+46	+15
of which: EEC (10 states)	−31	−64	−57	−57	−33	+7	0
OECD excluding EEC	−29	−44	−33	−19	−15	+11	+14
OPEC	−62	−57	−38	−25	+5	+19	+13

Source: See Note to Table 3.3.

relatively high. The recovery in the overall balance in 1983 and 1984 was largely based on the reduction of the deficit with oil-producing countries which went down by a half between 1982 and 1984.

The persistence of a significant deficit with industrialized countries is evidence of the fragile nature of French external trade which is highlighted by structural studies.

Structural Weaknesses

A detailed examination by INSEE of trade in industrial goods highlights certain structural weaknesses in the pattern of France's foreign trade.[12] Using a breakdown into 600 products, the analysis picked out from among 300 industrial and food products ninety 'strong point' sectors which were well in surplus in foreign trade terms and ninety-seven 'weak point' sectors which were heavily in deficit. One particular characteristic of France's industrial structure was readily apparent: whereas the specialization of France's main competitors is often highly concentrated, French ones are spread widely – there are strong and weak points in each of the twenty industrial branches of 'level 40' of the nomenclature of industrial activities. Moreover the strong points are generally where there are large industrial groups firmly entrenched on a world scale. Conversely, the weak points are in small and medium firms which are often very numerous. An example is in engineering, where the

12. M. Delattre, 'Points forts et points faibles du commerce extérieur industriel' (Strengths and weaknesses of foreign trade in industrial goods), *Economie et statistique*, 157, July–August 1983.

weakest point, the machine tools sector, has 174 firms employing more than twenty people, the four biggest of which account for only 21% of the turnover.

The differences in trade patterns at the world level (surplus with the developing countries and the Eastern bloc, deficit with industrialized countries) are reflected in several of the ninety-seven stronger sectors. In eighty-three of these the trade balance with developed countries is either in slight surplus or even in deficit, but with EEC countries the cover rate is 80% for one product in two and less than 50% for one product in four.

A comparison of productivity and competitivity levels in France and the big industrialized countries confirms the absence of large poles of competitivity. Philippe Guinchard's study of five big industrialized countries shows that France is the country which has the narrowest structure of comparative advantages.[13]

Conversely, Japan's surpluses are concentrated on a small number of products: steel, engineering goods, engineering construction, electrical and electronic goods. Here Japan is highly competitive in relation to other sectors and to other countries, which gives her a comparative advantage in these sectors. The optimum exchange rate policy for Japan therefore is one based on a permanently undervalued currency which means the export sector has a high price competitivity.

West Germany has a trade surplus in industrial goods which is mainly the result of its reputation for producing quality goods, even though it has no comparative advantage in industrial productivity. This situation is compatible with an overvalued currency which means that a modest growth in volume of exports is compensated by gains in the terms of trade.

France has neither the comparative advantages of Japan nor the firm export sector of West Germany. Price competitivity is sufficiently important for her not to be able to afford over a long period an overvalued currency, as the foregoing analysis has shown. But the comparative advantages of the export sector are not such that she can substantially benefit from a currency which is seriously undervalued. The findings of structural studies therefore reinforce macro-economic analyses in confirming the need for, but also the limitations of, exchange rate policies.[14]

13. 'Productivité et compétitivité comparées des grands pays industriels' (Comparative productivity and competitivity in the major industrial countries), *Economie et statistique*, 162, January 1984.
14. See also the analysis of M. d'Aglietta, A. Orléan and G. Oudiz, 'L'industrie française face aux contraintes de change' (French industry and exchange rate constraints), *Economie et statistique*, 119, February 1980.

Figure 3.14 Balance on current account as % of GDP

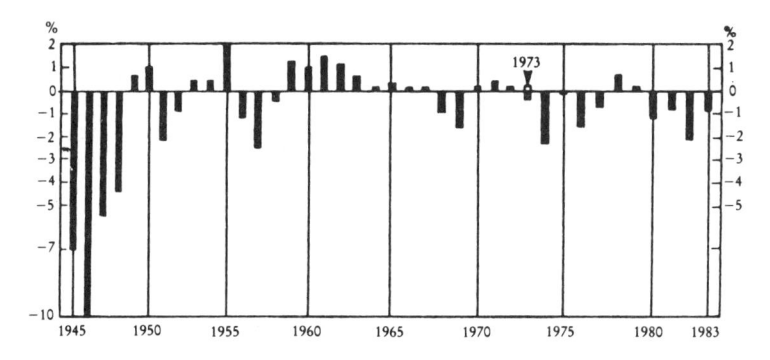

Source: E. Barbier-Jeanneney and J.-M. Jeanneney, *Les économies occidentales du XIXe siècle à nos jours* (Western economies from the nineteenth century to modern times), Paris, Presses de la Fondation Nationale des Sciences Politiques, 1985. The old sets of figures ended in 1973, and a new series began: in the old series, the current balance for 1973 is in surplus (0.4% of GDP); in the new one, it is in deficit (0.4% of GDP).

Devaluations and Economic Austerity: An Assessment of the Experiences of 1958 and 1969

The slowness with which the external balance was brought back into equilibrium by the three exchange rate adjustments contrasts with the apparent ease with which the deficit was wiped out by the 1958 and 1969 devaluations (see Figure 3.14). Allusion has already been made to the reasons that post-oil shock parity adjustments were less effective – the perverse effect from increased energy costs and the difficulty of competitive devaluations when currencies are tied together. However, another look at the 'successful' devaluations of 1958 and 1969 is interesting because it shows that on these occasions the recovery of foreign trade was brought about not only by increased competitivity but also by the gap between the restrictive policies which were the necessary adjunct of the devaluations and growth in other countries. As will be seen in the next section, the Swedish experience in 1982 led to similar conclusions.

For the purposes of the present analysis, use will be made as in the previous section of foreign trade equations, with separate consideration of the role of demand, tensions and competitivity, and estimated for the 1950–79 period for the whole of goods and services and not just the industrial sector. The findings shown in Figure 3.15 make possible the detailed analysis of fluctuations in volume of foreign trade according to their trend in the light of the three factors of demand, tensions and competitivity. It is competitivity which is the main influence on exports: export competitivity was in continuous decline from the devaluations at the end of the 1940s to those of 1957–8. The recovery after the 1958 devaluation lasted longer because of the relative stability of prices, but the worsening of the current balance in 1968 and the ensuing speculation made necessary a further devaluation which happened at a time of recovery in world demand. It brought a steep growth in exports and increased competitivity which helped to maintain this growth during the recession of 1971–2. Subsequently, during the periods when the franc was floating, between January 1974 and July 1975, and between March 1976 and the setting up of the EMS at the beginning of 1979, competitivity did not improve despite a significant depreciation of the franc.

Figure 3.15 shows that increased competitivity was not the only factor in the 1959 and 1970 recoveries – a decrease in domestic demand in 1958–9 and growth in other countries in 1969 were other important factors. The role played by the gap between restrictive domestic policy and recovery abroad, in the spectacular recovery which followed the December 1958 devaluation, has frequently been emphasized.[15] In contrast to the disguised devaluation which preceded it (the 20% operation of August 1957) the December 1958 devaluation brought about effective increases in competitivity. The August 1957 operation was a 20% levy on the sale of foreign currency and a payment of the same amount on purchases; this went on until the actual devaluation in June 1958 confirmed this disguised devaluation. This 20% depreciation of the franc was almost completely offset by the rise in domestic prices (16% from the first half of 1957 to the first half of 1958) and the partial abolition of export subsidies, so that over the same period the franc price of exports rose by 18%, giving a reduction of only 2% in currency terms. Conversely, most of the 14.9% devaluation of the franc in December 1958 was passed on to export prices which fell in currency terms by 8% in 1959.

The recovery of foreign trade however was helped by the restrictive policy introduced at the end of 1957 and reinforced by the

---

15. Cf. for example, the *Rapport sur les comptes de la nation* (Report on the national accounts) for 1959, where the term 'cyclical lag' appears several times.

Unavoidable External Constraints

Figure 3.15 Factors explaining changes in external trade from 1950 to 1979

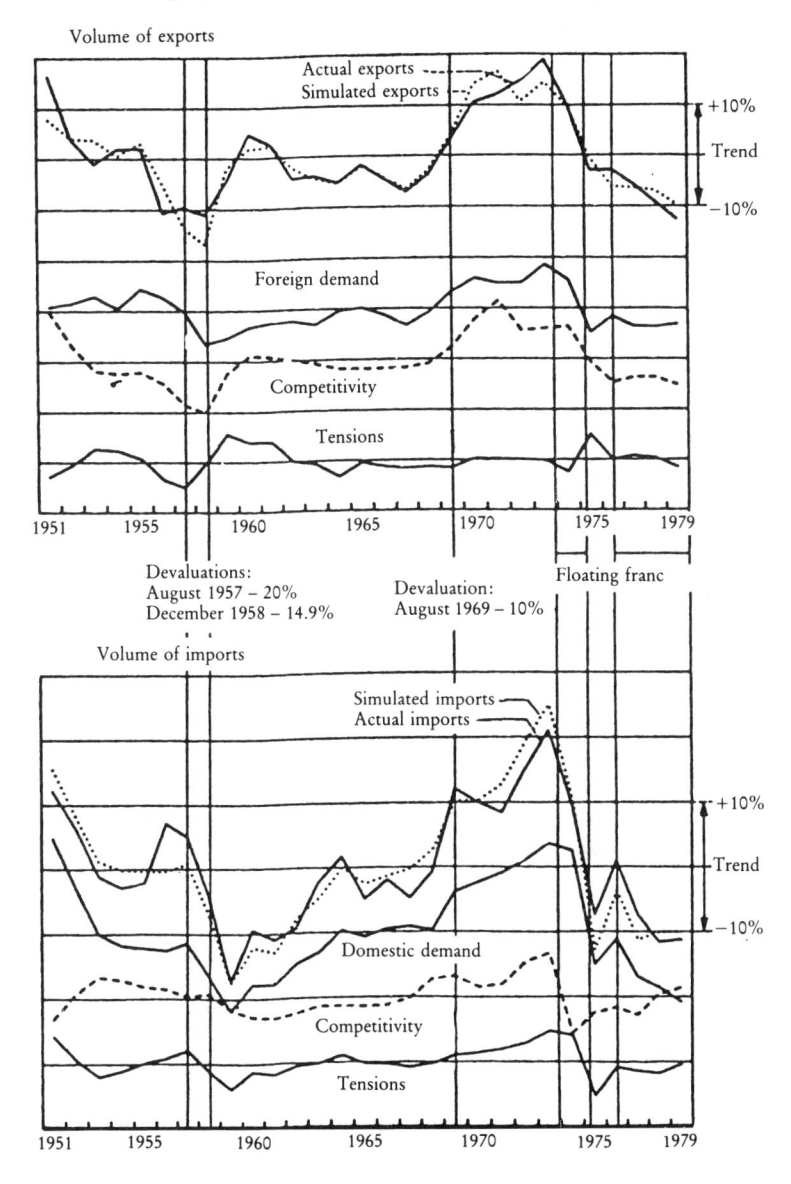

Source: F. Fournelle, P.-A. Muet and P. Villa, 'Le commerce extérieur en France depuis 1950' (External trade in France since 1950), *Annales de l'INSEE*, 49, January–March 1983.

Table 3.14 The recovery of external trade in 1959, 1970 and 1983 (% rate of change)

	Total trade in goods and services (annual average)				Trade in industrial goods (change over previous year)
	1958	1959	1969	1970	From 1983 (1st quarter) to 1984 (1st quarter)
Export cover rate by volume					
Actual	+8	+20	−6	+9.5	+13
Simulated	+5	+25	−1	+9.5	+18
Impact of world and domestic demand	−1	+7	−2	+1.5	+10
Impact of tensions	+8	+8	−2	+1.5	+4
Impact of competitivity	−2	+10	+3	+6.5	+4

Source: For total trade in goods and services – simulations by the Fournelle, Muet and Villa model. The equations used for these simulations are given in 'Le commerce extérieur en France depuis 1950' (External trade in France since 1950), *Annales de l'INSEE*, 49, January–March 1983, pp. 76–9. The statistics are given in the appendix to CEPREMAP working paper no. 8124. For trade in industrial goods – simulations by OFCE-quarterly model.

stabilization plan which accompanied the December 1958 devaluation. Table 3.14 details the respective influence of these factors in the recovery which took place. In 1958 the improvement came about essentially because a fall in domestic demand in relation to productive capacity boosted exports and reduced imports. This recovery became much stronger in 1959 as the world economy recovered, as domestic demand marked time, and as significant improvements in competitivity were made (10% over the previous year).

World economic revival was also a factor in the 1970 improvement in the external position, but this was less marked than in 1959 because the August 1969 devaluation occurred at a time of overheating of the economy which was only rectified in 1970 when the effects of economic measures connected with the devaluation brought the growth of domestic demand down to below that of demand from abroad.

There are several similarities between the 1982–3 case and these previous cases. In particular, the recovery was effective only when increased competitivity coincided with economic revival in other countries and the moderation of domestic demand (1959, 1970 and 1983); but whereas increased competitivity accounted for about half of the 1959 recovery and more than two-thirds of the 1970 one, it constituted only one quarter of the favourable effect in the year after the March 1983 devaluation. However, if it had not been for the rise in the dollar which added greatly to the cost of oil despite a significant reduction in the amount imported, the policy of economic austerity combined with the devaluation would have been enough to bring foreign trade back into balance by mid-1984.

Competitive Devaluation and Complementary Economic Measures: The Swedish Experience of October 1982

Should there have been one earlier and larger devaluation to restore competitivity quickly instead of achieving it gradually through three devaluations made necessary by speculation? The answer seemed fairly clear to socialist governments which came to power after the French one in 1981. In December 1982, the Spanish Prime Minister, Felipe Gonzalez, devalued the peseta by 8% as soon as he came to power, after announcing a policy of 'effort and austerity'. This had been preceded some months earlier by Olof Palme who marked his return to power by a 16% devaluation of the kroner and a concomitant policy of boosting the economy by budgetary means and holding down wage rises.

The Spanish devaluation was not so much a competitive devaluation as a psychological measure intended to counter speculation in anticipation of a fall in the peseta and to break the depreciation–inflation cycle of the Spanish economy. It brought a partial restoration of competitivity which had worsened considerably since 1978 (see Figure 3.16). On the other hand, the 16% devaluation of the Swedish kroner in October 1982, coming after a 10% devaluation by the previous government in September 1981 heralded a high level of competitivity unprecedented in the previous ten years.

The undoubted success of the Swedish government's policy was the result of a combination of favourable factors.[16] Since increased competitivity came just as world economic recovery was under way, exports to markets experiencing strong growth were boosted – the United States, the United Kingdom and West Germany took

---

16. For a detailed analysis, see, for example, the article by H. Monet, 'La politique sociale-démocrate de la Suède' (Sweden's social-democratic policy), *Les Cahiers Français*, 218, October–December 1984.

Reflation and Austerity

Figure 3.16 Indicator of real exchange rate against the Deutschmark

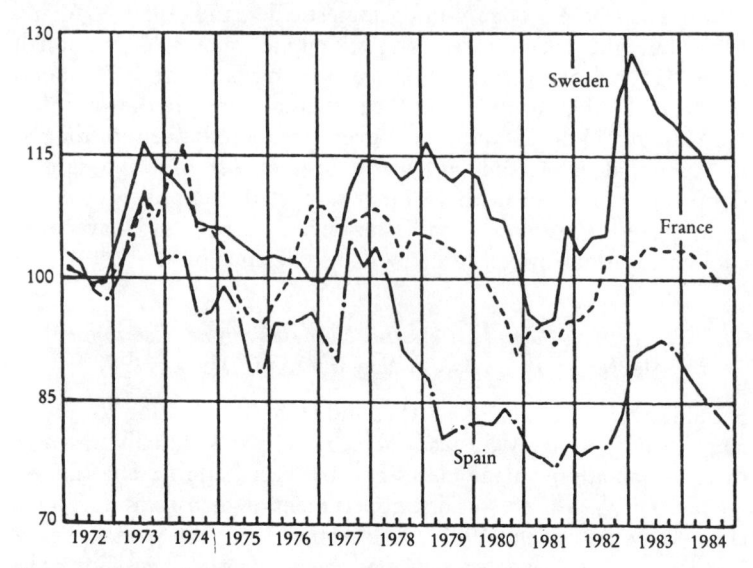

Note: An increase indicates an improvement in competitivity.
Source: Exchange rate corrected by relative consumer prices, OECD. The diagram is taken from the OFCE's report on the international economic situation *Observations et diagnostics économiques*, April 1985.

30% of Swedish exports. Moreover since European countries' external constraints were loosened by world recovery, the Swedish devaluation was not cancelled out by a chain reaction of devaluations by her main competitors. Sweden has a specialized pattern of production in high technology goods, and at the time of devaluation there was considerable productive capacity to respond quickly to a rapid rise in demand. A final point is that a policy of holding down wage rises meant that the inflationary impact of the devaluation was limited and firms' profitability was enormously improved.

The current balance recovered rapidly and was back in equilibrium after a short J-curve (see Figure 3.17);[17] in particular, the balance in goods and services began a long period of surplus from mid-1983. Industrial production experienced an exceptionally strong growth (see Figure 3.18), and was in the main export-led.

In all three countries, the recovery in the current payments position came about through a combination of increased competi-

---

17. The favourable effects of the 1981 devaluation partly offset the perverse effects of the 1982 one.

Unavoidable External Constraints

Figure 3.17 Balance on current account as % of GDP (Sweden, Spain and France)

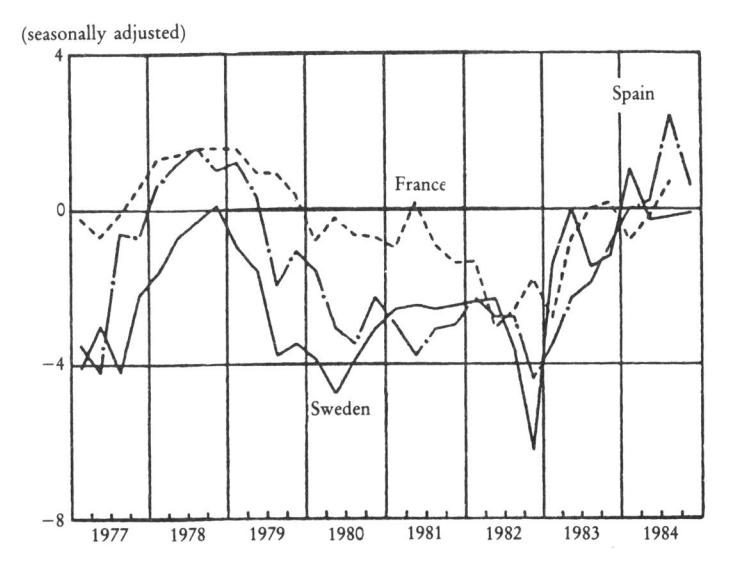

Sources: OECD and IMF.

Figure 3.18 Industrial production (Sweden, Spain and France)

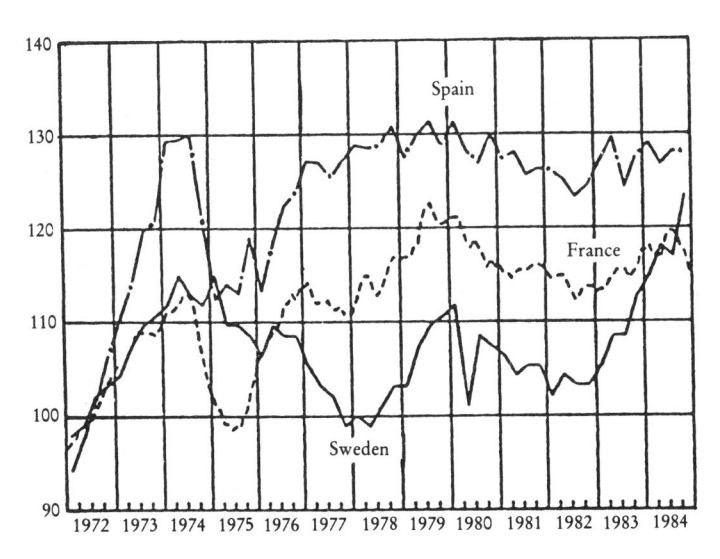

Sources: OECD and IMF.

tivity (though this was modest in France and Spain) and the gap between world recovery and a weak level of domestic demand. The Socialists in France had the misfortune, compared to their Spanish and Swedish colleagues, of coming to power one year too soon, though it is true that the extent and rapidity of the Swedish recovery was a function of a devaluation which was competitive and aggressive, features which were lacking in the Spanish devaluation and the three devaluations of the franc.

Foreign Debt and Financing the External Deficit

The equilibrium position of the balance of payments does not just depend on foreign trade. In a highly speculative world situation where a considerable mass of floating capital moves from one money market to another in search of capital gains or high interest rates, capital movements are strongly influenced in the short term (and sometimes in the long term) by exchange rates or in the case of fixed parities by currency holdings. An analysis of how the external deficit is financed shows however that the Socialist government, unlike the Americans, could not really hope to finance a foreign exchange deficit over a long period by capital inflows.

Financing the External Deficit

Table 3.15 gives details of France's balance of payments over the last few years, and shows how the deficit in goods and services, transfers and capital movements was financed. Since the first oil shock and the appearance of persistent deficits in the balance of current transactions, the financing of this deficit has been through mounting long-term debt incurred not only by government, but also by the banking sector and the big state undertakings. In the balance of payments, this net flow of debt authorized by the Treasury and guaranteed by the State is counted as a long-term capital movement, which means that the total of capital flows and the balance of current transactions gives only a partial view of the extent of the deficit which has to be financed. For this reason, in Table 3.15 'spontaneous' movements of capital have been separated from authorized borrowing which is shown as one of the components in the financing operation.

The total deficit on current account (line 1) and spontaneous movements of capital (authorized borrowing excepted – line 2) is the sum which has to be financed (line 3) either by long-term

Table 3.15 France's balance of payments[1], 1980–6

	1980	1981	1982	1983	1984	1985	1986
(1) *Current transactions*	−18	−26	−79	−36	−7	−3	+20
− external trade	−57	−55	−102	−63	−36	−48	−13
− services	+41	+38	+46	+60	+65	+83	+74
− capital revenues[2]	+16	+14	+7	−4	−11	−14	−11
− transfers	−18	−23	−30	−29	−25	−24	−30
(2) *'Spontaneous movements of capital*[3]	+28	−37	−33	−7	−2	+10	+40
− long-term[3]	−24	−55	−54	−45	−24	−22	−35
− short-term, private and banking sector[4]	+52	+18	+21	+38	+22	+32	+75
(3) *Balance of current transactions and 'spontaneous' movements of capital* (3)=(1)+(2)	+10	−63	−112	−43	−9	+7	+60
(4) *Authorised net medium- and long-term borrowing*	+18	+34	+79	+88	+36	+13	−48
(5) *Changes in currency reserves* (5)=(3)+(4)	+38	−29	−33	+45	+27	+20	+12

[1] Balance of payments 'excluding banking intermediaries'.
[2] Including balance of public sector interest payments and investments.
[3] Excluding authorized medium- and long-term borrowing.
[4] Including errors and omissions.

borrowing from abroad (authorized net borrowing – line 4), or by a reduction in gold and currency reserves (line 5).

The deficit on current transactions (line 1) was caused mainly by a worsening of the foreign trade situation, but it was aggravated over a period of time by the deterioration of the balance of capital revenue which, because of borrowing, went from a 16 billion surplus in 1980 to an 11 billion deficit in 1984 and 1985. The worsening balance of payments situation was principally caused in 1981 by spontaneous movements of capital.

The flight of capital just after the presidential election was particularly in the form of huge purchases of foreign securities by French residents until the 'investment currency premium' was introduced on 21 May 1981 as one of the first financial policy

Figure 3.19 Quarterly balance of direct investment and portfolio investment

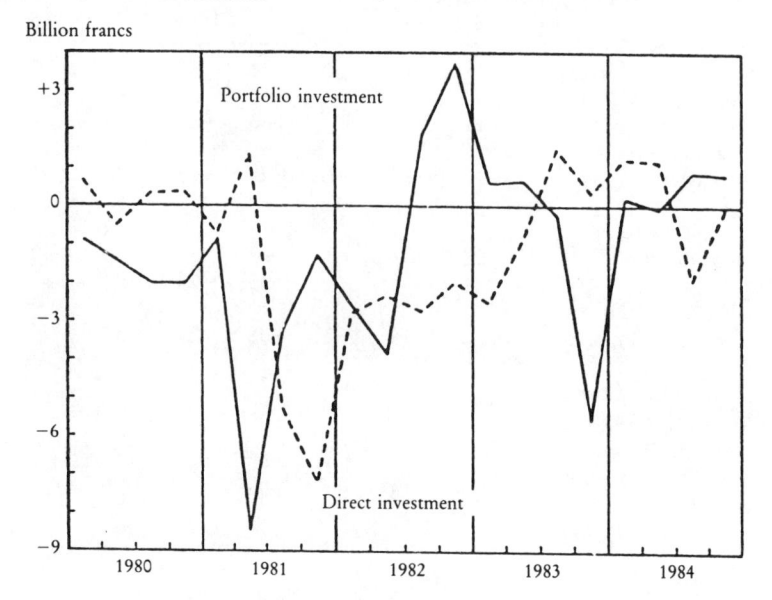

Source: Balance of payments (Banque de France).

measures of the Mauroy government. It made the acquisition of foreign currency to pay for a new investment conditional on there being currency from the sale of an existing investment, and meant that the portfolio investment deficit was brought down to the level of the previous year (see Figure 3.19). But from the second half of the year, the net flow of direct investment in turn fell into heavy deficit, and the balance of long-term capital movements did not regain its former position until 1984.

There were considerable fluctuations in short-term capital movements until the 1983 devaluation, with significant reductions in the annual surplus in 1981 and 1982. Overall, the balance of current transactions and spontaneous capital movements (line 3 of Table 3.15) which gave a 10 billion franc surplus in 1980 became a 63 billion deficit in 1981, 112 billion in 1982 and 43 billion in 1983. The financing of this deficit was carried out in 1981 and 1982 at the same time by short- and long-term borrowing and by calling on reserves.

Currency reserves (see Figure 3.20) were however significantly affected in the short term by speculation. Intervention in the money market to support the franc reduced reserves by 36 billion in the second quarter of 1981 and by 17 billion in the third quarter. The

Unavoidable External Constraints

Figure 3.20 Financing the deficit from current transactions and 'spontaneous' movements of capital

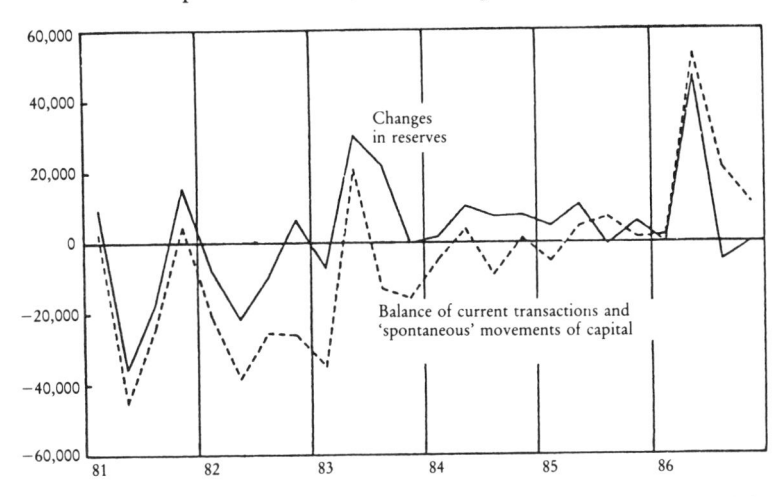

Note: The difference between the unbroken line showing changes in reserves and the dotted line showing the balance of current transactions and 'spontaneous' movements of capital represents the increase in medium- and long-term external debt (authorized net borrowing).

Source: Quarterly balance of payments excluding financial intermediaries.

October 1981 devaluation allowed only a temporary replenishment of the reserves; the franc had to be supported again until the June 1982 devaluation, after which the recovery of the reserves was mainly due to long-term foreign borrowing, particularly drawings on the 4 billion government loan contracted in October 1982. From February 1983 however renewed pressure on the franc led to further reductions in the reserves until the devaluation in March.

The replenishment of currency reserves after this devaluation was principally the result of the return of capital attracted by higher interest rates. Short-term interest rates on the franc did not in fact drop after the devaluation and remained on average 3 points higher than dollar investments and 7 points higher than the rate for Deutschmark investments. The recovery of the currency reserves was subsequently helped by a 4 billion ECU loan from the EEC in Summer 1983. Over the year the increase in foreign borrowing, together with a drop in the borrowing requirement, meant that French reserves rose by 45 billion francs. This trend continued in 1984 and 1985, while a return to equilibrium in the current balance meant less need for long-term borrowing and a recasting of the pattern of this borrowing.

Foreign Borrowing

The debate on foreign borrowing took an acute turn at the end of 1983 and throughout 1984. A possible reason was that with the initial success of the economic austerity policy, this was the only theme available to the Right, which stressed the 'economic bankruptcy of the Socialist government' and the situation they would inherit in 1986. However, when the Senate published the report of its enquiry committee assessing the 'structure and extent of France's foreign debt', this, despite worries during 1982 and 1983, had largely been brought under control even though the dollar continued to rise.

The official publication of France's foreign debt position is a recent practice. The first time was by Raymond Barre in a final report when he left office just after the 1981 presidential election. This kind of assessment, from flows of medium- and long-term borrowing in the balance of payments, was subsequently repeated in regular publications from the Ministry of Finance. This definition of foreign debt corresponds to authorized outstanding foreign loans of more than a year, contracted by French residents and disposed of or able to be disposed of in the money market, together with loans of more than a year taken out by the government to build up its currency reserves. At 31 December 1983, foreign debt defined in this way amounted to 451 billion francs and included government borrowing (63 billion), borrowing guaranteed by the government (327 billion) and borrowing by firms which was not guaranteed (61 billion). This definition of foreign debt is broader than that applied in many countries, which excludes non-guaranteed debt, and sometimes even limits the notion of indebtedness to government borrowing. Conversely, the French definition excludes short-term borrowing over a period less than a year as well as certain medium- and long-term borrowing by banks to finance their international operations.

The broader definition suggested by the Senate committee includes short-term borrowing by banks after discounting off-shore operations, but this makes no difference to France's net borrowing since short-term debt is offset by credits of the same amount (see Table 3.16). It is therefore of limited use for analysing net flows of interest payments and repayments which is the only real problem raised by the total amount of borrowing.

Indebtedness was in fact comparable with official reserves of currency (429 billion francs at the end of 1983) and loans to foreign countries (250 billion). That some of these loans are not wholly safe

Table 3.16 Differing assessments of foreign debt as at 31 December 1983

	Debts	Credits	Net borrowing
Long-term commitments (official definition)	451	250	201
Banks' short-term commitments excluding international operations	150	150	0
Commitment used in Senate report	601	400	201

Source: Senate, 301 (1983–4), report drawn up for the commission of enquiry into the structure and level of France's external debt. Session held on 9 May 1984.

is something which is not peculiar to France but affects all industrialized countries. The geographical breakdown is in fact similar to that of other developed countries: 55% to developing countries, 20% to countries of the Eastern bloc, 15% to OPEC members and 10% to OECD countries. The problem is less that of repudiation of debts by Third World countries as the effects of rescheduling them – in 1983 there was a loss of 20 billion francs to the French balance of payments.

New borrowing to finance the external deficit was not the only factor contributing to the increase in borrowing. Table 3.17 shows that the effect of floating currencies and in particular the continued rise in the dollar from 1980 to 1984 was almost as important as the net flow of borrowing in the increase of foreign debt,[18] whereas from 1974 to 1979 the impact had been nil. From the end of 1980 to the end of 1984, foreign debt rose from 94 to 528 billion francs, an increase of 434 billion. This increase was made up of 257 billion in new net borrowing (surplus of borrowing over repayments – line 1 of Table 3.17) and 177 billion due to the appreciation of currencies against the franc (line 2). From 1985, the fall in the dollar brought a decrease in foreign debt expressed in francs. Between the end of 1984 and the end of 1986, this fall meant that 110 billion francs of foreign debt were wiped out. The overall lightening of the debt burden brought about by currencies floating was somewhat smaller (98 = 76 billion + 22 billion) because of the April 1986 currency adjustment when the Deutschmark and the guilder rose against the franc. Added to this was the appearance in 1986 of surplus on current balance which allowed early repayment of loans and a further reduction of external debt by 45 billion francs.

18. In 1984, the dollar represented 57% of foreign debt, the Deutschmark 10%, the Swiss franc 8% and the yen 5%; the rest was divided equally between the guilder, the French franc, the ECU and the pound sterling.

Table 3.17 Medium- and long-term changes in the external debt

	Average annual change 1974–9 and commitments at 31 December 1979	1980	1981	1982	1983	1984	1985	1986
1. Borrowing net of repayments	+19	+18	+34	+78	+89	+38	+13	−45
2. Increase in commitment from previous period because of floating currencies	0	+11	+31	+30	+66	+39	−76	−22
3. Change in total borrowing (1 + 2)	+19	+29	+65	+108	+155	+77	−63	−67
4. Debt as at 31 December (billion francs)	94	123	188	296	451	528	465	398
5. Dollar rate as at 31 December	4.02	4.57	5.72	6.68	8.40	9.72	7.50	6.35
6. Debt as at 31 December (billion dollars)	23	27	33	44	54	54	62	63

Source: Ministry of Finance, 'Situation de l'endettement extérieur de la France', Notes Bleues nos. 178, 193 and 227.

Unavoidable External Constraints

Table 3.18 Debt charges (interest and contractual repayments in billion francs)

	1984	1985	1986	1987	1988	1989	1990
Scenarios							
(1) Ministry of Finance	66	77	88	99	119	–	–
(2) Senate 1	66	77	89	115	143	–	–
(3) Senate 2	68	82	97	123	155	–	–
(4) OFCE debt reduction	–	–	80	81	101	88	121
(as % of exports)			*7.1*	*6.7*	*7.9*	*6.3*	*8.0*
Debt charges as at 31 December							
(5) 1983	67	72	75	76	91	77	99
(6) 1984	–	78	82	84	104	89	122
(7) 1985	–	–	69	67	81	68	96
(8) 1986	–	–	–	56	56	53	67

Note: The scenarios take into account anticipated new borrowing as well as anticipated changes in exchange rates and interest rates. The timetable for debt charges as at 31 December is calculated at the exchange rates and interest rates applicable at the time. It does not provide a forecast of charges on future external borrowing, since it does not take into account new borrowing, or, conversely, anticipated repayments.

Sources: (1) Ministry of Finance, 'Situation de l'endettement extérieur de la France', Notes Bleues no. 178, 4–10 June 1984. Assumptions – 1 dollar = 8 francs in 1984, 7.6 francs afterwards; rates of other currencies at their 31 December 1983 level (Deutschmark = 3.06 francs); (2) and (3) Senate, see source of Table 3.16. Assumptions – 1 dollar = 8 francs in 1984, 7.4 francs afterwards; Deutschmark 3.16 in 1984, 3.68 in 1988; (4) P.-A. Muet, A. Fonteneau and F. Milewski, 'Le contre-choc pétrolier et la baisse du dollar: quelles marges de manoeuvre pour la politique économique?' (The oil counter-shock and the fall in the dollar: what freedom of manoeuvre for economic policy?), *Observations et diagnostics économiques*, 15, April 1986. Assumptions – 1 dollar = 7.1 francs in 1986, 7 francs afterwards; Deutschmark 3.18 in 1986, 3.23 afterwards; (5) to (8) *La balance des paiements de la France*, Annual report, 1983, p. 114, 1984, p. 109, 1985, p. 111, 1986, p. 113.

Financing the external debt: an assessment of the scenarios established in 1984 For an individual as for a government the possible constraints from indebtedness arise not from the gross amount borrowed but from the charges associated with the debt in relation to available income. The future position for foreign debt as at 31 December 1983 showed that annual charges (interest payments and repayments of capital) were rising and would reach their maximum in 1988 and 1990 (see line 6 of Table 3.18). For these two years servicing the debt outstanding at 31 December 1983 amounted to no more than 5–6% of the total value of exports, hardly more than in

1983 (4.4%). Nevertheless there was a danger that this figure would rise quite considerably if borrowing went on increasing because the return to equilibrium on the current balance was too slow. The Senate Report underlined the risk by giving three possible scenarios for 1988 relating to debt servicing and the main components of the balance of payments; shortly afterwards, in June 1984, the Finance Ministry published its own scenario.

The three Senate scenarios were drawn up by DRI-France which at the end of 1984 published a study comparable to the US banks' 1992 forecasts. The forecast total of borrowing is not given in the scenarios published by the Senate. They share, however, certain assumptions with the Finance Ministry scenario:

1 Deficit in spontaneous movements of long-term capital running between 40 billion and 50 billion francs from 1984, though it turned out to be less in reality: 24 billion in 1984, 22 billion in 1985 and 35 billion in 1986 (cf. Table 3.15).
2 Movements of short-term capital including variations in currency reserves globally nil (this was more or less the case in 1984–5 and there was a 44 billion surplus in 1986).
3 The dollar valued at 8 francs in 1984, and 7.40 francs afterwards.

Differences between them concerned the value of the franc against strong European currencies and, more fundamentally, how quickly the current balance would return to equilibrium. Whereas the Finance Ministry took the rate of European currencies as that obtaining at the end of 1983, the Senate assumed the value of the franc would continue to fall, with the Deutschmark at 3.16 francs in 1984 and 3.68 in 1988. Similarly it was assumed US interest rates would rise until 1985 (10.4% for the 3-month Euro-dollar) and then fall slightly (9.9% in 1988), whereas the Finance Ministry again took the rate as that obtaining at the end of 1983 (about 9.5%). The Senate Report, pointing to the worsening of the external deficit at the beginning of 1984, thought it unlikely, despite what Jacques Delors said in March 1983, that the current balance would return to equilibrium in two years, and illustrated its belief by advancing the three scenarios.

The first scenario was based on the official view of a return to equilibrium on the current balance followed by surpluses of around 30 billion to 40 billion. As in the Finance Ministry's scenario, keeping up currency reserves meant the need for a net positive flow of long-term borrowing from abroad until 1988. In the second scenario, there was still a current account deficit (22 billion) in 1984, with equilibrium in 1986 and a surplus of no more than 5 billion to 15 billion afterwards. The third scenario assumed an even higher deficit in 1984 (27 billion) and 1985 (15 billion) followed by surpluses of 25 billion in 1987 and 36 billion in 1988.

The persistence of a current account deficit and the assumption that the franc would fall against the stronger European currencies meant, in the two latter scenarios, the need for foreign borrowing net of repayments of 30 billion to 50 billion francs.

In fact, since the current balance more or less returned to equilibrium in 1984, and since investment abroad was running at 20 billion to 30 billion francs less than forecast, new borrowing (total borrowing less repayments) reached only 36 billion francs in 1984 and 13 billion in 1985 instead of the 40 billion and 72 billion in the 1984 forecasts. Moreover the external debt was fundamentally restructured in 1985 to extend capital repayments and take advantage of lower nominal rates. About a fifth of the debt (100 billion francs) was refinanced in this way. A final point is that following the oil 'counter-shock', the surplus on current account appearing in 1986 went mainly to the reduction of the debt, and net borrowing was 45 billion less than repayments. It can be seen therefore that the actual situation was far removed from the Senate's 'black' scenarios and was even better than the predictions of the 'optimistic' scenarios.

The new conditions resulting from the oil 'counter-shock' were highlighted at the beginning of 1986 by the OFCE using three scenarios describing various policies with regard to foreign debt. The scenario which has up to now proved to be the most likely one assumed that the surplus on current account and on spontaneous flows of capital would be used to reduce external debt and is therefore called the 'debt reduction scenario'. With net borrowing limited to 10 billion francs per year and repayments of between 40 and 90 billion francs, reduction of the debt meant that medium- and long-term external debt would be brought down to less than 5% of GDP by 1990. The two other scenarios also showed that even with a more expansionist domestic policy in France (reflation in one country) and certainly if such a policy were co-ordinated in the framework of the OECD (co-ordinated reflation scenario), external debt did not pose a problem in the medium term (see Figure 3.21). Payments to finance the external debt (interest and repayments falling due) were only 69 billion francs in 1986 instead of the 88 billion to 97 billion forecast by the 1984 scenarios and the 80 billion of the OFCE debt reduction scenario (Table 3.18).

The reduction of the nominal charges on the debt came about by

Figure 3.21 Medium- and long-term changes in the external debt (as % of GDP)

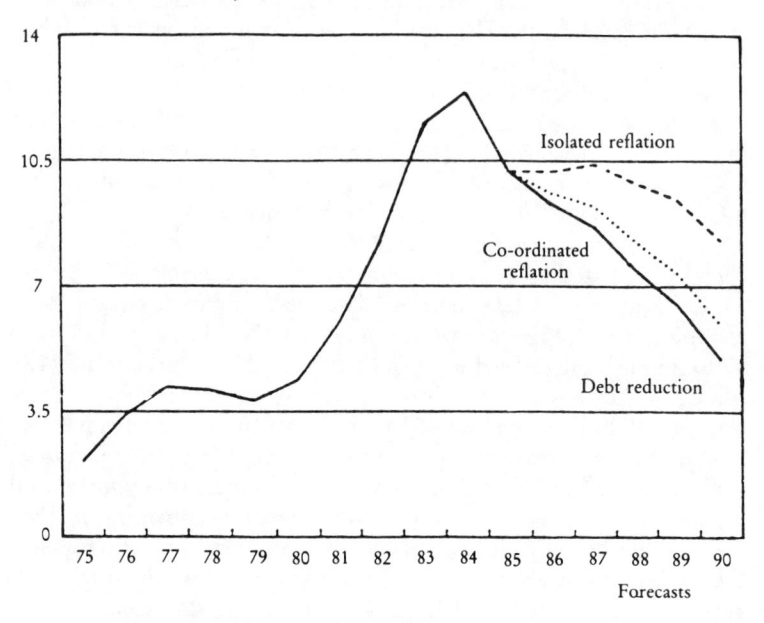

a combination of three factors: the fall in nominal rates of interest; the fall in the dollar against the franc; and the fact that in 1985–6 restructuring took place and repayments were made before they were due. This reduction is clear from the forecast relating to the debt accruing at the end of each year (second half of Table 3.18) – from the high point of 1984 (line 7) charges drop sharply and because of restructuring and repayments made before they were due, the high points in 1988 and 1990 are not as great.

Developments in recent years led to the conclusion that, even with extra gross borrowing, the level of payments to finance the debt is that forecast by the OFCE debt reduction scenario, and that the high points of 1988 and 1990 would not exceed 8% of exports. This is far removed from the 10.5% for 1988 forecast by DRI-France for the Senate Report and put at 13.5% for 1990–2 in an analysis published since then.

–4–

The Fight Against Unemployment

Bringing down unemployment was at the centre of the Left's economic programme, but this was something of a gamble. Since the middle of the 1960s the rate of unemployment had been rising. Before the economic crisis this increase was caused by demographic factors such as the post-war baby boom and the rise in the number of women in employment; from 1974 slow-down in economic growth became a major factor.

When the Left came to power the number of new jobs per year, in order to stop unemployment rising, needed to be higher than in 1965–70, when the employment position was favourable.[1] The international situation meant that the achievement of this was extremely difficult. Nevertheless the Left tried to boost employment by stimulating the economy and creating jobs in the public sector. At the same time it attempted, with limited success, to reduce working hours and expanded policies introduced in the 1970s to improve labour patterns, particularly youth training and a lower retirement age.

The reduction of the working week to thirty-nine hours in 1982 gave rise to feelings of disillusion in working people and especially in government circles: because of the prevalent emphasis on productivity, its effects were quite modest. This relative failure led the government to take a more decentralized line and introduce schemes linking the reduction of working hours with 'solidarity'. These were only partly successful, but they allowed an innovatory approach linking reduction of working hours to the reorganization of production.

The introduction in 1982 and 1983 of 'solidarity' schemes for early retirement and retirement at 60 was more successful. It lowered the average age of the labour force and helped considerably in keeping the number of unemployed on the two million mark

1. See M. Anyadike-Danes and J.-P. Fitoussi, 'Dimensions du problème de l'emploi en Europe et aux Etats-Unis' (Dimensions of the employment problem in Europe and the United States), *Lettre de l'OFCE*, 12, 22 February 1984.

Reflation and Austerity

between mid-1982 and Autumn 1983. This 'age management of the labour force' policy was also applied to the younger age range for whom new training programmes were set up. The Mauroy government however was only moderately successful in this area, and the rise in youth unemployment was stemmed only after the September 1984 measures.

Employment policy can therefore be divided into three stages between 1981 and 1985. During the first stage the emphasis was on creating jobs; the second stage tried to reduce the labour force by getting older employees to retire; the third stage delayed the entry of young people into the labour market. Since the last two approaches could be no more than temporary, it was necessary to look for the basis of a real growth in employment, but this was only partly dependent on economic policy in France.

Shorter Working Hours

Raymond Barre had been implacably opposed as Prime Minister to the idea of shortening working hours to reduce unemployment. Conversely the Left considered a reduction in working hours not only as a means of 'changing people's lives' through a better balance between work and free time, but also as the best way of fighting unemployment by a 'different share-out of work'.

When he introduced his measures to boost employment on 15 September 1981, Pierre Mauroy declared that a reduction of working hours was by far the most effective way of tackling unemployment; he added that it would be a real job-creating measure only if the working week was brought down to thirty-five hours by 1985. He said that its implementation should stem not from one single overall decision but from a negotiated reduction taking various forms, alongside a reorganization of work and a distribution of income which was in keeping with the distribution of work. The question of whether things worked out as Mauroy had hoped will be examined, after a historical survey of the length of the working week in France. Finally, an international comparison will be made in order to show France's position in relation to other major countries.

Brief Historical Survey of Legislation on Working Hours

The first laws on working hours go back to 1841 for child employment (eight hours a day for children between 8 and 12 years, twelve

The Fight Against Unemployment

hours for those between 12 and 16) and March 1848 for adults (ten hours in Paris and eleven hours in the provinces),[2] though this latter legislation was abrogated on 9 September 1848. In 1874 the employment of children under the age of 13 was forbidden. In 1892 new provisions were introduced – ten hours a day for children between 13 and 16, eleven hours for those between 16 and 18 and for women, and twelve hours for adult males. A weekly rest day was obligatory from 1906 and in 1919 the 'eight-hour law' was passed which provided the framework for regulating working hours until 1936, though there were many derogations from it.

On 21 June 1936 the Popular Front Parliament passed a law with the following provisions: annual two-week paid holiday; the actual length of the working week not to exceed forty hours; no overall reduction of income – 'there shall be no reduction in the standard of living of working people as a result of the application of this law'.

Moreover the possibility of overtime was strictly limited. This lack of flexibility very quickly led to a considerable reduction in the length of the working week, which in large firms went down from 46 to 40.5 hours in 1937. This cut in working hours appeared to have a favourable effect on the unemployment situation. Between October 1936 and October 1937, 160,000 jobs were created in manufacturing firms employing more than 100 people, and a further 70,000 to 92,000 new jobs (sources differ on the exact figure) on the railways, where the legislation was strictly applied.[3] Conversely, in small private firms, which dominated the labour market, employers were reluctant to take on extra labour: 'wherever labour could be replaced by machines, this was done'.[4]

However, the boost to employment and the reduction of unemployment were short-lived. The inflexibility of the forty-hour week caused a slow-down in economic activity, in that firms could not get enough skilled labour.[5] Despite the devaluations of October 1936 and December 1937, production fell in the first months of 1938, unemployment rose and employers resorted to short-time working.

2. Y. Barou and J. Rigaudiat, *Les 35 heures et l'emploi* (The 35-hour week and employment), Paris, La Documentation Française, 1983.
3. J.-C. Asselain, 'Une erreur de politique économique: la loi des quarante heures de 1936' (A mistake of economic policy: the forty-hour law of 1936), *Revue économique*, 25 (4), 1974.
4. Cf. J.-C. Asselain, 'La semaine de quarante heures, le chômage et l'emploi' (The forty-hour week, employment and unemployment), *Le mouvement social* (special issue on 'Le Front populaire'), 54, January–March 1966, pp. 181–204.
5. This point has been developed by A. Sauvy in *Histoire économique de la France entre les deux guerres* (Economic history of France between the wars), Paris, Economica, 1984.

Figure 4.1 Reduction in the working week since the 1890s

Length of working week in French industry (hours)

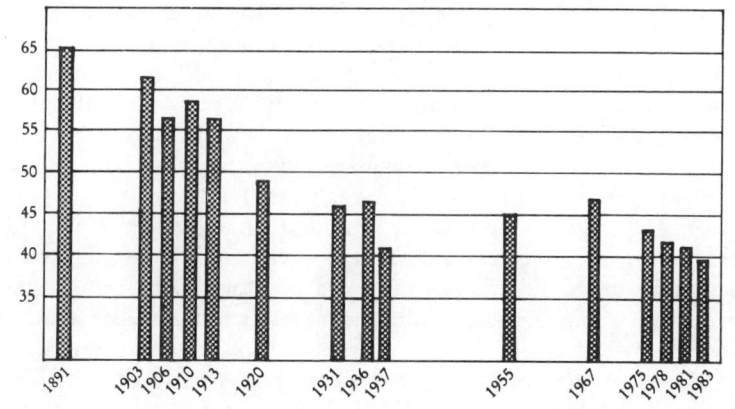

[Bar chart showing working week hours for years: 1891 (~65), 1903 (~61), 1906 (~56), 1910 (~58), 1913 (~56), 1920 (~49), 1931 (~46), 1936 (~46), 1937 (~41), 1955 (~45), 1967 (~46), 1975 (~43), 1978 (~41), 1981 (~41), 1983 (~39)]

Sources: *Travail et emploi*, 4 and 20.

The average working week at that time in large firms was 38.7 hours.

The 1936 scheme was made more flexible by the new Daladier–Reynaud government during 1938. A decree in March 1938 allowed overtime when an abnormal level of work warranted it, another in August 1938 allowed special dispensation for firms working on defence contracts, and further ones in November 1938 allowed the working week to be extended to fifty hours simply by giving notice, and subject to authorization by Ministry inspectors.[6]

The emergency measures introduced during the Second World War were abrogated on 26 February 1946 by a law which re-established the 1936 scheme, though with the possibility of up to twenty hours' overtime, with Ministry approval, 'to increase production'. Up to 1968, there was no significant change in working hours, but paid holidays were extended – to three weeks on 27 March 1956 and four weeks on 16 May 1963. To offset the labour shortage, working hours gradually increased by invoking the overtime provisions of the 1938 and 1946 laws. The average working week for the workforce as a whole went up from forty-four in 1946

6. A.-C. Decouflé and N. Svendsen, 'Contribution à une histoire des durées du travail dans l'industrie française du milieu du XIXe siècle à la seconde guerre mondiale' (Contribution to a history of working hours in French industry from the mid-nineteenth century to the Second World War), *Travail et emploi*, 20, June 1984.

The Fight Against Unemployment

to 46.1 in 1962, and for manual workers it was almost forty-seven hours (see Figure 4.2).

This increase continued until the 1963 'stabilization plan', but it was the Grenelle agreement of 17 July 1968, following the May 1968 'events' which began the significant downward trend which lasted until 1976. As overtime gradually dwindled and forty hours a week became the normal pattern again, the average length of the working week went down from 45.2 in 1968 to 41.8 in 1976. This reduction went against the French tendency to cut working hours by means of the law, and in fact came about through *agreements*. Between May 1968 and October 1969, more than 200 agreements, seventy-one of them covering the whole country, were concluded,[7] to cover various periods of time up to 1977. From 1976, the reduction in working hours slowed down and the working week stabilized at around forty hours. To start the trend moving again, the government in Spring 1978 encouraged negotiations on the rationalization and reduction of working hours, but these got nowhere. After the publication of the Giraudet Report in April 1980, negotiations restarted but again failed. It was the victory of the Left in 1981 which allowed the breakthrough below the forty-hour barrier (see Figure 4.1).

Thirty-Nine Hours, Provided That . . .

On 17 July 1981, the government, employers and unions, though without the CGT (the communist-dominated trade union) and the CGPME (the small businesses association) managed to reach agreement on a package of proposals called 'a protocol on working hours'. This was a general framework for negotiating 'a gradual and flexible reduction of the working week irrespective of the legal requirement', though the signatories agreed that the legal stipulation should be reduced to thirty-nine hours, that there should be a general right to a fifth week of paid holiday, that time lost for public holidays would not have to be made up, that there should be an annual overtime quota and that the maximum permitted length of the working week (including overtime) should be lowered. The timetable required negotiations to begin in each industry by 30 September 1981 and a meeting at the beginning of December 1981 would look closely at the negotiations and make sure that legislative and administrative provisions tied in with the contractual provisions.

7. Cf. Y. Barou and J. Rigaudiat, 1983.

Figure 4.2 Changes in the length of the working week (in hours) since 1950 in firms employing more than ten people

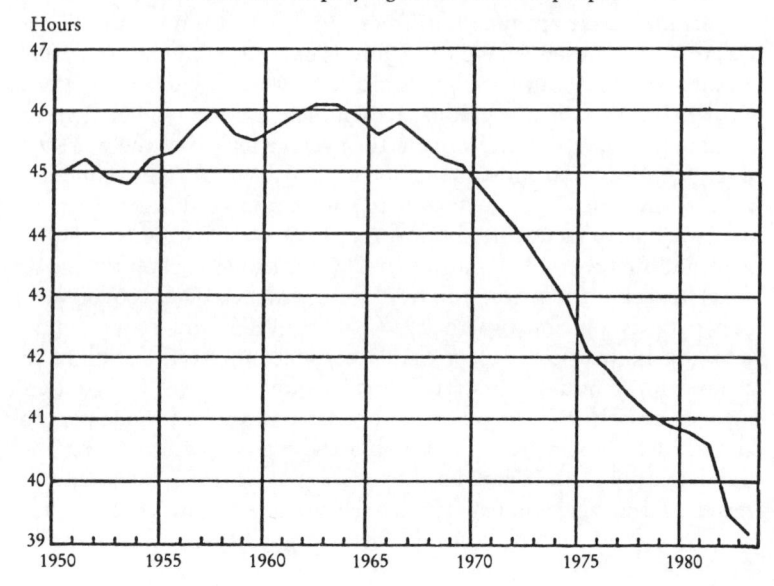

Source: INSEE.

In reality, the negotiations took much longer. When they were suspended on 20 December 1981, only a dozen industries with more than 10,000 employees had reached an agreement. Therefore, whereas it had been envisaged that a law would be the culmination of agreements in the various industries, the government decree of 16 January 1982 stemmed from a single government decision of general application rather than from a process of negotiation.

The provisions of this decree were as follows:

1 The legal length of the working week to be thirty-nine hours from 1 February 1982.
2 General right to a fifth week of paid holiday (to start with holidays taken between June 1982 and the end of May 1983); time lost for up to eight days of public holidays need not be made up.
3 Reduction of the maximum permitted length of the working week to forty-eight hours over one week (instead of fifty) and forty-six hours over twelve weeks (instead of forty-eight). Measures to deter resort to overtime on the part of employers involved not only an annual quota fixed by decree at 130 hours

The Fight Against Unemployment

per year per employee (2.75 hours per week), but also the right to time off equivalent to half of the overtime done. By opting for this method rather than one whereby overtime was paid at 50% above the normal rate, the government was trying to dissuade the employers from requiring overtime,[8] and to stop employees having a financial incentive to do it.

4 'Working hours of employees on permanent shift work, where production is a continuous cycle, must not on average over a year exceed 35 hours per week worked; this provision shall take effect from 31 December 1983 at the latest' (Article 24 of the decree).

5 There was a certain amount of flexibility with regard to the rational use of working time:
  (a) Weekend shifts: exceptions allowed, by collective agreement, to the rule about Sunday rest-day. Sunday shifts to be paid at least time and a half.
  (b) By collective agreement the lengths of working weeks could vary throughout the year provided the average over a year did not exceed thirty-nine hours.
  (c) For individual employees, hours could be carried over (and not counted as overtime), but the maximum was determined by decree – three hours from one week to the next, and ten hours in any one month.

6 On the question of remuneration (i.e. no loss of pay) for the shorter working week, the decree provided that those on minimum guaranteed wage should be paid the same for a 39-hour week as for a 40-hour week, and that the matter of remuneration for other groups of employees should be settled by the parties involved.

The Economic and Social Consequences of the January 1982 Decree

The reduction of working hours had many economic and social implications. Its effect on the actual length of the working week and the working year will be analysed, as well as the implications for wages, production, employment, firms' costs and social relationships within the firm.

The reduction in the working week was more than an hour in the

---

8. In fact, for two hours overtime above the quota of 130, the immediate cost is 2.5 times (1.25 × 2) the hourly rate and these two hours will therefore establish the right to an hour off. Overall, there will have been only one hour overtime for a cost equal to 2.5 times the hourly rate.

Table 4.1 Manual workers and white-collar workers (excluding large state undertakings): breakdown of weekly hours in each category (as %)

	Less than 39 hours	39 hours	Between 39 and 40 hours	40 hours	Between 40 and 42 hours	42 hours and above	Average weekly hours
Manual workers							
January 1981		4.2		56.2	14.0	25.6	40.8
January 1982		8.4		62.8	11.0	17.8	40.5
January 1983	21.4	48.5	3.3	10.9	8.5	7.4	39.3
January 1984	28.8	46.4	2.6	8.8	7.5	5.9	39.1
January 1985	30.3	47.5	3.1	6.9	7.0	5.2	39.0
January 1986	29.3	49.4	2.3	6.5	6.5	6.0	39.05
White-collar workers							
January 1981		3.0		74.6	10.9	11.5	40.5
January 1982		12.9		70.3	8.8	8.0	40.2
January 1983	19.3	63.3	3.4	6.6	4.3	3.1	39.1
January 1984	26.3	59.7	3.0	4.9	3.4	2.7	39.0
January 1985	28.3	59.1	2.7	4.4	3.0	2.5	38.9
January 1986	30.4	58.4	2.4	4.0	2.7	2.1	38.85

Source: Quarterly questionnaire by Ministry of Employment.

first half of 1982 Firms implemented, by and large, in terms of actual hours worked, the reduction in the legal length of the working week, whether this had been agreed at industry level under union pressure, or understood as an obligation arising from the January decree.

According to the quarterly statistics of the Ministry of Employment, weekly hours worked went down by 1.1 in the first half of 1982. Although this reduction was smaller in the case of weeks of less than thirty-nine hours, it can be said that there was a general reduction of this magnitude. On 1 January 1983, 73% of manual workers and 86% of white-collar workers were working less than forty hours a week whereas the figures for 1 January 1982 were 8.4% and 12.9% respectively (see Table 4.1). On average, the length of the working week was very close to the legal figure of thirty-nine hours, as against 40.5 hours on 1 October 1981.

The number of hours worked per year went down by sixty-three in 1982 In theory, the reduction in the number of hours worked per year ought to have been 4.3% or roughly ninety-five hours (made

Table 4.2 Change in yearly hours worked* from 1981 to 1982

	1981	1982	Difference Hours	%
Manual workers	1,888	1,821	−67	−3.6
White-collar workers	1,858	1,799	−59	−3.2
Both categories	1,873	1,810	−63	−3.4
10–49 employees	1,896	1,833	−63	−3.3
50–199 employees	1,875	1,812	−63	−3.3
200–499 employees	1,857	1,797	−60	−3.2
Over 500 employees	1,851	1,786	−65	−3.5

*Nominal hours worked, ignoring short-time work, strikes or absences of various kinds. The actual yearly total, taking into account part-time work and absences including strikes, is put at 1,690 for 1981 and 1,620 for 1982.
Source: D. Frayssinet, November 1984.

up of forty hours from the fifth week of paid holiday, forty-seven from the reduction of the working week and eight because May 8th was added to the list of public holidays). However, Ministry of Employment statistics relating to November 1981 and November 1982 show that the effect on hours worked per year was not as great as this. It was about 3.4% for all employees, equivalent to sixty-three hours.[9] Table 4.2 shows moreover that manual workers benefited more from reduction in working hours (sixty-seven hours) than other employed people (fifty-nine hours); this was because fewer manual workers than other categories (14% as opposed to 30%) got the fifth week of paid holiday in 1981.

The principle of reduced working hours without loss of pay was only about two-thirds effective According to an INSEE analysis in September 1982 of the effects of the reduction in the working week, using a sample of 3,000 industrial firms and 2,000 firms in the wholesale and retail trade,[10] the vast majority of employees did not suffer loss of income when their working hours were reduced. In fact, between 1981 and 1982, the purchasing power of the average annual wage per head increased by 0.7% as a yearly average. It is true that the average yearly increase between 1974 and 1981 had

---

9. See D. Frayssinet, 'La Durée annuelle du travail en 1981 et 1982: premiers résultats' (A preliminary analysis of the number of hours worked in 1981 and 1982), *Dossiers statistiques du travail at de l'emploi*, 9, November 1984.
10. O. Marchand, D. Rault and E. Turpin, 'Des 40 heures aux 39 heures: processus et réactions des entreprises' (Firms' reactions to shortening the working week from forty to thirty-nine hours), *Economie et statistique*, 154, April 1983.

been 2.5%, but there are risks comparing these two sets of figures: first, because the trend was sharply downwards after the second oil shock and second, because wages are dependent on several other factors (minimum guaranteed wage, unemployment, prices, wages policy). For these reasons, it would be more appropriate to use an econometric equation to determine the extent of income loss from reduced working hours. When this econometric equation was simulated on the OFCE's quarterly model, it was found that the concept of not losing pay because of reduced working hours was only two-thirds effective, though it should be noted that the standard error in the equation means the figure can only be put in the broad band of 55% to 80%.[11]

There was no loss of production According to the INSEE study just mentioned, reduction in working hours brought about a drop in production of 1%. However, as was pointed out by government experts in the report on firms' non-wage costs,[12] this finding is incompatible with the way production and productivity moved in 1982. The 0.7% rise in production and the sharp increase in productivity (2.9%) were more consistent with a better use of fixed capital than with a hypothetical fall in production. Moreover the fact that there were still production bottlenecks, that some delivery dates were not being met, and that firms' views of their productive capacities had not changed, is confirmation that production was hardly affected by shorter working hours. Firms therefore compensated for this reduction by productivity gains obtained from a faster work rate, fewer rest periods, seasonal flexibility of working hours, introduction of new equipment and reorganization or introduction of shiftwork (see Table 4.3). It is true however that there were a few firms which had difficulty in adapting to the new conditions brought about by shorter working hours.

In trade the effect of shorter working hours on employment practices was usually a reduction of opening hours (44% of cases) and a better use of individual employees' working hours; 11% of firms, generally the larger ones, said they were taking advantage of the new scheme for variable weekly working hours.

Productivity was emphasized at the expense of employment According to the simulations carried out by the Commissariat du

11. M. Boutillier, 'L'évolution récente des salaires' (Recent wage trends), *Observations et diagnostics économiques*, 5, October 1983.
12. Cf. joint report by the employers' association and the government – CNPF, *Les charges des entreprises françaises*, 1983.

The Fight Against Unemployment

Table 4.3 Effects of shorter working hours on employment practices

Effect reported by firms[a]	In industry	In trade
Introduction of new machinery	16	–
Increased work rate on existing plant, or reduction of non-working time	18	–
Introduction, reorganization or extension of shift work	16	4
Work sub-contracted	10	–
Take advantage of the new possibility to vary the working week	18	11
Reduction in the number of days or half-days when the firm or business was open	–	5
Reduction in the number of hours per day when the firm or business was open	–	44
More flexibility in individual employees' hours (staggered hours, shorter breaks)	–	25
No effect	41	26
No reply[b]	6	3

[a] Firms' replies are weighted according to size of workforce, so that, for example, 16% of industrial workers are employed in firms which said they introduced new machinery. A firm could of course give several replies to the single question on the effect of shorter working hours.
[b] The significance of non-replies is to increase slightly the percentages given for replies to each question, and particularly the one for 'no effect'.
Source: O. Marchand, D. Rault and E. Turpin, April 1983.

Plan (national planning commission) using the DMS model,[13] shortening the working week by one hour with no loss of monthly pay or productive capacity, should have created or preserved about 100,000 jobs over the first year. How far was this *ex ante* estimate in keeping with what actually happened in 1982? Two different kinds of analysis are available to answer this question: one group is based on questionnaires to firms (the micro-economic approach) and the others rely on actual employment trends during 1982 (the macroeconomic approach).

According to the INSEE study mentioned before, the effect of shorter working hours on employment was very slight: 10,000 to 20,000 jobs created or preserved in industry and 4,000 to 8,000 in trade. The Scientific Management Centre of the Paris Mining

13. See report of the Commissariat Général du Plan, *Aménagement et réduction du temps de travail* (Redistribution and reduction of working time), Vol. 1, Paris, La Documentation Française, December 1984, pp. 251ff.

Engineering Institute polled the personnel managers of twenty-two firms in the second half of 1982 and found that the effect on employment of the January decree was slight;[14] the returns showed that two-thirds of firms switched to a productivity approach whereas less than half of the same sample in 1981 said they would do this.[15]

But findings based on asking firms direct questions leaves out of account the indirect consequences of shorter working hours on job creation. For example, if a firm copes with shorter working hours by sub-contracting more work, it will reply that the reduction has had no effect on employment. For its part the firm which does the sub-contracting will not attribute an increase in orders, and therefore in jobs to meet them, to a reduction in working hours. A further point is that such polls have a limited scope – only 50% of firms were covered in the INSEE study. Finally, their conclusions partly contradict the strong correlation evident in the first half of 1982 between the new 39-hour week and the fact that the total for the industrial workforce held up well – it increased in the second quarter of 1982 for the first time since 1976.

The second possible methodological approach is to calculate the effect of shorter working hours on jobs by means of a macro-economic analysis of the number of people in employment. This type of method is used by the Ministry of Finance forecasting section, based on the view that the effect of shorter working hours on jobs is equal to the residual balance between the difference in total employed in 1981 and 1982 (a rise of 118,000)[16] and the increase attributable to improvements in the overall economic situation, to job creation in the public sector, and to the other aspects of employment policy (52,000). The conclusion is that there were 66,000 jobs created or redundancies averted during 1982 (see Table 4.4).

14. M. Pépin and D. Tonneau, 'Réglementation sociale et vie des entreprises: mise en oeuvre des ordonnances de janvier 1982 sur les 39 heures et la cinquième semaine de congé' (Firms and the legal framework of social policy: implementation of the January 1982 decrees on the 39-hour week and a fifth week's paid holiday), *Economie et prévision*, 59 (4), 1982.
15. M. Pépin, J.-C. Sardas and D. Tonneau, 'Réduction du temps de travail: une typologie du comportement des entreprises' (The shorter working week: a typology of firms' behaviour), *Economie et prévision*, 55 (4), 1982.
16. That is, the difference between changes in employment in the two periods. See D. Frank and J.-J. Trégoat, 'Une politique active en matière d'emploi et de lutte contre le chômage a marqué 1982' (1982 was marked by an active policy in employment and in the fight against unemployment), *Bulletin mensuel des statistiques du travail* (supplement), 104, 1983, p. 23.

Table 4.4 Effect on jobs of shorter working hours, according to the forecasting section of the Ministry of Finance*

	Services and manufacturing
(1) *Trend in employment – difference between 1981 and 1982*[a]	+118,000
(2) *Induced effect of certain legislative or executive provisions on employment*	−38,000
broken down into:	
Legalization of the status of illegal immigrant workers	(7–10,000)
Decrees of 5 February 1982 on temporary jobs	(notional)[c]
Abolition of the periods of practical training of the plan for the future of youth	(−27,000)
Introduction of schemes linking government help with early retirement	(−10,000)
Decree of 24 November 1982 (unemployment insurance)	(−8,000)
(3) *Direct impact on jobs of the various measures*	90,000
broken down into:	
Schemes linking jobs with investment in the textile industry	(20,000)
New jobs in Post & Telecommunications and hospitals[b]	(10,000)
New jobs in large state undertakings, excluding Post & Telecommunications	(15,000)
Relative improvement in general economic situation	(45,000)
Impact of shorter working hours (1) − (2 + 3)	66,000
Excluding banks, large state undertakings and hospitals	(51,000)

[a] Difference between the change in total number employed in non-agricultural market sectors (excluding construction) in 1981 (−84,000) and that in 1982 (+34,000).
[b] Shorter working hours not applicable.
[c] Exact figure not available; it is, however, negative. It is consistent with the total for (2) within the range given for the legalization of the status of illegal immigrant workers.
* For a more detailed analysis, see D. Frank and J.-J. Trégoat, 'Une politique active en matière d'emploi et de lutte contre le chômage a marqué 1982', *Bulletin mensuel des statistiques du travail*, (supplement) 104, 1983.

Compared with the INSEE study, the scope of this estimate is wider because it covers banks, large state undertakings and hospitals (15,000 new jobs). Moreover this method takes account of all changes affecting the number of hours worked per year, namely the reduction in the legal working week and the general right to a fifth week's holiday, whereas the INSEE study dealt only with the thirty-nine hours factor. In this way, *ex post* estimates of how many jobs the 1982 reduction created give results which are two or three times lower than *ex ante* estimates from macro-economic models. In other words, productivity gains were more significant than expected.

For most firms the cost was minimal It can be deduced from the various points just covered that the move to thirty-nine hours and a fifth week's holiday did not involve most firms in 1982 in significant direct extra costs. About a fifth of the reduction in working hours led to the creation or maintenance of 60,000 to 70,000 jobs, and the remainder to an increase in productivity which meant that there was no loss of income for about two-thirds of employees when they moved to a 39-hour week.[17] In estimating the cost to firms of the reduction in working hours, government experts assumed that there had been no loss of income at all,[18] and on this basis they had estimated the cost to firms at 3.3 billion francs in 1982, equal to 0.27% of the total wages bill (including contributions) of non-financial enterprises (excluding large state undertakings), and 8.3 billion in 1983, the first full year when the impact of new jobs and the fifth week showed.[19]

Working people reacted in different ways to shorter working hours Apart from the economic effects, the new legislation had indirect consequences inside firms which ought to be taken into account, as Michel Pépin and Dominique Tonneau argue in their detailed study of about twenty firms (see note 14). They found that adaptation to the new legal provisions meant that technical problems resurfaced which were connected with the notion of working hours.

17. It is of course doubtful whether such productivity gains can go on being made. The dilution of the advantages gained (by, for example, a limit on breaks, or a strict check on time worked), which occurred in some firms, will no longer be possible in future.
18. It should be remembered that econometric formulae contradict this hypothesis; cf. M. Boutillier, October 1983.
19. See CNPF, *Les charges des entreprises françaises* (Costs of French firms) 1983, pp. 64–6.

The Fight Against Unemployment

Among the problems which arose during negotiations between employers and workers were the following:

1 The very definition of working hours, and the need to take account of various breaks (paid or unpaid), preparation or change-over time, and rest periods.
2 Arguments over the notions of working week and hours worked per year.
3 The calculation of holiday entitlement, with problems of qualifying periods, equivalence between working days and days worked, and pay rises on the basis of seniority.
4 The definition of reduced working hours without loss of pay when this involved factors other than basic wage (overtime, bonuses).
5 On a more general level, a host of questions about employment practices: productivity gains, flexible working, organization of replacement labour, etc.

In discussing the behaviour of social actors, the authors of the study note that employees sometimes felt frustrated 'either because claw-back provisions, for example on break-times, meant that advantages turned out to be less than expected, or because the scope of the reduction did not satisfy the wishes of the majority'. In fact very often the unions demanded a reduction in working hours per day, whereas the workers themselves usually wanted to carry time forward or have longer weekends (see Inset 4.1).

Moreover it was not unknown for workers to have a negative view of the reduction in hours or the loss of certain benefits. For example those who already enjoyed shorter working hours saw the gap narrow between themselves and the generality of workers. A final point is that since the potential effect on jobs of shorter working hours was not glaringly obvious, employees were ready to accept the stress on productivity which allowed their level of pay to be maintained. Such considerations show that the move to thirty-nine hours was something of a disappointment for the government (in that the effect on jobs was slight), and for some workers.

In fact government, employers and workers all realized that to be economically effective the reduction in working hours had to be brought about by a decentralized contractual process rather than by heavy-handed action – the government had to encourage people to do something rather than oblige them.

> **Inset 4.1**
>
> *Shorter working hours and worktime patterns: employees' wishes*
>
> Question: if the working week was reduced to thirty-five hours, what would you want the most?
>
> | | 1982 | 1983 |
> |---|---|---|
> | An hour off the working day to improve the quality of your day (more time with your family, etc.) | 15.9 | 17.2 |
> | An extra half-day off per week | 34.6 | 29.2 |
> | Extra days off, to make long weekends or link public holidays with weekends | 29.4 | 33.4 |
> | Extra days added on to annual holidays | 12.0 | 8.9 |
> | Don't know | 0.4 | 2.5 |
> | No wishes | 7.7 | 8.8 |
> | TOTAL | 100.0 | 100.0 |
>
> Source: F. Boscher, C. Duflos and L. Lebart, 'Les conditions de vie et les aspirations des Français' (Lifestyle and aspirations of French people), *Consommation: revue de socio-économie*, 2, 1984.

From Obligation to Encouragement

For it to have a significant impact on jobs, the scope of the reduction of working hours had to be substantial, equipment and machinery had to be used more rather than less, and the 'no loss of pay' aspect had to be such that costs and competitivity were not affected. In circumstances such as these, financial support from the government is doubly justified – for employers who have to bear the cost of adaptation and investment and for employees who seem mostly to prefer pay raises to shorter working hours.

Government aid schemes to reduce working hours Aware of what it was asking employers and workers to do, the government introduced in January 1982 financial aid schemes to reduce working hours. These schemes provided for government help for those firms planning a reduction of at least two hours in the working week. The precise details of this reduction – particularly regarding 'no loss of pay' and the general organization of work – had to be agreed beforehand by both sides at the level of the firm. During 1982, government aid was in the form of partial or total exemption for

The Fight Against Unemployment

two years from employer's social security contributions for each *extra* job created by shorter working hours. For a reduction in working hours of between two and three hours, the exemption was of 75% of these contributions the first year and 50% the second year. For a reduction of three or more hours, the exemption for each new job was 100% the first year and 75% the second year. Because it was regarded as too restrictive and too limited, this scheme was made more flexible by a decree issued on 16 December 1982. In the new scheme government aid was not dependent on the number of new jobs created but on the effort put into reducing working hours, which, if it kept productive capacity at the same level, was regarded as capable of bringing new jobs. Therefore in 1983 government aid was available to any firm which reduced the working week to thirty-five hours before 31 December 1985 or reduced it by at least two hours between 1 September 1982 and 30 June 1984; agreed to keep its productive capacity at the same level by reorganizing where necessary, and improved its employment record compared with the trend over the previous three years in the particular industry.

For each hour of reduction and for each employee concerned, an annual grant of 1,000 francs was made for a maximum period of three years. An analysis of schemes set up in 1982-3 allows conclusions to be drawn about their extent (see Table 4.5) and their impact, particularly on how far the working week had been reduced by the end of the scheme in question, how many jobs had been created, how far there had been no loss of pay, and how production was organized.[20]

By 31 December 1982, 736 schemes had been set up of which 389 were in local government, affecting 121,107 employees, and 347 in private firms, involving 92,920 people. The total number for 1983 was smaller (277), especially in local government. Firms operating the schemes moved towards significant reductions in working hours: it was envisaged that by the end of the schemes, two-thirds of firms would be operating a working week of thirty-six hours or less; 605 of schemes set up in 1983 planned for a 35-hour week.

In 1982, the net figure of jobs created by reduced working hours from government aid schemes was 8,500 in local authorities and

---

20. See P. Barbezieux, 'Le bilan des contrats de solidarité–réduction de la durée du travail conclus en 1982' (Assessment of the 1982 schemes linking government financial aid with shorter working hours), *Travail et emploi*, 17, July–September 1983; and the same author's 'Bilan des contrats de solidarité–réduction de la durée du travail conclus en 1983', *Bilan de l'emploi 1983*, *Dossiers statistiques du travail et de l'emploi*, 3–4, June 1984.

Table 4.5 Impact of schemes linking government help with shorter working hours

	1982		1983		1984	1985	1986
	Local authorities	Firms	Local authorities	Firms	Firms	Firms	Firms
Number of schemes introduced	389	347	105	172	174	142	76
Numbers involved in shorter hours	121,107	92,220	15,728	69,248	28,713	14,800	7,126
Numbers of new jobs envisaged	8,481	6,043	988	1,633	176	n.a.	n.a.
New jobs potentially created or saved	–	–	–	5,198	2,153	n.a.	n.a.

Note: The potential effect on jobs is calculated as follows:

$$\frac{\text{Number of weekly hours fewer} \times \text{Number of employees involved in reduction}}{\text{New length of working week at end of scheme}}$$

Source: *Bulletin mensuel des statistiques du travail.*

6,000 in private firms. The number of new jobs was 6.5% of the number of people benefiting from reduced working hours. Since working hours were reduced on average by between 8% and 9%, the conclusion is that one-quarter of this went to increase productivity and three-quarters went to create jobs; the effect of the schemes therefore was much more beneficial as far as jobs were concerned than the move to thirty-nine hours. Moreover it was in small businesses, proportionately, that most jobs were created, but the move to thirty-nine had practically no effect on employment in this sector.

The 1983 change which allowed government aid to be given, under certain conditions, without the certainty of new jobs led to the creation of fewer jobs (2,600) but at least some redundancies were averted (5,200), particularly in the aircraft industry – 56% of employees covered by government aid schemes were from this sector.

As far as 'no loss of pay' was concerned, 55% of industrial firms and 40% of firms in the service sector reported that they only partially compensated the loss of pay arising from shorter working hours: in some cases employees had to take a direct and immediate cut in pay; a second method was to take the shorter working hours into account in future pay increases; and another approach was to adjust pay scales downwards.

Moreover, 72% of industrial firms and 62% of firms in the service sector said they changed employment practices after the reduction of working hours. This reorganization went furthest in cases where reductions were large and sudden, and took various forms: alternative shifts, 6-day working, introduction of a third shift, staggered working times. Despite the large amount of money put into them, the quantitative effect of the government aid schemes of 1982–3 was relatively small. So that firms in industries undergoing structural change (steel-making, the car industry, etc.) could be helped, the government introduced more flexibility into the schemes in 1984. Firms became eligible for financial aid where a reduction in working hours meant that redundancies might be avoided even though there could be no certainty that the workforce could be maintained at the same level for three years. At the same time, government aid was increased to between 1,000 and 1,500 francs per hour per employee over the year, and its degressive provisions were reduced.[21] This recasting of the scheme did not however have much effect on further reductions in working hours. Barely a quarter of that part of the budget allocated to reduction of working hours was used during 1984.

Measures to redistribute working time In addition to the overall reduction in working hours, the encouragement of part-time work and 'choosing one's own hours' was also supposed to contribute to 'the achievement of employment aims while meeting the aspirations of a section of the working age population', according to the sixth priority programme of the Ninth Plan.

There has been a sharp increase in part-time work in recent times. Whereas in 1980–3 the number of full-time workers fell by nearly 500,000, the total of part-time workers rose by 346,000. But despite this increase, part-time work is still not very widespread in France (see Table 4.6). This is because too few part-time jobs are available, not because of low demand for such jobs – there were, at the end of 1984, 140,000 people registered as wanting part-time work. In order to encourage firms to offer more part-time work, the government introduced financial aid to any firm taking on, on a permanent basis, an employee who would work on average between twenty-eight and thirty-two hours a week. In 1984 the amount of government aid

---

21. According to the Ministry of Employment, for an employee earning 6,000 francs a month, the State covers 81% of the cost to the employer in the first year, 71% in the second year and 61% in the third (or 57%, 50% and 43% respectively if social security contributions are taken into account), when the firm goes from a 39- to a 35-hour week, ignoring productivity gains.

Table 4.6 Part-time work as % of total number of employed in major countries

		Men	Women	Total
Sweden	1980	6.9	46.3	24.7
United Kingdom	1979	1.3	37.7	15.4
United States	1981	7.2	22.4	13.4
West Germany	1979	1.8	30.4	12.2
Japan	1980	5.2	19.3	10.0
Netherlands	1979	1.8	30.4	12.2
France	1980	1.8	23.2	7.5
Belgium	1981	1.3	16.4	6.4
Italy	1979	1.2	6.0	2.6

Source: OECD.

for each new job was 6,000 francs. This grant was subject to two conditions:

1 The new job(s) should not have been created by redundancies, for economic reasons, in the three months before or the twelve months afterwards, except for cases of premature retirement under the government scheme.
2 The number of part-time jobs in the firm must not be more than 25% of the total workforce.

Modelled on long-standing Swedish provisions, other policies to redistribute working time were introduced: leave to set up a business, sabbatical leave, leave for parents to pursue part-time education, gradual reduction of days worked per week prior to retirement, half-time working for young people beginning their first job, etc.

There is every reason to welcome the development of these ways of organizing work, first because it is what one section of the population wants, and second because it meets the needs of the present-day technological revolution. There is reason to believe, without wholly going along with the optimism of Michel Albert,[22] that increase in part-time work is one way of reducing unemployment.

---

22. See M. Albert, *Le pari français* (The challenge facing France), Paris, Seuil, 1982.

The Fight Against Unemployment

Reduction in Working Hours: Experiences in Other Countries

A quick look at the position in other major countries relating to working hours will put into perspective the policies of the Left government after 1981 concerning reduction and redistribution of working time. This will be followed by a brief survey of what has been happening recently in the United States and Europe in the area of redistribution of working time.

Working hours abroad In 1981, the working hours of French employees were as long as those of their foreign counterparts, if credence is given to the statistics of international organizations relating to the length of the working week in manufacturing industry. However, as A. Doyelle points out,[23] it is very difficult to establish a true comparison on the basis of data collected by international organizations; distortions are introduced in statistics on working hours by problems of conceptual definition, types of survey, their scope, the period they relate to, and the time between each one in a series. By analyzing a mass of data available however, it has been possible to put forward a comparison of working hours in 1980 in twenty countries. Figure 4.3 shows the main findings of this analysis relating to the actual working hours per year for full-time industrial workers, and then for employees as a whole.

It will be seen that the rank order for average working hours per year for all employees is different from that of industrial workers. This is due not only to differences between manufacturing industry and services but also to the differential development of part-time work (or short-time work) in the various countries. Japan and Canada, which have the highest number of working hours per year, as well as Sweden and Belgium, which have the lowest number, are in the same position on both tables; West Germany is in the middle. The United States and the United Kingdom are near the top for industrial workers but near the bottom for all employees. This situation is the opposite for France, Italy and the Netherlands. The updating of these statistics for the period after 1980 is not easy, but the Commissariat Général du Plan attempted this for 1982 from data collected by the OECD relating to actual yearly working hours per person.[24] From this updating it emerges that the reduction in yearly hours of industrial workers between 1980 and 1982 was

---

23. A. Doyelle, 'Durée du travail, un essai de comparaison internationale' (Work hours: attempt at an international comparison), *Travail et emploi*, 12, April–June 1982.
24. See Commissariat Général du Plan, *Aménagement*, 1984.

Reflation and Austerity

Figure 4.3 Actual annual working hours in France and other countries*

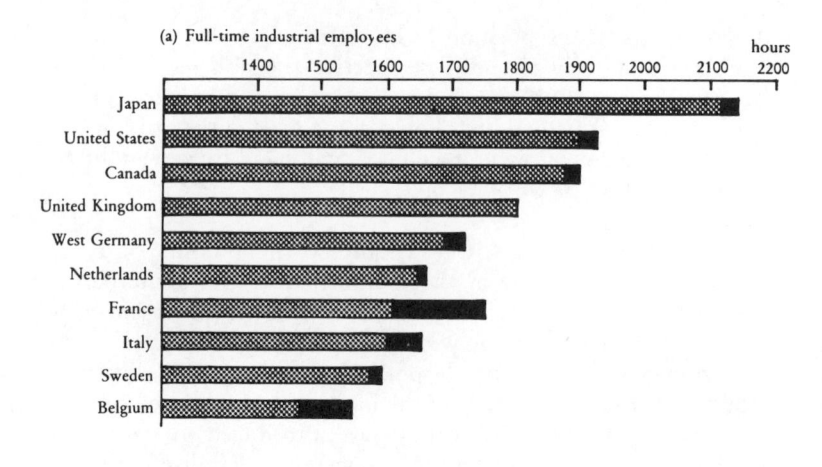

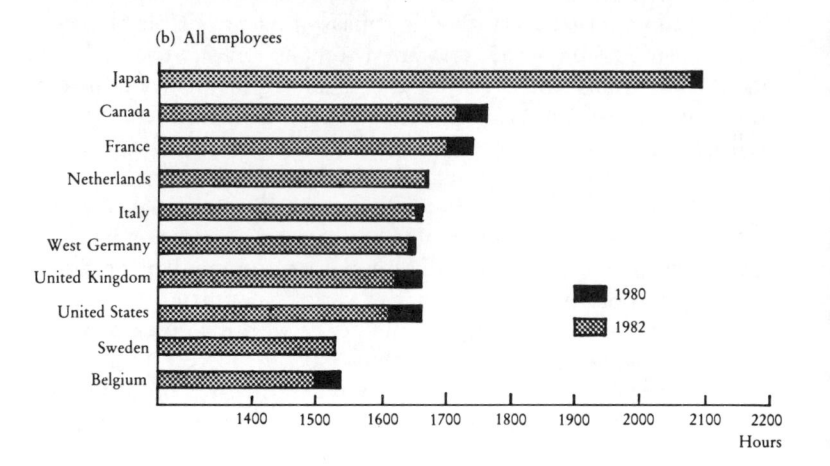

(a) Full-time industrial employees

(b) All employees

1980
1982

* Actual annual working hours equals weekly hours multiplied by the number of weeks actually worked (fifty-two weeks less paid holidays, holidays granted for long service, public holidays, days between public holidays and weekends not worked and not made up) less absences (illness, maternity leave, industrial accidents, strikes, etc.).

The Fight Against Unemployment

practically nil in the United Kingdom, the Netherlands and Sweden; it was between twenty and thirty hours in Japan, Canada, the United States and West Germany; fifty hours in Italy, eighty hours in Belgium and 120 hours in France. When it came to all employees, the spread was much smaller – Canada, the United States, the United Kingdom, Belgium and France dropped between forty and fifty hours; the Netherlands, Italy, West Germany and Sweden remained more or less the same. The conclusion is that as far as working hours were concerned, industrial workers in 1982 were in a relatively better position in France than in other countries, but that the relative position of other types of workers was less favourable since only Japan and Canada had longer yearly working hours.

Reduction and redistribution of working time in the United States and Europe In the United States weekly hours in manufacturing industry, taken over a long period, are about forty, but this figure is subject to considerable cyclical variations, with a significant fall during recessions (for example, 40.2 hours in May 1982 down to thirty-nine hours in December 1982) and recovery during economic upturn (see Figure 4.4). This cyclical variation also applies to the construction industry. Conversely, there has been a steady fall in weekly hours in the service sector since the 1950s. In trade, because of a move from full-time to part-time work, the level has fallen from forty hours to thirty-two hours at the beginning of the 1980s. In the United States, in contrast to Europe, 'an employment pattern of this nature does not cause problems for firms since fringe benefits, ease of declaring redundancies and flexibility of working hours are a direct function of official working hours and the seniority of employees',[25] and there is high mobility among people doing such jobs; nevertheless the medium-term trend in this sector seems to have been changing recently – there was a slight increase in hours worked during the economic upturn of 1983–4, apparently due to an increase in the hours worked by part-time employees.

Redistribution of working time has taken several forms in the United States, of which the main ones are as follows:[26] flexitime, where the full-time employee can choose working hours which are then adhered to as set hours; gliding time, where the employee can choose what time to start each day; variable days, where the employee can carry over time, as credit or debit, provided the daily

---

25. See S. Mathieu, 'Etats-Unis: une croissance hypothéquée' (Growth in the United States: a hostage to the future), *Observations et diagnostics économiques*, 8, July 1984.
26. Commissariat Général du Plan, *Aménagement*, 1984.

Figure 4.4 Length of working week in the United States, in the non-agricultural private sector

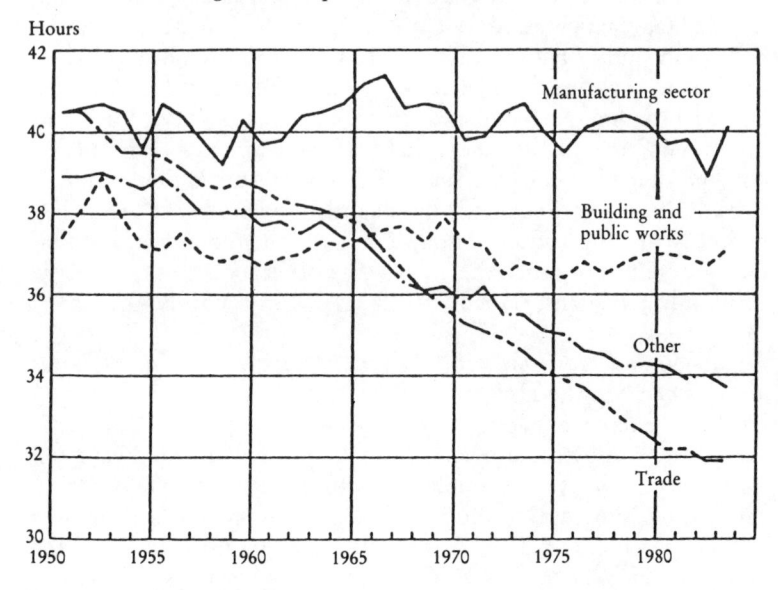

[Graph showing working hours from 1950 to 1980 for Manufacturing sector, Building and public works, Other, and Trade]

Source: S. Mathieu, July 1984.

average is eight hours; earning days off, where the employee works a 9-hour day for five days or a 10-hour day for four days one week and a 9-hour day for four days the following week; job-sharing, where a full-time job is shared between two people who have joint responsibility.

According to the American Management Association, one fifth of the US employees, a total of 21 million people, benefited from one of these schemes in 1983.

In most European countries, some degree of modification of working time has been introduced recently, but the emphasis has been on flexibility of working hours rather than an overall imposed approach. Ways of improving employment patterns have been as follows:[27]

1 Redistribution of the working week: in Belgium, three days of 12-hour shifts, or two 12-hour shifts at the weekend, with the possible addition of four hours on a Monday or Friday, or thirty-seven hours worked in four days at nine hours and fifteen

27. Commissariat Général du Plan, *Aménagement*, 1984.

The Fight Against Unemployment

minutes per day; part-time work in Italy, Belgium, the United Kingdom and West Germany; in the Netherlands, part-time work for young people starting their first job; various job-sharing schemes in the United Kingdom and West Germany.

2 Improvements affecting an individual's working life: in Belgium, raising the school leaving age to 18; in Belgium and Italy, lower retirement age with government help; in West Germany, gradually reducing the working week prior to retirement; combination of this with job-sharing in the United Kingdom.

3 Redistribution of work over a year: in Italy, the Netherlands and West Germany, negotiations on number of hours to be worked in a year; in Italy and the Netherlands, reduction in the yearly total of between thirty-six and forty-eight hours; in West Germany, of thirty-seven to forty hours; in Italy, greater flexibility regarding public holidays; a more flexible system of overtime working (Italy and West Germany).

Improvements in the working life of employees and a lower level of wage demands can be seen as the necessary counterpart of the costs involved in reducing working hours. Experiences in other countries show that innovation in this area is feasible provided agreements are negotiated at industry or plant level. The relative failure of recent French policies designed to redistribute working time shows that French attitudes need radical revision to bring back the momentum for shorter working hours.

The Creation of Public Sector Jobs and Direct Aid for Jobs

The second important element in employment policy was job creation in the public sector. At the same time, aid schemes initiated by the previous government to maintain and create jobs were expanded, and further direct aid for employment was introduced.

Job Creation in the Public Sector

François Mitterrand's 1981 presidential election campaign promised that '150,000 jobs will be created in social and public services to improve work conditions in this field and give better service to the public (health, education, postal service, etc.); 60,000 community-oriented jobs will be available for voluntary organizations and local authorities'. This proposal was not only diametrically opposed to those of other candidates, who wanted to reduce the number of

Table 4.7 Total number employed by central government between 1975 and 1984, as at 31 December (in thousands)

	May 1975	1976	1978	1980	1982	1984
Civilian ministries	1,895	1,953	2,067	2,093	2,176	2,209
Defence	451	449	455	461	458	453
Total:	2,346	2,402	2,522	2,554	2,634	2,662*

*249,000 of whom were part-time employees.
Source: A. Brenot-Ouldali and D. Quarré, 'Les effectifs des agents de l'Etat de 1975 à 1982' (Number of employees in central government between 1975 and 1982), *Economie et statistique*, June 1984; and INSEE, Archives and Documents, June 1987.

government employees; it was also a move away from the policies of the three years prior to the presidential election – whereas the number of government non-military employees had increased on average 2.4% during 1975–8, it had risen only by 0.6% in 1979–80 and virtually no increase was envisaged in the preliminary budget for 1981.

Were the 210,000 jobs promised in the public sector actually achieved? The answer to this question is obtained from budget statistics, as far as new jobs in government service and hospitals, and 'community-oriented' jobs are concerned, though local authority jobs will be left out of the reckoning because of the unreliability of statistics. New jobs in the large state undertakings will be looked at, however, even though they are not strictly 'public sector' jobs (see Table 4.7).

143,000 jobs were created in government service and hospitals The supplementary budget of 3 August 1981 created 34,869 government jobs, 12,000 of which were in the Post Office, and 2,827 government-financed jobs mainly in public undertakings and private education – a total of some 37,700 jobs (see Table 4.8). The budget for 1982 reinforced this initiative by being responsible for the creation of 41,300 government jobs and 5,300 further jobs outside government service; to these figures must be added 7,500 new jobs in the Post Office as a result of reduction of working hours.[28] New jobs in the draft budget for 1983 were fewer in

28. These jobs were put on a regular footing in the budget for 1983.

Table 4.8 Total net new jobs in the public sector during the Interim Economic Plan (1981–3)

	Budget for 1981	3 August 1981 package	Budget for 1982	Budget for 1983	Total for Interim Plan 1981–3
(1) *Jobs financed by the general budget*	1,888	22,866	35,599	13,258	71,723
broken down into					
Civilian jobs	1,163	21,866	33,916	12,588	68,370
Military jobs	725	1,000	1,683	670	3,353
(2) *Jobs financed by supplementary budgets*	−2	12,003	5,698	7,502	25,203
including					
Post & Telecommunications	—	12,000[b]	5,650	7,500[c]	25,150[b]
Total jobs financed by budgets:	1,886	34,869	41,297	20,760	96,926
(3) *Other Jobs paid by Government*[a]	—	2,827	5,293	2,609	10,729
Total: (1) + (2) + (3)	1,886	37,696	46,590	23,369	107,655
(4) *Subsidies to create jobs financed by the general budget*	—	7,250	14,910	6,535	28,695
broken down into					
Local initiative jobs	—	5,000	10,000	5,000	20,000
Jobs in social and cultural sectors	—	2,250	4,910	1,535	8,695
(5) *Jobs in hospitals, health care and social welfare establishments*	n.a.	9,340	18,000	8,000	35,340
General total: (1) + (2) + (3) + (4) + (5)	1,886	54,286	79,500	37,904	171,690

[a] Public undertakings, private education sector, and others.
[b] 4,000 of which were to fill vacancies.
[c] These jobs correspond in the budget for 1983 to the putting jobs created in 1982 on a regular footing following the introduction of shorter working hours. As far as the two years 1982–3 are concerned therefore, they are net new jobs; they have been kept in the 1983 column to give a better idea of what was contained in that budget.

Source: *Rapport sur la Fonction Publique en 1983* (Report on government administration in 1983), Paris, La Documentation Française.

number but still considerable – 13,258 government jobs and 2,609 other jobs.

During the period of the Interim Plan, therefore, a total of 107,700 new government and government-sponsored jobs were created. These mainly came under the Ministry of Education (34,800), the Post Office (21,150 plus 4,000 to fill vacancies), the Ministry of Economy and Finance (10,300) and the Interior Ministry (9,400). Moreover, permanent contracts were given to a large number of employees on short-term contracts, and the number of these fell 18% between 1982 and 1985 (from 338,000 to 277,000). To the total of new jobs in government service must be added the 35,340 in hospitals and health and social welfare establishments. The conclusion is that the aim of 150,000 new jobs was practically reached by the end of 1983.

The aim of creating 60,000 'community' jobs was only half realized Budgets during the period 1981–3 provided for subsidies for 20,000 jobs created by local initiatives and 8,700 jobs in the social welfare and cultural field. The aim of the programme on local initiative jobs was to help local projects for services and other activities which were not catered for by private firms or existing public services. Each job received government subsidies totalling 40,000 francs in 1983. The government programme created jobs for 17,900 people, as opposed to 20,000 envisaged – 2,700 during 1981, 11,100 in 1982 because local authorities were brought in, and 4,100 in 1983, when the local authorities did not receive aid because their plans were not in line with the spirit of the programme. It is not possible from available studies to assess accurately the net effect of this programme on the level of employment, mainly because of the substitution effects which there may have been between subsidized jobs in voluntary organizations and those in government service. However these subsidies were granted on the basis that they did not compete with existing firms or public services, and from the few studies made of beneficiaries, one can assume that there was a net creation of jobs and that 80% of the people involved had been without a job (though sometimes for reasons other than unemployment). A further point is that in filling most of these new jobs, priority was given to young people.

There was a considerable expansion of jobs in big state undertakings in 1981–2 . . . Whereas the number of employees on the state railways (SNCF) and the national coal undertaking (Charbonnages de France) had fallen sharply in 1980–1, it increased by 1.7%

The Fight Against Unemployment

(railways) or remained steady (coal) in 1982. In the Paris public transport undertaking (RATP), airlines and the electricity and gas undertaking (EDF–GDF), there was a considerable increase – respectively 6.9%, 3.9%, 5.5% (see Table 4.9).

Such increases were provoked not only by the government's wish to boost coal production and stem the rate of growth of unemployment, but also by the reduction in February 1982 of the working week to thirty-nine hours. The new jobs reduced unemployment but they also slowed the rise in productivity (because production fell), and worsened the already parlous financial position of most of the undertakings involved. To make up for this, the government had to increase significantly the level of subsidy (see Chapter 2); moreover when the 1983 austerity programme was introduced, the undertakings themselves had to stop recruiting labour, reduce investment and raise prices, which was disastrous for jobs in 1983–4.

In all, new jobs in government service (discounting local authorities), hospitals, large state undertakings and community projects totalled about 180,000. Taking into account induced effects and a lower labour force participation rate, these new jobs probably meant around 100,000 fewer unemployed in the period 1981–3. Obviously, the fall in the number of people employed in government service during the period 1984–6 had the opposite effect, and this will be examined later.

Government Support for Private Sector Employment

Apart from new jobs in the public sector, government employment policy also involved specific schemes to help job creation in the private sector. There were already a number of these before 1981; these were either kept on (apprenticeship), or modified and extended (grants to unemployed people starting up businesses, and schemes linking employment with training), or gradually abandoned (the exemption from employers' social security contributions when young people were taken on was ended in 1982). Other schemes were introduced in 1982–3 – those in the textile and clothing industry linking new jobs with investment, those linking new jobs with training and production, job creation grants in the small business sector, etc. The features of the main schemes will be surveyed, contrasting those for new jobs with those to boost economic activity, and an assessment of their effects on the level of employment will be made.

Table 4.9 Job creation in the large state undertakings*

	As at 31 December							% change on previous year						
	1979	1980	1981	1982	1983	1984	1985	1980	1981	1982	1983	1984	1985
Post & Telecommunications[a]	437,363	442,747	451,178	461,977	464,647	465,530	464,673	1.2	1.9	2.4	0.6	0.2	−0.2
SNCF (railways)	256,130	251,680	248,570	252,870	251,220	245,750	238,780	−1.7	−1.2	1.7	0.7	−2.2	−2.8
EDF–GDF (electricity and gas)	134,332	136,070	142,888	150,767	153,523	153,904	153,551	1.3	5.0	5.5	1.8	0.2	−0.2
Charbonnages (coal)	64,109	60,931	58,502	58,531	55,198	50,978	46,301	−5.0	−4.0	0.05	−4.5	−7.7	−9.2
Air France and Air Inter	38,618	38,909	39,557	41,096	41,650	42,481	42,867	0.7	1.7	3.9	1.3	2.0	0.9
RATP (Paris public transport)	36,148	36,018	36,238	38,754	39,267	39,326	39,184	−0.4	0.6	6.9	1.3	0.2	−0.4
General total:	966,700	966,355	976,933	1,003,995	1,005,505	997,969	985,356	−0.1	1.1	2.8	0.2	−0.7	−1.3
General total excluding Post & Telecommunications[b]	529,337	523,608	525,755	542,018	540,858	532,439	520,683	−1.1	0.4	3.1	−0.2	−1.6	−2.2

* In the national accounting sense.
[a] Permanent employees, corrected to take account of part-time employees, half-time employees and employees on reduced days prior to retirement.
[b] New jobs in Post & Telecommunications have been taken into account as new jobs in the public sector.
Source: Personnel departments of the undertakings concerned.

The Fight Against Unemployment

Job creation schemes These were many and varied, but among the main ones during 1981–4 were schemes to boost jobs for the under-25s, schemes in the textile industry linking new jobs with investment, and job creation grants in the small business sector. To these must be added government help for jobs created by local initiative, and jobs in the social welfare and cultural field which have been mentioned in the context of job creation in the public sector.

The aim of schemes to create jobs for the under-25s was to put young people into work even if this meant no net creation of jobs. A distinction must be made between the following:[29] apprenticeship schemes; exemption from social security contributions in the case of young people taken on, introduced as part of the 'pacts on employment', but abolished in June 1982; and schemes linking job creation with training, supplemented in 1983 by those linking job creation with career advice.

Schemes in the textile industry linking job creation with investment became possible by a decree on 16 April 1982 whereby government help was available to firms undertaking to invest in the industry and to increase employment; the government paid between 8% and 12% of the employer's social security contributions for a period of twelve months, with a possible extension for another twelve months. Schemes introduced in 1982 affected 2,700 firms in this sector.

Job creation grants of 10,000 francs for small businesses were introduced in February 1983. They were available to businesses which created at least one new job, and 13,300 grants were made in 1983.

Schemes to boost economic activity Two kinds of direct aid were introduced to foster economic activity – grants to unemployed people starting up new businesses and schemes linking job creation with training and production. Moreover, money to local councils to help set up new businesses was increased.

Grants to unemployed people starting up new businesses were introduced on 22 December 1980, in a law which modified an earlier experimental scheme launched by Raymond Barre in 1979. Until March 1984 it consisted of two elements – the payment from the unemployment fund (ASSEDIC) of a lump sum of up to six months unemployment benefit, depending on remaining benefit entitlement, and exemption from social security contributions for six

---

29. See below, the section on 'Youth training' (pp. 229–34) for more details.

months;[30] 9,200 unemployed people in 1979, 13,800 in 1980, 29,400 in 1981 and 40,000 in 1982–3 benefited from this scheme. Although Barre's idea had been attacked by the Left when it was introduced, it did the trick as far as the creation of new jobs was concerned.

Schemes linking job creation with training and production were introduced on an experimental basis in October 1983 and were intended to boost employment by increasing the national value added through co-operation between firms. Two or more firms linked up in a scheme to boost jobs and production – one firm took on labour to make new products, particularly unfinished goods for which there was a need on the domestic market, and the other(s) agreed to buy these goods. The scheme had the double advantage of boosting employment and helping to win back domestic markets. In 1984, government support was 40,000 francs per job per year over the three years of the scheme.[31] It was envisaged that 20,000 jobs would be created by 1985, but when the Communist minister behind the scheme, Jacques Ralite, left the Government in July 1984, this rather optimistic figure had to be revised downwards.

The effect of government help on jobs and unemployment The total number of jobs created by government subsidy is an imperfect measure of the success of a policy. Uncertainties such as whether the jobs would have been created or maintained in any case, and whether the new subsidized jobs merely replace unsubsidized ones reduce the actual number of new jobs. On the other hand the multiplier effects of these new jobs must be borne in mind. As for impact on unemployment, this depends on how far economic activity is changed by government aid schemes.

The relative effect of an employment subsidy policy on the level of unemployment compared to what it would have been without such a policy depends on the two kinds of effect mentioned, and these are extremely difficult to measure. For the sort of policy measures just examined, assessment is based, in the small number of studies carried out, on data obtained from those responsible for the schemes, and on questionnaires sent to the firms themselves.

In the case of apprenticeship, which involves at the same time an 'initial training' aspect and a 'job' component, it may be assumed

30. After the reform of UNEDIC on 1 April 1984, the government took over the provision of aid to unemployed people setting up their own businesses. There was a one-off grant of a minimum of 8,000 and a maximum of 32,000 francs in 1984.
31. See J. Ralite, 'L'efficacité des aides publiques à l'emploi' (The effectiveness of government aid for employment), *Economie et Politique*, July–August 1984.

The Fight Against Unemployment

that its impact on unemployment was slight, on the assumption that every extra 100 training places took only fifteen people off the unemployment register;[32] but this does not give a true picture of the particular part which apprenticeship plays in getting young people placed in jobs, and it is doubtful whether other kinds of training scheme would do this to the same degree.

Measures exempting employers from social security contributions in the case of young people taken on, and schemes linking job creation with training were assessed by looking at either the kind of jobs these young people went to, or the effect on jobs and unemployment. The conclusion is that the effect on employment levels was slight, since the grants were not big enough and did not last long enough to change the pattern of production. Moreover a sector-by-sector study of how far government help was taken up shows that most use was made of it by sectors with a large turnover rather than by those which created the most jobs. Conversely, employment levels may have been affected by the presence of clauses in the schemes which insisted that jobs should not disappear and that there should be no redundancies for economic reasons. All this points to the view that the effect of these government subsidies on unemployment was slight – 5% for contributions exemption and job creation training schemes; 15,000 to 20,000 jobs were saved in textiles in 1982 by schemes linking job creation with investment, according to Frank and Trégoat.[33]

As for grants to unemployed people setting up businesses, a study carried out in Summer 1982 by the Social Affairs Ministry showed that businesses created or taken over in this way employed on average 1.5 people one year afterwards.[34] Furthermore, some businesses had folded (about 20% in the first year according to the study) and others had flourished only at the expense of others in the same sector. A final point is that about a third of unemployed people who set up businesses did so without government help. The conclusion is that 40% of the jobs created by government help went to reduce unemployment, in other words there were 16,000 fewer unemployed in 1983 (see Table 4.10).

It is very difficult to estimate the effect on employment levels of

---

32. The assessments are taken from J.F. Colin, M. Elbaum and A. Fonteneau, 'Chômage et politique de l'emploi: 1981–83' (Unemployment and employment policy: 1981–83), *Observations et diagnostics économiques*, 7, April 1984.
33. D. Frank and J.-J. Trégoat, 1983.
34. C. Bloch-Michel, M. Mayo and J.Y. Rognant, 'Création d'entreprise par les demandeurs d'emploi' (Business creation by unemployed people), *Bilan de l'emploi 1982, Bulletin mensuel de statistique du travail*, 104, 1983.

Reflation and Austerity

Table 4.10 Effect on unemployment of financial aid to boost employment (in thousands)

	Average number benefiting in a full year			Effect on unemployment (annual average)		
	1981	1982	1983	1981	1982	1983
1. Aid to boost employment						
Apprenticeship	128	127	125	−19	−19	−19
Exemption from social security contributions for employing under-25s	86	107	9	−5	−4	−0
Schemes linking jobs with training	65	73	78	−4	−4	−4
Schemes linking jobs and investment in textile industry	−	−	−	−	−15	n/a
2. Aid to boost enterprise						
Grants to unemployed people to start businesses	20	32	40	−8	−13	−16

Source: J.-F. Colin, M. Elbaum and A. Fonteneau, April 1984.

the other aid for job creation. It is reasonable to assume that the impact of various grants to small businesses, for setting up a business, and in the context of strategic spatial (land use) planning was only slight.

Labour Force Management Policy

In order to manage the restructuring of manufacturing industry and to cope with the rise in unemployment, governments before 1981 had introduced, after the first oil shock but more particularly in 1977–8, schemes intended to keep down the total number of people employed. One type of scheme tried to encourage employed people to give up work. The workforce was to be reduced either through the 'income maintenance on redundancy' scheme set up in 1972 and the 'agreed allowance' from the national employment fund (Fonds National de l'Emploi), or by voluntary redundancy with 'income maintenance on giving up work' set up in 1977. The Left government abolished these income maintenance schemes; it brought retirement age down to 60 and instituted schemes of government help for people taking early retirement at 55.

The Fight Against Unemployment

The second aspect of managing the age structure of the workforce prior to 1981 was the system of 'job pacts' for young people introduced in July 1977. But the Left government thought that this policy was flawed, too costly, and ineffective; it put the emphasis rather on the task of putting young people into jobs, particularly those who leave school without qualifications.

The third aspect was to stop the inflow of immigrant workers from 1 July 1974 and to encourage those who were in France to leave by offering a free passage to their country. The Left government abolished this scheme in 1981 but re-introduced it in 1984.

Early Retirement and Retirement at 60: a Huge Success

Early retirement schemes, although originally intended to improve financial protection for older workers declared redundant and unlikely to find another job, were gradually changed into a means of encouraging older employees to give up work when they were extended to voluntary redundancies (see Inset 4.2). The continuing recession, the arrival in the 55–65 age bracket of the post-First World War baby boom, and the attraction of retirement at an increasingly early age on a relatively high pension,[35] are the main reasons why the number of people taking early retirement rose sharply – 150,000 in 1979, 330,000 in 1981 and nearly 700,000 in 1983 (see Table 4.11).

The change from 'income maintenance' to retirement at 60 According to a study of people ceasing work in 1981,[36] nearly half of those taking retirement did so through income guarantee schemes and more than a fifth through early retirement schemes financed by the national employment fund. The first type of scheme applied to workers aged 60 or above who left, voluntarily or otherwise, firms which had an agreement with UNEDIC (the unemployment fund) allowing for early retirement. The second type applied to workers of between 55 and 60 who were made redundant. By replacing this 'income maintenance' by optional retirement at 60, the Left government made retirement conditions available to all workers equally.

The new retirement age was effective from 1 April 1983, after

---

35. According to a SOFRES opinion poll published in the monthly *Notre temps*, 76% of people in the over-50 age group were happy to have retired or to be about to retire.
36. See G. Magnier, 'Les sorties de la vie active en 1981' (Cessation of work in 1981), *Travail et emploi*, 13, July–September 1982.

Table 4.11 Employees taking early retirement as at 31 December*
1979–84 (in thousands)

	1979	1980	1981	1982	1983	1984	1985
Guaranteed income							
on redundancy	93.7	118.0	159.5	196.7	201.1	187.1	159.3
on voluntary departure	62.9	95.5	145.9	193.2	231.0	221.2	190.7
Special grants from national							
employment fund	–	–	24.2	50.2	84.0	117.3	151.3
Schemes linking government							
help with early retirement	–	–	–	52.3	178.5	148.2	105.7
Total	156.6	213.5	329.6	492.4	694.6	673.8	607.0

* Each figure describes a stock, which varies according to number of new beneficiaries and those taking retirement.
Source: UNEDIC.

which date employed people who had worked at least 37.5 years had full entitlement to retire if they so wished. It might have been thought that retirement at 60 would have attracted fewer people than the previous system, since it was financially less advantageous and required more to qualify – employees had to have been members of a general social security scheme for ten years to gain from the new policy. Yet statistics from the national employees' retirement insurance fund show that this was not so; according to a study by their forecasting section,[37] extra applications made for retirement pensions because of the new retirement age were estimated at 116,000 in 1983, 206,000 in 1984 and 279,000 in 1985. Of course, not all extra pensions were paid out to people giving up work. Some of the new pensioners were already not working, others had already taken early retirement or regarded themselves as unemployed. The cost of the lower retirement age to the retirement pension fund was 1.3 billion in 1983, 5.4 billion in 1984 and 7.8 billion in 1985, though the abolition of the income guarantee meant that the cost of early retirement was less than before.

Government schemes for early retirement The end of the income guarantee schemes led to a rapid increase in early retirement among the age range of 55–59, either through job losses (special grants from the national employment fund introduced in November 1980 and

37. J.-P. Cendron, 'Prestations vieillesse du régime général: évolution rétrospective et prévisions à l'horizon 1986' (Retirement benefits from the general scheme: past developments and forecast for 1986), *Economie et prévision*, 68, 1985.

Inset 4.2

Schemes linking government help with early retirement

Decree no. 82–40 on government financial aid schemes was adopted by the Council of Ministers on 13 January 1982. Its aim was to boost new jobs to complement what firms would be doing on their own initiative. The schemes covered measures applicable to employers in industrial and commercial firms, agricultural businesses, public and government agencies and professional associations. Exclusions applied, in the private sector, to firms arranging temporary work and those employing caretakers of residential blocks and, in the public sector, to government employment and public administrative undertakings.

Three classes of support were introduced:
– help to reduce working hours (see later);
– help to facilitate early retirement;
– help for the gradual reduction of hours prior to early retirement.

Voluntary early retirement[38]

Where a firm agreed to take on an unemployed person on the voluntary departure of an employee aged 55 to 60, the latter was guaranteed an early retirement pension. The replacement for the departing employee had to be made within three months, though not necessarily to the same job. In the case of the new person taken on, priority had to be given to a person under 26 or a woman on her own with dependent children. The firm had to agree to keep its overall total workforce for a year after the last departure for early retirement (in full-time equivalent). The replacement had to be paid at least 70% of the departing employee for contracts signed in 1982; on 24 November 1982, this became 65% for that part of the wage under social security level and 50% for that part above.

Until April 1984, one-third of the financial aid was provided by the government and two thirds by UNEDIC. After this date, the government was responsible for all of it.

Gradual reduction of hours prior to early retirement

Where a firm agreed to take on an unemployed person when an existing employee moved from full-time work to part-time work, the latter was guaranteed income to cover 30% of the loss. The replacement to make up for the move to part-time work had to be within three months. The provisions on voluntary early retirement also applied here.

Source: Bilan de l'emploi 1982, p. 49.

38. Abolished on 1 January 1984.

Table 4.12 Schemes in 1982 and 1983 linking government help with early retirement

	1982	1983	Total 1982–3
Number of actual contracts signed	29,542	4,756	34,298
Total workforce of firms involved	4,307,757	464,958	4,772,715
Number of potential beneficiaries	318,782	18,207	336,989
Number of people taking early retirement	52,853	157,608	210,461
Vacancies registered with ANPE (national employment agency)	86,249	91,197	177,446

Source: G. Magnier, 'Les entreprises signataires de contrats de solidarité préretraite' (Firms participating in schemes linking government help with early retirement), *Dossiers statistiques du travail et de l'emploi*, 9, November 1984.

renewed in 1982) or through voluntary redundancy (government aid schemes for early retirement introduced at the beginning of 1982). These latter, compared to the previous system, had a much narrower scope. They were available to firms in a sound economic position, and were intended not only to encourage them to look first to young people and the unemployed to fill jobs vacated by older workers, but also to make them keep their workforce at the original level for a year after the departure of the last person to take early retirement. In spite of these relatively restrictive conditions, this policy was very successful because many people already wanted to take early retirement and because employers were able to lower the age profile of their workforce.

During 1982–3, 34,300 agreements were signed (see Table 4.12) affecting potentially 337,000 employees, out of a total in the firms involved of 4.7 million. In fact, two out of three people entitled took early retirement – the first payment of 52,850 pensions under the scheme was made in 1982 and of 157,600 in 1983, making a total of 210,000 people giving up work, or about a quarter of private sector employees in the age range of 55–59 at the beginning of 1982. The average age of people taking advantage of the scheme was 57; 40% were manual workers, 32% white-collar workers and 11% were managerial staff. The sectors losing most were banking and insurance, retailing, the car industry and the aircraft industry.[39]

39. See J.-P. Revoil, 'L'indemnisation du chômage et de la préretraite en 1983' (Unemployment and early retirement compensation in 1983), *Bilan de l'emploi 1983*.

The Fight Against Unemployment

Figure 4.5 Unfilled vacancies at end of month (in thousands)

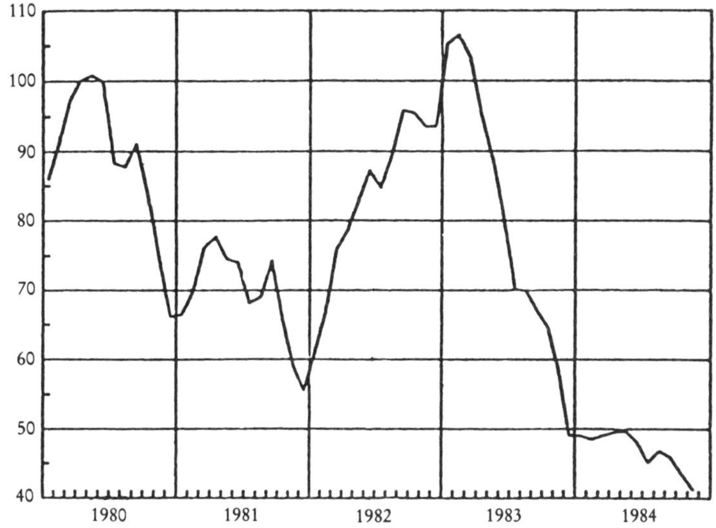

Source: Ministry of Employment.

Moreover, according to ANPE (national agency for employment), 177,500 job vacancies made possible by the scheme were registered with them between March 1982 and December 1983, leading to a spectacular rise in total vacancies in 1982–3 (see Figure 4.5).

According to a study carried out in November 1983,[40] the vast majority of firms kept to the conditions of their agreement, particularly the obligation of filling jobs falling vacant through early retirement – this happened in 95% of cases. Keeping the same total workforce was more difficult to adhere to, given changes in the employment and general economic situation during the period in question; for example, between April 1982 and October 1983, the total number of people employed in the private sector fell by 0.6%. Despite these problems, the percentage of firms which failed to carry out the terms of their agreement was small – 13% in the case of localized agreements and 6.6% for national ones – and non-replacement of vacancies was infrequent. In fact, there was an overall increase of 4.6% in the workforce of the firms participating in these schemes.

---

40. See *Dossiers statistiques du travail et de l'emploi*, 1.

A study published at the end of 1984 listed four reasons why firms involved themselves in schemes like these:[41]

1 The schemes allowed firms to give a 'social response' to demands made by their employees. It was something taken up by firms which were healthy but operating in a stagnant market, and its effect on jobs was limited.
2 Forward-looking, technologically advanced and financially viable firms used early retirement to tailor their staff to developments in the production process, without upsetting the jobs pattern too much.
3 The government aid schemes were a possible means of implementing reorganization. Because of early retirement, firms were able to change the pattern for job functions and qualifications, going mainly for productivity gains and the transfer of employees to tasks which frequently had a technological or commercial slant.
4 Early retirement gave firms a chance to restructure by updating equipment where markets were growing only slowly. The early retirement schemes were therefore used to take a long-term view and link changes in employment patterns with modification, often far-reaching, of their plant. The policy of early retirement and voluntary redundancy therefore constituted at the same time a response to a social need and an aid to firms' economic strategies.

However, it was decided to end the scheme on 1 January 1984 because it was costing too much. The only aspect of the policy which survived was the facility for gradual early retirement, which had in any case not been widely used since its inception.

Special allowances paid by the national employment fund These applied to workers in the 57–9 age group who were declared redundant for economic reasons. This scheme for early retirement has been widely used since 1981; at the end of 1985 151,000 people were receiving these allowances (see Table 4.11). This scheme allowed the workforce in industrial sectors undergoing restructuring to be reduced, particularly in the rubber industry, plastics, iron ore, metallurgy, glass and chemicals.[42] Very few steel-workers

41. See O. Galland, J. Gaudin and P. Vrain, 'Contrats de solidarité préretraites et stratégies d'entreprises' (Schemes linking government aid with early retirement, and firms' strategies), *Travail et emploi*, 22, December 1984.
42. See P. Marioni and M. Ricau, 'Préretraites et politique de gestion du personnel:

The Fight Against Unemployment

Table 4.13 Unemployment and early retirement benefits[a]

Billion francs	1980	1981	1982	1983	1984	1985
(1) Unemployment benefit	23.8	35.8	44.9	41.2	46.2	53.2
(2) Early retirement benefits[b]	8.8	14.1	24.4	42.7	49.3	48.1
(3) Total: (1) + (2)	32.6	49.9	69.3	83.9	95.5	101.3

[a] Excluding training grants, grants for setting up businesses, and management costs.
[b] Grants by government and by national employment fund.
Source: UNEDIC.

received this allowance, since the steel industry had its own social protection scheme introduced in July 1979 whereby employees over 50 could be on paid non-activity and those over 55 retiring early would receive a substantial pension.

The financial cost of early retirement schemes In 1984, the national fund for employment in industry and trade (UNEDIC) paid out 49 billion francs to people who had taken early retirement – 30 billion in income guarantees, 12 billion in the context of government aid schemes and 7 billion to cover allowances paid by the national employment fund. This figure contrasts with 25 billion in 1982 and 15 billion in 1981 (see Table 4.13). The increase was caused by a rise of 200,000 in the number of people taking early retirement between the end of 1982 and the end of 1983. Conversely, the decree of 24 November 1982 brought down the average amount paid to each person taking early retirement so that the real value of an allowance fell by 10% in 1983.

Youth Training

Young people, as the group which suffered most from the growth of unemployment, were the second of the two age groups targeted by the policy of 'managing the workforce'. This policy assumed great importance from 1977 when the Barre government introduced 'jobs pacts' in the field of youth employment. Later, some aspects of this policy were dropped, others modified, and additional features brought in. Despite these efforts, however, youth unemployment kept rising until Autumn 1984.

approche sectorielle' (Early retirement and staff management policy: a sectoral analysis), *Dossiers statistiques du travail et de l'emploi*, 7, September 1984.

'Jobs pacts' and the 'plan for the future of youth' The 'jobs pacts' were intended not only to help young people to enter adult working life by various grants and exemptions to employers who agreed to employ them or train them, but also to update and improve prospects for young people leaving school by providing periods of formal training. Various approaches were tried:

1 In the context of apprenticeship (120,000 young people a year since 1977), official aid meant exemption from social welfare contributions for those employers who took on apprentices and guaranteed them a proper training programme leading to a recognized qualification.
2 Between 50% and 100% exemption, for a year, from social welfare payments for employers in the case of each young person given a job. This scheme was abolished in June 1982.
3 Schemes linking jobs with training, which could apply to young people between 16 and 26, single women or the long-term unemployed. They were intended to help people from these groups who wanted a stable job but who did not have the right level or right kind of qualifications. Here government aid, consisting of a lump sum determined by the number of hours of training envisaged in each particular case, was intended to encourage the filling of vacancies which for the most part already existed.

The training programmes were of two different kinds:

1 Practical on-the-job training intended to give job experience to young people and certain groups of women who found it hard to get a job. These programmes, averaging six months, meant that firms could take on young people, who received from the government an allowance equal to 70% or 90% of the official minimum wage.
2 Periods of training and preparation for jobs, consisting of intensive training for six months followed by practical experience in a firm.

The degree of success of the various schemes is shown in Table 4.14. They were of benefit to an average of over 425,000 young people out of about 800,000 leaving school each year.

When the Left government came to power the previous government's scheme of 'jobs pacts' was replaced by the 'plan for the future of youth'. Since this was brought in fairly quickly, it incor-

Table 4.14 Overall effect of 'jobs pacts' and the 'plan for the future of youth'

	Pact 1 July 1977 to June 1978	Pact 2 July 1978 to June 1979	Pact 3 July 1979 to June 1980	Pact 3 July 1980 to June 1981	'Plan for the future of youth' July 1981 to June 1982
(1) Apprenticeship	117,302	111,430	122,124	126,379	123,995
(2) Schemes linking jobs with training	(35,617)	(51,702)	(65,601)	(64,357)	72,080
(3) Employers' exemption from social security contributions	229,949	94,943	151,558	144,374	107,985
(4) Practical training in firms	145,679	20,332	55,303	143,461	74,200
(5) Training in job skills	68,652	55,915	46,227	38,851	54,527
(6) Help for the older unemployed	–	–	3,408	2,662	–
(7) Number of premiums when first employee taken on	–	–	11,596	11,930	11,151
Total: (1) to (7)*	561,582	282,620	390,216	467,657	443,942

* For the first two pacts and the two years of the third pact, schemes linking jobs with training are not counted in the total, since they appear under the 'employers' social security exemption' heading. For the 'plan for the future of youth', the beneficiaries of these schemes appear as a separate component in the total, since the schemes did not involve exemption from social security contributions.

Source: OECD, *L'emploi des jeunes en France* (Youth Employment in France), Paris, 1984 (apart from apprenticeship and schemes linking job creation with training, for source of which see Table 4.15).

porated the main points of the previous policy but made training periods longer, extended the groups to which it applied and widened the scope of some of the provisions on subsidies. Overall, 444,000 young people benefited from the 'plan for the future of youth' between July 1981 and June 1982, that is, 24,000 fewer than the last of the 'job pacts' under the previous scheme.

New schemes to help young people aged 16–18 and 18–21 The new scheme announced by Pierre Mauroy in Autumn 1981 was based on the recommendations of Bertrand Schwartz's report on placing young people in work.[43] It was introduced in stages in March and September 1982 and was an overall approach to the problem of young people leaving school without qualifications, by providing them with a qualification and helping them in their transfer to adult working life. It consisted of periods of training mainly directed at the 16–18 and 18–21 age ranges – basic training and job advice, training for a first job and training for a qualification, with alternate periods of theoretical training and job experience. The policy was co-ordinated at the national level by the Employment Training Agency (Délégation à la Formation Professionnelle) and at the local level by committees and reception, information and advice centres set up by local authorities or local offices of central government. During the first year of operation, 70,000 young people between 16 and 18 received training and the figure rose to around 90,000 for 1983–4 and 1984–5 (see Table 4.15). Training programmes for the 18–21 age group involved about 45,000 young people.

Increase in vocational training in schools The 1982 scheme also laid great stress on vocational training in schools and the Ministry of Education aimed at giving this to 77,000 extra pupils in the school year beginning Autumn 1982 and 95,000 in 1983 (see Table 4.15). An analysis of the school population in 1983–4 shows that this aim was more or less achieved, since the number of pupils staying on at school was 88,000 in 1982 and 94,000 in 1983.[44] This contrasts with projections made on the basis of a gradual and steady rise in the numbers staying on at school which gave a figure of around 20,000 a year for 1982 and 1983.

The extension of schemes linking jobs with training These were

43. B. Schwartz, *L'insertion professionnelle et sociale des jeunes* (The integration of young people in work and in society), *Rapport au Premier ministre*, Paris, La Documentation Française, September 1981.
44. See *Bilan de l'emploi 1983*, p. 25.

Table 4.15 Help for youth employment 1982–6

	July 1982 to June 1983	July 1983 to June 1984	July 1984 to June 1985	July 1985 to June 1986
Apprenticeship	119,115	115,391	112,707	117,278
Schemes linking jobs with training and retraining	78,033	83,618	75,913	24,682
Skills training, 16–18 yr olds	70,132	88,919	94,801	77,464
Skills training, 18–21 yr olds	45,000[a]	45,000[a]	35,976	58,400
Young people staying at school[a]	77,000	95,000	80,000	n.a.
Community work schemes	–	–	158,642	337,932
Day release and similar schemes broken down into:				
Schemes of retraining and upgrading skills	–	–	3,044	69,967
Work experience schemes	–	–	12,277	98,279

[a] In the absence of statistics, target figures are given.

Sources: 'L'apprentissage de 1977 à 1983' (Apprenticeship between 1977 and 83), *Dossiers statistiques du travail et de l'emploi*, 2, 1984; 'Les contrats emploi-formation' (Schemes linking job creation with training), *Dossiers statistiques du travail et de l'emploi*, 8, October, 1984; for training for 16–18 year olds, *Bulletin mensuel de statistiques du travail*. For the other aspects, *Bilan de l'emploi* and *Direction de la prévision*.

introduced in 1977 and became an important part of the government aid programme for training young people and placing them in work (Tables 4.14 and 4.15). In July 1983 they were complemented by schemes linking jobs with retraining as a response to the needs of other groups of young people.

These schemes provided young people who already had a qualification with a short (150 hours) programme which retrained them within the firm for a different job; the government gave a lump sum (6,900 francs in 1983) to the firm if it agreed to employ the retrained person for at least a year.

The actual scheme linking jobs with training applied to young people who had no qualification for the particular job they had in mind. They were trained for between 200 and 1,200 hours. For each hour's training, the government paid a grant (46 francs in 1983) in two instalments to firms which employed the young person in question for at least one year in the case of training lasting less than 500 hours, or two years for training lasting 500 hours or more. The highly ambitious aims of these schemes linking jobs with training was not fulfilled in 1983–4 – between 1 July 1983 and 30 June 1984, only 83,600 young people benefited from the scheme (Table 4.15), whereas the target had been 200,000. The scheme was of most benefit to unemployed people (55% of those involved).

The new measures introduced in September 1984 On 26 September 1984 the Council of Ministers decided on a new plan to fight youth employment which had two new features – greater use of day release and community work schemes.

The first was the result of the 26 October 1983 agreement between employers and trade unions, and a law passed in February 1984. To make up for the debudgetization of contributions paid by firms for apprenticeship (0.1% of the wage bill) and post-experience training (0.2%), new schemes were introduced for 16 to 25 year olds. Those involving an actual job were schemes to acquire a qualification over a period between six months and two years, retraining programmes (for no fixed period, or at least for one year), and, more closely akin to training courses than the previous two, schemes to introduce young people to working life.

These new schemes were very slow off the ground. Between September 1984 and July 1985, only 15,000 people were involved as opposed to the original target of 300,000. It was only in 1985–6 that a significant number of people benefited (170,000) but this increase happened at the expense of the existing schemes – those linking jobs with training, and training programmes for 16 to 18 year olds. Overall therefore the number of extra young people receiving training rose by about 100,000 (Table 4.15).

The second feature of the September 1984 plan was more innovative in that it offered 'community project jobs' with the status of job trainee to unemployed young people under the age of 21. The work involved was intended to meet local needs in the area of social welfare, environment, provision of community facilities and cultural and sporting activities. The jobs were set up locally and supervised by local councils, voluntary organizations, charitable foundations, and public sector undertakings; they were intended to help the professional and social adaptation of young people between 16 and 21. The work was for eighty hours a month for a minimum of three and a maximum of twelve months, for a wage of 1,200 francs per month, plus allowances of up to 500 francs.

This scheme was very successful; the number of people involved by June 1985 was 160,000, with 340,000 more between July 1985 and June 1986. Taking into account people finishing – the average length of stay was six months – the total number of participants at any one time was about 190,000 after the end of 1985. Nearly 90% of people taken on were unemployed and about three-quarters of them had never had unemployment benefit before entry.

Youth training schemes reduced temporarily the size of the labour force Training programmes and the increased number of young people staying on at school were intended mainly in the long term to make the supply of labour better suited to the needs of the economy, including future changes. However the immediate effect of the policy on training was to remove temporarily from the labour market at least some of those who benefited from it. To assess the effect on changes in the total workforce and unemployment, the impact of schemes operated in one year has to be measured against that of the previous year's operations. For example, taking training programmes of the same length, any reduction in the total of new entrants means that people going back to employment outnumber those leaving it, and the variation in unemployment is therefore positive.

Moreover policies on training and placing people in jobs are intended at least partly to address the problem of hidden unemployment – people who are unemployed but not registered. Because of this, the effect of the total of registered unemployed is less marked. Statistics on registered unemployed show that it was particularly young people under 18 who benefited from the rejigging of training policy after 1982. Of the total registered unemployed under 25, the proportion of under 18s fell from 13.3% at the end of 1981 to 8.3% two years later, whereas the proportion of 18 to 21 year olds and 22 to 24 year olds continued to rise until 1984 (see Table 4.16).

Immigration Policy: Hopes Dashed

A constant assertion of the Left government was that it wanted immigrant workers and their families to be better integrated professionally, socially and culturally. This was put into practice particularly in 1981–2 when the status of about 110,000 illegal immigrant workers who had arrived before 1981 was legalized. At the same time, the policy introduced in the late 1970s of encouraging immigrants to return to their country of origin was dropped in 1981, although the ban on new immigration, in force since 1975, stayed,

Table 4.16 Youth unemployment between 1979 and 1985

	1980	1981	1982	1983	1984	1985
Number of under-25s unemployed	736,914	916,782	963,705	990,685	1,004,100	897,700
Percentage under-25s in total unemployed	45.2	45.5	45.2	44.5	42.9	36.5
Breakdown by age group						
Under 18s	14.8	13.3	10.2	8.3		
18 to 21 year olds	58.4	59.1	60.9	61.7		
22 to 24 year olds	26.8	27.7	28.5	30.0		
Total under-25s	100	100	100	100		

Source: Ministry of Employment.

and the fight against illegal immigration was stepped up. Moreover at the beginning of 1984, faced with increasing job losses in the car industry, the government reintroduced measures offering immigrants financial encouragement to return home. This move was linked with bilateral negotiations with the countries of origin on ways to find jobs for those immigrants who returned home.

The Development of Employment Policy and its Effect on Unemployment

There have been varying emphases in France's recent record on employment policy; stress on an 'active' employment policy and on working hours gave way to policies on managing the labour force by influencing the pattern of labour supply, and to adjustment policies for greater efficiency in a changing jobs market. The pendulum therefore swung, and will probably continue to do so, between two objectives which were stressed alternatively: to stop unemployment rising in the short term and to take care of the social implications of changes in employment patterns. The shortcomings of such an approach are obvious – by introducing costly programmes of temporary validity to fulfil the first objective, it fails in the context of the second objective to regulate in the short term the overall equilibrium of the labour market.

The Fight Against Unemployment

The Three Main Stages of Employment Policy in the Period 1981–5[45]

Table 4.17 gives an assessment of the effects of employment policy on changes in unemployment during the period 1981–3. The figures are approximate, but clear conclusions about the effects of employment policy are nevertheless possible.

In 1981–2 the government's 'active' employment policy halted the decline in the number of people in work ... This 'active' employment policy had four main features:

1 The principal result of general economic policy measures in 1981 and 1982 was to improve the overall economic context of employment;[46] economic recovery was fostered not only by an increase in welfare benefits and government spending but also by the devaluations of October 1981 and June 1982,[47] and this despite the tighter rein on the social security and unemployment benefit funds in the same period.[48]

2 These reflationary measures were accompanied by strenuous efforts to create public sector jobs; 150,000 jobs were created in two years in government service, large state enterprises and hospitals.[49]

3 At the same time, the government pressed forward with measures to encourage job creation – grants to unemployed people starting up businesses, schemes linking job creation with investment in the textile industry, etc.

4 Reductions in weekly and yearly working hours introduced by the decree of 16 January 1982 were part of the policy of stimulating employment. As already mentioned, this created or saved about 70,000 jobs.

The 'active' employment policy of 1981–2 halted, in the last quarter of 1981, the decline in the number of people in work (Figure 4.6). Whereas this figure fell by 84,000 in 1981, it rose by 72,000 in 1982 despite the poor international economic situation.

45. See M. Elbaum and A. Fonteneau, 'Les politiques d'emploi et leurs évaluations: le cas français au cours des années récentes' (Employment policies and their assessment: the French experience in recent times), *Cahiers lillois d'économie et de sociologie*, 5, first semester 1985.
46. See Chapter 2.
47. See Chapter 3.
48. See Chapter 5.
49. See above, Tables 4.8 and 4.9.

Table 4.17 Impact of employment policies (excluding general economic policy) on change in unemployment (in thousands)

Measures	Source: Assessments of OFCE – Ministry of Employment[a] 1981	1982	1983	Source: Bilan de l'emploi 1982[b] 1982	Source: Bilan de l'emploi 1983[c] 1983
	Change on previous year			Change over the year	
Shorter working hours, including schemes linking government aid with shorter working hours	0	−40	0	−50	−3
Creation of jobs in the public sector, including Post & Telecommunications and hospitals	−26	−63	−46	−50	−22.5
Aid to save jobs and boost employment (schemes linking jobs and investment in textiles, grants to unemployed to set up businesses, aid for youth employment)	−35	−41	−39	−35	−20
Early retirement and retirement at 60	−51	−68	−125	−55	−143.5
Youth training policy (training programmes, staying on at school, etc.)	−15	+5	0	+20	−39
Specific actions*	−7	−10	−47	−20	−20 to −70
Total:	−134	−217	−257	−190	−248 to 298

* Legalization of immigrants' status, measures to help long-term unemployed, short-time working, stricter rules for job seekers, 24 November 1982 decree.
[a] J.-F. Colin, M. Elbaum and A. Fonteneau, 'Chômage et politique de l'emploi 1981–83' (Unemployment and employment policy 1981–83) *Observations et diagnostics économiques, Revue de l'OFCE*, 7 April 1984.
[b] D. Frank and J.-J. Trégoat, 'Une politique active en matière d'emploi et de lutte contre le chômage a marqué 1982' (1982 was marked by an active policy on employment and the fight against unemployment), *Bulletin mensuel des statistiques du travail*, (Supplement) 104, 1984.
[c] T. Lacroix and J.-C. Guergoat, 'Le succès des préretraites a permis de stabiliser le chômage' (Unemployment stabilized by success of early retirement), *Dossiers statistiques du travail et de l'emploi*, 3–4, June 1984.

The Fight Against Unemployment

... and increased the labour force participation rate According to a study by INSEE in March 1982, the recovery in the number of people employed gave rise to a significant increase in the number of women and young people in jobs. Whereas in the period 1975–81 the rise in the number of women employed had contributed 120,000 per year to the rise in the total number employed, this figure was 260,000 in 1982 (see Table 4.18). The same phenomenon applied to young people under 25; it is one which is normally apparent when the employment situation improves, particularly in the commercial service sector and the central and local government sector. The general view is that the creation of 100 jobs in the service sector means 40–50 unemployed fewer, and 50–60 more people in the jobs market. In 1981–2, it is likely that the increased number of jobs sucked in extra people, mainly women, who had not been registered as unemployed. Because of this, unemployment continued to rise until Summer 1982 even though the number of people in work went up.

Between Autumn 1982 and Autumn 1983, the policy of 'managing the labour force' meant that unemployment steadied around the two million mark The main thrust of employment policy changed between 1982 and 1983: the stress on 'active' policies to stem the rise in unemployment was replaced by 'labour force policy'. This was against the background of a more restrictive macro-economic policy beginning with the 26 March 1983 plan, which cut back sharply the number of new public sector jobs. Moreover, after the notable successes of 1982, reductions in working hours fell back to the previous rate of 0.4% a year, and the new scheme linking government aid with reduction in working hours was only moderately successful. A fall of 200,000 between December 1982 and December 1983 in the number of people in work (see Figure 4.6) shows the severely reduced scope of the 'active' jobs policy, though the level of grants to unemployed people starting up businesses remained high.

The most significant measures in 1983 to fight unemployment were without doubt the schemes to encourage people to take early retirement. Added to the increase in redundancies for economic reasons financed by the national employment fund were schemes linking official aid with voluntary early retirement; these led to an increase in the number of people giving up work from some 50,000 in 1982 to 150,000 in 1983.

These measures taken as a whole plus the lowering of the retirement age to 60 in April 1983 helped, according to INSEE

Table 4.18 Breakdown of the annual change in the resident labour force, derived from number of people in employment at 31 March* 1954–85 (in thousands)

	1954–62	1962–68	1968–75	1975–82	1981	1982	1983	1984	1985
Annual change in labour force	+28	+140	+203	+242	+116	+326	+34	+27	+170
1. Demographic changes and migration	+86	+268	+228	+211	+242	+232	+218	+202	+154
2. Impact of labour force participation rate	−58	−128	−25	+31	−126	+94	−184	−175	+16
made up of:									
under-25s**	−20	−64	−61	−40	−103	−21	−60	−114	−43
over-54s	−32	−84	−79	−71	−119	−83	−248	−123	−20
women 25–54	−3	+25	+113	+156	+111	+259	+129	+79	+78
men 25–54	−3	−5	+2	−14	−15	−61	−5	−17	+1

* The change in the labour force over a year is broken down into:
  – Change attributable to demographic factors: the labour force participation rate in March of year $n − 1$ is applied to the change in total population (labour force and non-active population) between March of year $n − 1$ and March of year n. The flow comes from the natural movement of population and net migration.
  – Change attributable to the labour force participation rate. The change in this between March of year $n − 1$ and March of year n is applied to the population figure for March of year n. Changes in the participation rate in the case of young people are a function of changes in the proportion still in education and the participation rate of those no longer in education.

** Including those doing military service.

Source: INSEE, *Comptes de la Nation* (National accounts).

The Fight Against Unemployment

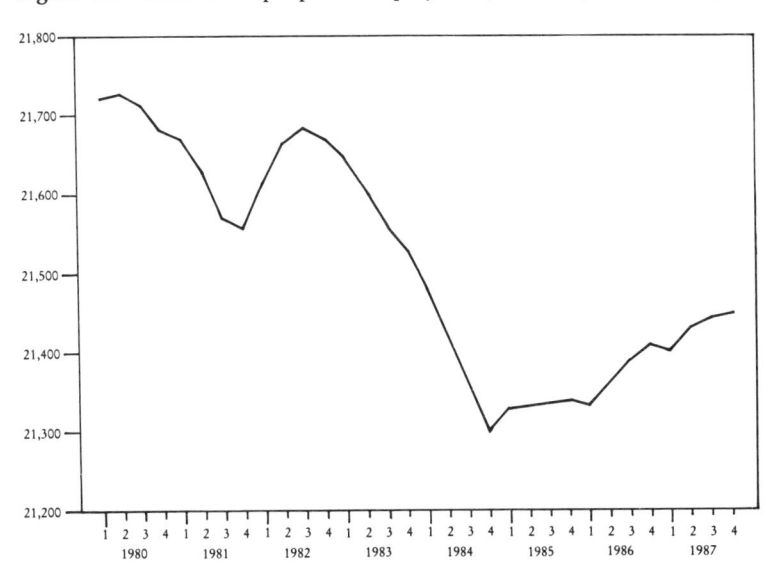

Figure 4.6 Number of people in employment, 1980–7 (in thousands)

employment statistics, to reduce the number of people in work by 250,000 in 1983 (see Table 4.18) as opposed to a fall of 100,000 in 1981–2. However, because of measures such as training programmes for 16 to 18 year olds, and the increased numbers staying on at school, the proportion of young people below 25 in work also fell.

Overall, the number of people leaving the labour market permanently or temporarily more or less offset, for the first time, the natural demographic increase in the labour force. Despite a decrease in the number of people in work, the level of unemployment steadied at the two million mark until Autumn 1983 (see Figure 4.7).

In 1984–5, the emphasis of employment policy was on restructuring industry and youth unemployment In 1984 there was a move away from intensive anti-unemployment measures, though at the end of the year a new programme of help for young people was introduced. There was a phasing out of 'active' policy measures, and there was no further reduction in working hours on an annual basis; moreover, new jobs in the public sector only just matched, or indeed were fewer than, the number of jobs lost. The year 1984 also saw the end of schemes of government aid for early retirement, not only because of their high cost but also because of the danger of a virtual elimination of those over 55 from the labour market.

–241–

Figure 4.7 Unemployment, 1980–8 (in thousands)

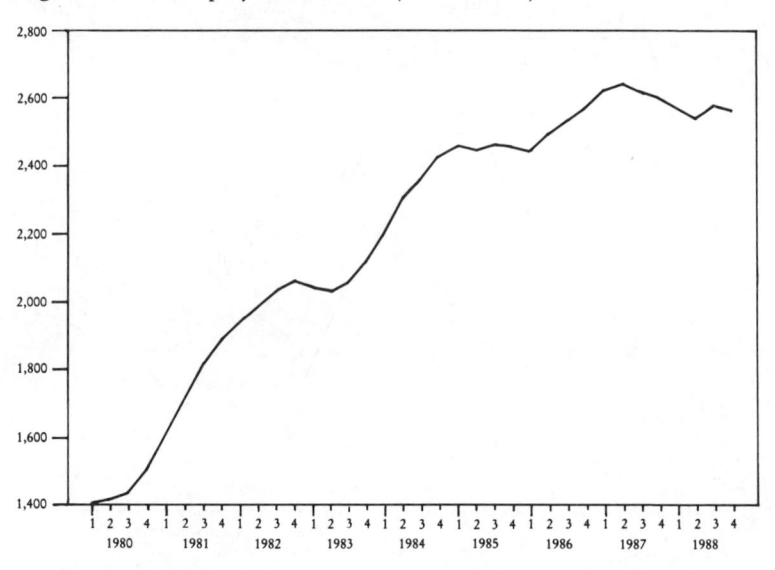

In Spring 1984, the main emphasis became the fine-tuning of the social aspects of industrial restructuring, with a variety of measures allowing each sector to be dealt with in the appropriate way. There were specific programmes for certain sectors (e.g. leave of absence for retraining in steel and shipbuilding), or for certain geographical areas (exemption from social security contributions in Lorraine, and special efforts to stimulate jobs in regional centres where traditional industries were being run down). Individual retraining schemes were introduced, e.g. for immigrant workers prior to returning home, and employees who lost pay in moving jobs were given a gradually reducing temporary allowance.

Since the modernization of industry was once again the government's priority, employment policy regained its traditional role of facilitating restructuring, though it had to operate in a way which was appropriate to the sector in question. Whether this new emphasis could be a lasting one was thrown in doubt however by the steady rise in unemployment between Autumn 1983 and Summer 1984, a fact which the government implicitly recognized by introducing in September 1984 a new plan to combat youth unemployment.

The Fight Against Unemployment

Figure 4.8 Comparison of unemployment rates* in France and certain OECD countries

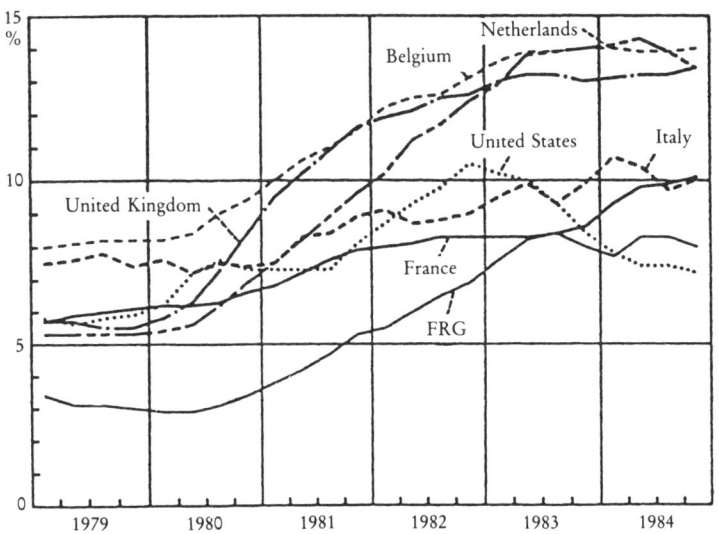

*The unemployment rate is the number of unemployed as a percentage of the labour force, according to the OECD definition.

Employment Trends and Unemployment in Other Countries

International comparisons in the field of jobs and unemployment are always difficult to make, given divergences in the measurement of unemployment, in the definition of various aspects of employment (e.g. part-time work), and in the classification of the unemployed (length of time unemployed, sex, age groups). During the period of 1981–4 the trend in other industrialized countries regarding numbers in work and unemployed was the opposite of that in France. Whereas in France unemployment remained practically at the same level in 1982–3, it rose sharply elsewhere, particularly in West Germany, the United Kingdom, Belgium and the Netherlands, as well as in the United States up to the end of 1982 (see Figure 4.8). Conversely, between mid-1983 and the end of 1984, unemployment dropped significantly in the United States and remained steady in the other countries, but it rose in France from 8% to over 10%. These disparities arose because economic policies were not synchronized and because the employment situation evolved differently in the various countries. Table 4.19 shows the numbers of people in work between 1980 and 1985 in France and in other

Table 4.19 Annual average total of people in work, in France and other countries, between 1980 and 1984 (total in thousands, and % change on previous year)

	1980		1981		1982		1983		1984	
	Total	%	Total	%	Total	%	Total	%	Total	%
United States	100,907	0.5	102,042	1.1	101,194	−0.1	102,510	1.3	106,702	4.1
Japan	55,360	1.0	55,810	0.8	56,380	1.0	57,330	1.7	57,660	0.6
European Community including:	110,854	0.6	109,458	−1.3	108,535	−0.8	107,793	−0.7	108,000	0.2
France	21,916	0.1	21,803	−0.5	21,834	0.1	21,729	−0.5	21,511	−1.0
West Germany	26,302	1.0	26,101	−0.8	25,632	−1.8	25,228	−1.6	25,174	−0.2
Italy	21,107	1.5	20,924	−0.9	20,875	−0.2	20,921	0.2	21,269	1.7
United Kingdom	25,306	−0.3	24,323	−3.9	23,987	−1.4	23,792	−0.8	24,035	1.0

Source: O. Marchand and E. Martin-Le-Goff, '200,000 emplois à nouveau perdus en 1984' (200,000 jobs lost again in 1984), *Economie et statistique*, 176, April 1985.

The Fight Against Unemployment

countries. In the United States, the net total of new jobs created was six million between the end of 1980 and the end of 1984. These new jobs were mainly in the service sector, and more particularly in the area of services to firms (financial services, engineering and other consultancy) and to individuals (restaurants, security services). More than 80% of these new jobs were created in firms with fewer than a hundred employees.

During the same period nearly three million jobs were lost in the European Community.

−5−

The Fruits of Austerity

Compared with West Germany and Japan, where the rate of inflation soon fell back to below its pre-first oil shock level, France did not manage to reduce its inflation rate and it was still running at an annual 9% level by the time of the second oil shock. The persistence of strong domestic inflationary pressure, at a time when exchange rates were favourable (the dollar was falling and the franc had settled against European currencies) was evidence of a price–wages dynamic which was particularly unfavourable.[1] This was confirmed by the high level of the indexation coefficients given by French econometric models in the period of economic crisis.

Right-wing governments before 1981 had had to accept this economic pattern, but it was overturned, rather paradoxically, by the Left government in a way which it had not foreseen in its election campaign. Disinflation took place in an international environment which was much less favourable than is usually thought. While it is true that there was a slow-down of the inflation rate in France's main trading partners, the sharp rise in the dollar throughout the period and to a lesser degree the depreciations of the franc within the EMS meant that imported inflation exerted permanent pressure on the disinflationary process in France. The rise in import prices between 1982 and 1984 was on average 2% higher than the rise in the price of GDP.

Expectations of continued inflation were ended by the effectiveness of the price and wage freeze in the second half of 1982, a situation which continued during 1983 and 1984, and this led not only to a marked drop in the rate of inflation but also a revival of firms' profitability unprecedented for at least thirty years. Disinflation and improvement in firms' profitability were the result of an important separation − the gap which opened up between the productivity of labour, which went up more than 3% on average in 1983 and 1984, and real wages, which stayed the same. The plough-

---

1. See Chapter 1 for comparative analyses of the inflation which followed the first oil shock.

The Fruits of Austerity

ing back of profits into investment took longer to come about because interest rate rises increased their overheads, but it took off in 1985 when interest rates fell and there was less borrowing by firms. This turn-round was brought about by the forceful policy of Mauroy and Delors in the winter of 1982–3. From mid-1984, disinflation gained a momentum of its own, helped by the low level of domestic demand brought about by a restrictive fiscal policy. This in fact was the other aspect of economic austerity; cuts in government spending were surprisingly high in view of the fact that the government gave itself two objectives – to keep budget overspending below the level of 3% of GDP, and to reduce taxation.

The decision in 1985 to reduce direct taxation of firms and individuals by one percentage point was influenced by the US approach to supply-side economics – that the economy would be more buoyant if taxes were lower. The US government had applied the first element of the classical liberal credo by a sharp reduction in taxes on individuals, but it shrank from introducing the second element – reduction of government spending. The result was that the US government used the pretext of supply-side economics to create the only example of Keynesian recovery of demand in the 1980s. This was a case however of a relatively closed economy which was financing its external deficit by taking advantage of the fact that its currency was the means of international payment. Such privileges were not accorded to the French economy, and tax cuts had partly to be accompanied by cuts in spending, which had the effect of limiting the expansionary impact to a slight tax advantage for households.

The recovery of firms' profitability meant the loosening of one constraint on investment, and from 1984 the main factors holding back investment were lack of markets and the high level of real interest rates. This lack of investment due to shrinking markets was dealt with very suitably by the policy of tax redistribution in favour of individuals, which offset the fact that wages were being held down. However, this was not an effective answer to economic crisis at the higher level of a nation which, to maintain external balances, could not grow faster than its trading partners. It is quite likely that policies of austerity applied by the majority of European countries were a necessary condition for long-term economic recovery. But since the prospects for European growth were not good, there was little chance that this would be brought about by market forces alone. Conversely, a co-ordinated European recovery based on far-reaching medium-term plans could well hold out hopes for an end to the recession. This will be the theme of this final chapter.

Disinflation and the Return of Profitability

Disinflation on the world level will be described briefly, before we turn to a quantitative analysis of the process which in France led to a slow-down of inflation and a return of firms' profitability; the effect on the recovery of investment will be examined.

Disinflation in Major Industrialized Countries

Disinflation after the second oil shock was such that inflation in industrialized countries fell to levels significantly lower than those before the first oil shock (see Table 5.1). At the end of 1984, inflation rates in major West European countries matched those of the end of the 1960s, cancelling out the effect of the two oil shocks. This general trend of disinflation was strongly affected by exchange rate movements. The rise in the dollar and the yen against the European currencies after 1980 and the rise in the pound up to 1982 helped disinflation in the United States, Japan and the United Kingdom, but hindered it in West Germany and France (last column of Table 5.1).

The slow-down of inflation was partly due to the exceptional length of the recession and the high level of unemployment, but also to the policy of holding down wages. Even though most countries had maximum levels for the growth of money supply, there is no evidence for supposing that monetary policies had any specific influence on disinflation, beyond the normal one which interest rate rises have on dampening down demand and increasing the value of the national currency. There is no doubt that knowledge of the intended ceiling on growth of monetary supply helps disinflation by changing people's expectations, but its influence is neither greater nor smaller (and in France probably much smaller) than knowledge of the official inflation rate target.

On the other hand, the slow-down in wage costs, which came about in many countries when the traditional mechanism for deciding and planning wage rises broke down, was the decisive factor in disinflation.[2] This happened in France when wages and prices were frozen as part of the package accompanying the June 1982 devaluation.

---

2. Cf. on this point the analysis of disinflation in the major OECD countries done by CEPII in the book quoted in Table 5.1.

Table 5.1 Consumer prices in the major OECD countries

	Percentage change over previous year							Disinflation			Effect of exchange rates between 1981 and 1983[c]
	1978	1979	1980	1981	1982	1983	1984	1985	Differential between maximum and minimum[a]	Differential between 1978 and 1985[b]	
United States	7.7	11.3	13.5*	10.4	6.1	3.2*	4.3	3.5	−10.3	−4.2	−2.5
Japan	3.8	3.6	8.0*	4.9	2.7	1.9*	2.2	2.1	−6.1	−1.7	−0.6
West Germany	2.7	4.1	5.5	6.3*	5.3	3.3	2.4	2.2*	−4.1	−0.5	+1.3
France	9.1	10.8	13.6*	13.4	11.8	9.6	7.4	5.8*	−7.8	−3.3	+1.4
United Kingdom	8.3	13.4	18.0*	11.9	8.6	4.6*	5.0	6.1	−13.4	−2.2	−3.1
Italy	12.1	14.8	21.2*	17.8	16.6	14.6	10.8	8.6*	−12.6	−3.5	n.a.

[a] Differential between maximum rate (generally in 1980) and minimum rate (generally 1983 or 1985), both marked by an asterisk for each country.
[b] Fall in inflation rate between 1978 and 1985.
[c] Average effect of exchange rate variations between 1979 and 1983 on the annual rate of consumer price changes during 1981–3.
Source: CEPII, *Economie mondiale 1980–90 – la fracture?* (The World economy in the 1980s: the final breakdown?), Paris, Economica, 1984, pp. 15–16.

Disinflation in France: From Freeze to Disindexation

The wages and prices policy introduced in June 1982 was intended to break the vicious circle linking price rises with wage rises. Where wages are wholly price-indexed and where the whole of wage increases feed through to price increases, any acceleration, however slight, of the price–wage spiral is compounded and amplified in an inflationary process which is checked only by delays in adjustments and in the operation of external factors – for example the fact that wages are partly indexed on foreign prices insofar as these are a factor in consumer prices. Econometric estimates by the main French models of the usual determinants of prices and wages show that wages are almost wholly indexed on prices and prices on wage costs, allowing for delays in adjustment. It was very much because of this that the high level of inflation after the oil shocks persisted.[3]

To counter this, two approaches were possible: either keep on with a very restrictive policy involving a fall in demand and a sharp increase in unemployment, which would act on wages and prices and set in train the disinflationary process; or conversely set it in train by ending people's expectations of continuing inflation.[4] It was the latter approach which Pierre Mauroy and Jacques Delors adopted first by imposing an effective freeze on wages and prices in the second half of 1982 and then by introducing the idea of planning wage rises on the basis of the rate of inflation aimed at. Obviously, both policies help to slow inflation, but wage policy played a decisive role by making inflation less costly in terms of jobs and growth. As J. Vignon wrote:[5] 'This strange period, when the monthly inflation rate fell to a surprising 0.3% or 0.4%, not only ended people's expectations of continually rising prices, but also gave the government time to plan for an update of the French version of nominalism.'

The total freeze on prices and wages was brought to an end by a series of agreements which were voluntary in industry and government-imposed in services and retailing. These agreements allowed limited price increases, and at the same time there was an

---

3. Cf. particularly the work by Patrick Artus, presented in Table 1.3, p. 42.
4. The possibility of such a process was well anticipated by Serge-Christophe Kolm in an article published just before the 1981 elections and reprinted in his *Sortir de la crise* (Emerging from the crisis), Paris, Hachette, Collection Pluriel, 1983, pp. 323ff.
5. J. Vignon, 'Le delorisme en économie' (Delors-ism in economics), *Les Cahiers Français*, 218, October–December 1984, p. 62.

The Fruits of Austerity

attempt to impose new rules to space out wage increases in the public sector. In this way the basis of a disindexation policy was laid by planning wage rises and increases in welfare benefits.

The government invited both sides of industry to agree on the future pattern of wage increases by signing contracts on a different basis from before:

1 The average wage increase for the coming year, and the timing of its introduction, would be determined in advance in accordance with national objectives (8% in 1983, 5% in 1984 and 4.5% in 1985); this would replace the system of quarterly backdated increases based on price levels.

2 There could be an adjustment at the end of the year but this should not be automatic and should take account of the national situation or of circumstances peculiar to the firm.

3 Negotiation should be on the basis of the total wages bill in a firm rather than comparison with previous wage levels; this would take account of the financial position of the firm.

A further point was that increases in social welfare benefits should take place twice a year (1 January and 1 July); the total involved should not be more than half the inflation rate aimed for by the government, and any adjustments should be *ex post*.

A Quantitative Analysis of Disinflation

Analytical method The effect of the freeze and disindexation on the way prices and wages are determined can be assessed by comparing them with the previous position, established by normal econometric methods. However, because prices and wages are interdependent, the analysis must be done in two stages. An indication of changes in the way prices and wages are determined is obtained by comparing what would have happened on the basis of the previous period with what in fact happened in the case of each one. The overall picture must also take account of any effects arising from the fact that prices and wages are interdependent,[6] a phenomenon summarized in Figure 5.1 which shows the main variables involved in the determination of prices and wages, and therefore in disinflation.

---

6. By using this approach in forecasting, we showed that it was possible to achieve an inflation rate lower than 7% in 1984 and around 5% in 1985. See 'Inflation à 5%: un pari réalisable?' (Inflation at 5%: an achievable goal?), *Lettre de l'OFCE*, 13, 28 March 1984.

Reflation and Austerity

Figure 5.1 Price–wage loop and the mechanics of disinflation

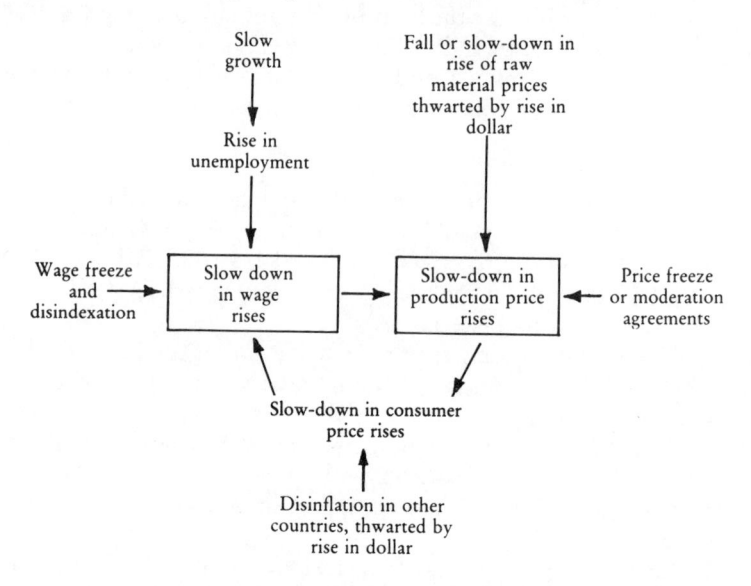

```
                    Slow              Fall or slow-down in
                   growth                rise of raw
                     │                  material prices
                     │                 thwarted by rise in
                     ▼                      dollar
                   Rise in                    │
                 unemployment                 │
                     │                        │
                     ▼                        ▼
Wage freeze      Slow down           Slow-down in           Price freeze
    and    ───▶   in wage      ───▶  production price  ◀───  or moderation
disindexation     rises                  rises                agreements
                     ▲                     ▲
                      \                   /
                       Slow-down in consumer
                           price rises
                              ▲
                              │
                       Disinflation in other
                       countries, thwarted by
                           rise in dollar
```

Changes in hourly wage rate depend mainly on three factors
1 Indexation on consumer prices; the assumption is that it is total, but that there is a delay of about five months.
2 Rise in the guaranteed minimum wage – the impact of this is adjusted to take account of a spread effect which is large in that the minimum wage is close to the average wage.
3 The situation of the labour market measured by the ratio of the number of registered unemployed to the number of vacancies.

To these traditional factors, the impact of which was assessed for the period 1964–81, were added the prices and wages freeze and the disindexation, the effect of which is estimated by comparing what was forecast with what actually happened.

Changes in domestic prices are brought about mainly by changes in prices abroad and by wage costs. Foreign disinflation (hindered throughout the period in question by the rise of the dollar) helps keep down the price of domestic production, first because it keeps firms' costs down by slowing down rises in the price of raw materials and imported capital goods, and second because it contributes indirectly to reducing firms' wage costs by keeping down price rises of imported consumer goods. To these various factors helping to keep costs down must be added the freeze and agree-

The Fruits of Austerity

ments to limit rises, the effect of which is assessed by comparing forecast and actual production prices.

The slow-down in wage rises was brought about by disindexation and the rise in unemployment The simulation of the wage equation in Table 5.2 gives an idea of the magnitude of the factors which contributed to the slow-down in wage increases. In the first half of 1982, the increase in hourly wage rates was very high – more than 16% over a year. The total labour force, which had been falling since the beginning of 1980, rose during this period,[7] and to this must be added indexation on a high level of inflation (12% over a year) and a shorter working week with no loss of wages. This latter factor caused a difference of 1.2% between forecast and actual change in the first quarter of 1982.

In the third quarter of 1982, the wages and prices freeze reduced by two percentage points the rise in hourly wage rates. On the basis of the previous situation, one-third of the reduction was gained by indexation and the freeze on prices, and two-thirds (1.3%) by the freeze on wages themselves. After the freeze, there was a slight catching up (0.6%) and, from mid-1983, the policy of disindexation, together with disinflation and a worsening of the labour market, led to a continual reduction in the rate of wage rises.

Disindexation slowed down wage rises mainly at the end of 1983 and during the first quarter of 1984. From the second quarter of 1984, the operation of the previous system of indexation would have given, because of disinflation, the same result as actually happened. However, a similar analysis by INSEE published in the *Rapport sur les Comptes de la Nation de l'année 1984* (National accounts, Report for 1984) gives a greater impact for disindexation. The INSEE model takes no account of rises in the minimum wage though it does bring in the influence of increased productivity of labour on wage rises. The differences between the two sets of results relate mainly to 1984. The assessment in each case of why wage rises slowed down between 1983 and 1984 is given in Table 5.3.

Hourly wage rates fell from 10.6% in 1983 to 6.6% in 1984 (see Figure 5.2). According to the OFCE model, of this 4% fall, the previous system of indexation counted for 1.7 percentage points and the deterioration in the labour market for 1.4 points, whereas the smaller rise in minimum wage had negligible impact. Disindexation therefore had only a 0.9% effect. According to INSEE, the previous system of indexation counted for 1.3 percentage points, increased

7. See Figure 4.6 (Chapter 4).

Table 5.2 Factors explaining changes in hourly wage rate (% quarterly change)

	1982 (1)	1982 (2)	1982 (3)	1982 (4)	1983 (1)	1983 (2)	1983 (3)	1983 (4)	1984 (1)	1984 (2)	1984 (3)	1984 (4)
Actual hourly rate	4.7	3.6	1.6	2.3	3.3	2.6	2.5	2.2	1.7	1.4	1.8	1.6
Labour market effect[a]	0.2	0.2	0.2	0.3	0.4	0.3	0.2	0.1	-0.1	-0.1	-0.1	-0.1
Inflation effect	3.2	3.2	2.6	2.3	2.3	2.4	2.3	2.2	2.1	2.0	1.8	1.6
Minimum wage effect	0.1	0.0	0.1	0.0	0.0	0.0	0.0	0.1	0.0	0.0	0.0	0.1
Difference between actual and simulated	+1.2[b]	0.2[b]	-1.3[c]	-0.3[c]	0.6[c]	-0.1	0.0	-0.2[d]	-0.4[d]	-0.5[d]	0.1	0.0

[a] Including autonomous effect.
[b] Effect of reduction of working hours without loss of pay.
[c] Effect of the freeze.
[d] Effect of disindexation.

Source: Econometric calculation in article by M. Boutillier, 'L'évolution récente des salaires' (Recent wage trends), *Observations et diagnostics économiques*, 5, October 1983, p. 110. The calculation was reassessed over the period 1965–84.

The Fruits of Austerity

Table 5.3 Comparison of two assessments of the slow-down in rise of hourly wage rates in 1983–4

(1) % change over the year, 1984		6.6
(2) % change over the year, 1983		10.6
(3) Slow-down		–4.0

Factors in the slow-down	OFCE equation		INSEE equation
(4) Worsening of the labour market	–1.4		–1.0
(5) Indexation on prices	–1.7		–1.3
(6) Other factors – minimum wage	–0.0	productivity	+0.5
(7) Unexplained change (disindexation)	–0.9		–2.0

Note: Change over the year calculated on the basis of the product of the four indices gives a rise of 11% in 1983; on the basis of the usual approximation, i.e. the sum of the four growth rates, the rise is 10.6%. This approximation has been used here in order to make comparison with the INSEE figures easier.

Source: OFCE equation – see Table 5.2; INSEE equation – *Rapport sur les Comptes de la Nation 1984* (Report on national accounts 1984), p. 37.

Figure 5.2 Prices and wages

% growth rate over previous quarter

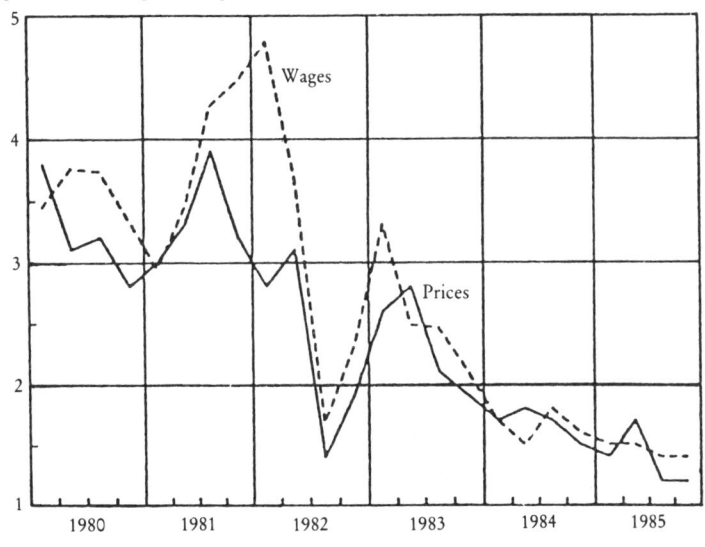

unemployment for one point, but on the other hand the rise in productivity added 0.5% to wage rises. Here disindexation accounts for a two percentage point reduction in wage rises.

However the full effect of the policy of disindexation on changes in wages is not shown in these figures. In fact, actual price rises, which contribute to the determination of wages, were smaller than they should have been because of disindexation, so that to assess the total effect of disindexation over the quarter, account must be taken of the effect of this disindexation on the slow-down in price rises, then the effect of this slow-down on wages, and so on.

Moreover, account must be taken of effects occurring in subsequent periods. In practice, there are two stages: first of all, actual changes in wages compared with what would have happened on the basis of the previous situation are analysed in order to assess the effect of the wage freeze and disindexation; then the same for prices to calculate the effect of the price freeze and agreements to limit rises. Then a simulation is undertaken of the price–wage spiral to obtain the overall effect of these policies on the way prices and wages changed (see Inset 5.1). Before giving the findings of this simulation, an examination will be made of the way production prices are determined.

The increase in production prices slowed because cost increases slowed   Table 5.4 shows changes in production prices and in the unit cost of production of non-financial firms, as well as the two main components of this – the cost of inputs and wage costs.

Disinflation started during 1982 as a result of the wages and prices freeze and a fall in input costs (although the annual average increase relative to the previous year was 12.1%, within the year the 1982 rise was 8%). This reduction in input costs was caused by a fall in raw material prices brought about because of the world recession, and because the price freeze meant that costs from the 1982 devaluations were not passed on. From 1983, the steady fall in wage costs and the cost of inputs was the main factor in disinflation, as well as the result of it.

An analysis of the difference between actual changes in production prices and what would have been expected over the long term points up the specific effect of the price freeze in the third quarter of 1982, but this was almost entirely cancelled out by the subsequent catching-up process.

The impact of the policy to limit price increases was that, from the third quarter of 1983, price rises were always lower than would have been the case according to the relation estimated on the

The Fruits of Austerity

Inset 5.1

A core model to analyse disindexation

To analyse the process of disindexation, a dynamic core model has been made summarizing on an aggregate level the main calculation of the price–wage loop of a quarterly model. The specification used and the coefficients are taken from the findings of the OFCE-quarterly econometric model. Since it was a matter of looking at the impact of shocks external to the price–wage loop on changes in prices and wages, these external magnitudes have been summarized in the following categories:
- import prices p_m
- shocks external to the production prices relationship ε_p
- shocks external to the wages relationship ε_w
- external shocks affecting retail prices ε_c

The model is specified in growth rates and in difference in relation to a base path. The equations are as follows:

(1) Quarterly rate of growth of wages ($\dot{w}$)

$$\dot{w} = 0.975 \left[\sum_{i=0}^{5} \dot{w}(-i) \right] + \varepsilon_w$$

(2) Quarterly rate of growth of production prices ($\dot{p}$)

$$\dot{p} = 0.7\, \dot{p}(-1) + 0.3\, (0.5\, \dot{w} + 0.5\, \dot{p}_i) + \varepsilon_p$$

(3) Quarterly rate of growth of consumer prices ($\dot{p}_c$)

$$\dot{p}_c = 0.7\, \dot{p} + 0.3\, \dot{p}_m + \varepsilon_c$$

(4) Quarterly rate of growth of input prices ($\dot{p}_i$)

$$\dot{p}_i = 0.7\, \dot{p} + 0.3\, \dot{p}_m$$

The indices between brackets indicate lags in quarters. The weightings used for the coefficients of indexation of wages on prices are as follows:

$$\alpha_i = \left(\frac{6}{21}, \frac{5}{21}, \frac{4}{21}, \frac{3}{21}, \frac{2}{21}, \frac{1}{21} \right)$$

To assess the impact of the freeze and disindexation, the differentials given in Table 5.2 have been used for wages. For prices, the impact of the freeze is calculated directly by indicative variables added to a price equation estimated over the period 1965–84, and prices policy by the differential between actual and

continued on p. 258

> **Inset 5.1** *continued*
>
> *A core model to analyse disindexation*
>
> simulated changes when these appear to be sufficiently large. In practice, the estimate of the price equation (for a specified level) shows persistently negative differences beginning with the fourth quarter of 1983. Converted into differences in growth rates, the following figures are obtained:
> Differentials on production prices (ε_p):
>
> | 1982.2 | 1982.3 | 1982.4 | 1983.3 | 1983.4 | 1984.1 | 1984.2 | 1984.3 | 1984.4 |
> |---|---|---|---|---|---|---|---|---|
> | −0.2 | −1.2 | +0.5 | +0.4 | −0.1 | −0.3 | 0.0 | −0.1 | 0.0 |
>
> Moreover, retail prices were more affected by the policy of keeping a close watch on prices than production prices were. Specific differentials not attributable to changes in production and import prices are as follows:
> Differentials on retail prices (ε_c):
>
> | 1984.1 | 1984.2 | 1984.3 | 1984.4 |
> |---|---|---|---|
> | −0.3 | −0.6 | −0.1 | 0.0 |

previous period. Nevertheless, actual reductions in price rises were slight (see Inset 5.1), perhaps because the simulation, by linking production price levels to unit cost levels, implicitly assumed that the impact of price policies would be temporary. The argument was that since there was unit elasticity of production prices to production costs, they would coincide in the long term.

During 1984, the slow-down of inflation was much more marked in the service sector, which was subject to a tight squeeze, than in the industrial sector. In fact, the removal of some price controls, together with an improvement in export margins, allowed some sectors of industry to pass on the steep rise in raw material prices – the dollar price of imported energy fell slightly, though its price in francs went up by 15.3% in 1984; similarly, the price of industrial raw materials fell by 2% in foreign currency terms but rose by 7% in francs.

Differences in inflation rates between sectors became less marked
These differences appear in retail prices (see Table 5.5). For the first time since the second oil shock, service prices rose slightly more slowly than those of manufactured goods. One of the main conse-

The Fruits of Austerity

Table 5.4 Production prices and costs of non-financial enterprises (% annual average)

	1978–81	1982	1983	1984	1985	1986
(1) Production prices	11.3	11.6	9.0	7.8	5.2	1.7
(2) Total unit cost	11.6	12.4	8.8	7.4	4.8	−0.5
– unit wage cost	11.3	13.0	9.7	6.6	5.4	2.8
– unit input cost	11.8	12.1	8.4	7.8	4.5	−2.3
(3) Improvement in profits:						
(3) = (1) − (2)	−0.3	−0.8	0.2	0.4	0.4	2.2

Note: The unit cost of production is equal to the sum of inputs, welfare contributions, financial charges and taxes connected with production, the whole as a proportion of the volume of production. In 1983, inputs represented 57% of production costs, and the wage bill was 35%.

Source: *Rapport sur les Comptes de la Nation* (Report on national accounts) 1986, INSEE.

Table 5.5 Changes in retail prices (% change over year), 1981–4

	1981	1982	1983	1984
Overall	13.9	9.7	9.3	6.7
Food	16.5	9.2	10.1	6.1
Private sector industrial goods	10.4	8.2	9.2	6.7
Private sector services	15.7	10.9	10.6	6.4
Public utilities	17.4	14.8	5.6	8.8
Rents, water	13.2	8.1	10.5	7.6
Health	11.9	5.0	9.5	3.4

Source: INSEE.

quences of the policy of agreed price increases was that consumer price changes in the various sectors became standard. Differential inflation rates between sectors, which had been as high as 5% or 6% in previous years, were very low in 1984 which reduced the structural factors in inflation.

An analysis by sector of the difference between actual and forecast changes shows that the biggest effect of price controls was in the service sector. Price changes in the industrial sector were what econometric forecasts would have made them, but the difference between this and actual changes in the case of services was over 1% in 1984.[8] A further point is that the strict watch on prices meant a stronger check on retail prices than on production prices.

8. The analysis by INSEE in its report on the current economic situation in February 1985 (p. 44) confirms this figure.

Table 5.6 Quantitative assessment of the freeze and the policy of disindexation (% change over year), 1981–4

	1981	1982	1983	1984
(1) Rate of change of production prices	13.5	8.7	9.0	5.5
(2) Disinflation since 1981	–	−4.8	−4.5	−8.0
Impact of:				
(3) Reduction in working hours	–	+0.6	+0.4	+0.2
(4) Freeze and disindexation	–	−2.9	−1.3	−3.3/−4.4
(5) Other factors = (2)−(3)−(4)	–	−2.5	−3.6	−4.9/−3.8

A quantitative overview of the freeze and the disindexation policy An assessment of the impact of the freeze, the disindexation policy and the price restraint agreements can be made using the dynamic flows of the model described in Inset 5.1. Table 5.6 gives findings on production prices during the period 1982–4 when domestic disinflation was strongest. For 1984, two assessments of the effect of wages policy are given – INSEE and OFCE.

The prices and wages freeze reduced inflation in 1982 by three percentage points. On the other hand, the rise in hourly wage rates brought about by the new 39-hour week raised it slightly (0.6%). Despite the slight setback at the beginning of 1983, disindexation and wage restraint agreements further contributed to disinflation, so that in 1984, prices and wages policy was responsible for half of the disinflation – this is shown by a comparison of lines 4 and 5 in Table 5.6. Other factors in disinflation were slow-down in growth, rise in unemployment and foreign disinflation, though this was almost entirely offset during this period by the rise in the dollar, and the fall in the franc within the EMS.

The slow-down of inflation was brought about more by prices policy than by wages policy (in the rough ratio of one-third to two-thirds). The mirror image is that the slow-down in wage rises was two-thirds due to wages policy and one-third due to prices policy. If the prices policy had not been accompanied by a deliberate restraint on wage rises, the cost of disinflation would have been borne by firms, whereas, because wage rises were held in check, firms benefited enormously from the disinflation policy by increasing profitability.

The Fruits of Austerity

Table 5.7 Main factors in changes in the profits–value added ratio for firms (annual rate, change within the period shown)

	From 1970 to 1972	From 1973 to 1977	From 1978 to 1982	1983 and 1984
(1) Change in annual rate, in the profits–value added ratio (in points)	–	−1.5	−0.2	+2.1
(2) Growth in labour productivity	+5.7	+4.05	+3.4	+4.25
(3) Less – growth in real wages	−5.9	−4.85	−2.15	−0.5
(4) Less – change in relative consumer prices in relation to value added	+0.4	−0.2	−1.0	−0.45
(5) Less – change in apparent rate of employers' welfare contributions	−0.2	−0.45	−0.4	−1.15

(1) = (2) + (3) + (4) + (5)
Source: P.-A. Muet and H. Sterdyniak, 28 May 1985.

Increased Profits did not necessarily go to Investment[9]

Disinflation and the recovery of firms' profitability stemmed from the difference between increased productivity of labour and zero rises in real wages. The factors leading to a fall in firms' profits after the oil shocks were looked at in Chapter 1. Initially, the main cause of this fall was that rises in the productivity of labour slowed down faster than rises in real wages. But from 1978 rises in the productivity of labour outstripped rises in real wages by more than 1% per year, though profits went on falling slightly (see Table 5.7). Moreover this turn-round was confounded by a rise in employers' social security contributions and a steady worsening of the terms of trade after 1979 as a result of the second oil shock. It was this deterioration of the terms of trade in fact which caused consumer prices to rise in the period 1978–82 by more than one percentage point more than value-added prices. And since wages were indexed on consumer prices and not on value-added prices, profits deteriorated to the same extent.

9. This section is based on the article by P.-A. Muet and H. Sterdyniak, 'Rétablissement des profits et stagnation de l'investissement: un paradoxe?' (Recovery of profits and stagnation of investment: a paradox?), *Observations et diagnostics économiques, Lettre de l'OFCE*, 25, 28 May 1985.

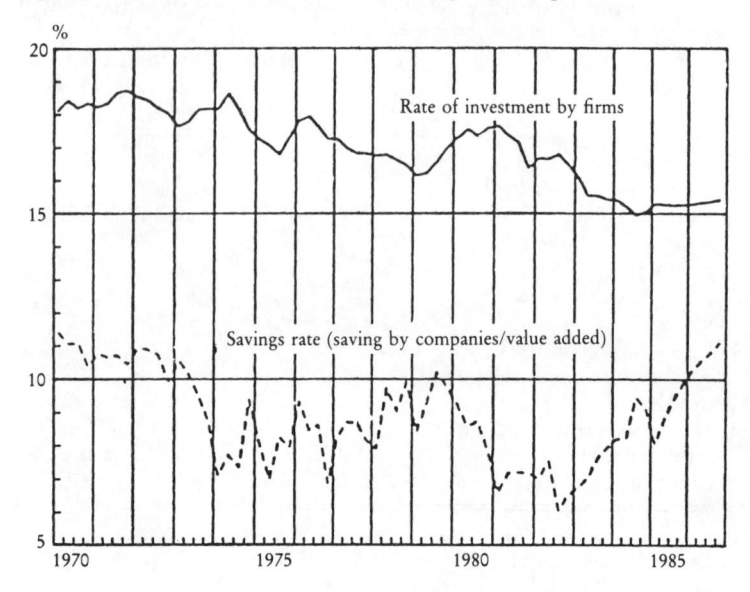

Figure 5.3 Investment by firms and savings by companies

The unfavourable impact of the terms of trade became smaller from 1982 onwards, but employers had then to cope with increased social security contributions. Profits recovered only when a sharp rise in the productivity of labour (4.25% per year on average in industry in 1983 and 1984) coincided with a zero rise in real wages. This gap, which was exceptionally large at eight percentage points over the two years, cancelled out the unfavourable impact of the other two factors and meant that the proportion of profit in the value added of firms went up by four percentage points. This recovery continued, so that by 1986 profitability, in terms of total profit and the reinvestment of profits, had returned to its pre-crisis level (see Figure 5.3).

The rise in profits however did not bring a marked recovery of investment. In fact, as was shown in the first chapter, three conditions need to be met for investment to increase: a growth in markets, sufficient money for reinvestment, and an expected rate of return higher than that from the money markets. It is this latter factor which is always the most difficult to assess. There was a big gap in the 1980s between the average economic return on capital investment and the return on investment in the money markets;[10]

10. See for example the analyses in the *Rapport sur le Comptes de la Nation 1984* (Report on national accounts 1984) pp. 125ff.

The Fruits of Austerity

and the recovery of the former in 1983 and 1984 was small compared to the level of real interest rates, so that investment in the market was much more profitable than capital investment. However it is difficult to draw conclusions from merely looking at average economic returns, which can differ markedly from the return on new investment. In particular, the marginal return expected on the basis of developments in the mid-1980s in the productivity of labour and real wages is much higher than actual average returns.

Moreover, econometric analyses covering the mid-1980s did not appear to confirm the view that sharp rises in real interest rates are a significant check on investment. When demand and profits are taken into account in looking at investment, the effect of real interest rates is at best slightly negative, and usually nil or even positive. There is the same conclusion with a model using the three constraints of expected level of demand, actual profits and the cost of capital (which brings in real interest rates).

The position is clearer however with regard to the respective influence of profits available for reinvestment and growth in markets. The analysis in Figure 1.13 (Chapter 1) showed that lack of money held back investment only in 1981 and the beginning of 1982. Even then, lack of buoyancy in the market would not have allowed a significantly higher level of capital investment. Later, the situation was reversed, and poor market opportunities gradually became more important than the actual level of profits, though both remained as constraints until mid-1983. From this date, the recovery of firms' profits removed this factor as a constraint.

In 1984, because of weak markets, investment by industry as a whole did not increase, whereas on the basis of profits available it should have gone up by more than 10%. This gap continued in 1985 and gave rise to the paradoxical situation where investment remained low at a time when reinvestment as a proportion of firms' added value was back to pre-first oil shock levels (Figure 5.3).

The Reduction of Budget Deficits

At the same time as it pursued a policy of disindexation and allowed firms a greater share of value added, the government tried to stabilize budget deficits at a level compatible with the improvement in the external balance. Because tax receipts fell when growth slowed down and because it wanted to moderate tax increases, the government had to hold down the rise in public spending and reduce the deficit in social welfare budgets. Moreover, public undertakings were urged to improve their financial situation.

Stabilization of the Budget Deficit at 3% of GDP

The constraint imposed by the president of the Republic in November 1982 that the budget overshoot should be limited to 3% of GDP was adhered to (see Table 5.8), but in view of the increase in net interest payments, this aim could be achieved only by a considerable reduction in spending.

The increase in interest payments . . . Between 1974 and 1980, the low level of budget deficits and real interest rates meant that the national debt settled at a figure of about 16% of GDP (Figure 5.4). After 1981 the national debt went up considerably because of the increased government borrowing requirement, together with the issue of bonds for nationalizations, and international borrowing to replenish currency holdings. By 1984, it was approaching 25% of GDP. At the same time, real interest rates as well as the proportion of long-term resources financing (which costs more) rose sharply (see Table 5.9).

An increase in rates and government borrowing led to a rise in interest payments, despite the introduction of new financial opportunities which postponed the payment of interest (renewable Treasury bonds with interest paid in arrears, etc.). In 1985, net interest payments paid by general government equalled 2.8% of GDP, as against 1.4% in 1981.

. . . required significant spending cuts Whereas government spending had previously increased by more than 6% per year in real terms, in 1984 and 1985 it was stable. All types of spending were affected by this slow-down – transfers, current costs, investments and consumption (see Table 5.10). In 1985, for the first time for many years, the total government wage bill went down in constant francs.

Given the present level of real interest rates on the one hand and the modest rise in production on the other, it is likely that interest payments will go on rising in value faster than GDP (for the conditions under which the debt would be stabilized, see Inset 5.2). In these conditions, central government departments and local authorities will have to clear a non-interest surplus if the 3% constraint is to be adhered to.

The Fruits of Austerity

Table 5.8 Net lending by general government (including Currency Stabilization Fund), as % of GDP

	1981	1982	1983	1984	1985
Central government	−1.2	−1.9	−3.3	−3.1	−2.9
Local authorities	−0.6	−0.8	−0.6	−0.3	−0.2
Social security	−0.0	+0.0	+0.8	+0.6	+0.5
Total of general government:	−1.8	−2.7	−3.1	−2.8	−2.6
Net interest paid	(−1.4)	(−1.35)	(−1.8)	(−2.0)	(−2.8)
Net lending excluding interest	(−0.4)	(−1.35)	(−1.3)	(−0.8)	(+0.2)

Source: *Rapport sur les Comptes de la Nation* (Report on national accounts) 1985, INSEE.

Figure 5.4 Public debt* at year-end and as % of GDP

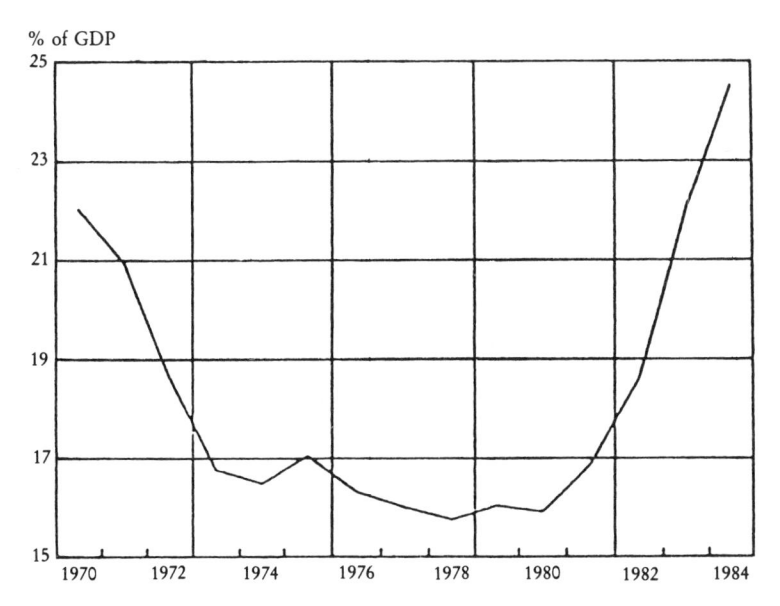

* Meaning the government's own borrowing and borrowing by Post & Telecommunications and the broadcasting authority but managed by the government, together with international borrowing by the government in 1982 and 1983.
Source: Treasury banking operations.

Table 5.9 Level and structure of interest payments by central government, excluding nationalizations[a]

	1977	1980	1981	1982	1983	1984	1985
Interest payments							
(billion francs)	13.6	26.1	44.8	48.2[b]	68.5	79.2	81.2
(percentage of GDP)	0.72	0.94	1.44	1.35	1.73	1.85	1.85
Structure of debt payment in %							
Long- and medium-term debt	8.7	24.6	27.2	31.5	31.9	34.7	45.2
Short-term debt	91.6	75.4	72.8	68.5	68.1	65.3	54.8

[a] Cost of interest charges and redemption of bonds issued for the nationalizations: 1982 – 3.4 billion francs; 1983 – 7.8 billion; 1984 – 6.3 billion.

[b] In 1982, Treasury bills on current account with 'interest paid in advance' were replaced by bills at monthly interest or bills with 'interest paid at final maturity'. The reduction in interest payments from the new arrangements was estimated at 10 billion in 1982. See C. de Boissieu and A. Gubian, 'Les indicateurs de la politique budgétaire et fiscale' (Indicators of budgetary and fiscal policy), *Observations et diagnostics économiques*, 9 October 1984.

Source: Budget final settlement legislation.

Table 5.10 Changes in government spending after 1981 (excluding interest payments) in constant francs (deflator: traded GDP) (annual % change)

	1981	1982	1983	1984
Gross wages	2.9	2.4	1.1	1.5
Defence and non-defence inputs	7.2	6.5	5.1	−1.7
Investment	−1.7	4.8	−5.7	−3.5
Transfers	7.4	7.9	2.4	0.3
Total:	5.8	6.6	2.0	0.2

Source: *Rapport sur les Comptes de la Nation* (Report on national accounts) 1984, INSEE.

The rise in real interest rates affected external debt As a percentage of GDP, external debt is influenced by two factors (see Inset 5.2) – the size of the deficit itself, discounting interest payments, and the difference between real interest rates and the rate of growth of GDP.

Until 1983, the level of real interest rates was always higher than the rate of growth of GDP, so that the stability of the debt ratio was

Inset 5.2

Conditions for stabilization of the public debt/GDP ratio

The persistence of a deficit in public finances is not incompatible with a stabilization of the debt/GDP ratio, but it depends very much on the respective value of the rate of growth of the economy and the real interest rate.

If E is public borrowing, D the deficit excluding interest payments, r the nominal rate of interest, p the level of GDP price ($\dot{p}$ the rate of inflation) and Q real GDP (g its rate of growth), then the public debt and the deficit are linked by the formula:

(1) $E = (1 + r) E_{-1} + D$

If we divide the two sides by GDP in value (pQ) and if we call d the public deficit (excluding interest payments) as a ratio of GDP, then the debt/GDP ratio (e) is:

(2) $\quad e = \left(\dfrac{E}{pQ}\right) = \dfrac{1 + r}{1 + g + \dot{p}} \left(\dfrac{E}{pQ}\right)_{-1} + d$

or, by using the usual approximations:

(3) $\quad e - e_{-1} \quad = \quad (r - \dot{p} - g)\, e_{-1} \quad + \quad d$

| change in the debt/GDP ratio | effect of the real interest/growth differential on existing debt | new borrowing |

Change in the debt/GDP ratio depends therefore on two factors:
– the burden of existing debt, that is, interest payments ($r\, e_{-1}$) reduced by the depreciation of the debt due to inflation ($-\dot{p}\, e_{-1}$) and to growth ($-g\, e_{-1}$)
– new borrowing made necessary by the deficit excluding interest payments (d).

When the real rate of interest ($r - \dot{p}$) is lower than the rate of growth (g), as was nearly always the case in France until 1983, the debt/GDP ratio can go down, despite new borrowing (1978 and 1980). Conversely, the rise in real interest rates helped to ease the burden of existing debt from 1983, as the following table shows:

continued on p. 268

	Inset 5.2 (continued)								
	1978	1979	1980	1981	1982	1983	1984	1985	1986
Change in debt/GDP ratio	−0.3	0.4	−0.1	0.9	1.3	2.4	1.6	1.8	1.2
Effect of:									
New borrowing	0.7	1.3	0.7	1.2	1.9	2.3	1.4	1.4	0.8
Existing debt broken down into	−1.0	−0.9	−0.8	−0.3	−0.6	0.1	0.2	0.4	0.4
– interest ($r\,e_{-1}$)	0.8	0.8	0.9	1.4	1.4	1.7	1.8	1.8	1.9
– inflation ($-p\,e_{-1}$)	−1.3	−1.3	−1.5	−1.5	−1.6	−1.5	−1.3	−1.1	−1.0
– growth ($-g\,e_{-1}$)	−0.5	−0.4	−0.2	−0.2	−0.3	−0.1	−0.3	−0.3	−0.4

Source: *Rapport sur les Comptes de la Nation* (Report on national accounts) 1986, INSEE.

compatible with a slight deficit discounting interest payments. In other words, growth and inflation were enough to offset in debt ratio terms the effect of new debt arising from nominal interest payments and even from an increase in the deficit itself (excluding interest payments), provided that this was not too large. Inset 5.2 shows for example that in 1978, discounting inflation and growth, the ratio of public debt to GDP should have risen 1.5 points – 0.8 from interest payments, and 0.7 from the non-interest deficit on government account. However, the reduction of the ratio was helped 1.3 points by inflation and 0.5 by growth (in volume terms), so that the debt ratio fell by 0.3 points. To summarize the effect of nominal interest payments, inflation and growth through the difference between real interest rates and rate of growth, it can be said that the debt ratio was reduced by 0.3 points because the 0.7% non-interest deficit in GDP was offset by the effect of the six-point difference between growth (3%) and real interest rates (−3%). With a debt ratio of 16%, the effect of this difference amounted to a one-point 'spontaneous' reduction of the ratio (0.16 × 6%).

The slow-down in growth in the 1980s, together with the sharp rise in real interest rates after 1983 (because of the rise in nominal rates, followed by disinflation) meant that this beneficial effect not only disappeared, but after 1983 exerted an upward pressure on indebtedness. In 1986, government debt ignoring interest payments amounted, as in 1978, to 0.8% of GDP; rather than a 0.3% reduction in the debt ratio, there was a rise of 1.2 points. This analysis, which could be applied to other debtor institutions (firms, or on the global level developing countries), shows that a reduction of indebtedness assumes that there is simultaneously strong growth and low real interest rates.

Reduction in Social Welfare Spending

The whole system of social security transfers is a decisive element in the flow of French national income. In 1986, welfare payments amounted to 27% of GDP and 37% of households' disposable income. Social welfare contributions by firms were about 37% of wage costs.

The level of economic activity is crucial for the financial equilibrium of social security funds – income depends on total gross wages, and expenditure is a function of autonomous demographic factors, social policy and the level of unemployment. Income therefore drops when growth slows, whereas expenditure remains the same or even, because of unemployment benefit payments, increases. The slow-down in growth therefore gives rise to a potential disequlibrium, and a periodic 'deficit' in social security funding. In the past, depending on the economic and political situation, this deficit has been dealt with in three ways – cutting expenditure, which sometimes meant that wastage was reduced, but could lead to distress; raising employers' contributions, which was a major factor in the rise in wage costs in France between 1974 and 1982; increasing employees' contributions, which caused much resentment when purchasing power was stagnating, and held down demand by households and economic activity in general.

Significant slow-down in rises in social welfare benefits after 1983 From the mid-1960s to the mid-1980s, three main periods can be seen in the development of social welfare benefits: 1968–73, 1973–82, 1982–6 (see Table 5.11). Between 1968 and 1973, the real value of benefits rose sharply (6.8% yearly average), though this was merely keeping pace with the rise in real GDP. Between 1973 and 1982, benefits continued this increase (6.4% annual average), but growth in GDP fell back sharply. After 1982, benefits rose more slowly (2.6%), though this was slightly more than GDP. As a percentage of GDP, social welfare benefits rose sharply (by eight points) between 1973 and 1982, but only by 0.6 points between 1968 and 1973, and 0.8% between 1982 and 1986 (see Figure 5.5).

An increased level of social welfare benefits is the result of three factors: the circumstantial rise in the number of recipients, rules

Table 5.11 Factors in the growth in welfare benefits (% annual average change in real value)

	1968–73 (1)	1968–73 (2)	1973–82 (1)	1973–82 (2)	1982–6 (1)	1982–6 (2)
Health benefits	**8.3**	**2.9**	**5.2**	**1.9**	**2.8**	**0.95**
Population	0.9	0.3	0.5	0.15	0.4	0.15
Indexation	4.4	0.6	2.4	0.3	1.1	0.1
or Health care consumption per head	8.4	1.7	4.7	1.1	3.7	0.85
Refunds	0.7	0.2	0.8	0.35	–0.4	–0.15
Retirement benefits	**6.8**	**2.85**	**6.2**	**2.6**	**3.0**	**1.2**
Demographic effect	1.4	0.6	0.2	0.1	1.4	0.6
Activity rate	0.8	0.35	0.7	0.3	1.0	0.4
Indexation	4.4	1.85	2.4	1.0	1.1	0.4
Policy	0.1	0.05	2.8	1.2	–0.5	–0.2
Family and maternity benefits	**3.7**	**0.8**	**3.7**	**0.7**	**0.3**	**0.05**
Number of recipients	0.3	0.05	–0.4	–0.1	–0.6	–0.1
Policy	3.4	0.75	4.1	0.8	0.9	0.15
Unemployment benefits (including early retirement)	**8.0**	**0.2**	**25.9**	**1.1**	**3.9**	**0.4**
Number of recipients	10.6	0.2	21.0	0.9	6.1	0.6
Indexation	4.4	0.1	2.4	0.1	1.1	0.1
Policy	–6.3	–0.1	1.6	0.1	–3.2	–0.3
Total benefits		6.8		6.4		2.6
Number of recipients		3.2		2.6		2.5
Indexation		2.6		1.4		0.6
Policy		0.9		2.4		–0.5
GDP		6.1		2.1		1.8

[1] Annual average growth rate.
[2] Contribution to increase in total benefits.
Source: A. Fonteneau, A. Gubian, H. Sterdyniak and C. Verpeaux, *Observations et diagnostics économiques*, 22 January 1988.

concerning indexation on wages, and policies extending or increasing benefit. The first two factors operate automatically, whereas the third one is a matter of politics. Health benefits are a function of the number of recipients which rises with demographic growth and greater demand per individual for health care, indexation which affects daily benefit payments, and policies which may increase the percentage of health care costs refunded. Retirement benefits are a function of the number of recipients, i.e. retired and early-retired people, which is determined by demography and the labour force participation rate. Unemployment benefits are a function of the number of unemployed and early-retired people. Unemployment

The Fruits of Austerity

Figure 5.5 Social welfare benefits as % of GDP

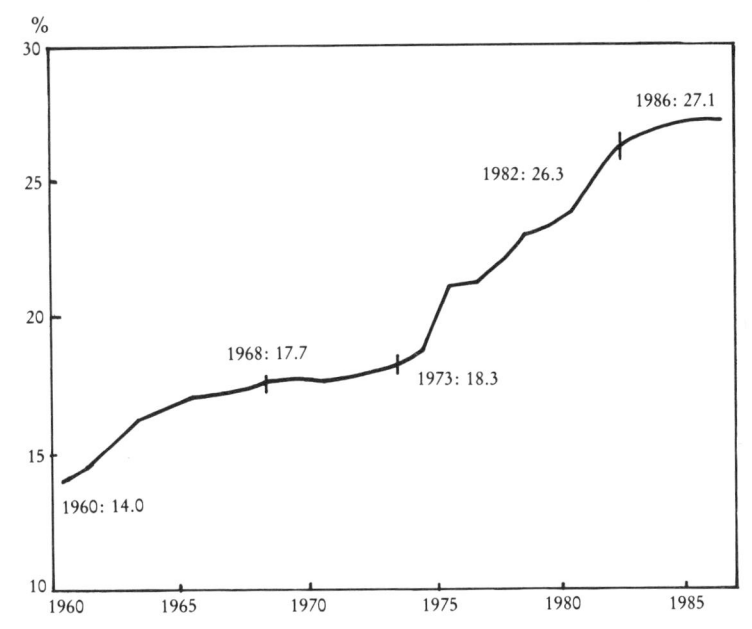

```
%
30
                                              1986: 27.1
25                          1982: 26.3
20      1968: 17.7
                         1973: 18.3
15
     1960: 14.0
10
   1960   1965   1970   1975   1980   1985
```

Source: Social welfare accounts, Ministry of Social Affairs and Employment; INSEE.

and retirement benefits are indexed on wages and therefore rises depend on how wage rates develop. The number of recipients of family welfare benefits depends of course on the total number of children (see Figure 5.6).

Between 1968 and 1973, the overall rise in benefits was due partly (3.2%) to the increase in the number of recipients when social security was extended to non-wage earners (self-employed persons), and partly (2.6%) to indexation on wages. Increases in actual rates of benefit were small, and only really applied to family benefits.

Between 1973 and 1982, the smaller increase in benefits was because indexation and total number of recipients (despite the rise in unemployment) had less effect than previously. The rise in unemployment accounted for 1.1% of the rise in total benefits, and a sharp rise in retirement benefit payments accounted for 1.2%.

Between 1982 and 1986, the 'total number of recipients' effect was about the same as in the previous period, since the greater number of retired people was offset by the smaller number of unemployed. Because real wages stagnated, indexation played no part in the rise in total benefits. The main factor, however, was the government

Figure 5.6 Social welfare benefits by category as % of GDP

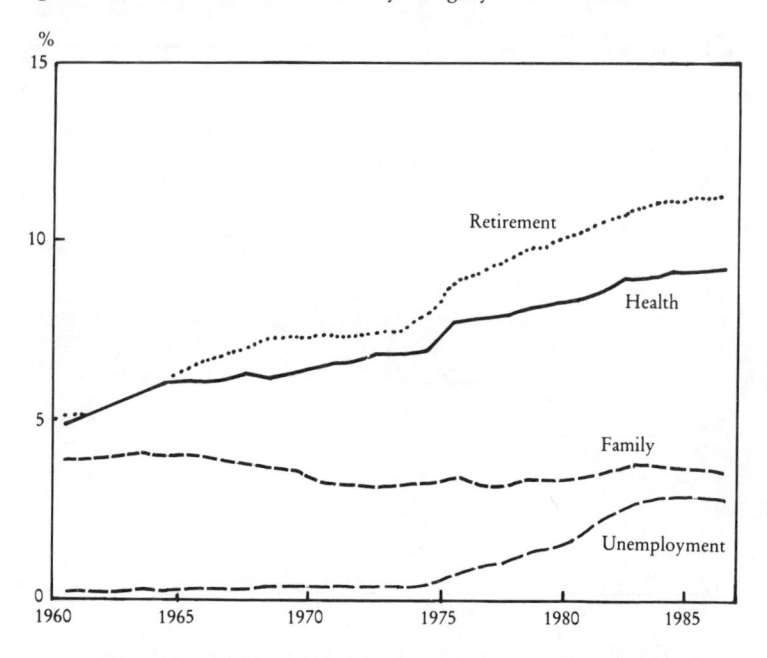

Source: Social welfare accounts, Ministry of Social Affairs and Employment; INSEE.

policy of increasing retirement and unemployment benefits by less than the rate of inflation; this accounted for three out of the four percentage points by which the growth in total benefits was reduced. At the same time, family welfare benefits did not rise, and a smaller percentage of health care costs was reimbursed.

The year 1983 was therefore the one when the brake was put on the policy of extending social welfare provision.

Financing social welfare provision The total income of social welfare funds increased at about the same rate as expenditure, rising from 16% of GDP in 1960 to 28.2% in 1986. It was between 1972 and 1982 that income, like benefit payments, rose fastest – by eight percentage points of GDP. Social security income can be grouped under four headings: employers' contributions, contributions by insured people (employees, self-employed, and those in receipt of a pension), tax receipts earmarked for social security funds (1%, plus later 0.4% of taxable income, civil servants' solidarity contribution, tax on tobacco, tax on spirits, etc.), and contributions by central and local governments (see Figure 5.7).

The Fruits of Austerity

Figure 5.7 Resources for social welfare provision by category and % of GDP

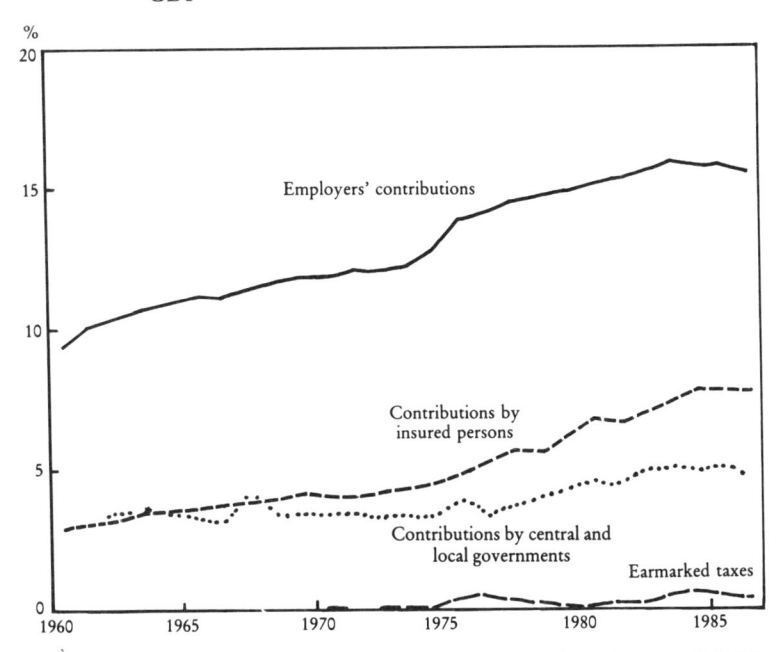

Source: Social welfare accounts, Ministry of Social Affairs and Employment; INSEE.

The main reason for the sharp rise in income is that employers' and insured persons' contributions (which in 1986 accounted for one-half and one-third respectively) increased significantly. The employers' share, which before 1973 had been stagnant, fell afterwards; contributions by insured persons continued to rise. Earmarked taxes began with the economic crisis and are not large (1.4% of social security income in 1986). Contributions by central and local governments fell until 1976, but rose slightly afterwards; an analysis of economic cycles shows that they rose when there was a sharp increase in expenditure (1967, 1975).

Any examination of the increase in contributions needs to take account of their assessment base – total gross wages, and the income of unincorporated entrepreneurs. Average rates calculated on this basis rose at the beginning of the 1960s, then less steeply until the first oil shock (see Figure 5.8). Their subsequent rise was greater, particularly between 1973 and 1982. The average contribution rates for employers was therefore 4.6 points between 1960 and 1965, 0.9 points from 1965 to 1973, 6.4 points from 1973 to 1982, and 2.4

Figure 5.8 Apparent welfare contribution rates

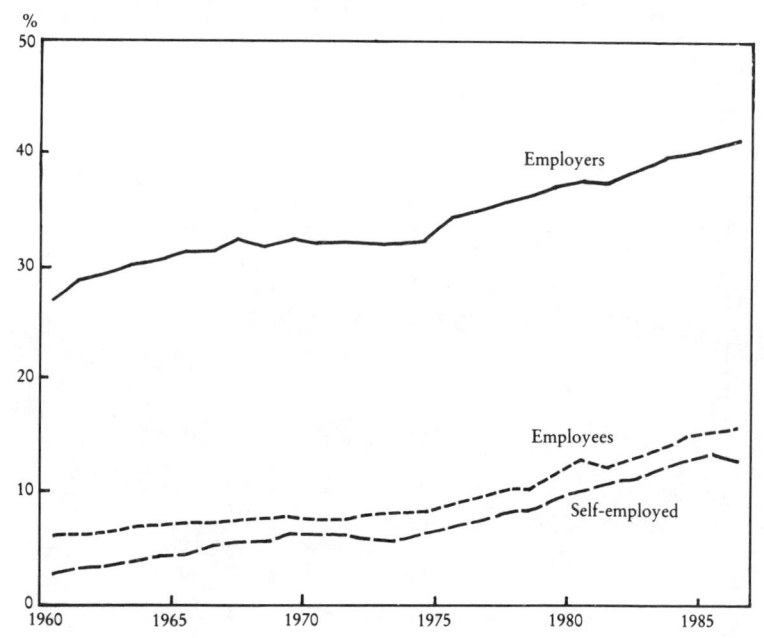

[Graph showing three lines from 1960 to 1985: Employers rising from ~27% to ~41%; Employees rising from ~6% to ~15%; Self-employed rising from ~3% to ~13%]

Source: Social welfare accounts, Ministry of Social Affairs and Employment; INSEE.

points up to 1986. The equivalent figures for employees are 1.1, 0.9, 5.0 and 2.5. Whereas between 1960 and 1965 it was the employers who paid for the increase in total benefits, since that period employers and employees have shared the cost of increases. Contributions by self-employed persons have kept pace with those of employees, though the rise was greater in 1960–9, because of extensions to their social welfare provision. The overall level of self-employed contributions however is much lower than that of employers and employees combined. It is true that the level of welfare provision is lower, but even in cases where their contribution rates are the same, these are applied to declared income levels which are lower than they should be because of tax evasion and fraud.

Since 1982, employers' actual contribution rates to the general social security scheme have not been increased, whereas those of employees have risen by 2.4 points. There are three reasons however why the average rate paid by employers has continued to rise:

The Fruits of Austerity

1 Increases in contributions to the unemployment benefit fund (at the end of 1982, in mid-1983 and at the end of 1985), and to the complementary retirement scheme.
2 The 1982 raising of the entitlement level for social security benefit by more than the increase in average wages; in this way total gross wages incurring contributions rose.
3 Measures introduced at the end of 1984 to speed up the collection of contributions.

As a percentage of GDP, employers' contributions, after a 3.3 point rise between 1973 and 1982, fell slightly; this is explained by the reduced share of gross wages in the value added. Contributions by households continued their modest rise, going from 7% in 1982 to 7.7% in 1986. There are thus two occasions when significant shifts happened: 1973, the start of a period when the need for higher social security income led the government to raise employers' and employees' rates which, because of existing levels, meant that employees then took on a greater share of the burden; and 1982, the start of a period when employers' contribution rates rose less fast and contributions as a percentage of GDP fell (Figure 5.7).

The slow-down in increase of welfare payments after 1983 meant not only that there was a slight surplus in social security accounts (see Table 5.8), but also that employers shouldered less of the burden of financing social welfare provision.

Reduction in the Deficits of Nationalized Undertakings

Despite a significant rise in capital grants and subsidies to nationalized undertakings (see Chapter 2), the financial results of the nationalized sector had worsened considerably during 1981–3. Losses incurred by the old nationalized undertakings amounted to 22 billion in 1982–3, whereas they had been virtually non-existent in 1980.

The deterioration was particularly significant in the case of EDF (electricity supply) – 8.4 billion franc deficit in 1982; and for GDF (gas supply) (see Table 5.12). The worsening of the EDF position is partly explained by dollar borrowing made in the second half of the 1970s to finance the electro-nuclear programme; that of Charbonnages de France (coal supply) and of GDF is partly accounted for by the government's unrealistic coal production targets for 1981, and the unfavourable terms of the new gas supply contracts with Algeria.

In the transport sector, RATP (Paris public transport system) had

Table 5.12 Net performance of nationalized undertakings[1] (in million francs)

	1980	1981	1982	1983	1984
(A) *Undertakings nationalized before 1981*					
Electricité de France	+84	−4,640	−8,363	−5,450	−900
Gaz de France	+49	−950	−2,560	−2,380	−3,025
Charbonnages de France[1]	+59	−67	−692	−768	0
SNCF	−675	−2,020	−5,300	−8,380	−5,540
RATP	(for reference only)[2]				
Compagnie Générale Maritime (CGM)	−360	−481	−736	−540	−380
Aéroport de Paris	+58	+28	+9	+17	+50
Air France	+10	−378	−792	+87	+530
SNIAS	+118	+153	+96	−357	+330
SNECMA	+70	−65	−45	−39	+40
Renault	+1,547	−690	−1,281	−1,576	−12,500
CDF Chimie	−550	−1,213	−834	−2,760	−865
Entreprise Minière et Chimique	+10	−312	−946	−159	+30
Total:	+420	−10,635	−21,444	−22,305	−22,230
(B) *Undertakings nationalized in 1982*					
Compagnie Générale d'Electricité (CGE)	+556	+586	+638	+662	+650
Saint-Gobain	+932	+566	−745	+405	+500
Thomson	+502	−170	−2,208	−1,251	0
Rhône-Poulenc	−1,884	−266	−787	+159	+1,989
Péchiney	+607	−2,465	−4,615	−295	+550
CII Honeywell-Bull	+180	−449	−1,351	−625	−500
CGCT			−325	−555	−550
Total:	+893	−2,198	−9,393	−1,500	+2,639
(C) *Steelmaking firms*					
Usinor–Sacilor	−3,261	−7,138	−8,341	−11,066	−15,700
Total (A) + (B) + (C)	−1,948	−19,971	−39,178	−34,871	−35,291

[1] Taking into account contributions to operating costs and employee retirement benefits, and for industrial groups the boundaries established by the observatory of national undertakings.
[2] Because the government and the Ile de France region gave a 'compensation payment' (5 billion francs in 1984) the net position of the RATP (Paris public transport undertaking) was virtually always in balance.
Sources: Accounts of the undertakings from 1980 to 1983, and information published in the press during 1984.

satisfactory results because of a significant increase in traffic (10% rise between 1981 and 1984). SNCF (national railways) was less commercially dynamic and its financial results were less good – its aggregate loss for 1981–4 was over 21 billion francs, and its medium- and long-term debt had reached 66 billion by 1983.

The Fruits of Austerity

Apart from the Compagnie Générale d'Electricité, nationalized industrial undertakings also showed a poor financial position. During the three-year period 1981–3, Pechiney had an accumulated deficit of 7.4 billion, Thomson 3.6 billion and CII Honeywell-Bull 2.4 billion (Table 5.12).

After 1984, the policy of bringing deficits down meant that the financial position of nationalized undertakings began to improve. This was particularly true for those firms nationalized by the Left government in 1982 – from a 1982 deficit of 9.4 billion, they moved to a 2.6 billion profit. However, 1984 was a disastrous year for Renault, as well as for Usinor and Sacilor, whose losses were 12.5 and 15.7 billion respectively.

Despite an improvement in 1984–5, the nationalized sector, which was intended to be the 'spearhead of the French economy', was a heavy burden on public finances. One might ask whether a 100% nationalization was necessary, at a cost of 25 billion between 1982 and 1985 (see Inset 5.3), when it would have been enough to take a 51% share in those industrial groups which needed to be controlled to carry out industrial policy and structural reforms.

Tax Reduction: Myths and Realities

According to the so-called 'Laffer curve', tax yield as a function of tax rate describes a bell-shaped curve. Receipts rise initially, reaching a maximum at a certain rate (though the proponents of the analysis find it hard to say exactly what level), beyond which economic agents are discouraged and prefer to reduce their economic efforts. Tax receipts therefore fall steadily and the tax base finally disappears – 'the rate devours the base'. President Mitterrand adopted this approach when, on the television programme 'L'Enjeu' on 15 September 1983, he said 'too much tax means no tax'; he decided on a policy of tax reduction beginning in 1985.

Mitterrand's remark prompted a public debate focusing on the appropriate 'income tax and welfare contribution rate'. The precise definition of this statistical indicator depends to a large extent on accounting usage, and this needs to be reviewed in order to have a clearer idea of the debate on the way levels of taxation developed. The methods and extent of tax reduction in the United States after 1981 and in France after 1985 will then be examined.

Inset 5.3

The cost of the nationalizations

Law of 11 February 1982
– Nationalization of five industrial groups (CGE, Saint-Gobain, PUK, Rhône-Poulenc, Thomson-Brandt), thirty-nine banks, and the finance houses of Paribas and Suez.[a]
– Establishment of the Caisse Nationale des Banques (CNB) and the Caisse Nationale de l'Industrie (CNI), to issue and manage the bonds exchanged for shares.

Decree of 17 February 1982
– The CNB and CNI provided with rules concerning organization and financing.
– The bonds take effect from 1 January 1982; they yield half-yearly interest based on the gross rate of return on certain non-indexed government loans; they are repayable over fifteen years, with an annual drawing of lots.

Cost of the nationalizations
– New liabilities at 31 December 1982 are a measure of the nationalizations and, as part of the government public debt, amounted to 38,873 million francs (17,730 for the CNI and 20,383 for the CNB).
– After 1982, the cost to the budget of interest and capital repayments was (in million francs) as follows:

1982	1983	1984	1985	Total 1982–5
3,428	7,848[b]	6,980	6,280	24,536

[a] In 1981, the firms Usinor and Sacilor were nationalized by consolidating loans from the FDES into capital grants (cost – 13,804 million).
[b] The cost of capital repayments appeared for the first time in 1983.
Sources: Budget final settlement laws 1982 and 1983, preliminary budgets for 1984 and 1985.

The Fruits of Austerity

The 'Income Tax and Welfare Contribution Rate': A Method of Measurement Dependent on Usage

The method of measuring the income tax and welfare contribution rate gives rise to at least two kinds of problem: what income taxes and welfare contributions (NICS in U.K.) should be included, and to what tax base should they be applied?[11]

In the current definition used by national income accountants in France, income tax and welfare contributions include taxes on production and importation, ordinary taxes on income and wealth, actual social security contributions and capital taxes paid by residents and non-residents to general government in France and the EEC.

The OECD uses a slightly more restricted definition for national accounts, which excludes taxes paid to the EEC, since capital taxes are regarded as transfers, and direct taxes paid by national and local government authorities. In 1984, the difference amounted to 1.3% of GDP.

'Income tax and welfare contributions' can also be defined in other ways. An assessment can be made of *all payments of an obligatory nature made by economic agents*. In this case, actual payments to general government must be supplemented by obligatory social welfare contributions paid to other institutional sectors, and by fictitious contributions, though some of the latter cover benefits of a 'charitable' nature. Such a definition is a higher measure of 'income tax and welfare contributions', and gives a rate which in 1984 was about three points up on the 'official' rate (48.2% as against 45.4%).

Conversely, if account is taken only of expenditure by the State, the definition is limited to income tax and contributions used by public authorities to *finance their spending net of transfers*.[12] The rate of tax and contributions net of transfers calculated in this way is a measure of the amount of real resources removed from the productive economy (see Table 5.13).

Another approach is to discount *obligatory payments between*

---

11. For a discussion of these questions, see for example: INSEE, *Comptes de la Nation 1984* (National accounts 1984), Vol. 2, p. 174; P. Mantz, A. Ramond, M. Tabouillot and M. Ungemuth, 'Le poids des prélèvements obligatoires: portée et limites de la mesure' (The influence of taxes and social welfare contributions: the impact and limitations of a policy), *Economie et statistique*, 157, July–August 1983; B. Théret and D. Uri, 'La pression fiscale: une limite à l'intervention publique' (Tax rates: a limit to public intervention), *Critique de l'économie politique*, 21, new series, October–December 1982.
12. See *Rapport sur les Comptes de la Nation 1984* (Report on national accounts 1984), Vol. 2, p. 174.

Table 5.13 Rate of taxes and contributions (T + C) as % of GDP

	1973	1974	1975	1976	1977	1978	1979	1980	1981	1982	1983	1984	1985	Change between 1973 and 1985 (in points)
1. T + C/GDP	35.7	36.3	37.4	39.4	39.4	39.5	41.1	42.5	42.8	43.8	44.6	45.0	45.6	9.9
Ratio of taxes to GDP	22.3	22.3	22.1	23.5	22.9	22.9	23.5	24.2	24.5	24.9	25.0	25.7	25.7	3.4
T + C paid to government	17.8	17.7	16.6	18.1	17.5	17.3	17.9	18.5	18.6	18.8	18.3	18.3	18.3	0.5
T + C paid to local authorities	3.9	4.0	4.3	3.3	4.3	4.4	4.5	4.7	4.8	4.9	5.2	5.7	5.9	2.0
T + C paid to other institutions[a]	0.6	0.6	1.2	2.1	1.1	1.3	1.1	1.0	1.1	1.2	1.5	1.7	1.5	0.9
Welfare contributions/GDP	13.4	14.0	15.3	15.9	16.5	16.6	17.6	18.3	18.3	18.9	19.6	19.0	19.9	6.5
2. Consolidated T + C[b]/GDP	33.8	34.4	35.4	37.3	37.4	37.4	38.8	40.1	40.2	40.9	41.7	42.0	42.8	9.0
3. Consolidated T + C net of transfers/GDP	12.5	12.4	11.2	12.3	12.2	11.5	12.6	14.5	13.2	12.6	12.6	13.0	13.3	0.8

[a] Other organs of central government, social security and the EEC.
[b] After obligatory internal payments to other departments.
Source: *Rapport sur les Comptes de la Nation* (Report on national accounts) 1985, INSEE.

The Fruits of Austerity

Figure 5.9 Rate of taxes and welfare contributions

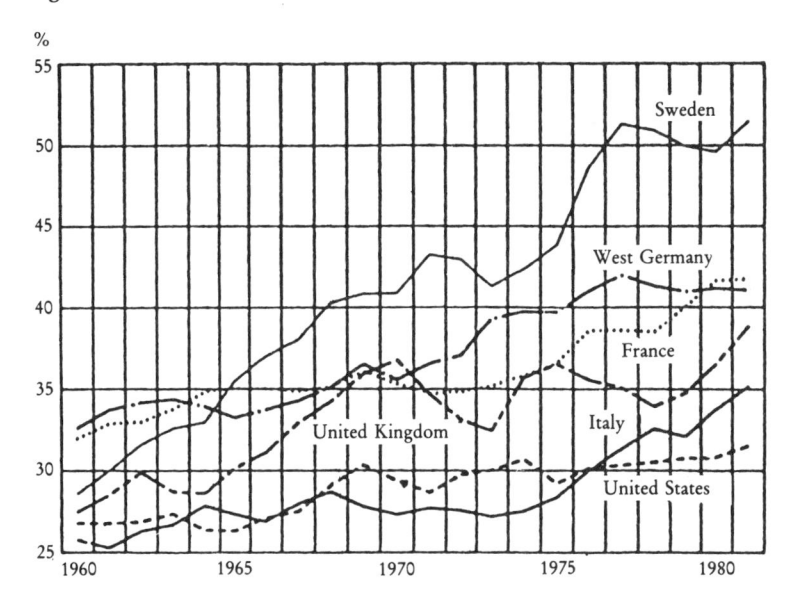

public authorities: welfare contributions paid by the government to social security funds, taxes paid by local authorities to the government, income tax paid by the government to itself, and so on. However, the rules and conventions within the French national accounting system make it difficult to establish a complete consolidation on this basis.[13] The various aggregates of taxes and contributions from the above definitions are usually applied to overall GDP and sometimes to traded GDP. Since income tax and contributions are an allocation operation, however, it would be more sensible to apply them to gross (or net) national income, or even to economic agents' primary income before tax and contributions.

Table 5.13 shows the development of the rate of unconsolidated and consolidated gross tax and contributions, and that of the rate net of transfers between 1973 and 1985. During these twelve years, the first two rates rose respectively by 9.9 and 8.9 points. Apart from two slight falls in 1977–8 and 1981, which are not very important because of time lags affecting the collection of income tax and corporation tax, there was a steady increase after the first oil shock. Other countries had the same experience, though the rise was slower, apart from Sweden (see Figure 5.9).

13. See P. Mantz et al., July–August 1983.

−281−

The picture is different if one looks at the development of the rate net of transfers, which was virtually unchanged during this period. The conclusion therefore is that the increase in rate of income tax and contributions after 1974 is brought about not by the allocation function of public authorities, but by a significant extension of their redistribution function. The big increase since the beginning of the economic crisis has not been in central government taxation (which has stayed around 18% of GDP), but in social welfare contributions and to a lesser extent in local taxes (Table 5.13).

Since it is principally a measure of the extent of redistribution, the rate of income tax and contributions is indicative of fundamental political choices. The debate on taxes and contributions should therefore link the level of these with that of welfare provision. In this way, people would have clearer choices. The debate should also take account of medium-term objectives, which might mean that employment-promoting tax reforms could be introduced.

Tax Reduction in the United States

When he entered office in 1980, President Reagan's approach to the economy was inspired by three principles: a fiscal policy favourable to business and promising supply-led recovery; a significant reduction of the budget deficit, so that the Treasury's role in financial markets could be limited; and a strict control over money supply. In retrospect, it is clear that US economic policy has been the very opposite of these original premises. There was indeed a recovery in 1983–4, but it was brought about essentially by a rise in consumption triggered by a sharp fall in income tax which was not accompanied by a reduction in government spending.

Between 1981 and 1985, the overall federal budget deficit rose from 2.6% to 5.4% of GNP. Tax reductions accounted for about half of this increase, the other half coming partly from a rise in defence spending which offset the fall in non-defence spending, and partly from the rise in interest payments because of the deficit and higher rates of interest (see Table 5.14 and Figure 5.10).

The higher deficit stimulated the economy, in accordance with Keynesian theory. Tax reductions boosted consumption and investment in housing by households, who were helped by a degree of relaxation of monetary policy from August 1982. The increase in household demand together with a rise in defence spending and tax allowances on investment led to a sharp rise in productive investment from mid-1983 (see Figure 5.11).

The combination of an expansionist fiscal policy and a restrictive

The Fruits of Austerity

Table 5.14 Factors in the change in the US federal deficit as % of GDP between 1981 and 1985

	1981	1985	1981–5
Overall federal balance made up of:	−2.6	−5.4	−2.8
Non-budget social security	−0.1	0.2	0.3
Budget shortfall	−2.5	−5.6	−3.1
Breakdown of change in the budget balance			
Revenue	−1.5	Expenditure	+1.3
tax on households' income	−1.1	Defence	+1.1
tax on businesses	−0.4	Excluding defence	−1.2
Social security and various	0.0	Social security and various	+0.4
Budget shortfall	−3.1	Net interest	+1.0

Source: Congressional Budget Office, *The Economic and Budget Outlook*, February 1988.

Figure 5.10 US federal budget – structural and cyclical deficit per calendar year, 1972–85

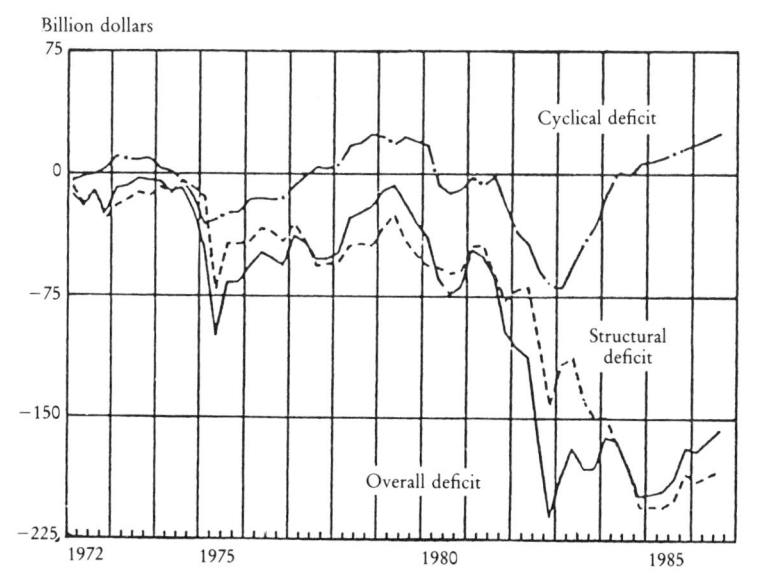

Source: Department of Commerce.

−283−

Figure 5.11 Change in GNP, household consumption and investment in the United States from 1973 to 1984

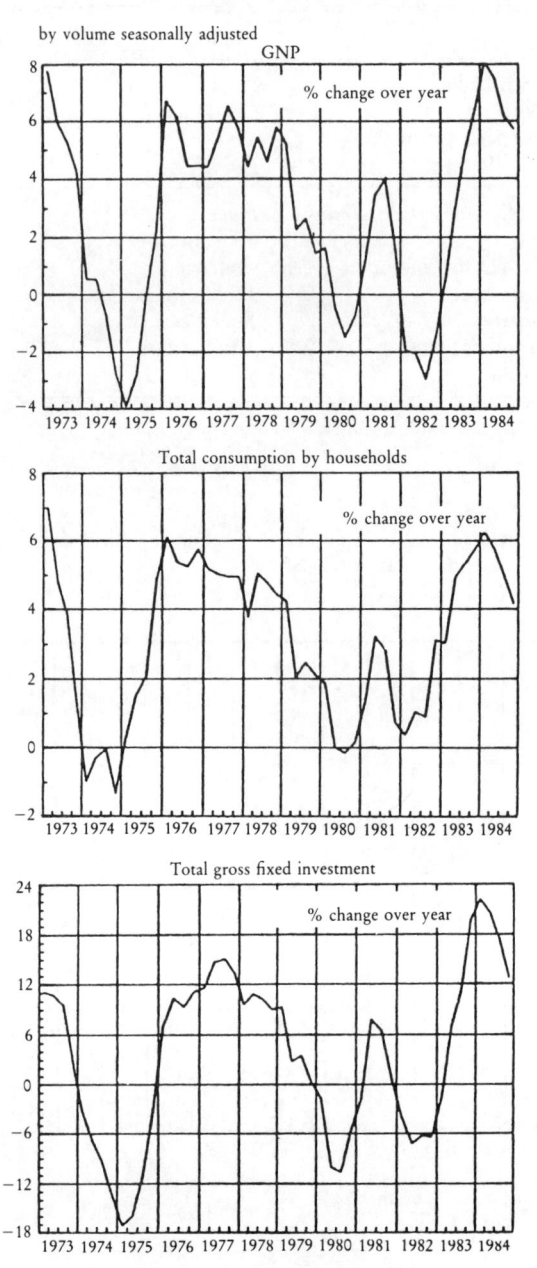

The Fruits of Austerity

Table 5.15 Contributions to change in real GNP in the United States from 1981 to 1984

	1980	1981	1982	1983	1984
Private consumption	0.3	1.2	0.9	3.1	3.5
Public spending	0.5	0.2	0.3	−0.1	0.7
Private housebuilding	−0.7	−0.2	−0.5	1.1	0.4
Other private investment	−0.3	0.4	−0.5	0.3	2.2
Inventory investment	−0.9	0.9	−1.2	0.5	1.9
Exports	1.0	0.0	−0.8	−0.6	0.4
Imports	0.0	−0.5	−0.1	−0.6	−2.2
GNP	−0.2	+1.9	−1.9	+3.7	6.8

Source: OECD Economic Outlook.

monetary policy caused nominal interest rates to rise. This led to a sharp rise in the dollar, which was a factor in disinflation and the rise in real interest rates. The fact of US growth and European stagnation, together with the rise in the dollar, led to a deficit on current account covered by a massive inflow of capital. In other words, the US economic recovery of the 1980s owed little to the supposed virtues of supply-side economics (see Table 5.15); but it offers an almost perfect illustration of the lessons of the IS-LM model applied to an open economy.

European countries had to cope with both the economic and the ideological consequences of US policy. The economic effects will be examined at the end of the chapter; we merely note for the moment the paradox that a socialist government in France in fact introduced budgetary austerity and reduced state economic intervention, which was the original approach of the US government.

Fiscal Policy in 1985–6: Reduction of Taxes

The rise in spending associated with the reflation of 1981–2, together with only slow economic growth and the desire to reduce the budget deficit led to a rise of about 0.7 points per year in the rate of income tax and welfare contributions between 1981 and 1984. Although this rise was smaller than the one point a year rise in the period 1973–80, it could have been too high in the long run. Mitterrand's decision to reduce the rate by one point from 1985 however was a concession to the classical liberal ideology gaining ground at the time. The actual reduction in the rate was in fact smaller than originally envisaged. Moreover, in order to keep the budget deficit at 3% of GDP, it was accompanied by a significant cut in spending, with the result that its macro-economic effect on economic activity was virtually nil.[14] However, by reducing the effect of wage restraint on households' disposable income, it was important in the economic context of 1985–6, at a time when wages were stagnant and firms' profits were making a strong recovery.

The tax cuts . . . The main tax cuts of the Fabius government in 1985–6 are summarized in Table 5.16, which shows that they mainly benefited households. In 1985, total tax cuts for households amounted to 23.5 billion francs, though telephone charges and taxes on oil-derived products went up. In all, there was a net gain for households of 10.5 billion, representing 0.2% of GDP. For firms, the tax cuts were wholly offset by a rise in local taxes. The budget for 1986 continued the tax reduction measures and introduced further cuts. There was an extra 3% off income tax, giving households another 7.8 billion. Furthermore, the repayment of the enforced loan of June 1983 (13.8 billion in capital and 4.2 billion in interest) was brought forward from June to January 1986. Firms benefited from a five-point reduction in tax on retained profits, which went down from 50% to 45% from 1 January 1986. However, this was wholly offset by the abolition of the special allowance on investment. The total cost to the budget was 5 billion francs.

. . . were accompanied by spending cuts . . . The assessment of how spending evolved is done on the following basis: for each head of expenditure, as well as for the budget deficit, a calculation is made of the difference between changes in each head of expenditure (as well as in the budget deficit) and the official forecast of growth of GDP in value;[15] this difference is regarded as being brought about by new measures, except for items where changes were wholly determined in advance by previous decisions, in which case the change is regarded as spontaneous. Planned cuts in spending amounted to 17.5 billion francs in 1985 and 8.3 billion in 1986 (see Table 5.17). About half of the cuts affected total gross wages (12,000 fewer jobs, no rise in the real value of government employees'

14. The expansionist or restrictive nature of economic policy is measured in relation to the growth which the economy would have experienced if expenditure in which changes were not decided in advance had risen the same as GDP, and if taxation had remained unchanged. This measurement is therefore essentially cyclical, in contrast to the structural balance which looks at fiscal policy in relation to growth in full employment.
15. These are forecasts by the Ministry of Finance in connection with the budget.

The Fruits of Austerity

Table 5.16 Tax cuts in the 1985 and 1986 budgets (in billion francs)

	1985	1986
Households		
(a) Gains		
– cut in income tax	10	6.2
– abolition of 1% of social security contributions and tax on tobacco	13.5	–
– cut in VAT rate	–	0.8
– postponement of rise in public utility charges	–	0.8
Total excluding repayment of enforced loan:	23.5	7.8
(Repayment before due date of June 1983 enforced loan	–	18.0)
(b) Losses		
– 16% rise in telephone charges	3.5	–
– increase in tax on oil-derived products	9.5	–
Total:	13.0	0
(c) Net gains excluding repayment of enforced loan i.e. (a) less (b)	10.5	7.8
(including repayment of enforced loan	–	25.8)
Firms		
(a) Gains		
– reduction in business tax	10.0	–
– 5-point reduction in tax rate on retained profits	–	5.0
– various allowances	1.3	0.4
Total:	11.3	5.4
(b) Losses		
– abolition of special allowance on investment	–	5.0
– 16% rise in telephone charges	4.5	–
– increase in tax on oil-derived products	4.9	–
– various taxes	1.9	1.9
Total:	11.3	6.9
(c) Net gains i.e. (a) less (b)	0	−1.5

salaries and pensions) while the other half concerned subsidies to firms. A further point is that the government made a slight reduction in its non-wage operating expenditure, and in its capital spending.

... and use of off-budget operations The difficulty in making rapid reductions in spending led the government to alter the scope of the budget by transferring some budgetary spending to other agents. In this way in 1986, the social security fund and the post and telecommunications service were obliged to meet respectively 11 billion and 2.9 billion francs of spending previously financed by the government (Table 5.17).

Reflation and Austerity

Table 5.17 Planned reductions in government spending in the budgets of 1985 and 1986 (in billion francs)

	1985	1986
(a) New policies		
– reduction in the number of government employees	–0.9	–0.3
– stagnation in the real incomes of government employees	–5.1	(–5.8)
– cut in subsidies to firms	–8.0	–3.0
– government spending on goods and services	–3.5	+0.8
Total:	–17.5	–2.5
(b) Removal of items from budget, composed of:	0	–13.9
– transfers to Social Security	–	–11.0
– transfers to Post & Telecommunications	–	–2.9

Note: The effect of the stagnation of the real incomes of government employees in 1986 (5.8) which was a continuation of 1985 fiscal policy is given for reference only, and is not taken into account in the 1986 total, since this covers only those measures which were introduced in the budget for 1986.

Overall (see Table 5.18), the gross reduction in taxes in the budgets for 1985 and 1986 had reached 50 billion francs in 1986. Two-thirds (32.6 billion) of these gross reductions were offset by tax rises on oil-derived products, the abolition of some tax allowances and an increase in public utility charges. The remainder (17.4 billion francs less tax and contribution revenue) was more than offset by reductions in spending (21.4 billion).

Taking expenditure and income together, the fiscal policy measures of 1985–6 can be summed up by saying that in 1986 they represented a 12 billion franc gain for households, a 13 billion loss for firms and a 2.7 billion cut in government operating expenditure, giving an overall surplus of 4 billion. But whereas the new measures in the budgets of these two years gave this slight surplus, spontaneous changes (particularly interest payments) on the other hand increased the deficit further, even though 11 billion of this was transferred to the social security fund (which meant a rise in employees' social welfare contributions in 1986).

The macro-economic consequences   The macro-economic effects of fiscal policy in 1985–6 are shown in Table 5.19. Changes to the 1985 budget had, overall, a neutral effect on production for that year, but they had an impact on the structure of demand – consumption by households was boosted by 0.3%, investment by firms pegged back 0.4% and government spending on goods and services cut by 1%. The employment level was slightly reduced, mainly because of the fall in the number of government employees; 0.4 percentage points

The Fruits of Austerity

Table 5.18 Impact on the budget of the new measures in 1985 and 1986 (in billion francs)

	Impact in 1985	Impact in 1986 1986 measures	Impact in 1986 1985–6 measures
(a) Tax cuts	−34.8	−13.2	−50.0
(b) Increases in taxes and levies	24.3	6.9	32.6
(c) Impact on change in revenue (a+b)	−10.5	−6.3	−17.4
broken down into:			
households	−10.5	−7.8	−18.9
firms	0.0	1.5	1.5
(d) Impact on changes in expenditure	−17.5	−2.5	−21.4
broken down into:			
– transfers to households	−6.0	−0.3	−7.0
– transfers to firms	−8.0	−3.0	−11.5
– own expenditure	−3.5	0.8	−2.9
(e) Impact on budgetary balance (c–d)	7.0	−3.8	4.0
broken down into:			
– households	−4.5	−7.5	−11.9
– firms	8.0	4.5	13.0
– own expenditure	3.5	−0.8	2.9

Sources: Lettre de l'OFCE, nos 18 and 28.

were added to price rises, because the increase in indirect taxes was not wholly offset by the reduction of business tax. The trade balance improved slightly (by 4 billion) because of the tax increase on oil-derived products.

By 1986, the cumulative effects of fiscal policy in 1985–6 were more significant – GDP rose by 0.1%, and household consumption by 0.6%.

Fiscal policy lessened the impact of a stringent wages policy The effects of the 1985–6 policies must be looked at in the general economic context. Although real wages were stagnant and the number of people in work fell, production continued to rise. The proportion of total gross wages in value added fell, while that of profits went up. The benefit to industry of the difference between stagnation of real wages and rising labour productivity in 1985–6 can be put at 60 billion francs per year. Industry's improved position meant that the government could reduce the aid it gave, and at the same time households, particularly the managerial class, benefited from the reduction in indirect taxes. In a way, this policy

Table 5.19 Macro-economic impact of the 1985–6 budgetary measures (difference in relation to base)

	Impact on level in			
	1985	1986		
	1985 measures	1985 measures	1986 measures	Total 1985–6
Real GDP (%)	0.0	0.0	0.1	0.1
Household consumption (volume, %)	0.3	0.5	0.1	0.6
Investment by firms (volume, %)	−0.4	−0.2	0.1	−0.1
Consumer prices (%)	0.4	0.6	0.0	0.6
Total number of employees (thousands)	−9	−6	4	−2
Balance on goods and services (billion francs)	4	3	−2	1
Balance on general government (billion francs)	6.7	3.5	−3.2	0.3

Sources: *Lettre de l'OFCE*, nos 18 and 28.

was the very opposite of the one pursued in 1981–2, when low wage-earners gained and high incomes were taxed more heavily. But while it increased the work motivation of managers and other high income groups, it had the opposite effect on those who had seen their real income stagnate or fall for three years.

There was an alternative policy – industry's profits could have been boosted just as much, and a less stringent wages policy could have been followed, if employers' social welfare contributions had been reduced, instead of cutting taxes paid by households. This would still have had a disinflationary impact, boosted profits, and raised households' income net of tax. It would have favoured incomes in the lower and middle range, though the effect on public opinion would have been less dramatic than the tax-cutting policy.

Arguments for a Co-ordinated Reflation

Have economic policies lost their effectiveness, as many economists have asserted? Will corrective economic policy automatically lead to economic recovery? These questions can perhaps be answered by a

The Fruits of Austerity

straight comparison of the US and the European experiences. By applying the biggest fiscal expansion in post-war times, the Reagan administration not only proved the relevance of Keynesian principles, but also provided the key to world economic recovery. Conversely, Europe became bogged down in disharmony and corrective economic policies; it let itself be pulled by the US locomotive without taking the option leading to the growth necessary to counter massive unemployment brought on by ten years of recession. Moreover, the European option could have avoided the imbalances caused by the United States expanding on its own, which could lead sooner or later to restrictive policies and a new recession.

It may be paradoxical that it has taken 'classical liberalism' involving 'the reduction of state control' to show how relevant Keynesian principles are; but it does not matter how an economic policy is dressed up – the important thing is what it is in itself.

Recovery through Investment or Consumption: The Wrong Debate

Economists and politicians, of Right or Left, often 'explain' that economic recovery is good only if brought about by investment, as opposed to 'bad' recovery fuelled by consumption. Leaving aside government investment or large projects (which are in any case usually financed by the State) there has never been an expansion of private investment which was not preceded by expansion of demand. Moreover when government investment leads to growth, it is because of the multiplier effect first on production, then on private investment. Tax incentives can boost investment temporarily by altering the time-scale for projects, but no businessman will invest simply because his profits have gone up and the cost of investment has fallen, if he is not certain that the extra production from his investment can be absorbed by the market.

Table 5.20 shows moreover that increased consumption and increased investment are complementary rather than mutually exclusive. The countries where investment rose sharpest between 1980 and 1984 also had the biggest rise in private consumption. Conversely, the countries which had a sharp fall in investment in this period (Belgium, the Netherlands) were those where consumption stayed the same or fell.

The debate between recovery through investment or through consumption is to a large extent an artificial one. Any rise in consumption leads by an acceleration effect to a rise in investment, and any rise in investment affects consumption through the multi-

Table 5.20 Growth, investment and consumption: changes in volume of the balance on goods and services between 1979 and 1984 (% average annual change)

	United States	Japan	United Kingdom	Italy	France	West Germany	Netherlands	Belgium
Gross domestic product	2.1	4.2	0.9	1.0	1.1	0.9	0.2	1.0
Imports	8.2	0.1	2.0	2.8	3.7	2.5	0.7	0.6
Household consumption	2.8	2.5	1.4	1.5	1.8	0.3	−0.8	0.0
Total investment	3.0	2.4	0.6	0.2	−0.3	−0.3	−1.7	−3.0
Exports	−0.1	11.1	1.4	2.0	3.5	4.9	2.1	3.4

Source: INSEE, *Rapport sur les Comptes de la nation* (Report on national accounts) 1984, Vol. 2. *Environnement international*; for France, *Comptes nationaux aux prix de 1970* (National accounts at 1970 prices).

plier. Moreover, the interaction of the two, contained in the traditional accelerator–multiplier, is the starting point for theories of cycles and growth. This debate overlaps with another which must be looked at in a context wider than that of France – the choice between supply-side policy and demand-side policy.

Supply-side Policy and Demand-side Policy: Micro and Macro Levels

The effectiveness of supply-side or demand-side policies is clearly very different depending on whether one is looking at the microeconomic or the macro-economic level. In general terms, the area where demand-side policies are effective is at the macro level; for supply-side policies, it is the micro level. Obviously, a firm will gain no benefit from raising the wages of its employees, in that the extra demand for its own products will normally be negligible. Conversely by lowering its production costs, it could expand its sales over those of its competitors.

On the national level, both policies will usually mean increased production. The more closed and extensive an economy is, the more effective demand-side policies will be. On the world level, supply-side policies will work only in a very marginal way, that is, by the increased demand brought about by a fall in production costs (this is the income effect of micro-economic theory).

On the other hand, all the competition effects (or substitution effects) which are important for the individual producer or the exporting country are inoperative at the world level. This is exactly what happens with devaluations. When one country devalues on its own, it can increase its share of the market, but if all its competitors devalue as well, the only effect is to raise prices all round. The same conclusion applies to wage restraint policies. Keynes' message of fifty years before is still very relevant:[16] 'If you are part of an international system, you can always improve your position by lowering wages more than your neighbours... You can thereby shift some of the world unemployment in your country over to theirs. But you cannot increase overall employment in the world by reducing wages. You must do that by increasing the size of industry.'

Any increase in effectiveness of demand-side policies with the scale of the economy in question is mainly because there is no longer a leak in the multiplier effect. This can be shown simply by

---

16. J. M. Keynes, speech to the 'Macmillan Committee', 19 February 1931.

Reflation and Austerity

Table 5.21 Multiplier effect of an increase in public spending equal to 1% of GDP

	Separate expansion			Co-ordinated expansion		
	1st year	2nd year	3rd year	1st year	2nd year	3rd year
United States	1.5	1.8	1.7	1.9	2.5	2.4
Japan	1.4	1.7	1.8	2.1	3.0	3.5
West Germany	1.2	1.4	1.3	2.3	3.3	3.6
France	1.1	1.3	1.4	1.8	2.6	3.0
United Kingdom	0.9	1.0	1.0	1.8	2.3	2.4
Sweden	1.0	1.0	0.9	2.2	2.9	3.2

Note: Assuming accommodating monetary policy and fixed exchange rates. For separate expansion, the multiplier does not take account of international links.
Source: Simulations by the OECD INTERLINK model presented in the article by F. Larsen, J. Llewellyn and S. Potter, 'International economic linkages,' *OECD Economic Review*, 1, Autumn 1983, p. 43.

going back to the model used in the first chapter. The multiplier of an increase in government spending is, in fact, all the greater because the leak from external trade (represented by the marginal propensity to import) is small. Using the figures given in Appendix 1.2 for the parameters of the multiplier, we can calculate the multiplier effect for various degrees of openness of the economy:

$$\text{Multiplier} = \frac{1}{1 + m - c(1 - a - t) - \alpha}$$

$$= \begin{cases} 1.0 \text{ with } m = 0.70 \text{ (Sweden)} \\ 1.4 \text{ with } m = 0.50 \text{ (France, West Germany)} \\ 3.3 \text{ with } m = 0.10 \text{ (OECD as a whole)} \end{cases}$$

For a country like Sweden which is wide open to foreign competition, the marginal propensity to import reaches 0.7 and the spending multiplier does not go beyond 1. In West Germany and France, this propensity is around 0.5 and the multiplier is over 1. For the whole of the OECD the marginal propensity to import is very low (0.1) and the multiplier is more than 3. This multiplier represents the effect of a policy of co-ordinated expansion in the OECD as a whole. The data from the OECD's INTERLINK model given in Table 5.21 confirm these findings.

When each country undertakes on its own budgetary expansion

The Fruits of Austerity

Table 5.22 Effect on the current balance of a budgetary expansion equal to 1% of GDP: change in the current external balance as % of GDP (a minus sign indicates an increase in the deficit)

	Separate expansion			Co-ordinated expansion		
	1st year	2nd year	3rd year	1st year	2nd year	3rd year
United States	−0.4	−0.4	−0.4	−0.2	−0.1	−0.1
Japan	−0.3	−0.3	−0.3	−0.1	–	–
West Germany	−0.6	−0.6	−0.5	−0.2	–	+0.2
France	−0.5	−0.6	−0.6	−0.1	–	–
United Kingdom	−0.6	−0.6	−0.6	−0.2	−0.2	−0.1
Sweden	−0.7	−0.7	−0.6	−0.3	−0.2	+0.1

Note: Assuming accommodating monetary policy and fixed exchange rates.
Sources: Simulations by OECD INTERLINK model, in F. Larsen *et al.* 1983.

equal to 1% of GDP, then GDP increases by 1.8% at the most in fairly closed economies (Japan, United States), by 1.4% in countries which face moderate competition (West Germany, France), and by only 1% in countries wide open to international competition (Sweden).

When, on the other hand, expansion policies are applied at the same time, the multiplier effect is two or three times higher. For example, it reaches 3.5 in West Germany and Japan, 3.2 in Sweden and 3 in France, but only 2.4 in the United Kingdom and the United States. The countries which benefit the most from expansion of world economic activity are those which export high-technology manufactured goods (West Germany, Japan, Sweden) for which the demand elasticity is greater than unity.

Not only are expansion policies much more effective when they are co-ordinated, but the main obstacles (external and public deficits) disappear.

Co-ordinated Reflation does not Increase External and Public Deficits

Table 5.22 shows that the external deficit caused by one country indulging in a budgetary expansion equal to 1% of GDP is of the order of 0.3% to 0.4% in the United States and Japan, and 0.6% in the United Kingdom, France and Sweden. It is understandable that European governments are loath to reflate when they know that the external deficit will increase by about 60% of the total budget stimulus. However, when economic expansion is co-ordinated throughout the OECD, the external deficit practically disappears in all countries and there may even be a surplus in those countries whose industrial exports are highly demand elastic (West Germany, Sweden). In fact, the OECD is practically a closed economy and increased raw material imports from the Third World mean that developing countries can import more from industrialized countries (the 'leak' is in practice limited to those OPEC countries with a low absorption capacity).

The consequences are just as beneficial for public finances. In fact, tax and welfare contribution revenue is highly sensitive to economic growth. According to OECD estimates, a 1% rise in GDP causes a 0.4% rise in taxes and contributions in the major European countries and the United States, 0.6% in Sweden, and only 0.2% in Japan. Therefore, when a government increases its spending in order to expand the economy, it recovers a significant proportion in greater tax revenue. The effect of the expansion on the public deficit is as slight in cases where the multiplier effect is large and the marginal rate of taxes and contributions high.

Thus, an isolated reflation of 1% of GDP gives rise to a public deficit of only 0.3% of GDP in the United States, because the expenditure multiplier is high. It is also 0.3% in Sweden, despite a low multiplier, in this case because the marginal rate of taxes and contributions is high.

If the expenditure multiplier remains lower than the inverse of the marginal rate of taxes and contributions, then budgetary expansion increases the public deficit. This is what happens when reflation is applied in isolation. When the expansion of the economy takes place on a co-ordinated basis, the multiplier is usually higher than the inverse of the marginal rate of taxes and contributions, and budgetary expansion reduces a budget shortfall rather than increasing it. Table 5.23 shows that after three years, an initial shortfall would turn into a surplus in all countries except the United Kingdom and Japan. In the case of Sweden, the improvement would be spectacular because taxes and welfare contributions are highly sensitive to economic growth.

Stagnation in Europe and non-co-operative equilibrium What was it that led European countries to pursue policies of economic retrenchment at a time when the United States was experiencing its fastest growth of the post-war period? An initial explanation might be the comparative lack of concern in European countries about the rise in unemployment, as opposed to the clear dislike of it in the

Table 5.23 Effect on the budget deficit of an increase in public spending equal to 1% of GDP: change in net lending by general government as % of GDP (a minus sign indicates an increase in the deficit)

	Separate expansion			Co-ordinated expansion		
	1st year	2nd year	3rd year	1st year	2nd year	3rd year
United States	−0.9	−0.5	−0.3	−0.7	−0.1	+0.3
Japan	−0.9	−0.8	−0.7	−0.9	−0.5	−0.2
West Germany	−0.8	−0.6	−0.6	−0.4	+0.4	+0.9
France	−0.9	−0.8	−0.7	−0.6	+0.1	+0.6
United Kingdom	−0.9	−0.8	−0.8	−0.7	−0.3	−0.1
Sweden	−0.6	−0.3	−0.3	−0.2	+0.7	+1.1

Notes: Assuming accommodating monetary policy and fixed exchange rates.
Source: Simulations by the OECD INTERLINK model, in F. Larsen *et al.* 1983, p. 84.

United States. There is some truth in this explanation, but it is obvious, particularly in the case of France, that this approach was less the result of deliberate policy decisions than the fact that the general thrust of economic policy had to cope with external constraints.

The major reason that retrenchment policies were followed in conjunction was that because there are many decision-making centres in Europe, they were forced to apply more restrictive policies than each one separately would have wished, in response to the second oil shock and then the rise in the dollar and in US interest rates. This analysis has been formulated in various ways in the last few years to show that if, in response to an inflationary shock, each country tries to reduce its inflation by stemming the fall in its currency against that of each trading partner, a non-co-operative equilibrium ('Nash equilibrium') is created, where interest rates are much higher than the levels which co-operation could have brought. The non-achievement of a co-operative equilibrium is explained by the well-known paradigm from game theory called 'prisoner's dilemma'. In economic terms, this dilemma would explain why co-ordinated economic expansion cannot be achieved even though it would benefit all countries.

In a situation of co-ordinated expansion, the 'traitor' country – the one which applies a restrictive policy within a co-ordinated expansion – improves its position without incurring too high a cost in terms of unemployment. It is therefore in the interest of each country to be the 'traitor' and the resulting equilibrium is the one where countries opt for the most negative solution. In such a situation, the existence of many decision-making centres has a collective cost, which can be avoided only if a supranational body imposes a co-operative solution, or if the game is played over and over again and there is perfect information about other countries' decisions. Decision-makers also need to be convinced of the benefits of co-ordinated expansion. In the field of economic thinking however the new classical ideology has had a strong influence, derived for some people from the weakest element in econometric models – the Phillips curve. They have relied on this to conclude that re-expansion policies involve a long-term inflationary risk.

Is unemployment in France 'natural'? (or, has the NAIRU increased?) In macro-econometric models such as those used in this book (OFCE-annual and OFCE-quarterly models), wages are, in the long run, wholly indexed on prices (the long-run Phillips curve is vertical and becomes a relationship between the growth rate of real wages and the rate of unemployment). There is therefore only one rate of unemployment which is compatible in the long run with the stability of the wage–profit ratio and with the stability of the rate of inflation. This rate of unemployment is in fact what monetarist writers call the 'natural rate', or what contemporary writers call the non-accelerating inflation rate of unemployment (NAIRU).

Since the inflationary process is unstable when wages are wholly indexed, inflation grows faster or slows down according to whether the actual unemployment rate is lower or higher than the natural rate (on the assumption that in the long run, the exchange rate adjusts to maintain purchasing power parity).

This concept of natural unemployment is meaningful only in the very long run, when the Phillips curve is stable, and when the model (and the economy it is supposed to represent) has a balanced growth path. However, it is often used in medium-term analyses to calculate the unemployment rate which would have stabilized inflation and the wage–profit ratio, after the shocks which have affected the economy are taken into account. This unemployment rate (NAIRU) is a direct function of the 'growth rate of non-inflationary real wages', that is, the growth rate in real wages which would not involve a rise in the ratio of wage costs in production, taking account of increases in labour productivity, employers' welfare contribution rates and the terms of trade. A slow-down of growth in labour productivity or a worsening of the terms of trade brings

The Fruits of Austerity

about a fall in this non-inflationary wage rate, and therefore a rise in the NAIRU.

Sachs and Wyploz[17] have argued that between 1963 and 1984, the NAIRU rose in the same proportion as the actual rate of unemployment (between 1% and 10% for the actual rate and between 1% and 9% for the NAIRU. But the Phillips curve which they use has a specification, the instability of which has been shown by numerous French econometric studies. The disequilibrium indicator for the labour market used in all French models (and particularly the two used in this book) is the ratio between unemployment and unfilled vacancies, which means that frictional unemployment which increases both sides of the ratio at the same time can be ignored. However, the approach of Sachs and Wyploz brings in the rate of unemployment and in fact corrects the resulting instability by a trend over time; by definition this leads to a natural rate of unemployment which increases indefinitely (obviously this specification has a bearing on the fact that they found the NAIRU to be so high during the period studied).

It is clear however that whatever the specification used, with disindexation, and then decreases in the value of the dollar and the price of oil since 1985, the NAIRU was bound to fall sharply after 1985. This is the conclusion reached by F. Lecointe, H. Sterdyniak and V. Przedborski[18] who used the OFCE-quarterly model's Phillips curve re-estimated over a long period of time (see Table 5.24).

The first part of Table 5.24 compares the changes in effective real wages (line 1) and 'non-inflationary real wages' (line 2). The latter are broken down into three components: labour productivity growth; changes in terms of trade; changes in the rate of employer social security contributions.

The gap between the *growth rate of non-inflationary real wages* and the *growth rate of effective real wages* represents the annual variation (in points) of the share of profits in value added. The NAIRU is the rate of unemployment which, over the period examined, would cause wages to grow at the same rate as non-inflationary real wages, allowing for actual changes in the minimum wage. This is because the long-run Phillips curve is a relationship between real wages, the rate of change of the real minimum wage, and the unemployment rate. The gap between the effective

17. J. Sachs and C. Wyploz, 'The economic consequences of President Mitterrand', *Economic policy*, 1 (2), April 1986.
18. F. Lecointe, H. Sterdyniak and V. Przedborski, 'Salaires, prix et répartition' (Wages, price and distribution) in J.-M. Jeanneney (ed.) *L'économie français depuis 1967* (The French economy since 1967), Paris, Seuil, 1989.

Table 5.24 Actual rate of unemployment and the NAIRU

	1967–73	1973–9	1979–82	1982–7
(1) Actual real wage ($\dot{\omega} = \dot{w} - \dot{p}_c$)	5.5	4.0	2.4	0.9
(2) Non inflationary real wages) $(\dot{\omega}^* = \dot{Q} - \dot{N} + \dot{p} - \dot{p}_c - \dot{s})$	5.7	3.0	1.2	2.5
broken down into:				
– labour productivity ($\dot{Q} - \dot{N}$)	5.7	3.9	3.2	2.5
– terms of trade effect ($\dot{p} - \dot{p}_c$)	−0.1	−0.4	−1.7	0.5
– employers' contribution ($-\dot{s}$)	0.1	−0.5	−0.2	−0.5
(3) Gap between non inflationary real wage and actual real wage (= change in annual rate in the profit share: $-\dot{\beta} = \dot{\omega}^* - \dot{\omega}$	−0.2	−1.0	−1.2	+1.6
(4) Impact of minimum wage ($-b\dot{m}$)	−0.3	0	−0.1	−0.1
(5) NAIRU (%)	2.2	6.0	8.6	6.3
(6) Actual rate of unemployment (%)	2.0	4.4	7.5	10.1

Notes: Phillips curve: $\dot{w} = \sum_i a_i \cdot \dot{p}_c (-i) + b\dot{m} + \Phi(U)$

with $\sum_i a_i = 1$

Wages share in value added: $\beta = \dfrac{wN}{pQ} \cdot s \dfrac{\omega}{\omega^*}$

NAIRU ($\bar{U}$): $\dot{\omega}^* = b\dot{m} + \Phi(\bar{U})$

$\dot{x}$ is the rate of growth of x

Source: F. Lecointe, H. Sterdyniak and V. Przedborski, 1989.

unemployment rate (line 6) and the NAIRU (line 5) therefore depends on: the difference between the growth rates of non-inflationary and effective wages (line 3); and the impact of the minimum wage on real wages (line 4).

In the balanced-growth period (1967–73), labour productivity and real wages moved at a nearly identical rate, while the terms of trade and employer social security contributions remained stable. The real minimum wage moved up 0.3 points and effective wages rose 0.2 points, slightly outpacing non-inflationary wages. These increases explain the acceleration in wage inflation and why the NAIRU was slightly greater than the effective unemployment rate.

In the wake of the 1973–9 and 1979–82 oil shocks, the growth rate of non-inflationary real wages fell sharply owing to a deceleration in labour productivity growth, worsening terms of trade, and the funding of the social security deficit by an increase in employer contribution rates. The slow-down, however, was more limited for effective wages. In other words, the effective rise in unemployment

The Fruits of Austerity

was smaller than the one which would have stabilized inflation (NAIRU).

Between 1983 and 1987, the gap which opened between the stagnation of real wages and the growth of labour productivity together with an improvement in the terms of trade led to a difference of nearly four percentage points on average between the actual rate of unemployment (10.1%) and the NAIRU (5.8%). At the end of the 1980s therefore, there was a large margin of manoeuvre for non-inflationary expansion of the economy.

Conclusion

> The western world already has the resources and the technique, if we could create the organisation to use them, capable of reducing the economic problem, which now absorbs our moral and material energies, to a position of secondary importance.
>
> J. M. Keynes, Preface to
> *Essays in persuasion*, 1931

The assessment of five years of left-wing economic policy is not an easy task, given the great difference between initial objectives and what was done in practice. From the viewpoint of what could be done in the economic situation in which the Left found itself, there was an undoubtedly positive side to its economic and social achievements; from that of a 'French-style socialism making a break with capitalism', the failure was dramatic. As Michel Rocard noted in the run-up to the 1986 parliamentary elections, it was the Left government's unpopularity which was the main result of the difference between intentions and actions: 'Even in the economic field, I am convinced that it is not so much our policy that the French people dislike – since they know that no other approach would spare them the effort which it involves – but the difference between our present policies and the excessive nature of some of our electoral promises' (speech at the 1985 Toulouse party conference).

The Failure of Ideologies

Any failure by the Left is first and foremost the failure of ideologies. A French-style 'Bad-Godesberg'[1] was apparent day after day when the Left was in power, as is shown by comparing early speeches

---

1. In 1959, the West German Social Democratic Party meeting at Bad Godesberg broke with Marxism by recognizing the private ownership of the means of production, and the need for markets.

Conclusion

with later declarations. The objective of a break with capitalism gave way to a recognition of the role of industry as the vehicle for growth: 'Firms produce wealth, create jobs, determine our standard of living and our place in the world' (François Mitterrand, appearing on television on 15 January 1984). The economic crisis and external constraint, which the Left largely ignored during the 1981 election campaign, quickly became matters of concern again. The question which was the stumbling block of the Joint Programme of the Left – how far to go in the nationalization of firms' subsidiaries – was again answered by events, since some subsidiaries were partly privatized without causing much discussion. In other words, the recognition of economic constraints and the advantages of the mixed economy slowly led the French Socialist Party towards a social democracy to which, for the Left, there seems to be no real alternative, at least in a developed economy and a democratic political system.

By discovering the virtues of the firm, the Left managed to reconcile workers with industry, thereby laying the foundations of a social democratic consensus which France lacked for so long, and which had a part to play, for example, in the success of disinflation.

However, while on the Left ideology finally gave way to realism, many on the Right did not take long to start adhering to a liberal ideology, even though it had never been applied when they were in power. Moreover, liberal ideology could not point to many successes: economic expansion in the United States was an indication of the relevance of Keynesian principles (see Chapter 5), and President Reagan's pragmatism knew exactly when to drop liberal principles, both on spending cuts and in the field of international trade. Furthermore, the two years of Chiraquian liberalism represented, as we predicted in the original French edition of this book (1985), a further clash between ideology and reality which brought no more benefits to the liberalism of the French Right than the earlier example had done to French-style socialism.

Although nationalizations were not the 'spearhead of the economy', they nevertheless meant an end to ten years of falling investment in the undertakings concerned, and the beginning of a restructuring which would have been hard to achieve given the low risk-taking propensity of French capitalism.[2] The ease with which the Chirac government was able to sell off the shares of undertakings

---

2. See the chapter by Christian Stoffaës in H. Machin and V. Wright, (eds) *Economic policy and policy-making under the Mitterrand presidency 1981–84*, London, Frances Pinter, 1985.

nationalized in 1981 shows, to a certain extent, that the nationalized sector had been managed efficiently.

However, an analysis of the facts stripped of their ideological dressing shows that the Left's policy after 1981 was no more the 'adventure', which many on the Right called it, than the previous policy of the Right before 1981 had been 'a contribution to the economic crisis', as the Left alleged.

Creditable Achievements in a Europe Hit by Recession

French economic achievements during 1981–6 were not great, but they compared well with those of other major European countries. Comparisons of growth rates are never easy because short-term economic policies are out of phase; for example, France and Italy introduced austerity at a later stage than West Germany and the United Kingdom. Whatever base is taken, however, French growth remains of the same order of magnitude as that of its major European partners. During 1981–6, the annual growth of GDP was 1.5% in France and West Germany, 1.2% in Italy, 0.9% in Belgium and the Netherlands, and 2.1% in the United Kingdom. The higher growth in the United Kingdom and lower growth in Italy is essentially because of the lack of synchronization of economic cycles mentioned earlier. If 1980 is included in the reckoning, the average growth of the four main countries of the Community is in fact identical at 1.5%.

The average rate of unemployment in France during the six years 1981–6 was one of the lowest in the Community – 9.0% as against 7.3% in West Germany, 9.8% in Italy, 10.7% in the United Kingdom, 11.8% in Belgium and 10.7% in the Netherlands. Taking into account the initial value (1980), the average rate of unemployment is higher by 2.7 points in France, 2.3 in Italy, 4 points in West Germany and Belgium, 4.7 in the Netherlands, and 5.1 in the United Kingdom.

A final point is that because France's economic policy was to a large extent counter-cyclical (though this was not totally deliberate, as we have seen in Chapter 2), French growth was the most steady of major industrialized countries, and France was the only country besides Japan not to experience a fall in GDP after the second oil shock.

On the other hand, the success of the austerity policy as far as inflation and the external balance are concerned must be seen in context. During 1981–6, price rises in France were greater on

Conclusion

average than those of her main partners (though this was also true in the 1970s), and external indebtedness rose sharply.

There are no miracles in economics. Economic expansion as well as austerity has benefits and costs, between which politicians have to decide. However, as was shown in Chapter 5, disinflation and the recovery of firms' profits was achieved at a lower cost in terms of unemployment and real incomes than in most other European countries. The success of the Left's prices and wages freeze (as opposed to the failure of previous ones) and its policy of disindexation was due in large part to the social consensus on which the government could draw, and which allowed the Left government to succeed in an area where it was least expected to do so. It would have been unthinkable in 1981 that by the end of the Parliament, the Left government would have brought down inflation to under 5%,[3] and indeed some 'forecasters' – using not very rigorous methods, it is true – were predicting 20% inflation with the coming to power of the Left.[4]

Absence of Vision in the Medium Term

A quantitative analysis of the 1981–2 reflation and of the circumstances in which it was applied hardly supports the view that there was an initial reckless phase to which austerity was the inevitable consequence. It was the world situation faced by the Left which made austerity inevitable. The 1981–2 reflation was on a fairly modest scale and would not have led to problems if world economic recovery, of which there were signs in 1981, had gathered pace, as was the case in the years after the first oil shock.

Of course, the Left made several mistakes during the initial reflationary stage. The first, and probably the most significant, was the desire to achieve in less than a year objectives which would have caused less stress to the economy if they had been spaced out over the full length of the Parliament. What is rather surprising in view of its earlier pronouncements is that the Left did not have medium-term programming, and the Plan never played the part assigned to it – perhaps imprudently – by Socialist policy statements.

---

3. This was the rate of inflation before the oil counter-shock which brought it down to 2% on an annual basis in the first half of 1986.
4. Macro-economic models indicated, on the other hand, that the main risk in economic expansion was not inflation but the external deficit, which has been shown to be true (cf. Chapter 2).

The second mistake was to underestimate the risks inherent in the May 1981 economic situation:

1 The franc was overvalued against the Deutschmark and the pressures on it even before the Left government took office made devaluation inevitable, though it would have been more effective if it had been applied immediately.
2 The French economy was already in a period of reflation because of what the Barre government had done just before the 1981 election, which made further reflationary measures more risky.
3 The effects of restrictive monetary policy in the United States were to a great extent underestimated, though this mistake was made by all forecasters in France and abroad. Instead of the expected fall in the dollar and the upturn in the economy in 1982, the dollar rose in value and there was an economic downturn which contributed, to a greater extent than the reflation policy, to a worsening of the external deficit in 1982 (see Chapters 2 and 3).

In view of the difficulty in predicting how the world economy would develop, it would have been better to go for a purely cyclical economic expansion by means of large government and industrial programmes, energy-saving projects, and large increases in welfare benefits and reductions in income tax for the poorly paid. This kind of specifically targeted reflation involved little in terms of long-term commitment, and could have been applied again when the time was ripe. It also had the enormous advantage of avoiding dramatic changes in economic policy.

If the franc had been immediately devalued by a modest amount within the EMS, this would have eased external constraints. Failing that, could these have been overcome by a competitive devaluation? This was the strategy of the Swedish Socialists in 1982, in domestic and external conditions which were much more favourable than in France in May 1981.[5] The economic risks of such a strategy are well known – inflationary surge and temporary increase in the external deficit because of the worsening of the terms of trade. The way to reduce the risk of inflation is also well known – a very tight control of incomes, both wage and non-wage. This was applied in Sweden in 1982, but it might not have worked in the post-May 1981 'state of grace' in France; it would have also made impossible any increase in the minimum wage.

From the political point of view, such a strategy involved risk in

5. See Chapter 3.

Conclusion

so far as it implied leaving the EMS. If France's commitment to Europe had been reduced in this way, some elements of the new left-wing majority would have been tempted to pursue a completely unorthodox economic policy. To the extent that a co-ordinated European policy was vital for economic expansion, any irresponsibility on the part of France would have caused enormous problems in the long term.

Moreover, as our analysis of the devaluations of the franc shows, competitivity gains would not have been enough to bring down quickly an external deficit of the scale of 1981–2, and a Left government could hardly hope to offset a worsening of the terms of trade by attracting capital on a massive scale. In other words, there was no alternative to the policy of austerity.

The French economy, held to an average growth of not much more than 1% a year, could not avoid a sharp rise in unemployment. If it had not been for a specially designed employment policy, unemployment would have risen to three million by 1985. Unemployment was stabilized at two million between Summer 1982 and Autumn 1983 because of the introduction of government early retirement schemes and the reduction of the normal retirement age to 60. The introduction of community work schemes (*travaux d'utilité collective – TUC*) meant that unemployment levelled out again in 1985 at a figure of 2.4 million. Of course these were only temporary measures in the context of a worsening labour market situation.

The Socialist government's employment policy however was not a total success. The most notable failure was the reduction of the working week to thirty-nine hours. The way it was implemented did not lead to a significant increase in jobs, and in fact delayed the introduction of a work-sharing policy which is still one of the keys to reducing unemployment in the long term.

Two Conditions for Reducing Unemployment: Go for Growth and Redistribute Working Time

Reducing the unemployment brought about by ten years of recession assumes that two conditions can be met at the same time. The first is that European countries must go for growth to reach a position where there is a net creation of jobs. However, this necessary condition is not sufficient to achieve 'acceptable' unemployment levels. The second condition is that a significant part of the productivity gains from growth should be devoted, in a decentralized way, to reducing working hours. For this to happen, there must of course be sustained growth.

In the mid-1980s, because of slow growth and policies to improve profit levels, the real value of wages fell, and this was why many wage earners found it difficult to accept 'income-sharing' as well as work-sharing. This was partly why employees did not press hard for a 35-hour week. However, a situation of higher growth and a maintenance of the wage–profit ratio at its mid-1980s level would mean that a choice was possible – a rise in real wages or reduction in working hours and more jobs.

To be wholly effective, a policy of work-sharing should be accompanied by a greater flexibility of the working week and the working year in order to put fixed capital to better use and to meet customers' needs better. As for the return to high growth, this is unlikely to come about merely through the operation of the market.

European Economic Expansion

Is Europe doomed to permanent decline? As in many other areas, we must avoid extrapolating too much from the short- to the medium-term. Just before the first oil shock, economists noted slow growth in the United States compared with the buoyant European economy, and were quick to speak of a structural decline of the US economy. In the 1980s the same economists asserted that Europe (now described as 'old') was showing how behind it was in technological, demographic and many other ways. Yet Europe is no more behind in the 1980s than it was before; it is simply that it is divided into states which individually no longer have much influence on their own economy. If Europe's problems were technological, it would be difficult to understand how for example French economic growth was three times lower than the US in 1983–6, whereas labour productivity was rising faster in France than in the United States.

Europe's difficulties are essentially macro-economic and stem from the growing contradiction between the fragmentation of political power and the internationalization of trade. Almost all the constraints on national activity-boosting policies would disappear at European level and, *a fortiori*, at world level. Budgetary expansion aggravates public deficits when carried out in isolation; but when applied in conjunction, it has no effect or even reduces them. Separate expansions of the economy come to grief on external deficits, but these are insignificant when expansion is co-ordinated.

Conclusion

Moreover, it is argued that budgetary expansion harms investment because of hypothetical crowding-out effects; but investment was constrained principally by demand in the 1980s.

It is true that real interest rates remain high; however, here again, they could be brought down by co-ordinated monetary policies and a return to fixed exchange rates, both of which are helped by general disinflation. Similarly, a recovery of profits removes one of the obstacles to a sustained recovery. However, for the virtuous circle of growth to be set going, it has to be started by a co-ordinated re-expansion and sustained by large medium-term programmes.

Europe has the human and technological means needed to bring about high growth; but it still has to bridge the gap between political power which it has inherited and economic power. The national framework is no longer relevant to macro-economic regulation.

Bibliography

Aglietta, M., A. Orléan and G. Oudiz, 'L'industrie française face aux contraintes de change' (French industry and exchange rate constraints), *Economie et statistique*, 119, February 1980

Albert, M., *Le pari français* (The challenge facing France), Paris, Seuil, 1982

Anyadike-Danes, M. and J.-P. Fitoussi, 'Dimensions du problème de l'emploi en Europe et aux Etats-Unis' (Dimensions of the employment problem in Europe and the United States), *Lettre de l'OFCE*, 12, 22 February 1984

Artus, P., 'Formation conjointe des prix et des salaires dans cinq grands pays de l'OCDE' (Joint determination of prices and wages in five OECD countries), *Annales de l'INSEE*, 49, January–March 1983

———, G. Laroque and G. Michel, 'Estimation of a quarterly macroeconomic model with quantitative rationing', *Econometrica*, 52 (6), November 1984

Artus, P. and P.-A. Muet, 'Un panorama des développements récents de l'économétrie de l'investissement' (A survey of recent developments in the econometrics of investment), *Revue économique*, 35 (5), September 1984

———, *Investment and factor demand*, North-Holland, 1989.

Asselain, J.-C., 'La semaine de quarante heures, le chômage et l'emploi' (The forty-hour week, employment and unemployment), *Le mouvement social*, 54, January–March 1966

———, 'Une erreur de politique économique: la loi des quarante heures de 1936' (A mistake of economic policy: the forty-hour law of 1936), *Revue économique*, 25 (4), 1974

Barbezieux, P., 'Le bilan des contrats de solidarité–réduction de la durée du travail conclus en 1982' (Assessment of the 1982 schemes linking government financial aid with shorter working hours), *Travail et emploi*, 17, July–September 1983

———, 'Le bilan des contrats de solidarité–réduction de la durée du travail conclus en 1983' (Assessment of the 1983 schemes linking government financial aid with shorter working hours), *Bilan de l'emploi 1983, Dossiers statistiques du travail et de l'emploi*, 3–4, June 1984

Barou, Y. and J. Rigaudiat, *Les 35 heures et l'emploi* (The 35-hour week and employment), Paris, La Documentation Française, 1983

Bibliography

Barre, R., *Une politique pour l'avenir* (A policy for the future), Paris, Plon, 1981
Baudet, P.-A., 'Dix ans de politique économique en RFA' (Ten years of economic policy in FRG), *Cahiers français*, 218, October–December 1984
Beaud, M., *Le mirage de la croissance* (The mirage of growth), Paris, Syros, 1983
Benassy, J.-P., 'Théorie du déséquilibre et fondements micro-économiques de la macro-économie' (The theory of disequilibrium and the microeconomic basis of macro-economics), *Revue économique*, 27 (5), 1976
Bloch-Michel, C., M. Mayo and J. Y. Rognant, 'Creation d'entreprise par les demandeurs d'emploi' (Business creation by unemployed people), *Bilan de l'emploi 1982*, Bulletin mensuel de statistique du travail, 104, 1983
de Boissieu, C. and A. Gubian, 'Les indicateurs de la politique budgétaire et fiscale' (Indicators of budgetary and fiscal policy), *Observations et diagnostics économiques*, 9, October 1984
Boscher, F., C. Duflos and L. Lebart, 'Les conditions de vie et les aspirations des Français' (Lifestyle and aspirations of French people), *Consommation: revue de socio-économie*, 2, 1984
Bourit, F., P. Hernu and M. Perrot, 'Les salaires en 1981' (Wages in 1981), *Economie et statistique*, 141, February 1982
Boutillier, M., 'L'évolution recente des salaires' (Recent wage trends), *Observations et diagnostics économiques*, 5, October 1983
Brenot-Ouldali, A. and D. Quarré, 'Les effectifs des agents de l'Etat de 1975 à 1982' (Number of employees in central and local government between 1975 and 1982), *Economie et statistique*, June 1984
Bucher, A. and H. Sterdyniak, 'Un investissement relativement soutenu' (An investment which was relatively sustained), *Observations et diagnostics économiques*, 5, October 1983
Cendron, J.-P., 'Prestations vieillesse du régime général: évolution rétrospective et prévisions à l'horizon 1986' (Retirement benefits from the general scheme: past developments and forecast for 1986), *Economie et prévision*, 68, 1985
CEPII, *Economie mondiale 1980-90: la fracture?* (The world economy in the 1980s: the final breakdown?), Paris, Economica, 1984.
CNPF, *Les charges des entreprises françaises: rapport au Premier ministre* (Costs of French firms: report to the Prime Minister), Paris, La Documentation Française, 1983
Colin, J.-F., M. Elbaum and A. Fonteneau, 'Chômage et politique de l'emploi: 1981–83' (Unemployment and employment policy: 1981–83), *Observations et diagnostics économiques*, 7, April 1984
Commissariat Général du Plan, *Aménagement et réduction du temps de travail* (Redistribution and reduction of working time), Paris, La Documentation Française, 1984

Bibliography

Commission du Bilan, *La France en mai 1981* (France in May 1981), Paris, La Documentation Française, 1981.

Debonneuil, M. and H. Sterdyniak, 'Apprécier une dévaluation' (Assessment of a devaluation), *Economie et statistique*, 142, March 1982

Decouflé, A.-C. and N. Svendsen, 'Contribution à une histoire des durées du travail dans l'industrie française du milieu du XIXe siècle à la seconde guerre mondiale' (Contribution to a history of working hours in French industry from the mid-nineteenth century to the Second World War), *Travail et emploi*, 20, June 1984

Delattre, M., 'Points forts et points faibles du commerce extérieur industriel' (Strengths and weaknesses of foreign trade in industrial goods), *Economie et statistique*, 157, July–August 1983

Doyelle, A., 'Durée du travail: un essai de comparaison internationale' (Working hours: an attempt at an international comparison), *Travail et emploi*, 12, April–June 1982

Dutailly, J.-C., 'Aides aux entreprises: 134 milliards en 1982' (Government help for business: 134 billion in 1982), *Economie et statistique*, 169, September 1984

Eckstein, O., *The great recession*, North-Holland, 1979

Eisner, R., *How Real is the Federal Deficit?*, Free Press, New York, 1986

Elbaum, M. and A. Fonteneau, 'Les politiques d'emploi et leurs évaluations: le cas français au cours des années récentes' (Employment policies and their assessment: the French experience in recent times), *Cahiers lillois d'économie et de sociologie*, 5, first semester 1985

Fonteneau, A., 'Les erreurs de prévisions économiques pour 1982' (Errors in economic forecasting for 1982), *Observations et diagnostics économiques*, 4, June 1983

——, and A. Gubian, 'Comparaison des relances françaises de 1975 et de 1981–82' (Comparison of the French reflation of 1975 with that of 1981–82), *Observations et diagnostics économiques*, 12, July 1985

Fonteneau, A. and P.-A. Muet, 'Le poids de la contrainte extérieure sur la France' (The impact of international constraints on France), *Lettre de l'OFCE*, 3, 23, March 1983

Fournelle, F., P.-A. Muet and P. Villa, 'Le commerce extérieur en France depuis 1950' (External trade in France since 1950), *Annales de l'INSEE*, 49, January–March 1983

Frank, D. and J.-J. Trégoat, 'Une politique active en matière d'emploi et de lutte contre le chômage à marqué 1982' (1982 was marked by an active policy in employment and in the fight against unemployment), *Bulletin mensuel des statistiques du travail* (supplement), 104, 1983

Frayssinet, D., 'La durée annuelle du travail en 1981 et 1982: premiers résultats' (A preliminary analysis of the number of hours worked in 1981 and 1982), *Dossiers statistiques du travail et de l'emploi*, 9, November 1984

Galland, O., J. Gaudin and P. Vrain, 'Contrats de solidarité préretraites et

Bibliography

stratégies d'entreprises' (Schemes linking government aid with early retirement, and firms' strategies), *Travail et emploi*, 22, December 1984

Guinchard, P., 'Productivité et compétitivité comparées des grands pays industriels' (Comparative productivity and competitivity in the major industrial countries), *Economie et statistique*, 162, January 1984

INSEE, *Rapport sur les Comptes de la Nation*, collection C, 101–2, 108–9, 117–18, 124–5

Janossy, F., *La fin des miracles économiques* (An end to economic miracles), Paris, Seuil, 1972

Jeanneney, J.-M. and E. Barbier-Jeanneney, *Les économies occidentales du XIXe siècle à nos jours* (Western economies from the nineteenth century to modern times), Paris, Presses de la Fondation Nationale des Sciences Politiques, 1985

Keynes, J.M., speech to the Macmillan Committee, *Hearings of the Macmillan Committee*, London, HM Printing Office, 1931

——, *The general theory of employment, interest and money*, London, Macmillan, 1973 [1936].

Klein, L., 'Longévite de la théorie économique' (The longevity of economic theory), *Cahiers du seminaire d'économetrie*, 20, 1979.

Kolm, S.-C., *Sortir de la crise* (Emerging from the crisis), Paris, Hachette, Collection Pluriel, 1983

Lacroix, T. and J.-C. Guergoat, 'Le succès des préretraites a permis de stabiliser le chômage' (Unemployment stabilised by success of early retirement), *Dossiers statistiques du travail et de l'emploi*, 3–4, June 1984

Larsen, F., J. Llewellyn and S. Potter, 'International economic linkages', *OECD economic review*, 1, Autumn 1983

Lecointe, F., H. Sterdyniak and V. Przedborski, 'Salaires, prix et répartition' (Wages, prices and distribution) in J.-M. Jeanneney (ed.), *L'économie français depuis 1967* (The French economy since 1967), Paris, Seuil, 1989

Lenormand, H., 'Une analyse des causes de la stagnation économique mondiale' (An analysis of the causes of world economic stagnation), paper given to the conference on multinational modelling, Brussels, 8–9 December 1983

——, and D. Vallet, 'Les responsabilités de la politique monétaire américaine dans les difficultés économiques mondiales' (The responsibilities of US monetary policy in time of world recession), *Economie prospective internationale* (journal of the CEPII), 18, 2nd quarter 1984

Llewellyn, J., 'Resource prices and macro-economic policies: lessons from the two oil shocks', *OECD economic review*, 1, Autumn 1983

Machin, H. and V. Wright (eds), 'Economic policy and policy-making under the Mitterrand presidency 1981–84', London, Frances Pinter, 1985

Magnier, G., 'Les sorties de la vie active en 1981' (Cessation of work in 1981), *Travail et emploi*, 13, July–September 1982

——, 'Les entreprises signataires de contrats de solidarité préretraite' (Firms

Bibliography

participating in schemes linking government help with early retirement), *Dossiers statistiques du travail et de l'emploi*, 9, November 1984

Malinvaud, E., *Unemployment theory reconsidered*, Oxford, Blackwell, 1983

Mantz, P., A. Ramond, M. Tabouillot and M. Ungemuth, 'Le poids des prélèvements obligatoires: portée et limites de la mesure' (The influence of taxes and social welfare contributions: the scope and limitations of the policy), *Economie et statistique*, 157, July–August 1983

Marchand, O. and E. Martin-le-Goff, '200,000 emplois à nouveau perdus en 1984' (200,000 jobs lost again in 1984), *Economie et statistique*, 176, April 1985

Marchand, O., D. Rault and E. Turpin, 'Dès 40 heures aux 39 heures: processus et réaction des entreprises' (Firms' reactions to shortening the working week from forty to thirty-nine hours), *Economie et statistique*, 154, April 1983

Marioni, P. and M. Ricau, 'Préretraites et politique de gestion du personnel: approche sectorielle' (Early retirement and staff management policy: a sectoral analysis), *Dossiers statistiques du travail et de l'emploi*, 7, September 1984

Mathieu, S., 'Etats-Unis: une croissance hypothéquée' (Growth in the United States: a hostage to the future), *Observations et diagnostics economiques*, 8, July 1984

Mauroy, P., *C'est ici le chemin* (This is the way), Paris, Flammarion, 1982

Miqueu, D., 'La politique économique des Etats-Unis' (US economic policy), *Les cahiers français*, 218, October–December 1984

Modigliani, F., 'Life Cycle, Individual Thrift, and the Wealth of Nations', *The American Economic Review*, 59 (3), June 1986, Nobel lecture given in December 1985

Monet, H., 'La politique sociale–democrate de la Suède' (Social–democratic policy in Sweden), *Les cahiers français*, 218, October–December 1984

Muet, P.-A., 'La modélisation macro-économique' (Macro-economic modelling), *Statistiques et études financières*, Special Number, 1979

——, *Théories et modèles de la macro-économie* (Theories and models in macro-economics), Paris, Economica, 1984

——, and S. Avouyi-Dovi, 'L'effet des incitations fiscales sur l'investissement' (The effect of tax incentives on investment), *Observations et diagnostics économiques*, 18 January 1987

Muet, P.-A., A. Fonteneau and F. Milewski, 'Le contre-choc pétrolier et la baisse du dollar: quelles marges de manoeuvre pour la politique économique?' (The oil counter-shock and the fall in the dollar: what freedom of manoeuvre for economic policy?), *Observations et diagnostics économiques*, 15, April 1986

Muet, P.-A. and H. Sterdyniak, 'Rétablissement des profits et stagnation de l'investissement: un paradoxe?' (Recovery of profits and stagnation of investment: a paradox?), *Observations et diagnostics économiques, Lettre de l'OFCE*, 25, 28 May 1985

Bibliography

OECD, 'Simulations of fiscal policy using the OECD model of international links', *OECD Economic Review, Special studies*, July 1980

——, 'Youth employment in France', Paris, 1984

Parti Socialiste, *Propositions pour l'actualisation du programme commun de gouvernement de la gauche* (Proposals for updating the joint programme for government by the Left), Paris, Flammarion, 1978

Pépin, M., J.-C. Sardas and D. Tonneau, 'Réduction du temps de travail: une typologie du comportement des entreprieses' (The shorter working week: a typology of firms' behaviour), *Economie et prévision*, 55 (4), 1982

Pépin, M. and D. Tonneau, 'Règlementation sociale et vie des entreprises: mise en oeuvre des ordonnances de janvier 1982 sur les 39 heures et la cinquième semaine de congé' (Firms and the legal framework of social policy: implementation of the January 1982 decrees on the 39-hour week and a fifth week's paid holiday), *Economie et prévision*, 59 (4), 1982

Price, R.W.R. and P. Muller, 'Structural budget indicators and the interpretation of fiscal policy stance in OECD economies', *OECD Economic Review*, 3, Autumn 1984

Ralite, J., 'L'efficacité des aides publiques à l'emploi' (The effectiveness of government aid for employment), *Economie et politique*, July–August 1984

Revoil, J.-P., 'L'indemnisation du chômage et de la préretraite en 1983' (Unemployment and early retirement compensation in 1983), *Bilan de l'emploi 1983*

Sachs, J. and C. Wyploz, 'The economic consequences of President Mitterrand', *Economic policy*, 1 (2), April 1986

Sauvy, A., *Histoire économique de la France entre les deux guerres* (Economic history of France between the wars), Paris, Economica, 1984

Schwartz, B., *L'insertion professionnelle et sociale des jeunes: rapport au Premier ministre* (The integration of young people in work and in society: report to the Prime Minister), Paris, La Documentation Française, September 1981

Théret, B. and D. Uri, 'La pression fiscale: une limite a l'intervention publique' (Tax rates: a limit to public intervention), *Critique de l'économie politique*, 21, new series, October–December 1982

Topol, R. and M.-A. Boudier, 'Les mauvais résultats du commerce extérieur industriel pèsent sur la croissance' (Poor external trade figures stifle growth), *Observations et diagnostics économiques*, 5, October 1983

Vignon, J., 'Le delorisme en economie' (Delors-ism in economics), *Les cahiers français*, 218, October–December 1984

Vilares, M., 'Un modèle macro-économétrique pour l'étude des changements structurels: théorie et application a l'économie française' (A macro-economic model for the analysis of structural change: theory and application to the French economy), in J.-P. Fitoussi and P.-A. Muet (eds), *Macro-dynamique et déséquilibre* (Macro-dynamics and disequilibria), Paris, Economica, 1985